For Maureen

can't wait to read

your entire dissertation

Elisabeth

GERMAN WOMEN'S LIFE WRITING AND THE HOLOCAUST

Complicity and Gender in the Second World War

This important study examines women's life writing about the Second World War and the Holocaust, such as memoirs, diaries, docunovels, and autobiographically inspired fiction. Through a historical and literary study of the complex relationship between gender, genocide, and female agency, this volume analyzes correct androcentric views of the Second World War and seeks to further our understanding of a group that, although crucial to the functioning of the National Socialist regime, has often been overlooked: that of the complicit bystander. Chapters on army auxiliaries, nurses, female refugees, rape victims, and Holocaust survivors analyze women's motivations for enlisting in the National Socialist cause, as well as for their continuing support for the regime and, in some cases, their growing estrangement from it. The readings allow insights into the nature of complicity itself, the emergence of violence in civil society, and the possibility of social justice.

ELISABETH KRIMMER is a professor of German at the University of California, Davis. Her previous publications include: *Religion, Reason, and Culture in the Age of Goethe* (2013); *Enlightened War: Theories and Cultures of Warfare in Eighteenth-Century Germany* (2011); *The Representation of War in German Literature: From 1800 to the Present* (Cambridge, 2010); *In the Company of Men: Cross-Dressed Women around 1800* (2004), *Hollywood Divas, Indie Queens and TV Heroines: Contemporary Screen Images of Women* (2004) and *Contemporary Hollywood Masculinities: Gender, Genre and Politics* (2011).

GERMAN WOMEN'S LIFE WRITING AND THE HOLOCAUST

Complicity and Gender in the Second World War

ELISABETH KRIMMER

University of California, Davis

CAMBRIDGE
UNIVERSITY PRESS

CAMBRIDGE
UNIVERSITY PRESS

University Printing House, Cambridge CB2 8BS, United Kingdom

One Liberty Plaza, 20th Floor, New York, NY 10006, USA

477 Williamstown Road, Port Melbourne, VIC 3207, Australia

314–321, 3rd Floor, Plot 3, Splendor Forum, Jasola District Centre,
New Delhi – 110025, India

79 Anson Road, #06–04/06, Singapore 079906

Cambridge University Press is part of the University of Cambridge.

It furthers the University's mission by disseminating knowledge in the pursuit of
education, learning, and research at the highest international levels of excellence.

www.cambridge.org
Information on this title: www.cambridge.org/9781108472821
DOI: 10.1017/9781108563758

© Elisabeth Krimmer 2018

First published 2018

Printed and bound in Great Britain by Clays Ltd, Elcograf S.p.A.

A catalogue record for this publication is available from the British Library.

Library of Congress Cataloging-in-Publication Data
NAMES: Krimmer, Elisabeth, 1967– author.
TITLE: German women's life writing and the Holocaust : gender, genocide and female
agency in the Second World War / Elisabeth Krimmer, University of California, Davis.
DESCRIPTION: Cambridge ; New York : Cambridge University Press, [2018] | Includes
bibliographical references.
IDENTIFIERS: LCCN 2018012047 | ISBN 9781108472821
SUBJECTS: LCSH: World War, 1939–1945 – Women – Germany. | Women – German –
History – 20th century. | World War, 1939–1945 – Participation, Female. | Holocaust
survivors' writings, German – History and criticism. | National socialism and
women. | Germany – Social life and customs.
CLASSIFICATION: LCC D810.W7 K75 2018 | DDC 940.53/18082–dc23
LC record available at https://lccn.loc.gov/2018012047

ISBN 978-1-108-47282-1 Hardback

Contents

CHAPTER I

Introduction
Gender, War, and the Holocaust

"Do you understand that I need to understand ... how a human being can remain indifferent[?] The executioners I understood; also the victims, though with more difficulty. For the others, all the others, those who were neither for nor against, those who sprawled in passive patience ... those who were permanently and merely spectators – all were closed to me, incomprehensible."

Elie Wiesel, 1982[1]

In 1945, the American authorities charged Ilse Koch, the infamous "Bitch of Buchenwald" whose husband ran the Buchenwald concentration camp from 1937 to 1941, with numerous cruelties toward prisoners. She was accused of hitting inmates if they looked at her the wrong way, of selecting tattooed prisoners to be killed, and of turning "the skin of tattooed inmates into lampshades, gloves, knife sheaths, [and] book covers."[2] When Koch was tried for her offenses, notions of gender drastically impacted the arguments of both the prosecution and the defense. Koch emphasized her dependent status *vis-à-vis* her husband: "I was a housewife and I think my power is being overestimated because if I have three ... children, then I am so occupied all day long that I have neither the intention nor [the] time to take care of camp matters."[3] To counter this perception, the prosecution pointed to a directive by Commandant Koch "to the SS to the effect that orders by her [*Frau* Koch] were to be obeyed to the same extent as if he had given them."[4] Koch initially received a life sentence, but Lucius Clay, the American military governor of Germany, overturned the ruling for lack of evidence (and because the beginning of the Cold War made it politically expedient). Koch's story does not end there, however. Counteracting Clay, the US Senate called for a hearing on Ilse Koch and appointed the Ferguson Commission to investigate her case. Again referencing gender, the commission found her guilty as charged: "Most of the defendants tried with her could avail themselves of the plea that they were part of a military organization and as such were obliged to carry out orders regardless of how much they personally opposed them. In contrast, every act committed by Ilse Koch as shown by the evidence was that of a volunteer. ... Being a woman made her participation more unnatural and more deliberate."[5] In spite of these recommendations, the Americans, who were eager to avoid double jeopardy, did not try her again, but released her to the German authorities, who sentenced her to life in prison for offenses against German citizens.

As Koch's story shows, gender interferes with the perception of political and moral agency on every level. It can serve to minimize and even erase women's responsibility for the Nazi war and genocide, but it can also heighten the sense of culpability.[6] And the obfuscation of guilt and complicity is not the only way in which gender impacts our perception of women's roles in war and genocide. In addition to altering perceptions of guilt, notions of gender can also make female suffering and victimization invisible. This erasure of both guilt and suffering has much to do with concepts of war that exclude the experiences of women. John Keegan, the illustrious historian of war, notably defines warfare as "the one human activity from which women, with the most insignificant exceptions, have always and everywhere stood apart."[7] To this day, the Second World War is generally perceived as a male enterprise even though women accompanied the army as auxiliaries and nurses and even though civilians, that is, women, old people, and children, comprised two-thirds of its victims.[8] Tellingly, as feminist historian Linda Grant de Pauw points out, until recently the deaths of civilians were simply "not classified as 'casualties'" but rather as "collateral damage."[9] In other words, even though women contributed to the war effort on many levels and even though civilian deaths outnumbered military deaths by far, women did not feature in the official record of the war.

It would appear that, when it comes to women in the Second World War, we are dealing with two different kinds of invisibility. Both the active participation of women in war and genocide, their contributions to the war effort as secretaries, army auxiliaries, and nurses, their roles as eager helpers and even perpetrators in Hitler's killing fields,[10] *and* their suffering as refugees, rape victims, and concentration camp inmates need to become part of the official narrative of the Second World War. It is the goal of this book to contribute to this shift in perception by highlighting the many ways in which concepts of gender trouble our ideas of war and confuse our perception of guilt and suffering. Specifically, I argue that the disinterest in female war stories carries in its wake a concomitant neglect of structures of complicity, which are to be distinguished from instances of perpetration. Thus, in recovering women's voices, we also begin to understand the fundamental parameters that are at the heart of what I call a "grammar of complicity": a web of ruptured narratives, conceptual and visual blind spots, and silences.

In order to shed light on female complicity in the Second World War and the Holocaust, I examine various forms of life writing, including diaries, memoirs, "docunovels," and autobiographically inspired novels. But before I do so, I would like to explicate the contexts and discourses that shape our perception of these texts: the nexus of gender and warfare, the concept of complicity, the roles of women in the National Socialist regime, and the genre of memoir. Since all instances of female agency and victimization that form the subject matter of this book occur within the context of warfare, I begin by parsing the conceptual blind spots that attend to discussions of gender and war. I then focus on one specific blind spot, namely the interrelation of gender and complicity. Although recent studies have shown that women were among the ranks of some of the worst Nazi perpetrators, the majority of the female citizens of the Third Reich must be categorized as bystanders who were complicit with, but not themselves agents of Nazi crimes. More often than not, their guilt pertains to sins of omission. They did not act cruelly themselves, but were complicit with the cruelty of others. In order to provide a framework in which we can understand their actions, I discuss the concept of complicity in general and the roles and standing of women in the Third Reich in particular. Finally, I have chosen to juxtapose memoirs with some works of (autobiographically inspired) fiction because these fictional works help to situate the memoirs in the discursive contexts that shaped either these texts or our reception of them. Moreover, at times, fictional works offer solutions to the dilemmas that remain "raw scars"[11] in memoirs. Since memoirs rely on a set of assumptions quite different from those that apply to fiction, I give a brief overview of the specific challenges presented by this form of life writing.

Women and War

It has often been pointed out that war has a drastic impact on gender roles. For example, in her edited collection *Brutality and Desire: War and Sexuality in Europe's Twentieth Century*, feminist historian Dagmar Herzog notes the "convulsive and potentially transformative impacts of wars on gender roles and relations."[12] In some contexts, wars have even been endowed with an emancipatory energy: as husbands and fathers become soldiers, wives and daughters gain authority and power in the domestic realm; similarly, as male employees and workers are drafted for frontline service, women gain access to public arenas and to forms of employment that were previously closed to them. Several studies have shown that the First and Second World Wars offered women new forms of freedom and new opportunities, including "skilled, high-paying jobs in heavy industry; new positions in government bureaucracies, educational institutions, the armed forces, and on the front lines as ambulance drivers, medics, and resistantes."[13]

Undoubtedly, wars change gender roles, but it is equally true that gender changes war. In the edited collection *Arms and the Woman: War, Gender, and Literary Representation*, literary scholar Helen M. Cooper calls gender a "crucial organizing principle in the war system."[14] To be sure, gender, both as reality and as ideology, exerts a profound influence on the execution and representation of war and genocide. Consequently, attending to the roles of women in war is crucial not only for our understanding of women's history but also for our perception of warfare: if we focus on the experiences of women, we realize that aspects of war that are frequently relegated to the periphery and dissociated from the "actual" violence of war – the experience of the refugee, the suffering of the concentration camp inmate, but no less the bureaucratic work involved in conducting a war – are in fact central to its functioning. This is all the more true in the Second World War, which blurred the boundaries between battlefield and home front in significant ways. By directly targeting civilian populations either through genocidal policies or through so-called counterinsurgency strategies such as the "Commissar Order" (*Kommissarbefehl*),[15] but also through carpet bombing and displacement of large populations, meaningful distinctions between front line and rear became increasingly redundant. In light of this melding of front and rear, it stands to reason that, if our notion of war is funneled through the perspective of the soldier, it is liable to remain "obsessed with the experience of a very small portion of the large populations implicated in modern warfare" and, consequently, much of what constitutes modern warfare is left out.[16] As Hanley puts it, "canons and cannons have more in common than the accident of sounding alike."[17] If, however, we succeed in including the voices of women, we not only gain insights into how warfare affects women but also begin to develop a fuller and more complex understanding of the scope and nature of modern wars and genocide. In particular, I argue that turning our attention toward the experiences of women allows us to gain a deeper understanding of a group that was crucial for the execution of the Holocaust, but that has often been overlooked: that of the complicitous bystander.

Complicity

Ranging from historical studies of concentration camp guards to numerous biographies and films about the worst offenders of the National Socialist regime, there is a great deal of literature about Nazi perpetrators. There is also an increasing amount of research on those who were victimized in the Holocaust and the Nazi war of conquest. In contrast, there is little on those women and men who can be classified as complicit bystanders.[18] Although bystanders constituted the majority of the German population, few historians, as Elizabeth Harvey reminds, "have concerned themselves with those whose narratives are those of collaboration and compromise with racist movements and repressive regimes . . . sometimes playing down, but sometimes presenting with pride, their past attitudes and actions."[19] And yet the successful execution of the Nazis' genocidal program would have been unthinkable without the passivity, apathy, or silent assent of this group. As Simon Wiesenthal points out, the Nazi "minority reigned because of the cowardice and laziness of the majority."[20] I believe we should take Wiesenthal's insight to heart. Indifference, inertia, and timidity lack the sensationalist appeal of stories of atrocity and cruelty, but they are nonetheless directly and causally linked to the Holocaust. Recent studies show that the majority of the German population never approved of genocidal policies, but they also show that widespread support for the mass killing of Jews was not necessary for the seamless execution of the Holocaust. Rather, an "anti-Jewish consensus" in the German population was enough to make the Holocaust possible.[21]

I believe that the sparsity of studies that focus on bystanders is related to the dearth of studies on women's participation in war and genocide. Indeed, historian Karen Hagemann makes a similar point when she calls "women's participation in the Wehrmacht . . . one of the best-repressed subjects in postwar Germany" and wonders whether this omission has to do with the fact that women's involvement "illustrate[s] most clearly the everyday participation of the many."[22] In many ways, women would seem to be the prime contenders for the title of bystander. Because they were, at least for the most part, excluded from leadership positions, they do not typically rank among the worst offenders of the regime and are consequently more likely found among the bystanders. Similarly, because women, unlike men, were identified with the domestic realm, they could more easily shed public obligations and are thus less likely to incur the responsibility tied to official functions. But this distance from the political domain does not necessarily exonerate the female sex. To be sure, some have claimed that women, precisely because they are frequently seen as apolitical and lack experience in the public sphere, should be forgiven their sins of omission, their failure to resist where resistance was necessary. But one might also conclude that the contributions they did make weigh all the more heavily since, unlike the actions of the soldier who was drafted to serve, they can justifiably be categorized as voluntary.[23]

Even if we disregard the complications introduced by gender discourses, the question of complicity is a highly complex and contested moral quandary. Complicity, as Lepora and Goodin point out, "comes on a sliding scale."[24] In determining the degree of a person's complicity, many factors are relevant. There is the gravity of the offense with which one is complicit and the question of "shared purposes" with the principal offender.[25] There is the moral valence of one's own contribution: is it wrong in and of itself or morally neutral? Is it an essential contribution or rather inconsequential? There is also the fact that, in the context of the Holocaust, we are dealing not only with acts of commission but also with sins of omission.[26] As Gordon Horwitz argues, "the failure to act, the failure to inquire, the failure to remember, each represent a contribution to the killing project."[27] Furthermore, the seriousness of the moral failure implied in complicity is also directly proportional to the degree to which one's action was voluntary and conducted in full knowledge of the purpose to which one was contributing. Especially the latter two criteria pose problems in the context of the Holocaust.

Many who failed to oppose the regime have argued that they were not cognizant of the Holocaust. Although these proclamations of ignorance may be truthful in individual cases, there is reason to doubt that vast segments of the German population remained completely in the dark about the murderous consequences of Nazi racial policy. Indeed, numerous studies have shown that much information was available through different channels. For example, even those who had never heard of extermination camps could have become aware of the magnitude of the genocidal killings through average soldiers who had participated in the mass executions of Jewish men, women, and children on the eastern front.[28] More importantly, even those who remained utterly untouched by the Nazis' genocidal rage must have been aware of the escalating discrimination against and persecution of Jewish citizens, plainly evident in the Nuremberg Laws, the highly visible violence of *Reichskristallnacht*, the public auctions of dispossessed Jewish property, and the deportations, whose victims frequently had to gather in public squares and were marched through town on their way to the train station under the gawking eyes of locals.[29] Given this wealth of information, it would seem that, in many cases, ignorance of the plight of the Jews was willful and culpable, a form of "prudent disregard," as Horwitz notes of the civilian population of Mauthausen that learned to turn a blind eye to genocidal atrocities in the local concentration camp.[30] In other words, we are dealing not with a lack of information, but with reinterpretations, evasions, and rationalizations.[31]

While some excuse their passivity with ignorance, others who went along with or failed to protest the criminal actions of the regime argue that they acted under duress; a claim that one should certainly take seriously since it is well known that the Nazis sanctioned oppositional behavior in various ways ranging from banal to life-threatening, and one could never be sure at which end of the spectrum the official response would fall. In some cases, a refusal to participate in the discrimination of Jews impeded one's chances at professional advancement; in other cases, casual criticism of the regime could lead to arrest, imprisonment, and even death.[32] But there are also numerous instances when men and women defied the regime through small acts of kindness or straightforward refusals to engage in wrongdoing and did not suffer any negative consequences.[33] Clearly, the crux of the matter consists in the fact that, while, in retrospect, it is easy to disentangle perceived risks from actual dangers, at the time such differentiations were arguably much harder to come by. After all, arbitrariness and unpredictability form part of the design of tyrannical regimes and contribute significantly to their effective control of populations. As a result, there are many cases where it is impossible to draw a clear line between bystanders and collaborators or even between collaborators and perpetrators.[34] At the same time, however, there is much to suggest that there were more opportunities for defiance and resistance, however small, than people dared or cared to avail themselves of.[35] Moreover, even if it remains difficult to reconstruct with any certainty all facts and perceptions that determined individual decisions in any given situation, we can gain a better understanding of the general parameters that circumscribed women's actions in the Third Reich by turning our attention to the reality and ideology of National Socialist gender politics.

Women in the Nazi State

Until the 1980s, feminist research conceived of the Third Reich as an exceedingly sexist, patriarchal state that reduced women to the three Ks of "*Kinder, Küche, Kirche*" (children, kitchen, church) and promised the "emancipation of woman from emancipation."[36] (Tellingly, the Nazi Party was the only major party that had not endorsed women's suffrage, in line with Hitler's conviction that women's liberation is a product of the Jewish intellect.[37]) In recent decades, however, feminist scholars have complicated this notion: women were not always or exclusively victims of National Socialist ideology and politics. Rather, their position in the National Socialist state was complex and multidimensional. While the Nazis severely limited women's access to the political and professional arenas, they also opened up numerous new opportunities for "Aryan" women and invited them to participate in the transformation of German society on a national scale.[38]

Initially, women were slow to support the National Socialist German Workers Party (NSDAP). The frequently cited allegation that women elected Hitler to power has long been revealed to be an unfounded, misogynist variant of the stab-in-the-back legend.[39] Although 48 percent of all female voters supported Hitler, they represented only 15 percent of all German women, hardly a sign of disproportionate female enthusiasm for the Nazis. Especially in the early years of the NSDAP, male party members outnumbered female party members by far. In 1935, for example, only 5.5 percent of all party members were female, almost half of whom were housewives.[40] During the next ten years, however, more and more women joined Nazi institutions and organizations. Thus, in 1941, roughly 6 million women, that is, every fifth German woman, were members of the formally independent *NS-Frauenwerk* or the *NS-Frauenschaft*, which was integrated into the NSDAP.[41]

The Nazis were expert at recruiting women for the cause by appealing to both baser and higher instincts. Some women felt validated by Nazi racial ideology and clung to their purported superiority over Jews and Russians;[42] others did not consider confinement to the home a change from their previous situation but rather appreciated the glorification of their roles as housewives and mothers; conversely, those who were publicly minded responded to Nazi rhetoric that called for sacrifices for the nation. Over and over again, Nazi women's leader Gertrud Scholtz-Klink appealed to women's desire to serve a greater purpose and to live up to the "sacred duty of every single person in the service of the people's community."[43] Scholtz-Klink kept reminding women that the *Führer* was counting on them and, in so doing, elevated women's sense of self-importance: "The *Führer* has given us the responsibility for all German people."[44] Similarly, in a speech on September 8, 1934, Scholtz-Klink appealed to women's desire to play a decisive role in the history of the German people: "Then she herself notices one day: I myself am history! And a deep insight comes over her: what is *Volk*? – I am *Volk*."[45]

Paradoxically, the patriarchal Nazi state, which excluded women from almost all party offices and functions, succeeded in recruiting large segments of the female population for a common cause in ways that the Weimar Republic had not. Scholtz-Klink's words did not fall on deaf ears, but were received eagerly by many young German women who were burning to make a difference. Renate Finckh, for example, a member of the Hitler Youth who wrote a memoir about her time in the League of German Girls (*Bund Deutscher Mädel*) (BDM), remembers the pride she felt when she was asked to serve her "*Volk*": "To be truly needed for a higher goal filled me with happiness and pride."[46] To Finckh, the Nazis offered "an emotional home, a safe shelter and soon also a place of recognition."[47]

Clearly, some aspects of National Socialist ideology and practice enhanced the self-esteem of Aryan women, allowed for the development of leadership skills and an active role in public life via organizations such as the *Deutsches Frauenwerk*, the *Deutsche Arbeitsfront* (German Labor Front), or the League of German Girls, and appealed to their desire to make a difference and work toward a purpose larger than themselves.[48] However, while the Nazis allowed for certain, nationally defined forms of female self-actualization, women's empowerment had distinct limits. Particularly in the early years of the regime, a number of policies sought to foreclose employment for women. Thus, a 1933 act called for the dismissal of double earners, that is, of married women whose husbands were gainfully employed. Similarly, the marriage loan program promised interest-free loans to newlywed couples if the wife left her employment until the loan was repaid.[49] In addition, the Nazis imposed numerous restrictions on female professionals. In 1936, Hitler decided that women could not become judges or lawyers, while female doctors faced increasing hurdles. And yet, in spite of these ideological limits, in later years, obstacles to female employment frequently gave way to the exigencies of a struggling war economy. In other words, the longer the war lasted, the more reality interfered with policy. While the Nazis never changed their ideas about women and work or female participation in the army, they either quietly ignored ideological gender precepts or reinterpreted female labor as service for the fatherland.[50] Thus, while the Nazis rejected the notion of a female soldier to the end, the so-called second army of female auxiliaries grew drastically. Driven by the pressures of a war on two fronts, the Nazis could not afford to be consistent in their effort to exclude women from public and professional life. Thus, the campaign against double earners ceased; women who received marriage loans were again allowed to work; and the quota that had reduced the number of female students to no more than 10 percent of the entire student body in December 1933 was lifted in 1935. By 1941 most men served in the army and almost 50 percent of all students were female.

Scholars who advocate a universal victim status of women in the Third Reich tend to emphasize that formal decrees excluded women from leadership positions in the National Socialist Party and in the administration of the Nazi state. This is certainly true, but it does not follow from this that women bore no responsibility for the Nazi war and genocide. Rather, numerous German women participated in the execution of Nazi policy on all levels, even if those policies were formulated by men:[51] female secretaries typed lists of executions and records of expropriated Jewish property; they composed the minutes of Nazi conferences and scheduled appointments for sterilization courts. Female telephone operators communicated the logistical arrangements of deportations;[52] female neighbors and housewives denounced strangers and acquaintances;[53] and wives and girlfriends provided emotional support to their male companions who were engaged in the business of genocide.

Women who fulfilled these functions were not only aware of the genocidal nature of the Nazi state but were also instrumental in ensuring the efficient implementation of Nazi policy and, by extension, the stability of the Nazi regime. To be sure, in many cases, women's participation was not as clear and direct as the actions of female guards in Nazi concentration camps, but consisted rather in mundane and indirect contributions, such as running a farm while the husband was away, or expressed itself not as action but as the absence of action, such as an unwillingness or inability to resist the policies of the Nazi regime. Consider, for example, all the women physicians or housewives' associations that were all too willing to purge their Jewish members.[54] Even then, however, one cannot speak of innocence since, as Schlink explains, "the act of not renouncing, not judging and not repudiating carries its own guilt with it."[55]

Clearly, the assumption that female guilt is limited to "corruptibility by the patriarchal society" has been discredited beyond repair,[56] and any attempt at a "'disposal of the female past' via the notion of the 'grace of a female birth'" is doomed to fail.[57] If, in spite of these findings, female complicity is often overlooked even today, it is precisely because women's contributions to war and genocide typically consisted of either inaction or activities that would be characterized as constructive, supportive, and even caring in a civilian context. Because women's involvement in the Nazi regime was frequently indirect, their political agency remained invisible. Recent research suggests that in the postwar period and continuing into the present women were not held to the same standard as men, and were, as Sarti has shown, "less likely to be convicted . . . of crimes against humanity and war crimes."[58] Of course, women who were complicit with the Nazi regime had every interest in encouraging this disparity. By representing themselves as bystanders who remained at a distance from the public realm, they not only trivialized their own capacity for political agency but also minimized any responsibility for the atrocities of the Second World War.[59] In spite of such efforts at obfuscation, however, women's contributions and complicity remain legible in their life writing from and about this period. Thus, this book relies on a corpus of memoirs, diaries, docunovels, and autobiographically based novels by female authors in order to analyze the various ways in which women supported Hitler's regime even as they suffered under the war that it had started.

In highlighting female bystanders, I do not mean to discount the fact that some women actively resisted the Nazi regime nor the fact that some numbered among the perpetrators and actively participated in the killing. We know that women were active as rescuers and resistance fighters, just as we know that, if the circumstances strengthened and encouraged violent dispositions, women too excelled at the business of genocide. And yet, if I have chosen to focus not on heroines or killers, but on women who collaborated with the Nazi regime, it is not only because these women constituted the majority of the female citizens of the Third Reich,[60] or because the many ambiguities and contradictions in their stories tell us much about the functioning of the Nazi regime, but also because their behavior offers valuable lessons about the nature of complicity, the emergence of violence in civil society, and the possibility of justice in general.[61]

In sum, my purpose in studying the life writing of female bystanders is twofold. First, these texts enrich our understanding of women's history by offering insights into women's motivations for enlisting in the National Socialist cause, into their continuing support for the regime, and, in some cases, into their growing estrangement from it. They teach us why and how women became what Christina Thürmer-Rohr has called "*Mittäter*," but they also show how women suffered from the consequences of National Socialist policies even if they had initially endorsed them. Second, it is precisely because women tended to be at the margins rather than the center of the regime, because their contributions tended to be indirect rather than straightforward, because women tended to be spectators rather than perpetrators of violence, that their life writing can help us understand how various forms of passive support kept the Nazi regime alive. Ultimately, these narratives of collaboration and compromise are at the heart of what made the Nazi terror possible.

Life Writing

Much recent scholarship has drawn attention to the growing popularity of memoirs.[62] In her fascinating study *Popular Trauma Culture: Selling the Pain of Others in the Mass Media*, Anne Rothe points out that the so-called misery memoirs, that is, memoirs that focus on various kinds of traumatic experiences, constitute "the largest growth sector in book publishing worldwide."[63] In light of this trend, it is hardly surprising that much of what we know about women and the Second World War is conveyed in memoirs. However, it is not just the marketability of the memoir that accounts for its preponderance among female-authored narratives about the Second World War. Rather, the genre of memoir is, as Couser points out, very democratic and thus "more available to amateurs than other genres."[64] This openness to nonprofessional writers also implies that the memoir is particularly accessible to women. Indeed, "women are more commonly than men the authors of nobody memoirs."[65]

There is much to be said in favor of memoirs. In personalizing history and historicizing the personal, memoirs make history accessible. Memoirs also allow previously marginalized and silent populations to give voice to their experiences. But there is also much to guard against. Unlike the novel, the memoir makes truth claims. Because of this, it has "more traction (pulling power) than fiction,"[66] but it also invites questions about its veracity, many of which have to do with the highly unreliable nature of the human memory and memoir's concomitant vulnerability to fantasy.[67] Much recent research, including the work of noted psychologist Daniel Schacter, suggests that the process of remembering is driven not by factual accuracy, but by the impetus to make meaning. As Schacter explains, "people rarely recalled all of the events ... they often remembered occurrences that made general sense, or that fit their expectations of what should have happened ... recollections of ... participants changed – sometimes substantially – across multiple retellings of the story."[68] Numerous studies have shown that the human memory does not work like the disk of a computer. Rather, the process of remembering is itself active and apt to change the contents of our memory: "stored memories fade, change, and alter spontaneously over time . . . when we remember a past experience, it is encoded anew into the memory system."[69]

In Greek mythology, the nine muses are the daughters of Zeus and Mnemosyne. Thus, poetry is born from memory. However, while mythology represents the concepts of narrative and memory as closely related, recent neurological and psychological research suggests a certain incompatibility between them: while narrative is enamored with details, local color, and specificity, the human "long-term memory does not favor discrete episodes . . . summary is apparently truer to the way memory actually works."[70] This lack of detail is particularly pertinent when the memories in question relate to traumatic experiences. Although, as Krystal, Southwick, and Charney explain, "stress enhances the recall of salient stimuli in the environment . . . [it] impairs recall of peripheral details."[71] Consequently, when memoirs offer a level of detail that is difficult to reconcile with the design of the human memory in general, that is, when they, as Heinemann remarks, have "the look and density of fiction,"[72] we are left to wonder just how much the author has taken advantage of creative license. Indeed, memoirs are likely to "'indulge,' more than historiography does or is willing to admit, in figuration or imagination," perhaps precisely because they "cannot claim the temporal immediacy or the plotlessness of diary and chronicle."[73] The attendant question of veracity that arises from this "indulgence" is all the more pressing since the memoir's special status and appeal consist precisely in its truth claim. And yet, to rely on one's talent as a writer and enrich one's memoir with descriptive detail does not necessarily mean that the experiences and historical events that form its subject matter are not told truthfully. Indeed, it may simply mean that the truth of a life is told more effectively.

In addition to the shortfalls of memory, the question of veracity can be compounded by other factors: first, memoirs, unlike novels, "are governed – and frequently constricted – by considerations of tact";[74] in other words, authors may wish to omit or alter information to protect their loved ones or themselves. Second, some women who decided to write about the war were children at the time, and children, as recent studies show, are particularly "apt to confuse real and imagined events."[75] Thus, when dealing with the memoirs of those who were children during the war, we would do well to bear in mind that what appear to be childhood memories may very well be secondhand narratives told by the parents of the memoirists or, conversely, firsthand experiences reinterpreted to appease the parent generation.[76] It stands to reason that such memoirs, whose authors must be considered innocent by virtue of their age, are ideally suited to deflect the political and moral responsibility of the parent generation.

In recent decades, the genre of memoir has been tainted by a proliferation of high-profile forgeries, including a fake Holocaust memoir by Binjamin Wilkomirski. In some ways, however, such forms of premeditated fraud deflect attention from a much more systemic problem: the fact that memoirs can lie about the past even if they are not intentionally deceptive. The process of remembering is not only selective and unreliable, but also highly dependent on the "retrieval environment."[77] Every individual human memory is, as Maurice Halbwachs has shown, an inherently social faculty, "a part or an aspect of group memory,"[78] and as such it is designed to respond to the values of an individual's social environment. In other words, the human memory is beholden to the present as much as to the past, and the individual whose memories turn out to be untruthful may have tried to deceive others consciously or may have fallen victim to his or her own lies and be "simultaneously the inventer and the believer."[79] Many recent studies have confirmed that a person's memory is highly susceptible to manipulation through, among others, leading questions or misinformation.[80] However, even if there is no intent to manipulate, we must assume that the present context determines past memories simply because "the reconstruction of the past always depends on frames of meaning and contexts of significance generated in the present."[81] Frequently, such adjustments and alterations either "serve to legitimate a present social order" and/or function as "biographical ... repair strategies."[82]

Unsurprisingly, memoirs of the Second World War, many of which were written decades after the war, are riddled with precisely such "biographical repair strategies." Because the perception of the Third Reich underwent drastic alterations in the process of *Vergangenheitsbewältigung* (coming to terms with the past), Second World War memoirs frequently navigate uneasily between the author's immersion in Nazi ideology at the time and various levels of distance and critique stimulated by postwar discourses. Because a memoir does not so much express an identity as it creates one, "images of the past are strategically invented to suit present needs."[83] And this act of "self-invention" will unfold differently in the discursive environment of the 1990s from what it would have been like in the 1950s. Consequently, it is often difficult to tell if the silences and gaps in personal narrations of the past originate in the cropped vision of the time or if they result from deliberate omissions in the process of remembering,[84] if we are dealing with actual memories or with a "personal myth," that is, a "fundamentally distorted narrative of self or life story."[85] In her analysis of

Holocaust memoirs, Kremer notes that "the survivor-writers conflate three characteristically separate roles: the victim who experiences, the eyewitness who reports, and the imaginative narrator who reconstructs or transfigures historic events."[86] While we know that all three roles impact narrative accounts of the past, it can be next to impossible to disentangle this mélange of competing voices.

While it is often difficult to separate the impact of the past from the demands of the present, we do know that certain patterns differentiate memoirs of bystanders and perpetrators from the memoirs of victims. In her study of three generations of victims and perpetrators of the Nazi regime, Gabriele Rosenthal concludes that stories told by the families of Holocaust survivors are organized around the central motifs of strength and resistance whereas the families of perpetrators emphasize their own victimization.[87] Angelika Ebbinghaus's book on women in National Socialist Germany confirms these findings. Ebbinghaus notes that many women who contributed actively to the implementation of National Socialist policies saw themselves as victims: "Their compassion extended only to themselves. They remained in the role of the victim even though they were perpetrators."[88] This emphasis on their own suffering in the stories of bystanders and perpetrators not only sidelines questions of complicity and guilt[89] but also speaks to a misguided search for redemption. It would seem that, by recycling "the Christian suffering-and-redemption trope of spiritual purification through physical mortification,"[90] memoirists who record the trials and tribulations of life in wartimes hope to atone for a guilt they have yet to admit. Indeed, at times, the self-identification as victim and concomitant obfuscation of one's own culpability culminate in accusations directed against the Jewish victims of the Nazis "who cannot be forgiven for the wrong done to them."[91]

Finally, any study of memoirs of the Second World War would be remiss if it did not address the impact of trauma on the process of remembering and writing. In particular, every analysis of memoirs that record the experience of war and of genocide needs to account for the fact that they deal with the kind of violent experiences that are often seen to immerse "the victim in the scene so profoundly that it precludes the kind of specular distance necessary for cognitive knowledge of what has happened."[92] Indeed, traumatic experiences are frequently defined as resistant to and even destructive of language. While I cannot discuss this question in depth, I do wish to note that I am skeptical of theoretical approaches, such as that advanced by Cathy Caruth, that conceptualize trauma as ineffable. Although I have benefited much from the plethora of enlightening insights in Caruth's work, I agree with Trezise's critique of some of her foundational premises. In his study *Witnessing Witnessing: On the Reception of Holocaust Survivor Testimony*, Trezise calls Caruth's theory of trauma "epistemically unfounded" because there is "no conceivable subject position from which it is possible to know what supposedly remains, by definition, unknowable."[93]

Trezise's critique of Caruth expresses some of the concerns that also inform Ruth Klüger's story about a Holocaust victim who returns from the dead to attend a lecture on Nazi atrocities. Taken aback by theories about the unspeakability of the horror inflicted by the Nazis, the ghost counters that there is no lack of words to describe what happened. In his case, the appropriate phrase would be "shot in the neck."[94] To be sure, and as Klüger is well aware, the fact that we have words to describe Nazi cruelty can in no way ensure that these words convey the full depth of the suffering inflicted on its victims. But even if we assume that there is a remainder that is confined to unspeakability, we would do well to remember that many writers of Holocaust memoirs are far more concerned with the unwillingness of others to listen to their stories than with the difficulty of putting them into words. As Trezise reminds us, such concerns should "give us pause before making a claim to the effect that the Holocaust or trauma of any kind is 'unspeakable.' We could stop to consider how, in a concrete situation of address, it might be heard by a Holocaust survivor and whether, among other translations, by no means the least plausible might sound like this: 'I don't want to listen.'"[95] And while the motivation for such an unwillingness to listen to accounts of the Second World War and the Holocaust may lie in a reluctance to engage with and be made a witness to suffering, it may also originate in a refusal to confront our own capacity for complicity and guilt.

Chapter Overview

The past two decades have seen a proliferation of memoirs of the Third Reich. This flood of publications has much to do with increased public attention to and acceptance of discourses on German victimization in the wake of German reunification, but it is also motivated by the simple biological fact that contemporaries of the war are dying and are often seizing their last chance to tell their side of the story as well as by the recent boom of the memoir genre in American and European culture.[96] As Fuchs and Cosgrove have argued, such memoirs have frequently "exposed the limits of Germany's official remembrance culture that for decades sidelined people's private memories of the war."[97]

In the following chapters, I discuss memoirs by army auxiliaries, by nurses in the German army, by German refugees and rape victims, and by Holocaust survivors. Each chapter begins with a brief discussion of the respective historical contexts and discursive frameworks. These introductions, which rely on historical studies but also on a theme-oriented analysis of a large group of memoirs that I do not discuss in depth, are followed by extensive interpretations of select works. Although I have attempted to present these memoirs in chronological order, they tend to defy clear-cut timelines. Many were written immediately after the war but published decades later. Some were written recently but integrate diary entries and thus seek to establish a dialogue with a younger self. Moreover, many of these memoirs are not in sync with public discourses of *Vergangenheitsbewältigung*. Texts written in the 1970s sometimes contain insights that are identified with later research on the Third Reich while some memoirs that were written in the past ten years remain largely untouched by public and academic debates on National Socialism.[98]

Although I have chosen to pair analyses of works by women who supported the Nazi regime with readings of texts by Jewish women who were victimized by the Nazis, I do not wish to argue for a national community of all victims of Nazism that includes both non-persecuted and persecuted Germans. Rather, I endeavor to steer clear of the "inherently competitive rhetoric of victim talk," precisely because I am acutely aware that, "while all victims suffer, not everyone who suffers is a victim,"[99] or rather, not everyone who suffers is exclusively a victim. Instead, my decision to include a chapter that examines the concept of complicity of non-Jewish German women from the perspective of Jewish victims of the Nazi regime is motivated by the conviction that an account of the roles of German women in the Second World War would be incomplete if it did not include the experiences of those German women who were designated as "Other" and excluded from the national community. We learn much about complicity by analyzing the various strategies of self-justification in the texts of women who actively contributed to the functioning of the Nazi regime. But we also learn much by turning our attention to the victims of the regime who suffered the consequences of such complicity.

Throughout, I approach stories that highlight the suffering of bystanders and perpetrators with caution. To begin with, these texts are problematic sources. Their authors may not remember the war accurately and, even if they do, they may choose not to record what they remember faithfully. Due to the obscurity of many of the female memoirists discussed here, it is difficult to evaluate the stories contained in these texts objectively. For the most part, the marginal roles they played have not attracted the attention of scholars of history. Thus, one cannot evaluate their texts based on factual information provided in authoritative biographies or studies. However, even in the absence of independently verifiable information, it is possible to identify omissions, inconsistencies, and internal contradictions within each text and thus to trace "the conflicted process of simultaneous denial and critical self-reflection"[100] that defines many of these narratives.

In addition to the uncertain nature of these memoirs as source material, I am acutely aware of the argument that Germans of the Second World War generation have forfeited the right to tell stories about their own misery. As the descendant of a survivor put it: "How dare they speak of German suffering when it was their country that had started it all."[101] And yet, there is a case to be made that the life narratives of Jewish and non-Jewish Germans form part of a larger story, albeit in very different ways. If we assume with Misztal that there is "a link between collective memory and social solidarity,"[102] and if we hope to actualize this potential for solidarity in the future, we will need to integrate all these story lines into our collective archive of the Second World War. Such an archive will not only offer insights into previously under-researched aspects of the Second War but also lay the foundation for a deeper understanding of what we might call "the grammar of complicity."

Every chapter in the book is designed to highlight crucial elements in an emergent structure of complicity: narrative ruptures, conceptual and visual blind spots, and silences. All of these elements can be read as "defensive reactions against the knowledge of belonging to a nation of perpetrators"[103] and all of them signal disturbances in the relation between self and world; these disturbances manifest as an inability to form a coherent narrative of the self, as a failure to integrate disparate facts into the dominant storyline, as a gradual erosion of any sense of reality; they give rise to omissions, denial, inconsistencies, non sequiturs, and contradictions. Indeed, all too often, a narrative inconsistency, expressive of "the twilight between knowing and not knowing,"[104] signals complicity.

I open my investigation with a chapter on women who, albeit in different ways, contributed to the success of Hitler's army. This chapter, entitled "Ruptured Narratives," offers readings of five autobiographical texts by four authors: a report based on the diary entries of army auxiliary Lore Vogt, written in 1945 and 1946; a docunovel by former auxiliary Hildegard Gartmann, published in 1971; the memoirs of Ilse Schmidt, also an army auxiliary; and two memoirs by "Hitler's pilot" Hanna Reitsch.

All these texts teach us not only that women were much closer to the front lines than is commonly acknowledged, but also that they were informed about the Nazi genocide, and, to various degrees, complicit with it. I argue that the inability to come to terms with this complicity finds expression in narrative ruptures that manifest themselves in non sequiturs, fragmented thoughts, abrupt shifts in focus, and the mantra-like repetition of almost identical stock phrases and anecdotes. These ruptures arise as the authors attempt unsuccessfully to reconcile memories of the past with the discursive pressures of the present; the brutal reality of the war with the National Socialist rhetoric of the *Endsieg*; the sense of exhilaration and agency felt at the time with the perception of victimization prevalent in the postwar period; and Nazi gender ideology with the lived experience of serving as an auxiliary (or, in Reitsch's case, as a test pilot) in Hitler's army. All texts discussed in this chapter evince awareness of the Holocaust, but they do so in twisted form. Some authors claim that they had heard stories about the Holocaust, but did not believe them. Others remain silent about the Holocaust, but then speak about a Jewish desire for revenge that remains curiously unmotivated. Schmidt's memoir in particular reveals that the effects of wartime silence about the Holocaust are pervasive. The fact that the Holocaust remained unspoken at the time led to the gradual erosion of any firm grasp of reality and created a climate in which actual ignorance and willful denial became indistinguishable and accountability unthinkable.

Chapter 3, entitled "Cropped Vision," turns its attention to the figure of the nurse. It contrasts idealizations of the "angel in white" in literary fiction with representations of nursing in memoirs by German army nurses and by inmate nurses in concentration camps. While Chapter 2 is primarily concerned with the impact of structures of complicity on narrative strategies, "Cropped Vision" also deals with the visual record of the war, that is, with the photographic record included in some of these memoirs. A reading of the memoirs by army nurses Erika Summ and Inge Ochsenknecht shows how these women learned to turn a blind eye to any and all experiences that were likely to disturb their emotional and cognitive equilibrium, including their own conformity with a genocidal regime. In other words, they habituated themselves to a form of cropped vision that highlighted German victimization but failed to take account of suffering inflicted by Germans. In contrast, inmate nurses in Nazi concentration camps bore the full brunt of Nazi atrocities. As I show, in order to cope with the immensity of suffering in the camps, inmate nurses were forced to refocus their gaze and redefine the meaning of care. In the absence of the most basic medical supplies, they offered solace, emotional comfort, and a commitment to commemorate after death those whom they could not help in life.

While Chapters 2 and 3 focus on women who actively participated in the Nazi war effort and consequently highlighted women's political agency and their various contributions to the National Socialist regime of terror, Chapters 4 and 5 deal with narratives by and about women whose complicity is offset by their own victimization. Chapter 4, entitled "Interrupted Silences," engages with the complicity of rape victims in the National Socialist regime of terror. It begins with a discussion of the historical context and theoretical framework for discussions of rape, and argues that stories of wartime rape present a dual challenge: a response that fails to acknowledge the suffering of the victims is likely to replicate the silence attached to this crime and/or to align with the perpetrators and reactivate the trauma of rape. Conversely, a response that ignores the issue of complicity inherent in these stories erases the political and historical context in which these rapes occurred and thus fails to do justice to those who were victimized by National Socialist Germany. In order to elucidate these dilemmas, I first discuss the representation of rape in *Germany Diary 1945–46* by Red Army soldier Wladimir Gelfand. I then contrast Gelfand's account with representations of rape in Alexander Solzhenitsyn's *Prussian Nights* (1974) and in Lev Kopelev's memoir *To Be Preserved Forever* (1976). The second section focuses on memoirs of German rape victims, in particular on Gabi Köpp's memoir of the trek. Following the discussion of memoirs, I then analyze the political deployment of the mass rapes in Ingo Münch's historical study, and a tendency to downplay the suffering of rape victims in works by left-leaning historians. I argue that, in all these accounts, rape is represented through a series of interrupted silences that reveal as much as they conceal. All too often, the experience of rape is silenced or drowned out either because of the shame associated with it or because of the political agendas of the authors. Thus, rape becomes invisible even in texts that explicitly address the topic of wartime rape. Finally, I conclude with an interpretation of two fictional representations of rape that offer a potential solution to the dilemma presented by the complicit victim: Julia Franck's *Blindness of the Heart* and Jenny Erpenbeck's *Visitation*. These recent fictionalizations of wartime rape experiment with new discursive strategies that no longer mandate silence about rape but also steer clear of emplotments that minimize female complicity. Throughout, I argue that we should heed the stories of rape victims, not least because such stories teach us to question pat dichotomies of victims and perpetrators and of silence and discourse; but we should also not hesitate to critique the ideological blind spots that inform them and reject the legacy of racism that they may imply.

Much like stories of wartime rape, representations of the trek, that is, of the German flight west from the Russian army toward the end of the Second World War, are intensely political documents.[105] Chapter 5, entitled "Parallel Stories," parses the narrative and conceptual difficulties that arise when members of the perpetrator nation narrate their own victimization. I ask not only how these authors offer testimonies of their own suffering and whether or not they acknowledge national guilt but also whether they reflect on their own complicity in the national endeavor. Although the experience of the trek, much like that of the refugee in general, is highly gendered,[106] gender is not one of the defining categories in the reception of these texts. In contrast, I seek to contribute to the critical discourse on German victimization and complicity not only by focusing on texts by female memoirists who have largely been ignored but also by highlighting how the author's gender affected her experience of the trek and her attempts to narrate this experience. I focus on autobiographically inspired texts by five female writers who took part in the trek west: the essay "Nobody Went East Anymore" by Marion Gräfin Dönhoff; the memoirs *Trek: An American Woman, Two Small Children and Survival in World War II Germany* by Mary Hunt Jentsch, *Surviving Was More Difficult Than Dying* by Erika Morgenstern, and *And Deep in the Soul the Distance: The Story of a Displacement from Silesia* by Katharina Elliger. The chapter concludes with an analysis of Christa Wolf's novel *Patterns of Childhood*.

While all previous chapters dealt with the self-perception of non-Jewish German women, "A View from the Outside In" discusses the representation of German women's complicity in the memoirs of Holocaust survivors. It includes three memoirs by Jewish women who "lived on the Aryan side" because their texts offer a particularly intimate look at the complicity of German women: Betty Lauer's memoir *Hiding in Plain Sight: The Incredible True Story of a German-Jewish Teenager's Struggle to Survive in Nazi-Occupied Poland* (2004) details how the author, who survived the war in Nazi-occupied Poland by pretending to be a Polish Christian, experienced the German occupying force; Inge Deutschkron's *I Wore the Yellow Star* (1978) and Marie Simon Jalowicz's *Gone to Ground: One Woman's Extraordinary Account of Survival in the Heart of Nazi Germany*, published posthumously in 2014, both chronicle the author's lives as hidden Jews in wartime Berlin; finally, Ruth Klüger's

Still Alive: A Holocaust Girlhood Remembered (1992) includes sophisticated reflections on the role of women in the Third Reich and on the
nature of guilt and complicity. I argue that reading the memoirs of
female Holocaust survivors offers a powerful counterargument to what
Kaplan calls "the myth of German innocence." All authors discussed in
this chapter highlight the constant exposure to anti-Semitism in everyday life as well as numerous interactions and encounters with Germans
of both genders who passively condoned or actively supported the
regime. I have chosen the title "A View from the Outside In" because
all these texts are marked by a crippling feeling of isolation and exclusion from an environment that used to be home, illustrated by scenes in
which persecuted Jews peek into the houses of Germans who are
unperturbed by the violent persecution of their former neighbors.

   In the past couple of decades, the field of Holocaust studies has adopted
Marianne Hirsch's term "post-memory" to deal with the generational
differences in the remembrance of the Nazi war and genocide. For my
own perspective on this period, however, the term "post-guilt" seems more
appropriate – with "post" implying both a distance from the guilt of the
previous generation and an inextricable involvement with it. I grew up as
a child of parents who, although they were too young to participate actively
in Nazi politics, endorsed aspects of Nazi ideology even after the war in
more or less explicit terms. My father, in particular, praised the Nazis for
creating employment and building *autobahnen*. When pressed, he would
insist that "we," a collective entity whose precise contours remained uni-
dentified, had no idea what was going on in Dachau, a town that was but
a few miles away from Eching, where I grew up. When it comes to my
mother, however, all I remember is a pervasive silence. It is partly because
of this silence that the following pages highlight the involvement of women
in the Third Reich as well as their suffering.

   While this project is tied to my life story, it is conceived, first and
foremost, as an urgent political intervention. In the age of global media,
we have become spectators and thereby witnesses of all the world's atrocities. Complicity, one might claim, is the postmodern state of being in the
world. I believe that, in learning about how the memoirists discussed in
these pages dealt or failed to deal with the ethical challenges of the Second
World War and the Holocaust, we also stand to learn about our own
implications in the humanitarian crises of our own time. In all my readings, I seek to remain aware of the fact that *ex post facto* accusations of
complicity are all too easy. As Gitta Sereny warns, "I don't know now at
which point one human being can make the moral decision for another

that he should have the courage to risk death."[107] Thus, we would do well to heed the advice of Kundrus, who reminds us that we should not jump to conclusions but rather take great pains to consider the context in which women were acting as well as the enormous differences between individual women's lives.[108] And yet I also believe that the political project of democratic government is doomed to fail if we go too easy on our manifold forms of complicity and compliance. As Trezise points out, "responsibility both precedes and exceeds the ability to fulfill it."[109] In interrogating the moral valence of German women's complicitious choices of the past, the goal is not to condemn past actions but to use them as a mirror for our own inadequacies and, ultimately, to develop a framework for our future.

Notes

1. Wiesel, *The Town beyond the Wall*, 148–149.
2. Whitlock, *The Beasts of Buchenwald*, 81.
3. Whitlock, *The Beasts of Buchenwald*, 222. According to Richter, Nazi women could "mit einer milden Strafe rechnen, wenn es ihnen gelang, ihr Leben als in erster Linie durch häusliche und erzieherische Aufgaben bestimmt darzustellen" ("count on mild punishment when they succeeded in portraying their lives as predominantly determined by domestic and educational duties") ("Das Andere hat kein Geschlecht," 186).
4. Whitlock, *The Beasts of Buchenwald*, 200–201.
5. Whitlock, *The Beasts of Buchenwald*, 249. See also Sarti, *Women + Nazis*, 155.
6. See also Kuretsidis-Haider on the demonization of female Nazi perpetrators ("Täterinnen vor Gericht," 204), Toussaint on a tendency to downplay the violence of female Nazi perpetrators because they do not conform to gender stereotypes ("Nichts gesehen – nichts gewusst"), Gehmacher on the popular representation of the wives of prominent Nazis ("Umfeld"), and Wachsmuth on the tendency to perceive female relatives as passive and apolitical victims of the Nazis ("Tradierungsweisen von Geschlechterbildern").
7. Keegan, *A History of Warfare*, 75.
8. See Naimark, *Fires*, 82, and Enloe, who writes that "so much of military history and current commentary on weapons, wars and defence spending is written as though women didn't exist" (*Does Khaki Become You*, v).
9. de Pauw, *Battle Cries and Lullabies*, 19.
10. Lower's work shows that women were not only "gleeful onlookers but also . . . violent tormenters" (*Hitler's Furies*, 3). She argues that we should take these female perpetrators seriously even if "the documented cases of direct killing are not numerous" (4).
11. Schwab, *Haunting Legacies*, 5.
12. Herzog, *Brutality and Desire*, 1.

13. Scott, "Rewriting History," 23. Longenbach makes a similar point: "The suffragettes, as Virginia Woolf would recall in *Three Guineas*, unconsciously 'desired our splendid war' precisely because it ripped apart Edwardian society as their own bombs could not" ("The Women and Men of 1914," 113).

14. Cooper, Munich, and Squier, "Introduction," xv.

15. The Commissar Order called for the summary execution of all Soviet prisoners who were identified as political functionaries, a category that allowed for a wide range of interpretations.

16. Hanley, *Writing War*, 6. See also Hagemann, who argues that the "systematic integration of gender perspectives will yield new interpretations . . . of both world wars" (Hagemann, "Preface," x).

17. Hanley, *Writing War*, 18. See also Alexijewitsch, *Der Krieg hat kein weibliches Gesicht*, 13–14 and Higonnet, "Introduction," 2.

18. In addition to Raul Hilberg's magisterial work, the behavior and motivations of bystanders are the subject of studies by Frances Henry, Gordon J. Horwitz, and Victoria J. Barnett, and of an edited volume by Klee, Dressen, and Riess. Barnett lists three factors that account for the behavior of bystanders: "the dynamics of totalitarianism; the development and role of prejudice; and the underlying dynamics of the widespread 'indifference' that existed" (*Bystanders*, 69).

19. Harvey, "Remembering and Repressing," 278.

20. Wiesenthal, *The Sunflower*, 19. See also "There were millions of such families anxious only for peace and quiet in their own little nests. These were the mounting blocks by which the criminals climbed to power and kept it" (91).

21. "anti-jüdischer Grundkonsens" (Bajohr, *offenes Geheimnis*, 43). See also Mühlhäuser, who argued that "Es sei eben nicht das heftige Verlangen nach dem Judenmord gewesen, das ihn ermöglichte, sondern die lähmende Gleichgültigkeit, das hinnehmende Desinteresse gegenüber dem Schicksal der Juden oder der Häftlinge der Konzentrations und Vernichtungs- und der Bevölkerung in den besetzten Gebieten" ("it was not the ardent desire to murder Jews that made it possible but the paralyzing indifference, the accepting disinterest toward the destiny of the Jews or the inmates of concentration and extermination camps and toward the population in the occupied territories") (Mühlhäuser, "Vergewaltigungen," 389).

22. Hagemann, "Home/Front," 24. Many scholars refer to Thürmer-Rohr's concept of "weibliche Mittäterschaft" ("female complicity"). However, Thürmer-Rohr does not initially discuss the Third Reich but rather focuses her remarks on nuclear war (see *Vagabundinnen*).

23. As Margit Reiter has shown, the marginalization, depoliticization, and concomitant exoneration of women characterizes not only public discourses but also family memory (*Die Generation danach*, 190).

24. Lepora and Goodin, *On Complicity and Compromise*, 8.

25. Lepora and Goodin, *On Complicity and Compromise*, 9.

26. Lepora and Goodin discuss the case of a Nazi mailman. They conclude that "the postman's contribution factor would be low"; however, "since the

badness of the principal wrongdoing, the Holocaust, is so very large, the overall pro tanto blameworthiness of the postman for his contribution to the wrongdoing might be quite high, his low contribution factor notwithstanding" (*On Complicity and Compromise*, 119).

27. Horwitz, *In the Shadow of Death*, 177. See also Karl Jaspers's statement that "blindness for the misfortune of others, lack of imagination of the heart, inner indifference toward the witnessed – that is moral guilt" (64).

28. See Friedländer, "The Wehrmacht, German Society, and the Knowledge of the Mass Extermination of the Jews," 24.

29. See Bajohr, *offenes Geheimnis*, 46–49.

30. Horwitz, *In the Shadow of Death*, 35.

31. See Cohen, *States of Denial*, xi and 1.

32. See Henry, *Victims and Neighbors*, 98.

33. Klee, Dressen, and Riess point out that those who refused to participate in the mass execution of Jews might be transferred, but they were not shot or arrested (*The Good Old Days*, xx; see also 76–86).

34. See Trezise, *Witnessing Witnessing*, 86.

35. For example, Horwitz shows that not a single inhabitant of Mauthausen who gave food to emaciated concentration camp inmates who were marched through town was imprisoned (*In the Shadow of Death*, 153). Barnett points out that Henry, in her study of the town of Sonderburg, "discovered only two cases in which people who helped Jews or openly criticized Nazi policies were punished" (*Bystanders*, 4).

36. Rupp, *Mobilizing Women for War*, 16. Gravenhorst and Tatschmurat point to the "Tendenz der bundesrepublikanischen Frauenforschung Frauen, wenn es um ihre NS-Beteiligung geht, zumindest partiell zu entschulden" ("tendency of women's studies in the Federal Republic to make excuses for women, at least in part, where their NS-participation is concerned") ("Vorwort," 11). According to Herkommer, women were, for the most part, seen as victims from the 1970s to the mid-1980s. In the mid-1980s, the focus shifted to women as potential perpetrators (*Frauen im Nationalsozialismus*, 9). For a concise summary of research on the role of women during the Third Reich, see also Herkommer, "Women," and Frietsch and Herkommer ("Nationalsozialismus und Geschlecht: eine Einführung," 25–30). Lanwerd and Stoehr argue that research on women in the Third Reich from the 1970s was more differentiated than contemporary accounts acknowledge ("Frauen- und Geschlechterforschung zum Nationalsozialismus seit den 1970er Jahren," 24–25).

37. Kaplan in Bridenthal, Grossmann, and Kaplan, *When Biology Became Destiny*, 210. See also Johnson, "Nazi Feminists," 60.

38. See Koonz, who points out that in the early years of the regime, "Nazi women had carte blanche to innovate as they saw fit" and "enjoyed greater latitude than did their more traditional counterparts in apolitical women's organizations" (Koonz, "The Competition for Women's *Lebensraum*, 1928–1934," 218–219). However, Koonz also notes that "within a year of Hitler's takeover, no woman leader from the 'old days' had survived in any major office" (226).

39. See Stephenson, *Women in Nazi Germany*, 15, and Tröger, "Between Rape and Prostitution." The counter-historical feminization of fascism is evident in the work of Joachim Fest: "Gewiß sind die Elemente abgöttischer Verehrung in der 'männlichen Bewegung' nicht minder wirksam gewesen; aber jener schrankenlos überreizte, entschieden hysterische Ton ... nahm seinen Ausgang doch vom Gefühlsüberschwang einer bestimmten Gattung ältlicher Frauen, die das unbefriedigte Triebmaterial ihres Innern im Taumel nächtlicher Großkundgebungen vor der ekstatischen Gestalt Hitlers zu aktivieren versuchten" ("Certainly, the elements of idolatrous worship were no less present in the 'male movement'; but this unlimited overwrought, decidedly hysterical tone ... originated in the emotional excess of a certain type of older women who sought to activate their unsatisfied internal drives in the frenzy of nightly mass rallies in front of the ecstatic figure of Hitler") (cited in Herkommer, *Frauen im Nationalsozialismus*, 14).
40. For more information, see Lehker, *Frauen im Nationalsozialismus*, 67ff.
41. For more information, see Benz, *Frauen im Nationalsozialismus*, 14–15.
42. According to Bernardoni, anti-Semitism allowed German women to project the sense of interiority onto Jews (Bernardoni, "Ohne Schuld und Sühne?," 133). See also Komann, who suggests that the National Socialist focus on racial belonging made gender seem secondary (Komann, "Wie ich Nationalsozialistin wurde," 164), and Roth, who argues that "no doubt race relations had priority over gender relations in Nazi ideology" (Roth, "Equality, Neutrality, Particularity," 9). Koonz notes that Nazi women saw themselves as "members of an elite" (Koonz, *Mothers in the Fatherland*, 11).
43. "Alles Lernen, alles Kämpfen nicht eine 'Sache an sich' ist, sondern eine heilige Aufgabe jedes einzelnen im Dienste an der Volksgemeinschaft" (Scholtz-Klink, *Verpflichtung und Aufgabe der Frau im nationalsozialistischen Staat*, 8). See Berger on Scholtz-Klink's tendency to turn service and sacrifice into a privilege and a form of heroism ("Die Reichsfrauenführerin Gertrud Scholtz-Klink," 109). See also Koonz, *Mothers in the Fatherland*, xvii–xxxv.
44. "Der Führer hat uns die Verantwortung für das gesamte deutsche Volk übertragen" (Scholtz-Klink, *Verpflichtung und Aufgabe der Frau im nationalsozialistischen Staat*, 16).
45. "Dann merkt sie eines Tages von selbst: ich bin ja selber Geschichte! Und es überfällt sie die tiefe Erkenntnis: was heißt denn Volk? – Volk bin ich" (cited in Benz, *Frauen im Nationalsozialismus*, 48).
46. "Für ein höheres Ziel wirklich gebraucht zu werden, erfüllte mich mit Glück und Stolz" (Finckh, *alltägliche Faschismus*, 71; see also Finckh, *neue Zeit*, 78, 92, 140).
47. "Eine emotionale Heimat, einen Hort der Geborgenheit und bald auch eine Stätte der Anerkennung" (Finckh, *alltägliche Faschismus*, 71). See also Bridenthal, Grossmann, and Kaplan, who point out that many women who were pro-Nazi "still fondly recall their sense of freedom from parental authority and their camaraderie with other women in the League of German Girls" ("Introduction," 22).

48. See Reese, *Growing Up Female in Nazi Germany*, 9; Steinbacher, "Einleitung," 9; and Krauss on female careers ("Rechte Frauen," 10). See also Kundrus, who points out that the financial support for soldiers' wives allowed women greater independence (*Kriegerfrauen*, 293). On "female collaboration as personal empowerment," see also Leck, "Conservative Empowerment and the Gender of Nazism," 151.

49. See Fontaine, *Nationalsozialistische Aktivistinnen (1933–1945)*, 74–75; Bajohr, *Die Hälfte der Fabrik*, 220.

50. For more information, see Lehker, *Frauen im Nationalsozialismus*, 57; Stephenson, *Women in Nazi Germany*, xiv–xv; Benz, *Frauen im Nationalsozialismus*, 195.

51. For detailed discussions of women's involvement and culpability, see Herkommer (*Frauen im Nationalsozialismus*), Kompisch (*Täterinnen*), and Gravenhorst and Tatschmurat (*Töchterfragen*). See also Hagemann, who claims that women "bore substantial responsibility for the functioning of the system" ("Home/Front," 24) and Sarti, who notes that women "played an important role in all levels of the war" (*Women + Nazis*, xv).

52. See Kohlhaas, "Weibliche Angestellte der Gestapo 1933–1945"; Zipfel, "Wie führen Frauen Krieg?," 464; Bock, "Ordinary Women in Nazi Germany," 89.

53. See Helga Schubert's *Judasfrauen*.

54. Bridenthal, Grossmann, and Kaplan, "Introduction," 21. Bridenthal, Grossmann, and Kaplan further point out that this lack of resistance has much to do with the fact that the women's movement "was sympathetic to Nazi appeals to motherhood, racial hygiene, social health, and eugenics, which had always been central concerns of the middle-class women's movement" (22).

55. Schlink, *Guilt about the Past*, 15.

56. "Korrumpierbarkeit durch die patriarchale Gesellschaft" (Windaus-Walser, "Frauen im Nationalsozialismus," 68). The most prominent exponent of this theory is Margarete Mitscherlich, who claimed that women became anti-Semitic because they adopted the prejudices of their fathers, brothers, and husbands for fear of losing their love (see Herkommer, *Frauen im Nationalsozialismus*, 26).

57. "'Entsorgung der Vergangenheit' mithilfe der Vorstellung einer 'Gnade der weiblichen Geburt'" (Meyer, "Brief an Lerke Gravenhorst," 140). Cf. Szepansky, who speaks of the "Gnade der weiblichen Sozialisation" (mercy of female socialization), claiming that women are raised to be sensitive and this sensitivity creates an emotional distance to the inhumanity of Nazi rule (*Blitzmädel, Heldenmutter, Kriegerwitwe*, 15).

58. Sarti, *Women + Nazis*, 41.

59. See Schüddekopf, who in his study *Der alltägliche Faschismus*, notes that the women he talked to positioned themselves on the margins of history (12).

60. See Weckel and Wolfrum, who note that "Nur in niederen Rängen, etwa als Angestellte der SS und Gestapo, nahmen Frauen aktiv teil am NS-Verbrechen, doch in erheblich geringerer Zahl als Männer" ("Women actively participated

in NS-crimes only in the lower ranks, such as employees of the SS and Gestapo, and in significantly lower numbers than men") ("NS-Prozesse," 10).

61. In her study of women in the Iraq War, Oliver concludes that "it is the disavowal of ambiguities . . . that contributes to a culture of violence" (*Women as Weapons of War*, 4).

62. Different scholars work with different definitions of memoir. For a useful definition, see Trezise: "A memoir is a first person narrative pertaining to a segment of the author's life in which he or she witnessed events of general or historical significance. Unlike autobiography, which encompasses the whole of an individual's life up to the time of writing, memoir covers primarily if not exclusively the segment in question. Unlike the diary or journal, it is written from a perspective that clearly postdates the demarcated series of events to which it refers" (Trezise, *Witnessing Witnessing*, 251). For more information on the genre of autobiography, see Smith and Watson, *Reading Autobiography*. For women and autobiography, see Smith, *A Poetics of Women's Autobiography*.

63. Rothe, *Popular Trauma Culture*, 6.

64. Couser, *Memoir*, 26.

65. Couser, *Memoir*, 146.

66. Couser, *Memoir*, 170.

67. See Gilmore, *The Limits of Autobiography*, 42.

68. Schacter, "Memory Distortion," 8.

69. Schacter, "Memory Distortion," 5–6.

70. Couser, *Memoir*, 73; see also 78.

71. Krystal, Southwick, and Charney, "Post Traumatic Stress Disorder," 157.

72. Heinemann, *Gender and Destiny*, 118. Heinemann suggests that "many Holocaust memoirs use a combination of fictional and non-fictional elements" (9).

73. Trezise, *Witnessing Witnessing*, 98.

74. Miller, "Entangled Self," 541.

75. Schacter, "Memory Distortion," 5.

76. See Misztal, *Theories of Social Remembering*, 76.

77. According to McClelland, "recall is not a retrieval, but a reconstruction . . . woven into a coherent whole, with the aid of preexisting knowledge. Details may be distorted to increase coherence . . . simultaneously constrained by traces left in the mind by the event we are remembering itself, by background knowledge of related material, and by constraints and influences imposed by the situation surrounding the act of recollection" ("Constructive Memory and Memory Distortions," 69).

78. Halbwachs, *On Collective Memory*, 53.

79. Prager, *Presenting the Past*, 124.

80. See Schacter, "Memory Distortion," 13.

81. Prager, *Presenting the Past*, 70.

82. Connerton, *How Societies Remember*, 3; "biographische . . . Reparaturstrategien" (Rosenthal, *Der Holocaust*, 15). See also Schacter, who points out that "distortion

might be particularly pronounced when recall is attempted long after a single experience that has not been retrieved or thought about in the interim, or when an experience was not particularly well encoded at the outset" ("Memory Distortion," 25).

83. Misztal, *Theories of Social Remembering*, 50. See also Jeffrey Prager, who calls memories "screens that express perceptions of the past generated by interests that postdate the past experiences" (*Presenting the Past*, 53).

84. See Harvey, "Remembering and Repressing," 291. See also Lehker, who notes that it is difficult to tell the difference between the author's point of view at the time and the author's point of view at the time of writing the autobiography (*Frauen im Nationalsozialismus*, 69).

85. Schacter, "Memory Distortion," 10.

86. Kremer, *Women's Holocaust Writing*, 25.

87. Rosenthal, *Der Holocaust*, 25. Rosenthal also notes that victims are often silent ("die partielle Sprachlosigkeit der Verfolgten") whereas bystanders and perpetrators like to tell stories about the past, but their stories are designed to hide, not reveal Nazi crimes (37).

88. "Sie bedauerten immer nur sich selbst. Sie verharrten in der Rolle der Opfer, obwohl sie die Täterinnen waren" (Ebbinghaus, *Opfer und Täterinnen*, 13). See also Bar-On, who notes the same trend when he comments on an interview with a Nazi perpetrator: "He actually felt sorry for himself. I had always hoped he might say something about the victims" (*Legacy of Silence*, 250). Reiter highlights the role of gender in victim discourses when she points out that grandmothers and mothers have done much to cement the focus on the victimization of one's own family (*Die Generation danach*, 49). See also Mahr, who confirms these findings in her analysis of seventy autobiographies from the Nazi era (*Kriegsliteratur von Frauen?*, 305).

89. Mahr concludes that most female memoirists of the Nazi era did not establish a link between their own actions and German guilt (*Kriegsliteratur von Frauen?*, 425).

90. Rothe, *Popular Trauma Culture*, 2.

91. "Denen man die an ihnen begangene Schuld nicht verzeihen kann" (Rosenthal, *Der Holocaust*, 349).

92. Leys, *From Guilt to Shame*, 8.

93. Trezise, *Witnessing Witnessing*, 46. According to Trezise, "Caruth confuses consciousness and assimilation: because the traumatic event cannot be readily integrated into a narrative or other symbolic framework, she mistakenly infers that it cannot have been consciously experienced or be consciously recalled" (52).

94. Klüger, "Dichten," 220.

95. Trezise, *Witnessing Witnessing*, 225.

96. On the popularity of the genre of memoir, see Gilmore, *The Limits of Autobiography*, 17. In addition to memoirs written by contemporaries, there are also numerous memoirs by children and grandchildren of victims and perpetrators; see Luhmann and Stone, "Pitfalls." Moreover, this is not the first

German memoir boom. As Peitsch points out, a large number of memoirs were published immediately after the war. In 1945, the predominant genre was the antifascist memoir, but as early as 1947 this trend gave way to memoirs authored by Germans in "inner exile" and by former Nazis (*Autobiographik*, 55).

97. Fuchs and Cosgrove, "Introduction," 2.
98. This is in line with recent scholarship that problematizes the focus on generations in German literary studies; see Eigler, who questions "presumptions about neatly separated generational cohorts or a one-to-one relationship between individual biographies and collective history" ("Beyond the Victim Debate," 78).
99. Rothe, *Popular Trauma Culture*, 8 and 24.
100. Fuchs and Cosgrove, "Introduction," 12.
101. Goschalk, "When Children of Holocaust Survivors Meet Children of Nazis," 339.
102. Misztal, *Theories of Social Remembering*, 52.
103. Schwab, *Haunting Legacies*, 95.
104. W. A. Visser't Hooft, cited in Cohen; on the different forms and mechanisms of denial, see Cohen, *States of Denial*, 7–9.
105. Douglas calls them "a political hot potato" (*Orderly and Humane*, 3).
106. On refugees and gender, see Marfleet, *Refugees in a Global Era*, 198–199.
107. Sereny, "Into That Darkness," 276.
108. Kundrus, *Kriegerfrauen*, 308.
109. Trezise, *Witnessing Witnessing*, 92.

CHAPTER 2

Ruptured Narratives
German Women and Hitler's Army

In both the popular imagination and much scholarly literature, the Second World War is constructed as an exclusively male endeavor. It is assumed that women were far from the front lines, relegated to the household and nursery by National Socialist policies. In truth, however, the much-touted National Socialist ideal of the housewife was a fiction that soon fell victim to the very real needs of conducting a world war. As Karen Hagemann points out, the Second World War was a total war "that mobilized both the 'front' and the 'homeland.'"[1] Before long, women not only assumed public functions that newly deployed men had left unfilled but also moved closer and closer to the front lines themselves. In doing so, they became complicit in the Nazi war and genocide.

Even though the Nazi mobilization of women lagged behind that of England, the United States, and Russia, it reached proportions that were previously unheard of in German lands.[2] According to Franka Maubach, both the number of women involved in war-related work and the variety of functions women fulfilled are without historical precedent.[3] And yet, to this day, the writings of women who served in Hitler's army have received little attention, their voices drowned out by the blanket assumption that women are "marginal to the military's core identity, no matter how crucial in reality are the services they perform."[4] As I show in what follows, this omission is highly problematic: thinking about war from a different, female, perspective not only corrects androcentric views of the Second World War[5] but also offers insights into the workings of a totalitarian regime. In particular, an analysis of texts by women who served in Hitler's army helps us understand why and how women became complicit in the German war of conquest and genocide and how they account for (or fail to account for) their contribution to the Nazi reign of terror.

In the following, I provide information about the status, functions, and self-perceptions of female army auxiliaries in the service of the Third Reich. In order to do so, I draw on recent scholarship and on a wide range of memoirs. I then analyze five autobiographical texts by women who, albeit in different ways, contributed to the success of Hitler's army: a report based on the diary entries of Lore Vogt, written in 1945 and 1946; two memoirs by "Hitler's pilot," Hanna Reitsch; the docunovel *Blitzmädchen* by Hildegard Gartmann, published in 1971; and the memoirs of Ilse Schmidt, written in the 1980s and 1990s. I have chosen these texts because they were written in different decades and thus represent different moments in the process of *Vergangenheitsbewältigung*. The five texts are also markedly different in how they approach the issue of complicity, with attitudes ranging from blanket denial to remorseful reflection. Since some of these authors have received little critical attention, I provide a summary of the most salient biographical facts. My main interest, however, concerns the narrative strategies employed in these texts: How do these women portray their motivations for enlisting and their experiences during the war? How do they represent their involvement in the Nazi war and genocide? What literary devices do they employ when they justify their actions or express remorse?

In her study of women in Hitler's killing fields, Wendy Lower concludes that the few women who wrote memoirs or spoke about the war at length

> did not admit to themselves or to us, either then or many years later, in courtrooms or their own memoirs, what their participation in the Nazi regime had actually entailed. . . . They failed to see – or perhaps preferred not to see – how the social became political, and how their seemingly small contribution to everyday operations in the government, military, and Nazi Party organizations added up to a genocidal system.[6]

While this is certainly true, it is also important to note that denial comes in many forms. As I show in what follows, the nature, scope, and strategies of such repudiations of responsibility differ markedly depending on the author's personality, social status in the Nazi regime, and time of writing and publication. Because a memoir does not so much express an identity as it creates one, "images of the past are strategically invented to suit present needs."[7] And this act of self-invention will unfold differently in the 1990s from what it would have been like in the 1950s.

The five texts listed earlier allow insights into the motivations of female members of the German army from strikingly different perspectives. My arrangement of these texts traces an ascending line of awareness, beginning with unvarnished enthusiasm for the regime and moving to a focus on German victimization and, finally, to growing insight into one's own complicity. Vogt's text, although it betrays an awareness of potential readers,[8] was based on diary entries and not meant for publication. Since Vogt died in 1947, she did not have an opportunity to revise her narrative to bring it in line with postwar discourses of *Vergangenheitsbewältigung*. Consequently, her text allows insights into the worldview of an eager female army auxiliary and devoted follower of Hitler. The discussion of Vogt's text is followed by an analysis of two memoirs by Hanna Reitsch, whose work as a test pilot constituted a significant contribution to the military success of Hitler's Germany. Even though Reitsch, unlike Vogt, had many years to think critically about the Third Reich, she chose not to do so. Reitsch's two memoirs, published in the 1950s and 1970s, defy attempts to identify clear-cut phases in a chronology of *Vergangenheitsbewältigung*. However, I have included Reitsch not only because her texts remind us that the historical trajectory of *Vergangenheitsbewältigung* is marked by unevenness but also because her perspective is unique: unlike Vogt, Gartmann, and Schmidt, she was not at the bottom of the totem pole but rather communed with the upper echelons of the Nazi hierarchy. Indeed, much as Reitsch herself seeks to deny it and in spite of National Socialist gender discrimination, Reitsch's access and power were considerable, and her writings are as close as we can come to the perspective of a female "officer."

The following section focuses on Hildegard Gartmann's docunovel *Blitzmädchen*, which was published almost three decades after the end of the Third Reich in 1972 and draws on the author's experience as an army auxiliary. In calling *Blitzmädchen* a docunovel (*Dokumentarroman*), Gartmann, as James Young puts it, "simultaneously relieves [her]self of an obligation to historical accuracy (invoking poetic license), even as [s]he imbues [her] fiction with the historical authority of real events."[9] *Blitzmädchen* does not spout Nazi slogans, but rather casts army auxiliaries as victims. Following a literary tradition that spans from Erich Maria Remarque's bestseller *All Quiet on the Western Front* (1929) to Heinz G. Konsalik's *The Physician of Stalingrad* (*Der Arzt von Stalingrad*) (1956), *Blitzmädchen* highlights conflicts between common soldiers and their SS officers in order to portray the suffering of ordinary Germans at the hands of the regime while erasing the Jewish victims of genocide along with female complicity. Where Gartmann's docunovel does mention atrocities, it titillates its readers' pornographic imagination by sexualizing Nazi brutality.

The final section focuses on the memoir of army auxiliary Ilse Schmidt, who completed her memoirs in the 1990s, that is, two decades after the publication of Gartmann's docunovel. Of all the authors discussed here, Schmidt is the only one who makes an effort to come to terms with her involvement in the National Socialist reign of terror, but even Schmidt ultimately leaves little room for the victims of the war.

Women in Hitler's Army

Despite much Nazi rhetoric about the true domestic calling of the female sex, women's lives in the Third Reich were highly militarized. Members of the League of German Girls were "drilled to march in formation and trained in field exercise and sometimes marksmanship with air rifles"[10] while adult women were recruited to perform various services for the fatherland. On February 15, 1938, Hermann Göring announced the Duty Year (*Pflichtjahr*) for young women between the ages of seventeen and twenty-five, which included farm work and domestic help and was required in order to be eligible for employment in factories or offices.[11] Similarly, as of the spring of 1934, prospective female students were required to participate in the Labor Service (*Reichsarbeitsdienst*) (RAD) for a minimum of six months.[12] They too worked mostly on farms and as family helpers. Although the RAD became compulsory for all young women aged seventeen through twenty-five in 1939,[13] only 150,000 of the 600,000 girls who were eligible for the RAD each year were actually drafted for service.[14] In 1941, the "Decree on the Further Wartime Deployment of the Reich Labor Service for Female Youth" added an additional six months of "Auxiliary War Service" (*Kriegshilfsdienst*) to this requirement.[15] Starting in the fall of 1943, when RAD members could be employed in armaments factories and even in the army, the RAD, along with the Red Cross, became the primary source for the recruitment of female auxiliaries.[16]

While RAD women worked within the boundaries of the Reich, army auxiliaries could be stationed abroad. Maubach counts 500,000 female helpers with the *Wehrmacht*, 500,000 with the *Reichsluftschutzbund*, 400,000 nurses and assistant nurses with the Red Cross, and 10,000 women who worked in concentration camps.[17] According to Hagemann, there was "one woman to every twenty soldiers. Only one third of these women were performing compulsory service."[18] Women were active in all branches of Hitler's army, and at least 500,000 were stationed in the East.[19] Signal-communication assistants (*Nachrichtenhelferinnen*) were entrusted with the new communication technologies (telephone and telegraph), which became an almost exclusively female domain during the war.[20] Women also served as *Stabshelferinnen*, that is, as secretaries, translators, accountants, or drivers in the army, and as plane spotters

(*Flugmeldehelferinnen*) in the air force, where they were in charge of reporting activity by enemy planes and calculating a plane's trajectory as well as the likely time of attack. Toward the end of the war, one third of all maintenance work on airplanes was conducted by women, and anti-aircraft defense was handled almost exclusively by women, although leadership positions remained in the hands of men.[21] Although all these women were defined as auxiliaries, that is, helpers, their roles frequently exceeded mere support work.[22]

In theory, the Nazi regime, like the US and British armies, prohibited women from handling guns and participating in armed combat.[23] An ordinance issued by the Supreme Command stipulated that "women and girls cannot be called upon to handle firearms in the fight against the enemy."[24] As the war progressed, however, the Nazis began to consider armed service for women.[25] While many Nazi leaders agreed with Scholtz-Klink that a woman's weapon was the ladle,[26] a minority, including Speer, Göring, and Goebbels, was in favor of arming women. Their efforts, however, were stifled by Hitler himself. Although Hitler never warmed to the idea of women in battle, eventually he too had to bend to the exigencies of the war.[27] On August 24, 1943, Hitler authorized the use of women in anti-aircraft defense where they operated searchlights and handled anti-aircraft artillery and firearms.[28] In February 1945, when it was already too late to implement any changes, Hitler approved Bormann's plan for a female battalion, and in March 1945, the Supreme Command of the army allowed the use of anti-tank grenades by women.[29] Regardless of these decrees, however, it is important to remember that many army auxiliaries did carry guns whether Nazi regulations approved of it or not – some had acquired them secretly; others were equipped by the military "for their personal protection."[30] And, of course, even women who were unarmed themselves were frequently exposed to armed combat, especially during the German army's hasty retreat.

Although female army auxiliaries were employed by the different branches of the military, they remained civilians without proper military standing.[31] Women had the opportunity to rise in the ranks from "*Helferin, Oberhelferin, Unterführerin, Führerin*" to "*Oberführerin*" and "*Hauptführerin*,"[32] but even toward the end of the war, only half of all army auxiliaries wore uniforms, ostensibly because of the need to save fabric[33] and their access to the military infrastructure was restricted. When army auxiliaries were stationed in the Reich, they were given ration cards and sent to civilian hospitals. When they served abroad, they could be treated in military hospitals and received the same meals as the soldiers.

Ironically, while the Nazis denied these women military status, the Hague Conventions did not: all army auxiliaries in uniform were treated as enemy combatants.

Although the United States, Britain, and the Soviet Union were more successful in including women in the war effort,[34] Germany experienced its own version of the Rosie the Riveter phenomenon: in spite of all hardship, the war presented many women with new opportunities and previously unknown freedom. In her pioneering study on German army auxiliaries, Maubach notes that in looking back many auxiliaries considered the war years the most wonderful time of their lives.[35] Toward the beginning of the war, national and individual expansion truly went hand in hand for these young volunteers. Many women who joined the army were motivated by a thirst for adventure, a desire to escape the narrow confines of traditional domesticity, to free themselves from parental authority, to travel and see the world.[36] Lipinski, an air force auxiliary, for example, writes: "I wanted to experience adventures! I wanted to see foreign countries."[37] And travel they did. The bulk of the auxiliaries was sent to the "Generalgouvernement," that is, the German administered part of Poland, and to France, but auxiliaries were also stationed in the Balkans, Russia, Romania, Yugoslavia, Norway, Italy, and Greece. Many memoirs of army auxiliaries are infused with a sense of excitement as their authors go sightseeing or spend a day at the ocean.[38] Finally, at least in the early years of the war, an office job with the army presented an attractive alternative to backbreaking labor in agriculture, the drudgery of domestic service, and highly unpopular employment in the armament industry.

During the early years of the war, many army auxiliaries enjoyed a level of luxury that they had not known before. They lived in occupied villas and were waited on by local women who cleaned and cooked for them and did their laundry. "We lived like Dubarry," a former army auxiliary comments.[39] Many an auxiliary also took pleasure in her status as one of few women among a large crowd of soldiers and officers. At the time, women who engaged in such romantic and/or sexual relationships were frequently labeled with the derogatory term "officer's mattresses" (*Offiziersmatratzen*).[40] However, we may assume that there was also a darker side to this presumed enjoyment of male attention. In her memoir, army nurse Erika Summ reports that several German secretaries in the Ukraine were the victims of sexual harassment and even rape by their male colleagues and superiors, who exploited their inferior, dependent status.[41] Summ oversaw several abortions that resulted from these rapes. Moreover, there is some evidence that, rather than being universally admired, female auxiliaries were resented by their male colleagues and seen as *"un remède contre l'amour."*[42] In his detailed study of the secret recordings of German POWs in American camps, Felix Römer reports that many German soldiers found the idea of a woman in arms unthinkable.[43] Particularly during the rapid retreat of the German army, such resentment could be lethal: some auxiliaries were left behind during the evacuation and even thrown off the trucks to make room for male soldiers.[44]

For many auxiliaries, the initial enthusiasm began to fade during the winter of 1941–1942. In spite of referrals by job centers (*Arbeitsämter*) and widespread recruitment campaigns, particularly by the League of German Girls, there was a dearth of volunteers.[45] Few women who joined the army now were eager to serve, and many were disillusioned even further as the front lines moved ever and ever closer to their quarters. After Stalingrad, the motto of freeing a soldier for the front (*einen Soldaten für die Front freimachen*) turned from a source of national pride into one of guilt and shame as it became clear that the soldiers they replaced were likely to die in the East. Moreover, much as these women loved to see other countries, many came to realize that the local populations resented their presence. Army auxiliary Elisabeth Himmelstoß, for example, who was stationed in France, notes that "many eyes look upon the uniform that I wear with hatred."[46] Others, however, were not bothered by such hatred and rather enjoyed the superiority afforded by their racial and national status.

Since most of the women in Hitler's army did not write memoirs or speak about their experience in public arenas, it is difficult to know how many of them were motivated by genuine enthusiasm for Nazi ideology – even more so since those few who wrote about the war were likely to "exaggerate, mislead, self-glorify, or mollify."[47] Typically, female memoirists of the war, who, as part of their formal training had all been exposed to Nazi indoctrination about the final victory and Slavic and Jewish "*Untermenschen*," pay little attention to politics while their personal lives occupy front and center. As one of the women interviewed by historian Rosemarie Killius puts it: "It was war and yet one went to the theater all the same. . . . All in all it was a happy and rich time."[48] Many auxiliaries define themselves as apolitical,[49] which might be a truthful representation of their interests at the time (and a possible explanation why they joined the Nazi cause to begin with), but it may also be a postwar ploy designed to minimize their responsibility in the Nazi war and genocide.[50] Indeed, such a self-imposed exile from politics could be a useful strategy of exculpation. Beate Meyer, for example, discusses the case of a Nazi secretary who was well aware of the genocidal practices of the regime but insisted that such policies belonged in the realm of politics, in which she was not involved.[51]

In addition to authors' various strategies of denial, their own preconceptions may prevent readers from grasping the full extent of the complicity of female army auxiliaries. In particular, prevailing gender stereotypes have accustomed us to think of women as victims and of women's work as menial and inconsequential. For example, traditional notions of the work secretaries do are difficult to reconcile with the concept of a female "desk murderer," whose "routine procedures generated unprecedented crimes."[52] And yet, army secretaries not only typed deportation lists but also, in some cases, influenced the composition of these lists. They drafted protocols of interrogations under torture, or conveyed *Einsatzbefehle*, that is, commands for mass executions. Indeed, secretaries were integral to the functioning of the Nazi machine of terror. In the *Gestapo*, for example, 35–45 percent of all employees were office personnel.[53]

In spite of their omissions, memoirs of female army auxiliaries allow insights into the complicity of women in Hitler's army and in the Nazi genocide. Since many auxiliaries served in the East, they had firsthand knowledge of the war and the Holocaust.[54] Army auxiliary Katja Lipinski, for example, witnessed mass executions and merciless brutality toward Jewish and Polish civilians.[55] The responses to such immediate experiences of the Nazi genocide differ vastly. Some memoirists are plagued by their role in the Holocaust; others deny all knowledge of it – often against all plausibility. Most frequently, however, we encounter neither straightforward denial nor anguished remorse but rather narrative ruptures, head-turning at times, as the author transitions seamlessly from horror and cruelty to the enjoyment of everyday pleasures.[56] For example, on the same page, one of the women interviewed by Killius expresses her shock at the bloody execution of deserters and then talks about how much fun she had in Verona.[57] More often than not, we must read between the lines to comprehend an author's true appreciation of the Third Reich. Ruth Kirsten-Herbst, for example, an anti-aircraft auxiliary, emphasizes repeatedly that she was drafted against her will and did not believe in a German victory. In the same breath, however, she insists that the end of the war, rather than Nazi tyranny, signals the true beginning of Germany's moral decline (and of denunciations!).[58] If remembering is indeed, as Connerton maintains, the ability "not to recall events as isolated; it is to become capable of forming meaningful narrative sequences,"[59] then the task of remembering is accomplished only incompletely in these memoirs. The numerous contradictions of Nazi ideology itself, the felt obligations toward the author's family and friends, and the pressures of responding to postwar discourses of *Vergangenheitsbewältigung* all produce narrative ruptures that manifest themselves in non sequiturs and logical contradictions, fragmented thoughts and elisions, abrupt shifts in focus and tone. Conversely, in the memoirs of devoted Nazis, an attempt to suture such ruptures is evident in the mantra-like repetition of almost identical stock phrases and anecdotes that function like magical incantations invoked to keep the ideological edifice of National Socialism from crumbling.[60] To many of these women, the war truly was both the best and the worst of times, and their narratives reflect their inability to come to terms with this duality and with their own complicity in the Nazi crimes against humanity. But even if the inability to account for the past is common, denial and narrative fractures come in many shapes and guises. In the following, I parse four different strategies of dealing with one's own involvement in the Nazi regime.

Lore Vogt: The Diary of a Committed Nazi

Lore Vogt's report is based on diary entries made during her time as army auxiliary. It was edited by Jutta Rüdiger, the BDM national leader from 1937 to 1945, who was instrumental in recruiting BDM girls for service in the army.[61] By her own admission, Rüdiger corrected syntax and idioms and omitted passages that she considered unclear, but she appears to have left the bulk of the narrative unchanged.[62] If she had changed it, one would be hard pressed to explain why she produced a text that runs counter to her own agenda: while Vogt relishes participation in armed combat and highlights how well the female auxiliaries performed even in the thick of battle, Rüdiger insists both in the foreword to Vogt's text and in her memoir that women are biologically and psychologically ill suited to withstand the hardships of warfare.[63] And yet, while Vogt's text contradicts Rüdiger's claims about the incompatibility of women and warfare, the emphasis on the enthusiasm of a young volunteer serves her well since it reduces her own culpability in recruiting women for Hitler's war. Even so, I am wary of attempts to shift blame from Vogt to Rüdiger since they so easily align with a tendency to single out a few select perpetrators while ignoring the complicity of the many.

Although edited, the text is still marked by its generic origin as a diary: past-tense narrative and descriptive passages alternate with action-oriented sequences consisting of short, paratactical sentences that read like outbursts and convey a sense of immediacy and emotional intensity.

Since Vogt died in December 1947 in Garmisch, she never had the opportunity to revise her report to bring it in line with postwar discourses of *Vergangenheitsbewältigung*, and her editor, Rüdiger, for better or worse, did not see a need to hide the text's anti-Semitic thrust and fervent belief in National Socialism. At the time of writing, Vogt was barely twenty years old and we must assume that she was exposed to a great deal of Nazi indoctrination. We simply cannot know if Vogt would have begun to think critically about her experiences if she had not died young. As it is, her report is a striking testimony to a woman's enthusiastic identification with National Socialist ideology, and readers cannot help but wonder if many memoirs by female auxiliaries would be like this if they had been written in 1945.

Vogt was born in 1924 in Brünn. In 1944, when the German military called for volunteers, the twenty-year-old Vogt, an enthusiastic member of the BDM, stepped up. Originally ordered to join the communication corps, Vogt convinced her superiors to reassign her as an anti-aircraft gunner (*Flakwaffenhelferin*). On November 15, 1944, she boarded a train for Vienna, where she was redirected to Rendsburg in Schleswig-Holstein. This trip via Hamburg and Berlin provided her with firsthand impressions of bombed-out cities. In Rendsburg, she received the uniform with the insignia of eagle and sword and was then transferred to Stolpemünde for basic training in anti-aircraft defense. Vogt and her comrades learned how to determine the type and location of an enemy plane in order to calibrate the trajectory of an anti-aircraft gun. She was excited about her new responsibilities and about swearing an oath to the *Führer*: "with fresh strength and joy we looked forward to what was to come."[64] Throughout, Vogt rejoices in her sense of agency, gladly bears all deprivations, and declares with pride that she is a soldier. Clearly, the Nazis knew how to mobilize women's desire to make a contribution to the national cause for their purposes, and Vogt, like many young women at the time, enjoyed nothing more than the feeling of being needed.

Although anti-aircraft gunners were classified as noncombat personnel, Vogt defined herself as a soldier and wanted to see action.[65] And her wish came true: anti-aircraft auxiliaries typically belonged to the air force and were supposed to remain in Germany, but Vogt's unit of 200 volunteers was on loan to the Waffen-SS and stationed in Prague from January to March 1945. Thus, Vogt, who, according to regulations was not supposed to be anywhere near the front lines nor allowed to handle weapons, was fully armed and in the line of fire. Vogt's story shows that, in a losing war, differentiations between front and rear disappear all too quickly. During the German army's rapid retreat in 1944 and 1945, women frequently found themselves in the midst of battle. Vogt and her colleagues not only operated searchlights, radar, and sound-locating equipment, they also learned how to use hand grenades, a 0.8 mm pistol, anti-aircraft guns, and even anti-tank grenades.[66] Since Prague was on the corridor for bomber planes on the way to Munich, Dresden, and Brüx (Most), Vogt found herself in the midst of armed conflict. Much as Nazi policies forbade arming women, the reality of a total war made traditional notions of what is and is not proper for women in the military obsolete – a fact that becomes abundantly clear if we pay attention to the neglected genre of army auxiliary memoirs.

Vogt's report provides ample proof that we are not dealing with an innocent bystander drafted against her will but rather with a committed Nazi. Again and again (and as late as Christmas 1944 and even March and April 1945), Vogt declares with conviction that Germany will win the war: "Still we walked upright and trusted the *Führer*. Germany will not perish."[67] She is proud of her unit and "cheerfully" embraces her work in anti-aircraft defense – a job she describes as "taking these little birds down."[68] When Hitler decides to grant her unit the right to wear the Hitler Youth badge, she is over the moon. When she receives news of Hitler's death, she is devastated but quickly decides to keep fighting.[69] Vogt also wholeheartedly embraces National Socialist racial theory. She calls the Czechs dogs and "riffraff," resents the presence of the Czech people in Prague because they ruin that beautiful city for her, and laments that a British "terror attack" killed only Germans, but unfortunately no Czechs.[70]

When the Czechs start to fight the Germans in May 1945, Vogt's unit is among those who seek to quash the uprising. In a hail of bullets,[71] Vogt and her companions "man" the guns: they fight, tend to the wounded, and feverishly burn documents. With great satisfaction, Vogt notes every Czech-occupied building that goes up in flames and every arrest and execution of Czech fighters by Germans. When she learns on May 8 that the war is over, she comments that her life is now worthless.[72] As Vogt and her unit march out of the burning city, they sing: "Nothing can rob us of our love for and faith in our country."[73] To Vogt, the defeat of the Germans must be caused by treason, and Germans who surrender are by definition traitors and scoundrels.[74] It would appear that Vogt's military prowess is matched only by her ideological fervor. Vogt's memoir suggests that the National Socialist militarization of women's lives from an early age is not simply ornamental, but translates into a very palpable commitment to fight for Hitler.[75] While we cannot exclude the possibility that Rüdiger accentuated Vogt's ideological fervor, it is equally possible that Rüdiger chose to publish Vogt's text precisely because the young recruit's *Weltanschauung* matched her own.

Although Vogt's activities so clearly run counter to the supposed non-combat status reserved for female army auxiliaries, Vogt insists that her work does not diminish her femininity: "We were definitely not rough warriors – always only women."[76] It would appear that Vogt has internalized Nazi military regulations that stipulate that women are never soldiers and that one should make allowances for their feminine nature,[77] even if her actions in Prague make a mockery of such notions. Disregarding all contradictions, Vogt seeks to reconcile Nazi gender ideology, her thirst for action, and the very real demands of a total war. She feels fully integrated into her unit and respected by "our men."[78] Indeed, Vogt even makes a case for female soldiers when she reports that the behavior of the army auxiliaries was morale building: impressed with how the auxiliaries handled themselves during the battle in Prague, the male soldiers derived strength from the presence of women.[79]

Vogt joins the trek west as a passenger on an SS tank. Here, her ambiguous status as a civilian on loan to the SS works against her. Since some of the female army auxiliaries wore uniforms and had the SS-specific tattoo of their blood group, the Americans considered them members of the SS. When Vogt is taken prisoner, she accuses her American captors of unfair treatment and hypocrisy.[80] She complains bitterly about her time as a prisoner of war, lamenting that she is treated badly and left to starve.[81] Vogt's memoir ends when she is reunited with her parents. She concludes with a declaration of deeply felt loss: "We will never come to terms with the end of the war: our Germany is no more. Thoughts cannot comprehend it: a people, no more empire, no more *Führer*."[82]

While Vogt highlights her own supposed victimization by the Americans, she does not once refer to the Nazi mass murder of Jews, although she repeatedly mentions Jews in passing.[83] Later on, when she is in captivity, she is horrified at the prospect of being transported in a car marked with the Star of David. When she has to fill out forms, she is upset about "Jews who grin impudently."[84] Back in Munich, she inquires about the new political regime and concludes that the country is now ruled by released concentration camp inmates who rage terribly and steal.[85] Here and elsewhere, Vogt elides the racial ideology that served to justify genocide and instead identifies concentration camp inmates with criminals. It would seem that Vogt's denial is of a different order than that of Nazis who wrote their memoirs decades after the war. Vogt, who authored her text in the 1940s, does not feel the need to profess innocence or ignorance. Rather, the genocidal atrocities of the Nazi regime simply remain unspoken – although they haunt the narrative in Vogt's paranoid dread of "grinning Jews."

Like many memoirs by female army auxiliaries, Vogt's narrative is characterized by numerous rifts. However, because it was written in close proximity to the war (1945 and 1946), these rifts are of a different nature. Vogt, who did not intend her report for publication, does not even attempt to downplay her ideological affinity with National Socialist ideology and she does not hide her anti-Semitism. There is no internal or external pressure to reconcile her fervent belief in Hitler with postwar discourses about the Third Reich and the Holocaust. Rather, in Vogt's case the rift that marks her report runs between the ideology she embraced and the historical reality she portrayed. To the contemporary reader, Vogt's unquestioned belief that Germany will win the war, pronounced as late as April 1945, is striking. Similarly, her insistence that she is "no rough warrior" as she shoots her way out of Prague is jarring. Throughout, Vogt's narrative is characterized by glaring contradictions. In many other ways, however, the text is disturbingly consistent. Vogt's belief in the superiority of the German master race and her devotion to Hitler form a coherent whole. In order to achieve such consistency, Vogt relies on stock phrases – "Germany will not perish" – that she recycles throughout. Indeed, the more reality threatens to destabilize her ideology, the more incessantly Vogt relies on her political mantras. If Vogt's narrative is fractured, it is not because of attempts to deny or obfuscate her actions and beliefs during the war but rather because the reality of the war asserts itself and undermines the ideological consistency of her rhetoric.

Hanna Reitsch: *Fliegen, Mein Leben* and *Das Unzerstörbare in meinem Leben*

Unlike the other women discussed in this chapter, Reitsch authored not one, but four memoirs, two of which deal with her life during the Third Reich. *Fliegen, Mein Leben* was written after Reitsch's release from American captivity and published in 1951. Her second memoir about the National Socialist regime, *Das Unzerstörbare in meinem Leben*, was first published in 1975. Tellingly, although there are more than two decades between the publication of these two texts, Reitsch did not change her story one bit. In spite of the growing pressures of discourses of

Vergangenheitsbewältigung, Reitsch, who, unlike Vogt, did live long enough to adjust her representation of the Third Reich to postwar expectations, made few concessions. Indeed, contemporary discourses about the Holocaust entered Reitsch's memoir only insofar as they strengthened her denial. Published three decades after the war, *Das Unzerstörbare in meinem Leben* relies on the same stock phrases that characterized Lore Vogt's narrative in 1945.

Reitsch was not only more prolific than the other women discussed here, she also exerted considerably more influence during the Third Reich. Where Vogt adored Hitler from afar, Reitsch had tea with him. Where Gartmann's protagonists looked out for enemy planes, Reitsch conducted daredevil tests designed to improve the performance of the entire German air force. In the absence of female army officers, Reitsch's work provides an important counterweight to the perspective of the female auxiliary: the life writing of a woman who moved in Hitler's inner circle, worked with all levels of the German air force, and commented on and even initiated policy proposals, including a plan for German suicide bombers.

Hanna Reitsch was born on March 29, 1912 in the Silesian town of Hirschberg as the daughter of a Prussian ophthalmologist and a Tyrolian mother. She describes her family as happy and harmonious. They traveled, made music, and went on hiking expeditions. Reitsch reports being particularly close to her mother, a devout Christian who admonishes her to do good if she wants to go to heaven.[86] Again and again, Reitsch emphasizes that her education instilled a "firm moral and spiritual foundation," whose cornerstones are respect, dignity, honor, and the fatherland.[87]

From an early age, Reitsch was a tomboy who believed that she had been born a girl by mistake.[88] Even as a small child, she felt a longing to fly. After a lengthy campaign for parental permission, she was finally allowed to take a course at the School for Glider Pilots in Grunau – the Versailles Treaty forbade the use of motor planes – where she met her "pilot father" ("*Fliegervater*") Wolf Hirth. Hoping to become a flying doctor in Africa, she enrolled in the Colonial School for Women in Rendsburg. She then studied medicine in Berlin and Kiel, but dropped out to become a test pilot at the research institute for glider planes in Darmstadt, where she participated in numerous expeditions to exotic locales, including Finland, France, Spain, Argentina, and Brazil. Reitsch interpreted these trips as missions for peace and understanding, but they also served the larger purpose of Nazi propaganda with Reitsch herself as a "symbol of Aryan pride and achievement."[89] When the war started, she tested new planes for the purpose of quality control, identifying any problems that could lead to crashes. She writes: "I never knew in the morning if I would still be alive in the evening, but I considered myself the luckiest person in the world, grateful that I was tasked with such great responsibilities."[90]

The main beneficiary of Reitsch's work during this period was the military. For example, the troop-carrying glider DFS-230, whose landing brakes Reitsch helped to improve, was crucially important during the invasion of Belgium in 1940 because it was completely silent and thus ideal for use behind enemy lines. Reitsch also tested the Messerschmidt 321 Gigant, which was intended for use during a potential German invasion of England. Furthermore, she tested a glider that was to serve as a flying gasoline tank, a device to cut the steel cables of barrage balloons, and a catapult for planes with a heavy load and little room to maneuver.[91] In recognition of her accomplishments, Reitsch was bestowed the title of "captain" in 1937, which made her the first female *Flugkapitän* in the world. In 1941, Göring awarded her the golden military flight medallion, followed by a reception, where Hitler presented her with the Iron Cross Second Class. In 1942, she became the only woman to receive the Iron Cross First Class.

In 1937 and again when the war started, General Ernst Udet recruited her for the test center for military aircraft in Rechlin, where she worked on improvements for all types of military planes. She also flew a rocket plane, which led to her first severe accident: she had multiple fractures of the skull, and her nose had to be reconstructed. It was particularly hard on her that her reconvalescence barred her from working during a time when the German army started losing: "To my last hour I wanted only to help my homeland."[92] When she was fully recovered, General Robert Ritter von Greim called her to the eastern front, where she arrived in January 1944. Both Greim and Reitsch saw her presence as morale building: "I now knew and had seen it in their gleaming eyes what it meant for the men that I came to them from home."[93] Conversing with soldiers, she took it upon herself to explain the true meaning of perseverance in spite of utter hopelessness.[94] Concerned about Germany's future and the possibility of total capitulation, Reitsch together with SS *Sturmbannführer* Otto Skorzeny devised a plan that relied on suicide bombers who would destroy crucial infrastructure in enemy cities.[95] She claims that she suggested this plan to Hitler, who declined because he did not consider Germany's situation serious enough to require such drastic measures.

As this episode shows, Reitsch was on intimate terms with the highest leaders of the Nazi regime, a member of what Trevor-Roper calls Hitler's "oriental court of flatterers and toadies."[96] She appears proud of such familiarity with the upper echelons, but also goes to great pains to show that, based on her congenial interactions with the Nazi greats, she could not have suspected anything untoward. Thus, she praises Hitler's easy-going manner and confidence, but then backtracks that their meetings took place in an official context and did not allow any insights into his personality.[97] Similarly, she reports that she visited Himmler in July 1943 to thank him for the flowers and chocolates he had sent during her reconvalescence. Reitsch states that they discussed women's social position in the Third Reich and the importance of Christianity, and insists that Himmler encouraged her to voice her criticism openly in all future conversations. She even claims that she confronted Himmler with "rumors" about gas chambers and that Himmler subsequently placed a disclaimer in German newspapers, whereupon Reitsch disqualified the "rumors" as enemy propaganda.[98] Clearly, Reitsch expects her readers to believe that, even though she moved in the inner circles of the Third Reich, even though her hometown of Hirschberg housed one of the sub-camps of Gross-Rosen, and even though she herself had spent time on the eastern front, she was completely unaware of the Holocaust.[99]

In both memoirs, Reitsch, whose work as a test pilot contributed significantly to the improvement of the German air force, maintains that flying is a completely apolitical activity: "My thoughts belonged to the wind, the clouds, and the stars. The political intrigues of the world did not reach up there."[100] According to Reitsch, flying calls forth a metaphysical experience of unity with nature and allows her to forget all earthly fear and pettiness.[101] In short, she portrays herself as both intimately involved with the ruling elite of the Third Reich and yet completely detached from National Socialist politics.

Surprisingly, Reitsch's self-exculpation gained credence in the postwar period, as Hitler's pilot successfully relaunched her career. In 1959, she taught gliding in India as the personal guest of Pandit Nehru. In the 1960s, Kwame Nkrumah, the autocratic president of Ghana, invited her to set up the National School of Gliding.[102] In 1961, President Kennedy invited her to the White House as part of a reception for the Association of Women Helicopter Pilots, the Whirly-Girls. In 1972, the International Order of Characters, an aviation organization, named her pilot of the year and gave her the nickname "Supersonic Sue." She remained active until her death of a heart attack in August 1979.

It is not an overstatement to say that Reitsch's memoirs are completely devoid of self-reflection. Throughout, Reitsch sees herself as a victim who sacrificed everything for the fatherland, risked her life to save others, and,

in return, experienced nothing but hardship, particularly during her fif-
teen-month captivity in an American internment camp. Like Leni
Riefenstahl, her equal in talent and lack of a moral compass, Reitsch is
convinced that she is totally innocent.[103] She attributes her imprisonment
to revenge on the part of the victors, claiming that she was dragged into the
political arena where she never belonged.[104] She laments that "libelous"
reports – particularly the works of William L. Shire and Hugh Trevor-
Roper, who wrote about her infamous visit to Hitler's bunker in the last
days of the war – sought to paint her as an important Nazi. She then
remarks that *at the time*, that is, in the immediate postwar period, being
called a Nazi was tantamount to being a criminal, implying that this
equation of Nazi and criminal has since been revised. Again and again,
Reitsch insists that she knew nothing about crimes committed by
Germans. Rather, her contact with Nazi leaders was simply the result of
her professional obligations. In the same breath, she assures readers that she
and all young Germans wanted peace even if the world does not acknowledge this and then proceeds to talk about Germany's lack of living space
and about how Germany used to be weak and needed to amass arms to
protect itself.[105]

As her reference to more space for the German *Volk* indicates, Reitsch's
narrative is drenched in National Socialist ideology and rhetoric. She refers
to her native Silesia as "German cultural soil" while her family's suicide in
the wake of Germany's defeat – Reitsch's father shot himself, his wife, his
daughter, three grandchildren, and the maid – is simply a "tragic death in
May of 1945."[106] In both memoirs, Reitsch's refusal to confront her past
manifests itself in the rigidity and formulaic nature of her language. She
repeats certain claims in mantra-like sameness. Several anecdotes found
entrance into both memoirs in almost identical prose. There is much talk
about destiny and about being guided by a higher power. Reitsch even casts
her father's murder-suicide in a gentle, religious light, portraying it as a
return to God to avoid falling into the hands of the Russians.[107]
Feldmarschall Ritter von Greim, whom Hitler appointed as Göring's
successor as head of the air force and who also committed suicide in May
1945, is referred to as one of the greatest and noblest officers of the German
army and as a father to the Russian prisoners who worked for him. His
decision to end his life and not stand trial is justified in her eyes since his
responsibilities extended only to purely German affairs and thus ended
with the end of the war.[108] Later on, Reitsch implies that all post-1945
judges were Jews who denied Germans justice.[109] She considers it a sign of
her magnanimous spirit that she tolerated imprisonment by the Americans

without hatred or bitterness and even prayed for them: "Father, forgive them for they do not know what they are doing."[110] Again and again, she draws attention to her positive attitude in spite of everything done to her and professes to speak with complete honesty about her Nazi past in spite of the Allies' censorship after the war. After all, as Reitsch maintains, the Germans think critically while the Americans exhibit a uniformity of thought and tend to be blinded by propaganda.[111]

In spite of Reitsch's abhorrent politics and her complete unwillingness to accept any responsibility for her role in the Third Reich, her memoirs continue to find avid readers: *Fliegen, Mein Leben* was published in its fourth edition in 2001 and *Das Unzerstörbare in meinem Leben* in its seventh edition in 1992. Surely, some of this interest is motivated by Reitsch's access to Hitler and her ability to provide intimate glimpses of the Nazi leadership. In addition, the popularity of Reitsch's life writing may also be due to the fact that the diminutive Reitsch – she was five feet (154 centimeters) tall – succeeded as a woman in an almost exclusively male profession under a notoriously misogynist regime. To be sure, Reitsch experienced gender discrimination throughout her career. When she first took lessons, she was told that girls should stick with pots and pans. When she performed badly at a gliding competition, she was presented with a kitchen scale and a meat mincer. When she learned how to fly big planes, she had to work with officers for whom the presence of women on the tarmac was a red flag and who were looking for excuses to send her home. Throughout her career, she was a target of male resentment, which she claims to have overcome through her task-oriented attitude and excellent performance. Reitsch reports that many envied her and resented her success, and she is aware that her gender had a part in this.[112] Strategically astute, she would rebuff her opponents by pointing out that the needs of the fatherland were more important than male privilege while casting her job as female support work and herself as one of the many women "who helped the brave soldiers on the front ... in their own way."[113] In Reitsch's account, knitting socks for soldiers and testing rocket planes are practically one and the same. Reitsch, who wore a uniform of her own design because the army would not provide her with one, learned to maintain a precarious balance between minimizing her own role while simultaneously highlighting her accomplishments.

If Reitsch succeeded in spite of all obstacles, it was not only because she enjoyed the patronage of several influential Nazi functionaries, including Ernst Udet and Ritter von Greim, but also because she possessed a singular ability to turn a blind eye to anything she did not want to see, be it gender discrimination or Nazi atrocities. In his biography of Reitsch, Piszkiewicz wonders if "Hanna's head injuries might have disconnected her higher cognitive processes."[114] But Reitsch's refusal to so much as mention the Holocaust by name is not caused by cognitive impairment. Rather, her success as a female civilian in Hitler's military and her enormous capacity for denial are two sides of the same coin. Of all women discussed in this chapter, Reitsch is the only one who might, with some justification, be categorized as a perpetrator. And yet, although her contributions to the Nazi regime were far greater than those of Gartmann or Schmidt, her writings lack any hint of an awareness of her own complicity.

Hildegard Gartmann's docunovel *Blitzmädchen*

Hildegard Gartmann's docunovel *Blitzmädchen*, which was published in 1971, presents a fictionalization of the author's own experiences in the war. In designating the text a docunovel, Gartmann frees herself from the need for historical accuracy while still laying claim to an aura of authenticity. *Blitzmädchen* narrates the last months of the war beginning on New Year's Eve 1944.[115] As might be expected given the late date, Vera Fern, the narrator of *Blitzmädchen* – named after the bolts of lightning sewn onto the uniforms of *Nachrichtenhelferinnen* – did not volunteer but was drafted. Before she joined the army, Vera attended art school with the goal of becoming a dance instructor. In the army, she stood guard on a tower sixty kilometers east of Posen, looking out for enemy airplanes and reporting any sightings to the central anti-aircraft command in Posen – a job that could be low key and boring but could also become quite dangerous: Because such towers were located in exposed positions that offer a view of the surrounding countryside, they were easy targets for enemy planes.

Blitzmädchen's style is evocative of works by Vicky Baum and the *Neue Sachlichkeit* of the Weimar Republic. The story is told in present tense by a first-person narrator, and dialogues outweigh descriptive passages by far. Much of the plot focuses on the traditional fodder of Second World War fiction: the conflict between the top brass and the average grunt.[116] Here as in many Second World War novels and films, the distance between leaders and followers is magnified by their differing commitments to the Nazi regime with the clear intent of accentuating the culpability of the upper echelons while minimizing that of the lower ranks. While Vera and her comrades are presented as apolitical, the abusive female group leader Käte Potter is a dedicated Nazi. Tellingly, though, the text does not engage with

Potter's obsession with Nazi ideology; for the most part, it simply presents it as a nuisance. Rather than discussing and contradicting Potter's views, the *Blitzmädchen* roll their eyes, yawn when they are being indoctrinated, and play pranks on her.[117] Much of the plot is organized as a game of cat and mouse between Potter and her female underlings who are constantly trying to get the better of her and who, much like the good soldier Švejk, feign incompetence to stay out of danger. Whenever their superiors are not around, Vera and her friends abandon their post because they resent that their youth is being wasted: "no cinema, no dance, not even a night out."[118]

Throughout, Gartmann's fictionalization of her experience as an army auxiliary trades in the clichés of the soldier's novel. The female leader Potter is a stereotypical diehard Nazi who is completely devoid of humanity: When Beate, one of the auxiliaries, dies because of a miscarriage, Potter considers her death just punishment for being a whore.[119] Potter is also a hypocrite of the greatest order. Although she herself is guilty of major transgressions, including sexual promiscuity and alcohol abuse, she berates the auxiliaries for minor infractions. Conversely, the *Blitzmädchen* spend a lot of time and energy plotting revenge. When they think that Potter froze to death, they rejoice.[120] And when the drunken Potter passes out, they take photos of her in a compromising position so as to be able to blackmail her if the need arises. As a result, the war waged by Nazi Germany on Russia and on the Jews recedes into the background, along with their own complicity, while conflicts between Nazi leaders such as Potter and their German victims take center stage. It would appear that we are meant to identify or at least sympathize with Vera and the other young women in her unit whose malicious pranks are presented as good fun and legitimate revenge; and yet, in light of their own callous actions, readers might also conclude that the young auxiliaries are themselves profoundly affected and corrupted by the same forces of dehumanization that they purport to oppose.

Paradoxically, Gartmann's protagonist claims to be both uninterested in politics and immune to Nazi propaganda and racial ideology.[121] Since the women in Vera's unit have contact with wounded soldiers in a hospital – at some point they clean up a room containing amputated limbs – they are acutely aware that Germany is losing the war. They also know that the local population hates the Germans – Poles throw rocks at them and call them "Nazi pigs." Consequently, Vera and her friends fear that the Poles might take revenge when the war is over.[122] The text hints at the reasons for this hatred – a soldier tells Vera that the Germans shot 500 Poles because three Germans had been killed – but such sparse pieces of information remain

background noise, the foil for the conflict that the text is primarily concerned with: the war between the average German and the Nazi leaders:
"The fat cats get drunk and we kick the bucket."[123]

Although *Blitzmädchen* alludes to Nazi atrocities, the narrator assumes a
stance of "wilful ignorance."[124] Thus, Vera is acutely aware of the "disappearance" of the Jews – when a synagogue in Posen is turned into a public
pool, she comments that the synagogue is no longer needed since there are
no more Jews in Posen – and of rumors that "they had killed all the Jews."
At the same time, she insists that "we did not believe it. Why would they
kill the Jews? They did not do anything to us."[125] There is no attempt to
reconcile the glaring discrepancy of the complete absence of Jews on the
one hand and the refusal to accept a sinister explanation for this absence on
the other. Similarly, although the text repeatedly mentions a prison camp
that is being guarded by the local SS, *Blitzmädchen* offers next to no
information about the inmates of the camp nor does it specify how they
are treated. The same holds true for the Polish victims of the Nazi expulsion campaigns in Arthur Greiser's Wartheland where Vera is stationed.[126]
There are casual references to resettled Baltic Germans, but no explication
of the injustice and terror involved in driving the local Polish population
from their homes.[127] Instead, the text adopts the Nazi term "partisan" for
any Pole who is killed by the SS and refers to SS actions as counterinsurgency efforts.[128]

Instead of integrating information about the local concentration camp
and the Nazi campaigns of ethnic cleansing into the narrative, *Blitzmädchen*
seeks to pique its readers' pornographic curiosity by representing sexually
perverted SS atrocities. Indeed, *Blitzmädchen* all but identifies political
corruption with sexual perversion. When the protagonist visits the SS head-
quarters, she witnesses and describes in graphic detail the sexualized torture
and murder of a Polish woman while emphasizing her own helplessness and
inability to rescue her.[129] Later on, *Hauptsturmführer* Keil, the local SS
commander and an aficionado of elaborate orgies with abundant champagne
and caviar, forces a group of male and female "partisans" to have intercourse
under threat of death and then proceeds to shoot them all.[130] Tellingly, not
one of the memoirs by female army auxiliaries discussed here sexualizes Nazi
cruelty or even highlights sexuality, whereas the consciously fictionalized
Blitzmädchen endows all SS atrocities with a prurient slant.[131] We do not
know if these detailed descriptions of SS perversion were introduced to
appeal to a reader's appetite for sensationalized SS porn or if they are in
fact authentic.[132] To be sure, Gartmann uses the term "docunovel" rather
loosely and does not rely on the technique of montage that many docunovels

employ when citing historical sources. Regardless of its authenticity, however, the focus on sexual perversion underlines the text's claim that Nazi atrocities were committed by a small group of mentally ill men whereas women such as Vera were not complicit with but rather victimized by the National Socialist regime.[133]

While the text uses the representation of SS orgies to highlight Nazi corruption, it portrays the auxiliaries' sexual transgressions as by-products of the war. In *Blitzmädchen*, the constant fear of death motivates a thirst for life that manifests as sexual desire.[134] As Vera's unit waits for the order to leave their outpost,[135] the front moves closer, and the parties get wilder. Treks pass through town, Vera and her friends are attacked by airplanes and strafed with machine gun fire, and their resolve not to die as virgins grows. When Vera sleeps with Keil's friend Wenk, whom she met in a bar where German officers drink and have sex with Polish women, she justifies it with a reference to the war.

In light of the text's focus on the corrupt nature of the Nazi elite, it is hardly surprising that the final showdown unfolds not as a conflict between Russians and Germans, or between Poles and Germans, but between army auxiliaries and Nazi superiors. Potter kills Ada, one of the girls, and is in turn killed by Margot. Then SS commander Keil threatens to shoot all German refugees in a passing trek.[136] Keil also attempts to shoot Vera and Margot but is himself shot by a POW before he can go through with it. To the end, *Blitzmädchen* highlights the victimization of average Germans by their Nazi leaders while crimes against Poles, Russians, and Jews play a minor role and complicity is conveniently sidelined. On the final pages, Margot blames the SS commander for the misfortune that has befallen her and her friends: "Keil, the beast, I hate him. We are paying for his atrocities against the Poles" – even though, just a few pages earlier, the same Margot, who knew all about Keil's crimes, had a blissful affair with him – a "talented artist" both "in bed and on the piano."[137]

Much like Vogt, Gartmann highlights the natural femininity of her protagonists while insisting that they are fully capable of handling the demands of their job.[138] Vera and her friends define themselves as soldiers, but soldiers in skirts.[139] In some ways, *Blitzmädchen* embraces traditional gender roles, particularly in its representation of Nazi perpetrators. Keil's fanaticism requires no explanation, but Potter's ideological affinity with National Socialism is an aberration because it violates gender expectations: "Gradually we began to doubt whether she is truly a member of the female sex."[140] Repeatedly, Gartmann uses the gender of her protagonists to emphasize their innocence and victimization.[141] And yet, although the text tends to present women as naturally peaceful victims, its basic structure casts doubt on such easy dichotomies. After all, Vera and her friends are both feminine and efficient soldiers, and the female leader Potter is both a woman and a Nazi leader.[142] Moreover, when Vera's friend Beate dies of a miscarriage, *Blitzmädchen* offers a critique of the underprivileged status of female auxiliaries in the German army: Beate dies not only because army hospitals are overwhelmed with casualties but also because they are not equipped to deal with pregnant women.

Much like Vogt's account, the fictionalized *Blitzmädchen* is marked by narrative ruptures. Although the text was published almost two decades after the end of the war, its narrative is disjointed and inconsistent. Graphic descriptions of sexualized torture, vague references to prison camps, and lukewarm denial of any knowledge of the Holocaust exist side by side without a discernible attempt to reconcile these disparate perspectives. The text relies on gender to distance its female protagonists from the Nazi reign of terror even as it portrays the young women's intimate involvement with various aspects of the war. Gartmann's docunovel hopes to garner sympathy for protagonists who bristle at the immorality of Nazi leaders, but unwittingly unveils how deeply these women are themselves affected by the dehumanizing thrust of National Socialist ideology. In *Blitzmädchen*, the fact that Margot sleeps with Keil, the embodiment of SS sadism, even though she is aware of his crimes, requires no explanation. Nor does the text ponder whether letting Potter freeze to death is indeed a justified form of punishment for her ideological blindness. We do not know how much of *Blitzmädchen* is authentic and how much is fictional, but we do know that, in spite of its desire to highlight the victimization of Hitler's female helpers and to portray a small group of sick men as responsible for Nazi atrocities, the text ultimately features female protagonists who are themselves corrupted by the Nazi regime. Even though Gartmann marshals gender and rank to obfuscate the involvement of female auxiliaries in Nazi crimes, their complicity emerges in the fissures and ruptures of the text.

Ilse Schmidt: *Die Mitläuferin: Erinnerungen einer Wehrmachtsangehörigen*

Ilse Schmidt started writing her memoir decades after the war. During her years of silence, she had suffered from post-traumatic stress disorder (PTSD). Random events, such as a whirring fan, triggered panic attacks and caused feelings of anxiety and shame. In an effort to confront her illness and encouraged by Ingeborg Drewitz, Schmidt decided to record her experiences during the war. She reports that the process of wading through the "thicket of memories" was accompanied by physical symptoms, including nausea, sleeplessness, and anxiety.[143] She completed a short version in the 1980s, which was stored in the *Bundesarchiv-Militärarchiv*.[144] The longer version, published in 1999, is written in present tense; its short sentences and sentence fragments convey the impression that Schmidt is still in the moment – an impression that is reinforced even further as Schmidt repeatedly interrupts her narrative to comment on the difficulty of writing about the war.

Ilse Schmidt, *née* Struwe, was born in 1919 in Brandenburg. She attended a secondary school followed by a trade school where she learned shorthand, typing, and accounting. At home, she took care of her sick mother, who died when Ilse was fourteen, and worked in her father's fruit-and-vegetable store. Her father joined the party for opportunistic reasons, driven by fear of unemployment and loss of status, but her family also included a Communist uncle and Social Democrats as well as diehard Nazis. Like most female auxiliaries, Schmidt notes that she herself was not interested in politics. She was, however, attracted to pretty uniforms and had a short-lived relationship with a *Sturmabteilung* (SA) man.

When an uncle in the employ of the secretary of the navy advised her to join the navy as an auxiliary, Schmidt seized this most welcome opportunity to escape from her stifling home environment. Six weeks after her twenty-first birthday, she happily embarked for Paris where she worked in the navy propaganda department, taking dictation, and archiving newspaper articles. Outside of the office, she availed herself of the many opportunities for amusement.[145] In spite of such professed enjoyment, however, Schmidt's writing is marked by a sort of split consciousness. On one and the same page, Schmidt waxes enthusiastic about French fashion, praising the "delightfully carefree time,"[146] and reports waiting for a date with air force men who do not show up because they were shot down. Clearly, in order to remain "carefree," army auxiliaries had to become habituated to the omnipresence of death in everyday life. But the strenuous effort involved in repressing anything that might interfere with the vision of a carefree life remains visible in the fractures of the text.

After Paris, Schmidt was transferred to the Bordeaux office of the navy newspaper *Gegen Engeland* and quartered in the home of an old French lady. She came to admire French *savoir vivre* and felt uncomfortable with her German companions' nationalism. In June 1941, she was deployed to Belgrade where she lived in a villa and had a Serbian maid. Here too she was assigned to the propaganda department in charge of "informing" the

German-speaking population about the war. In remembering this deployment, Schmidt reflects on what it meant to be a woman in an army of men. On the one hand, she was aware that becoming an army auxiliary allowed her to escape a life of domestic drudgery. Since all cooking and cleaning was handled by women of the occupied nation, Schmidt was free to pursue her career or enjoy leisure activities. On the other hand, she moved in an environment characterized by rampant sexism: when an officer all but ordered his men to accompany him on a visit to a brothel, Schmidt looked on in silence; when soldiers at a train station started yelling, "fuck her, the old pig," she pretended not to notice.[147] We would do well to take note of this aspect of working in a male-dominated milieu, especially in light of the oft-repeated claims that army auxiliaries enjoyed their minority status as coveted love objects among hundreds of admiring men.

After a bout of scarlet fever followed by a vacation and a brief stint with the theater and dance department in Belgrade, Schmidt was transferred to Rowno in the Ukraine, where she arrived in March 1942. Schmidt remembers that she had a Jewish maid, but cannot remember the exact nature of her work there.[148] She does, however, recall vividly that she observed executions from her bedroom window and that her superior, who noticed her discomfort, advised her not to think about it anymore.[149]

Schmidt reports further gaps in her memory brought on by a nervous breakdown during the German army's rapid retreat after the defeat at Stalingrad. She was left behind by her commanding officer, and barely made her way out. Schmidt, who even at the time was increasingly plagued by memories of her experiences in the East, then worked for Admiral Wilhelm Canaris in the office of counter-espionage in Berlin before applying for transfer to Rome to escape the daily bombing campaigns. Since the Allies had not landed in Sicily yet, Italy was relatively unaffected by the war, but, instead of enjoying the relative calm, Schmidt felt guilty about avoiding the dangers to which others were exposed.[150] She had an affair with a married man, but began to care about politics and realized that her paramour was a Nazi. When the war caught up with her, she experienced a bombing raid on Verona, moved north with the troops, and was taken into captivity by the Americans in May 1945. Friends helped her pretend that she was sick to get her back to Germany, where she ended up working in a POW hospital near Stuttgart, then in a psychiatric hospital near Braunschweig. After the war, she married a lieutenant she had met in Paris who had survived Stalingrad and spent six years in a Russian POW camp.

What stands out in Schmidt's memoir is how difficult the author finds it to talk about the violence, injustice, and murder that she witnessed on numerous occasions. Undoubtedly, there are many reasons for this silence: it might be caused by the repression of traumatic experiences, an ardent desire to look the other way, denial, deliberate lies, or the long-term effects of the secrecy imposed by the Nazi regime.[151] Moreover, in addition to the cognitive and emotional mechanisms of repression and denial that helped young women such as Schmidt deal with their complicity in the Third Reich, there are the profound effects of war and terror on all forms of intimacy, including the ability to communicate with and confide in another. During wartimes, strangers quickly become fast friends and then separate again just as easily. Romantic couplings are often fleeting either because the partners are transferred to other locations or because they have previous commitments. (Schmidt's involvement with a married man in Belgrade was one of several affairs facilitated by the man's prolonged absence from his spouse.) In Paris, Schmidt dated an intelligence officer, but they both made a point of never discussing work with each other. Most of the time, Schmidt does not even know if her partners are Nazis. It would seem that both the war and the Nazi regime eroded the kind of trust that would have allowed people like Schmidt to verbalize her experiences. Without such verbalization at the time, however, the task of reflecting on and processing experiences many years after the war becomes infinitely more difficult. As Huyssen explains, "the past is not simply there in memory but . . . must be articulated to become memory."[152]

In addition to the strictures of war and political oppression, individual predispositions and familial background contributed to Schmidt's initial silence. Schmidt herself attributes her inability to speak about the Nazi atrocities to her oath of secrecy, to fears of negative repercussions, and to an upbringing that taught her to ignore unpleasant realities. Her mother's favorite admonishment was "for the sake of dear peace, be quiet" while her father expected unconditional obedience.[153] Schmidt believes that in this her childhood resembled that of many Germans who remained silent and closed their eyes to reality. Thus, familial socialization and the political pressures of a regime in which, as Hannah Arendt explains, "everything plays out between news that nobody dares to talk about and propaganda lies that nobody believes" work together to create a stifling atmosphere of silence and denial.[154] When Schmidt is in Belgrade, she is repeatedly confronted with photos of mass shootings as part of her job, but does not dare discuss such evidence with anybody. After a while, she stops opening the envelopes and simply passes them on to her superior. Similarly, when Schmidt and a friend happen upon partisans who were hanged on lampposts, they do not talk to each other (or anybody else) about what they have seen. In the Ukraine, Schmidt observes how a crowd of Jewish men, women, and children are rounded up. She learns later that they were shot, but is afraid to speak out. Instead, she feels depressed and cries uncontrollably. According to Schmidt, the same avoidance strategy also characterized the behavior of her fellow army auxiliaries, all of whom do not talk about the war.[155]

The silence of Schmidt and her contemporaries not only sustained the Nazi regime of terror, it also prevented victims from receiving justice after the war. As Hannah Arendt explains, there is an intimate connection between silence and denial: "Since humans need their fellow men who can understand and confirm what they know and have experienced, for their own knowledge and experience, that which everybody knows somehow but can never say out loud loses all tangible reality."[156] In Schmidt's memoir, such a diffusion of reality and the resultant confusion about her motivations and those of others are plainly evident. At times, Schmidt seems genuinely unsure if her choices were motivated by an aversion to the Nazi regime. Thus, she is uncertain if the failure of her relationship with an SA man had something to do with his time on the eastern front and the fact that, in a letter, he had talked about cutting off the beard of an old Jewish man. Similarly, she wonders if her transfer to Serbia was a form of punishment for her fraternization with the French. With such basic confusion about one's motivations and the consequences of one's actions, however, accountability becomes impossible.

Unlike Gartmann, who portrays female army auxiliaries as victims of the Third Reich, Schmidt makes an effort to understand the significance of her work as an integral part of the Nazi death machine. She mentions an incident in which she explained to her superiors the underlying, critical meaning of a story published in a Serbian newspaper. At the time, she felt proud that she understood what her male superiors did not. Later, however, she realizes that her cleverness may have cost the Serbian writers of the piece their lives because "even the most insignificant cog has a function and many of these cogs make up the whole big machine."[157] Along the same lines, Schmidt begins to understand the importance of army auxiliaries for the Nazi war of conquest. When she is transferred to Poltawa, 600 kilometers from Stalingrad, she realizes that the soldiers whose jobs are now being done by female army auxiliaries were sent to Stalingrad. She wonders, "What am I doing in this male war? Men make war. Men kill. And they need women as hand maidens in their war."[158] As this citations shows, even though Schmidt begins to grasp the impact of her actions in the larger context of the war and even though she ponders her own complicity, she still sees herself primarily as a victim. To Schmidt, female army auxiliaries are pawns in a male war, yoked to a cause that they do not fully understand.

Schmidt's memoir suggests that she was no anti-Semite, but rather traumatized by the violence she witnessed and ashamed for her countrymen.[159] At the same time, however, a lot of attention is paid to her own suffering whereas the details of the massacres she was privy to remain vague. In her introduction to Schmidt's memoir, Annette Kuhn speaks of the gaping rift between the horror of the events and the sparse pieces of information given by Ilse Schmidt.[160] Along the same lines, Maubach points out that in Schmidt's account, the number of victims of the Nazi terror is greatly reduced: Schmidt estimates that 300 Jews were held in the Rowno ghetto, even though the actual number of victims is closer to 5,000.[161] Schwarz's critique of the same passage is even more pronounced. Schwarz compares Schmidt's account to that of a contemporary, a German engineer in Rovno, who testified at the International Military Tribunal in Nuremberg. This witness notes that the streets were lined with corpses. Schwarz comments tersely that, in light of this testimony and also of the fact that Schmidt's office window faced the courtyard where executions were routinely carried out, "her dramatically retold story of the deportation loses credibility."[162]

When Schmidt witnesses the preparation for a massacre, her first reaction is to call on the victims to defend themselves more vigorously: "Do more! That's not enough! Defend yourselves."[163] Hours later it occurs to her that she herself does not fight back either. At the end of her memoir, Schmidt asks, "who am I, what should I have done, why did I not do anything,"[164] and concludes that the only thing she is no longer guilty of is silence. Even though at times Schmidt's sense of victimization threatens to occlude her complicity, her trauma is clearly defined not only by her suffering but also by an acute awareness of her own culpability.

In spite of her effort to break the silence and reflect on her experiences, Schmidt's memoir remains marked by the same ruptures that characterized her life during the Third Reich. Memories of her home life, romantic affairs, and acquaintances in the occupied territories are vivid while attempts to integrate the victims of the Nazi regime into her narrative remain incomplete. The narrative flows when Schmidt speaks of her social life and her impressions as a foreigner in other countries. She also conveys a vivid sense of the fear of violence and of the intense panic with which she responded to her growing realization of Nazi atrocities, but she has no memory of the actual work she did in the Ukraine and offers only fleeting glimpses of the Jewish victims of the regime. In one of her short comments on the process of writing, Schmidt reports a recurring dream in which she recovers a box that was buried deep in the ground. At first, she cannot open the box, but when she finally succeeds, she finds her hidden self. It would appear that this box is an apt metaphor for Schmidt's book: her narrative is marked by the struggle to understand her former self, to write about feelings she could not verbalize or even acknowledge at the time. But it is telling that it is Schmidt's self, and not, as one might expect, the crimes of the Third Reich that are buried and in need of recovery. In reading Schmidt's memoir, one wishes that Schmidt could have paid tribute to the victims by recovering through research what she failed to notice at the time: by November 1941, 15,000 Rowno Jews had been murdered.[165] As it is, the book remains primarily an exploration of self, with sideways glances at the criminal nature of the Nazi regime. Even so, however, Schmidt's memoir differs from other similar accounts because the author recognizes that, in some small way, her work at the time contributed to the functioning of the Nazi machine of war and genocide.[166] Of all texts discussed in the chapter, Schmidt's *Die Mitläuferin* is the only one that engages in an effort to account for the author's complicity.

Conclusion

In recent years, several scholars have drawn attention to the various strategies that served to minimize women's involvement in the Nazi war and genocide. Kompisch, for example, notes that the demonization and sexualization of a few female perpetrators, such as Ilse Koch, created a safe distance between these monstrous outliers and the average German woman during the Third Reich. Kompisch also points out that whenever women professed ignorance about Nazi atrocities or declared that they were *forced* to participate in criminal actions, their claims were believed all too easily.[167] The motivation for such credulity is all too obvious: because women were barred from leadership positions in the party, they represent the silent majority. Consequently, acknowledging the full scope of women's participation in the Second World War and the Holocaust would be one more step toward recognizing the involvement of everyday Germans in the terror of the Nazi regime. And yet, if we read the memoirs of women who worked for the German army, such everyday involvement is plainly evident. Autobiographical texts by army auxiliaries such as Vogt and Gartmann teach us not only that women were much closer to the frontlines and far more involved in armed combat than is commonly acknowledged, they also show that women were informed about the Nazi war and genocide, and, to various degrees, complicit with them.

Neither Vogt nor Reitsch nor Gartmann reflect critically on their role in the Nazi regime. Vogt's and Gartmann's complicity emerges in the narrative ruptures, omissions, and contradictions that characterize both texts. Consider, for example, the extraordinary sense of agency at the time and the growing feeling of victimization after the war. Tellingly, Vogt fondly remembers the "soldier's happiness that we experienced all the same"[168] even as she complains bitterly about being mistreated in American captivity. Or think of Schmidt who is delighted when she alone understands the true meaning of a code used by partisans and who, when she applies for transfer to Rome, declares "that I took my life into my hands for the first time, decided about my future by myself and reacted independently."[169] It is this gap between the positive experience of travel, independence, and action on the one hand and the exposure to violence and genocide on the other, between the author's personal story, the reality of war, and, in later decades, the awareness of discourses of *Vergangenheitsbewältigung*, that produces the narrative ruptures evident in Vogt's, Gartmann's, and Schmidt's texts.

Many young German women longed to be part of a bigger cause and to be needed, and the Nazis excelled at exploiting this enthusiasm for their purpose. Young women such as Vogt and Schmidt appreciated the freedom they gained through their association with the National Socialist Party. As the Nazis began to lose the war, however, the struggle for survival overshadowed any remaining sense of agency. Even so, Vogt, a Nazi enthusiast who volunteered as late as 1944, remained convinced of the righteousness of her cause until the bitter end and consequently felt no need to justify her actions. Vogt spoilt for action and derived her sense of self-worth from her participation in the war. Her text is a shocking testament to the chauvinism and racism that motivated her association with the Nazis. While Vogt's youth is an extenuating circumstance, Reitsch never revised her perception of the Nazis or of her own role in their regime, even though she had plenty of time to do so. Because Reitsch shielded herself from any unpleasant reality even during the Third Reich, her account is marked not by inconsistency but by repetition and stock phrases.

Unlike Vogt and Reitsch, Gartmann's protagonists claim to despise the Nazis. Although they contribute to the war effort on many levels, they see themselves not as cogs in the Nazi machine, but as victims of the Nazis and thus feel no need to justify their actions. Finally, some memoirs are marked by remorse and regret. Decades after the war, Ilse Schmidt began to understand that, in some small way, her actions had helped to prolong a criminal war and had even contributed to the persecution and murder of millions of innocents. Of all the memoirs discussed in this chapter, Schmidt's text is by far the most instructive, precisely because Schmidt was neither an avid Nazi nor an opponent of the regime. Her memoir teaches us about the dangers of defining one's own life as apolitical and about the nefarious consequences of silence. Schmidt's memoir suggests that her silence, as well as the silence of her fellow army auxiliaries, lies at the heart of her failure to respond to the atrocities she witnessed. Because she did not verbalize her experiences at the time, her reality eroded. Actual ignorance and willful denial became indistinguishable. There may be little one can do about the gigantic capacity for denial of outliers such as Reitsch, but there is much to be gained by heeding the lessons implied in Schmidt's memoir.

Notes

1. Hagemann, "Preface," ix.
2. Germany never fully implemented the compulsory service for women permitted by the Defense Law of 1935. In January 1943, when the Nazis were losing the war and the need for manpower became dire, they introduced a labor conscription law that targeted women between the ages of seventeen and forty-five (excepting those who had one small or two school-age children), but did not fully implement it as the Nazi leadership was concerned about its impact on the morale of frontline soldiers, the *Wehrfreudigkeit in der Truppe* (Kundrus, *Kriegerfrauen*, 262). Because there was no general mobilization of the female sex (Bajohr, *Die Hälfte der Fabrik*, 253), "almost two-thirds of married women of working age were not employed" (Stephenson, *Women in Nazi Germany*, 54). The fact that wives of soldiers received up to 85 percent of their husbands' previous remuneration and that this allowance was reduced if these wives earned a salary did not help matters. (In contrast, the United States offered a low allowance and did not reduce it if women worked.) All in all, the German labor conscription law did more harm than good: its social injustice led to many complaints since female members of the upper classes – the wives of officers and party functionaries – were typically not pressed to find employment (see Lehker, *Frauen im Nationalsozialismus*, 108; Stephenson, *Women in Nazi Germany*, xvii; Gersdorff, *Frauen im Kriegsdienst 1914–1945*, 50). In comparison, Britain made war service compulsory for young, single women in 1941 (see Summerfield, "'She Wants a Gun Not a Dishcloth!'" 119). DeGroot writes that nine out of ten single women and eight out of ten married women served in the British army or industry ("Cordite," 100). Finally, while the

United States, Germany, and England used women in noncombat roles, in the Soviet Union, women were involved in combat "serving as snipers, machinegunners, artillery women, and tank women" (Elshtain, *Women and War*, 178). The Russians also created three all-female air force regiments, one of which, the 588th Night Bomber Regiment, was called "The Night Witches" (Jones, *Women Warriors*, 144; see also Pennington, "'Do Not Speak of the Services You Rendered'"). Koepcke estimates that 800,000 to 1 million women served in the Red Army (*Frauen im Wehrdienst*, 104). According to Conze and Fieseler, the press depicted female soldiers as "isolated cases" ("Soviet Women as Comrades-in-Arms," 222), even though half a million carried weapons and served at the front (212).

3. Maubach, *Stellung*, 10.
4. Enloe, *Does Khaki Become You*, 6.
5. See also Hanley, who explains that "unless we undermine the soldier's monopoly on representing himself at war, our memories of war will overtly or covertly serve his interests. We can challenge this monopoly only by redefining what war literature is about" (Hanley, *Writing War*, 124).
6. Lower, *Hitler's Furies*, 10–11.
7. Misztal, *Theories of Social Remembering*, 50. See Prager, who explains that memories are "screens that express perceptions of the past generated by interests that postdate the past experiences" (Prager, *Presenting the Past*, 53).
8. For example, Vogt states that she does not want to bore her audience ("Bericht über den Einsatz als Flakwaffenhelferin," 38).
9. Young, *Writing and Rewriting the Holocaust*, 52.
10. Reese, *Growing Up Female in Nazi Germany*, 4.
11. See Reese, *Growing Up Female in Nazi Germany*, 25; Bajohr, *Die Hälfte der Fabrik*, 228.
12. See Benz, *Frauen im Nationalsozialismus*, 197.
13. As of 1939, "all girls between seventeen and twenty-five who were not in full-time employment, school, or occupational training and were not needed as 'helping family members' in agriculture must join the Reich Labor Service (RAD)" (Hagemann, "Home/Front," 20–21); see also Winkler, *Frauenarbeit im Dritten Reich*, 57, 85, and 89.
14. Seidler, *Blitzmädchen*, 9.
15. For more information, see Benz, *Frauen im Nationalsozialismus*, 15; Koepcke, *Frauen im Wehrdienst*, 75; Hagemann, "Home/Front," 21.
16. Kompisch points out that many assistant nurses were recruited as army auxiliaries (Kompisch, *Täterinnen*, 217; see also Maubach, "Expansion," 103).
17. Gersdorff offers a precise count of the distribution of women within the armed forces: when the war started on September 1, 1939, 140,000 women were employed in the army; 50,000 of them were white collar workers and 90,000 were blue collar workers; 300,000 women were employed in the reserve army; the infantry employed 8,000 women in communication and 12,500 auxiliaries; the air force employed 130,000 and the navy 20,000 (Gersdorff, *Frauen im Kriegsdienst 1914–1945*, 74).

18. Hagemann, "Home/Front," 24.
19. See Lower, *Hitler's Furies*, 6.
20. For more information, see Seidler, *Blitzmädchen*, 35.
21. Most anti-aircraft stations were manned by two soldiers and six auxiliaries (see Seidler, *Blitzmädchen*, 42). See also Seidler, *Blitzmädchen*, 148 and Hagemann, "Kraft," 100.
22. See Blum, "'Einen weiblichen Soldaten gibt es nicht,'" 47.
23. The United States went to great lengths to confine women to noncombat status: for example, while women controlled "searchlight operations, targeting and hit confirmation" in mixed artillery crews, male recruits had to fire (Enloe, *Does Khaki Become You*, 123). Of course, this differentiation is rather artificial. As Annemarie Heinz writes: "Die Befehle, die ich weitergebe, setzen nicht nur die Scheinwerfer in Gang, sie ermöglichen die Zielfindung der Kanonen. ... Wir sind zu Handlangern des Todes geworden" ("The commands that I pass on not only turn the lights on, they also facilitate the targeting of cannons. ... We are the henchmen of death") (Heinz, *Anna, die Soldatin*, 73). See also Szepansky, *Blitzmädel, Heldenmutter, Kriegerwitwe*, 48.
24. "Zur Bedienung von Feuerwaffen im Kampf gegen den Feind dürfen Frauen und Mädchen im allgemeinen nicht herangezogen werden" (cited in Gersdorff, *Frauen im Kriegsdienst 1914–1945*, 73). Women were also warned that the use of a weapon might expose them to harsher treatment by the enemy (see Gersdorff, *Frauen im Kriegsdienst 1914–1945*, 374).
25. Service of women in the Wehrmacht on a large scale was first suggested at a meeting of state secretaries in the Ministry of Propaganda (Willmot, "Women in the Third Reich," 13).
26. See Rupp, *Mobilizing Women for War*, 38.
27. See Maubach, *Stellung*, 17, and Lehker, *Frauen im Nationalsozialismus*, 43. In 1936, Hitler declared: "Solange wir ein gesundes männliches Geschlecht besitzen ... wird in Deutschland keine weibliche Handgranatenwerferinnen-Abteilung gebildet und kein weibliches Scharfschützenkorps" ("As long as we have healthy men ... Germany will not form a battalion of female throwers of hand grenades or a female corps of sharpshooters") (cited in Seidler, *Blitzmädchen*, 8).
28. See Maubach, "Expansion," 108.
29. See Benz, *Frauen im Nationalsozialismus*, 201; Stephenson, *Women in Nazi Germany*, 95; Gersdorff, *Frauen im Kriegsdienst 1914–1945*, 72, and Kundrus, "Nur die halbe Geschichte," 721. Szepansky points out that some anti-aircraft auxiliaries were instructed in the use of machine guns (*Blitzmädel, Heldenmutter, Kriegerwitwe*, 240); see also Spieckermans, who writes about her "Geschützausbildung" (training in the use of guns) ("Als Flakwaffenhelferin im Einsatz 1944/45," 32).
30. "Ausstattung mit Handfeuerwaffen für den persönlichen Schutz, soweit im Einzelfall erforderlich, auch mit Panzerfaust pp. ist zulässig. Soweit Frauen und Mädchen im Heimatkriegsgebiet zum Wachdienst eingesetzt sind, wird Ausstattung mit Handfeuerwaffen genehmigt" ("Being equipped with

handguns for personal protection, insofar as it is required in individual cases, also with bazookas is permitted. Insofar as women and girls are deployed for guard duty on the home front being equipped with handguns is approved") (Gersdorff, *Frauen im Kriegsdienst 1914–1945*, 531). See also Koepcke, *Frauen im Wehrdienst*, 76, and Heinz, *Anna, die Soldatin*, 44–45.

31. See Koepcke, *Frauen im Wehrdienst*, 75; Gersdorff, *Frauen im Kriegsdienst 1914–1945*, 60; see also DeGroot on the "inferior, semi-detached status of auxiliaries" who "did not enlist, they were enrolled; they were supervised, not commanded" ("Arms and the Woman," 14).

32. On the ranks for women, see Seidler, *Blitzmädchen*, 19.

33. "Zur Ersparung von Spinnstoffwaren" (Gersdorff, *Frauen im Kriegsdienst 1914–1945*, 356).

34. "In June 1944, women were 39.4 per cent of the total British workforce" (Enloe, *Does Khaki Become You*, 182). While the United States chose not to conscript women for war work, the promotional campaigns of the War Manpower Commission and the Office of War Information were successful: "Germany's labor force increased by only 1% from 1939 to 1944, while the American female labor force increased by 32% from 1941 to 1945" (Rupp, *Mobilizing Women for War*, 75).

35. Maubach, *Stellung*, 73. It is also important to keep in mind that Hitler's female army was very young, typically between eighteen and twenty-five years old (see Lower, *Hitler's Furies*, 15).

36. As Enloe points out, even today recruitment strategies are designed to appeal to "the private aspirations and needs of those women who have the fewest alternatives for education, income, and autonomy" (Enloe, *Does Khaki Become You*, 134).

37. "Abenteuer wollte ich erleben! Fremde Länder wollte ich sehen" (Lipinski, *Frauen an die Front!* 32). Responding to this thirst for adventure, the military authorities, concerned about women who enjoyed their time abroad a bit too much, repeatedly sought to institute strict guidelines: "Von jeder deutschen Angestellten wird erwartet, daß sie insbesondere in der Öffentlichkeit alles vermeidet, was dem Ansehen der Deutschen im besetzten Frankreich irgendwie abträglich sein könnte. Dazu gehört auch der Besuch von Gaststätten über Mitternacht hinaus. In Ausnahmefällen trägt der deutsche Begleiter die Verantwortung. Gelage, Alkoholmißbrauch sind verboten, desgleichen lautes Benehmen und Einhaken auf der Straße" ("Every female employee is expected to avoid everything, particularly in public, that could be detrimental to the reputation of Germans in occupied France. This includes frequenting pubs after midnight. In exceptional cases the German companion is responsible. Wild parties and the consumption of alcohol are prohibited, as are loud conduct or linking arms in the streets") (cited in Gersdorff, *Frauen im Kriegsdienst 1914–1945*, 330). In contrast, there was great sympathy for men who needed to release pressure. Responding to a female complaint about an evening in a casino that referred to male officers as "barbarische[r] Sauhaufen" (barbaric pigs), the authorities insisted that

"Unsere Offiziere, die täglich ihr Leben für die Zukunft des deutschen Volkes einsetzen, dürfen nicht in die Lage gebracht werden, daß jede verständnislose Gans sie in so entwürdigender Weise kritisiert") ("Our officers who daily risk their lives for the future of the German people should not be put in a position in which every stupid goose can criticize them in such a humiliating way") (cited in Gersdorff, *Frauen im Kriegsdienst 1914–1945*, 334).

38. Harvey's study about German women who participated in the colonization of the East lists the following motivations: "opportunities for sight-seeing and self-enrichment," as well as "reluctant conformity, career-minded opportunism, a patriotic sense of duty, or an ideological commitment to the regime's colonizing 'drive to the East'" (Harvey, "Remembering and Repressing," 276–277). Harvey notes that many women saw the war as "a welcome opportunity to demonstrate their independence and their competence as women, to acquire professional experience and to 'see something of the world'; to escape from familial pressures and the stress of living under Allied bombardment, or a humdrum job" (Harvey, "Remembering and Repressing," 291). See also Winkler, *Frauenarbeit im Dritten Reich*, 123.

39. "Wir haben gelebt wie die Dubarry," cited in Killius, *Frauen für die Front*, 152.

40. See Herzog's comments on the "consensual pleasures made possible by the anonymity and mass mobility of times of war and the accompanying disruptions of traditional constraints and communal and familial monitoring mechanisms" (Herzog, "Introduction," 5).

41. Summ, *Schäfers Tochter*, 130.

42. Cited in Kardorff, *Berliner Aufzeichnungen 1942–45*, 93. Alexijewitsch shows that female Russian soldiers dealt with the same prejudice (*Der Krieg hat kein weibliches Gesicht*, 57, 112).

43. Römer, *Kameraden*, 118. See also Maubach, "Gender Relations," 169.

44. See Szepansky, *Blitzmädel, Heldenmutter, Kriegerwitwe*, 97.

45. In contrast, women who joined before 1941 were volunteers. According to Maubach, there were no forced recruitments before 1941 (Maubach, *Stellung*, 107).

46. "Viele Augen sehen haßerfüllt auf die Uniform, die ich trage" (Himmelstoß, *Und ich konnte nichts ändern!* 131). See also Lipinski: "Manch haßvoller Blick der Einheimischen traf uns. Verständlicherweise mochten sie uns nicht. Wer mag schon Besatzer aus einem 'Herrenvolk' über sich?" ("The locals cast many a hateful glance on us. Understandably, they did not like us. Who likes being lorded over by occupiers from a master race?") (Lipinski, *Frauen an die Front!* 4).

47. Lower, *Hitler's Furies*, 152.

48. "Es war Krieg und trotzdem ging man noch ins Kino. . . . Alles in allem war es in Frankreich eine sehr glückliche und abwechslungsreiche Zeit" (Killius, *Frauen für die Front*, 56 and 63; see also 146). See also Ruth Kirsten-Herbst, who writes, "Trotz Krieg und Bomben gefiel es mir ganz gut" ("In spite of war and bombs, I liked it very much") (*Mädchen an der Front*, 7), and Ilse Gräfin von Bredow, who trained horses for the army and whose memoir treats the

war years as a treasure trove of amusing anecdotes about the folly of mankind while eliding the murderous actions of the regime.

49. Killius's collection contains many statements along these lines, e.g., "Das Politische war zweitrangig, der Beruf, das Privatleben war wichtiger" ("Politics was secondary, one's job, one's private life were more important") (*Frauen für die Front*, 39), or "Es war Krieg. Aber das stand ganz im Hintergrund" ("It was war. But that was completely in the background") (40), or "Ich war auch politisch wenig interessiert als junges Mädchen. Ich war eben jung und hatte andere Dinge im Kopf" ("I had little interest in politics as a young girl. I was young and had other things to think about") (50).

50. See Christiane Grote and Gabriele Rosenthal on women's self-definition as apolitical as a strategy of exoneration ("Frausein als Entlastungsargument für die biographische Verstrickung in den Nationalsozialismus?"). See also Mahr, *Kriegsliteratur von Frauen?* 122.

51. Meyer, "Anpassung, Selbstbehauptung und Verdrängung," 179.

52. Lower, *Hitler's Furies*, 99.

53. Kompisch, *Täterinnen*, 84; Zipfel, "Die Welt ist so schön, und wir zerstören sie," 178.

54. See Zipfel, "Die Welt ist so schön, und wir zerstören sie," 174; "Wie führen," 465–467.

55. Lipinski, *Frauen an die Front!*, 16; see also 30.

56. Rosenthal speaks of "Deckgeschichten ... Erzähllücken" ("cover stories ... narrative gaps"). She points out that Germans who were not persecuted told stories that presented them as victims, but only hinted at and did not expand on scenes of real horrors, fear of death, the murder and dying of others, persecution, and a failure to help or resist (Rosenthal, *Der Holocaust im Leben von drei Generationen*, 36). See also Sayner, who notes "a tension between a suggested critical awareness by the protagonist and a repetition of positive characteristics of the past" (*Women without a Past?*, 182).

57. Killius, *Frauen für die Front*, 81.

58. "Uns ergriff eine Ahnung davon, was die nächste Zeit bringen sollte: Auflösung aller sittlichen Ordnungen, Mißtrauen gegen jedermann, Denunziationen ... Neuartigkeit der Situation" (Kirsten-Herbst, *Mädchen an der Front*, 97).

59. Connerton, *How Societies Remember*, 26.

60. Noting this preference for stock phrases, Maubach claims that what she calls "szenische Erinnerungen" ("scenic memories"), i.e., associative stories or stories of episodes that are rarely told or told for the first time, tend to be closer to the actual events than stereotypical, rehearsed narrative formulae that have become part of the personal repertoires of war stories (*Stellung*, 38).

61. For more information on Rüdiger, see Stephenson, *Women in Nazi Germany*, 77. Rüdiger claims that the party wanted her to select a group of BDM girls for service while she herself insisted that they rely on volunteers (*Ein Leben*, 125). Since Rüdiger's memoir shows little desire to obfuscate or deny her

National Socialist worldview – she proudly defends her conviction that Jews are different – it is likely that this is her genuine opinion.

62. Rüdiger was given the manuscript by Ruth Windisch, who had been Vogt's leader in the BDM and then served as her *Flakwaffenoberführerin* in Prague.

63. See Rüdiger, *Ein Leben*, 130; Rüdiger, "Foreword," 7.

64. "Mit frischer Kraft und Freude sahen wir dem Kommenden entgegen" (Vogt, "Bericht über den Einsatz als Flakwaffenhelferin," 18). See also Vogt, "Bericht über den Einsatz als Flakwaffenhelferin," 21.

65. "Wir wären schon lieber im Einsatz gewesen, um am Kampf teilzuhaben" (Vogt, "Bericht über den Einsatz als Flakwaffenhelferin," 23). See also Vogt, "Bericht über den Einsatz als Flakwaffenhelferin," 22.

66. See Vogt, "Bericht über den Einsatz als Flakwaffenhelferin," 29 and 42. See also "Seit einigen Tagen stehen Mädel aus unseren Reihen an den Geschützen" ("for several days now girls from our group have been manning the guns") (Vogt, "Bericht über den Einsatz als Flakwaffenhelferin," 32).

67. "Immer noch gingen wir aufrecht und vertrauten dem Führer. Deutschland wird nicht untergehen" (Vogt, "Bericht über den Einsatz als Flakwaffenhelferin," 45; see also 24 and 37).

68. "Frohsinn" (Vogt, "Bericht über den Einsatz als Flakwaffenhelferin," 29); "diese Vögelchen herunterzuholen" (Vogt, "Bericht über den Einsatz als Flakwaffenhelferin," 17).

69. Vogt, "Bericht über den Einsatz als Flakwaffenhelferin," 47.

70. "diese Hunde" (Vogt, "Bericht über den Einsatz als Flakwaffenhelferin," 56); "Gesindel" (Vogt, "Bericht über den Einsatz als Flakwaffenhelferin," 49 and 58); "das goldene Prag … Wie schön wäre es, wenn nicht immer slawische Laute diese Andacht stören würden" (Vogt, "Bericht über den Einsatz als Flakwaffenhelferin," 39; see also 33).

71. "Kugelregen" (Vogt, "Bericht über den Einsatz als Flakwaffenhelferin," 53).

72. "Das Leben war ja nun keinen Schuß Pulver mehr wert" (Vogt, "Bericht über den Einsatz als Flakwaffenhelferin," 53).

73. "Nichts kann uns rauben, Liebe und Glauben zu unserem Land" (Vogt, "Bericht über den Einsatz als Flakwaffenhelferin," 54). Indeed, singing is Vogt's default reaction to the sight of urban destruction.

74. Vogt, "Bericht über den Einsatz als Flakwaffenhelferin," 66 and 57.

75. See also Lehker, who points out that the militarization of girls began in the BDM, where they were habituated to entrance exams, uniforms, IDs, performance records, and badges (Lehker, *Frauen im Nationalsozialismus*, 37), and continued later with military rituals, such as the awarding of the mother's cross (49).

76. "Wir waren bestimmt keine rauhen Krieger – immer nur Frauen" (Vogt, "Bericht über den Einsatz als Flakwaffenhelferin," 28).

77. "Trotz ihres soldatischen Einsatzes keine Soldaten … auf ihre frauliche Eigenart … Rücksicht … nehmen" (cited in Gersdorff, *Frauen im Kriegsdienst 1914–1945*, 469).

78. See Vogt, "Bericht über den Einsatz als Flakwaffenhelferin," 64.

79. "Über unser Verhalten in den Prager Kampftagen und bei diesem schweren Marsch gestaunt und selbst dabei Kraft geschöpft" (Vogt, "Bericht über den Einsatz als Flakwaffenhelferin," 64). Conversely, women who do not join the fight and whom "jeder Amerikaner, ja Neger ... für eine Tafel Schokolade haben [kann]" ("every American, every negro ... can have for a bar of chocolate") disgust her (Vogt, "Bericht über den Einsatz als Flakwaffenhelferin," 66).

80. "Frieden und Waffenruhe und Kriegsgefangene – gibt es das?" (Vogt, "Bericht über den Einsatz als Flakwaffenhelferin," 60).

81. She does have fond memories of singing in the POW camps with a group of other women who became known as the Pilsener Nordkasernenspatzen.

82. "Über das Ende des Krieges werden wir wohl nie hinwegkommen: unser Deutschland ist nicht mehr. Die Gedanken können es nicht fassen: ein Volk, kein Reich, kein Führer mehr" (Vogt, "Bericht über den Einsatz als Flakwaffenhelferin," 86).

83. For example, she remarks that one of the barracks is being built by Jews (Vogt, "Bericht über den Einsatz als Flakwaffenhelferin," 37).

84. "Juden, die uns frech angrinsen" (Vogt, "Bericht über den Einsatz als Flakwaffenhelferin," 65); see also Vogt, "Bericht über den Einsatz als Flakwaffenhelferin," 61.

85. See Vogt, "Bericht über den Einsatz als Flakwaffenhelferin," 77.

86. See Reitsch, *Unzerstörbare*, 18.

87. "Festes sittliches und geistiges Fundament" (Reitsch, *Fliegen*, 19). See also Reitsch, *Fliegen*, 30.

88. "Als ob ich nur versehentlich ein Mädchen geworden wäre" (Reitsch, *Unzerstörbare*, 17).

89. Jackson, *Hitler's Heroine*, 49.

90. "Ich wußte damals nie am Morgen, ob ich am Abend noch leben würde, aber ich fühlte mich als glücklichster Mensch der Welt, voll Dank, daß mir solche verantwortungsvolle Aufgaben übertragen wurden" (Reitsch, *Unzerstörbare*, 79).

91. For more information on Reitsch's work for the military, see Piszkiewicz, *From Nazi Test Pilot to Hitler's Bunker*, 40–41.

92. "Ich wollte nur bis zur letzten Stunde meiner Heimat helfen" (Reitsch, *Fliegen*, 282).

93. "Ich wußte nun und hatte es an dem Aufleuchten der Augen gesehen, was es für die Männer bedeutete, daß ich aus der Heimat zu ihnen kam" (Reitsch, *Fliegen*, 291).

94. See Reitsch, *Fliegen*, 292.

95. She even signed on herself: "I hereby apply to be enrolled in the suicide group as pilot of a human glider bomb. I fully understand that employment in this capacity will entail my own death" (cited in Piszkiewicz, *From Nazi Test Pilot to Hitler's Bunker*, 75–76).

96. Trevor-Roper, *The Last Days of Hitler*, 80.

97. "Seine ungezwungene und einfache Art strömte eine Zuversicht aus, die sich jedem, der in seine Nähe kam, mitteilte"; "Dieser offizielle Empfang konnt

[*sic*] eine tiefere Einsichtnahme in das Wesen und die Persönlichkeit Hitlers nicht vermitteln" (Reitsch, *Fliegen*, 268).

98. Reitsch, *Fliegen*, 286.
99. Surprisingly, Jackson's recent biography supports this view. The book contains numerous inaccuracies and problematic statements. For example, Jackson casts Reitsch as a young woman who "made Hitler her ultimate paternal guide" because "her own father sadly committed suicide" (9), even though her father's suicide occurred after Hitler's suicide. Jackson also claims that Reitsch criticized the persecution of Jews during *Reichskristallnacht* and on several other occasions, but does not provide source attribution for these claims. According to Jackson, Reitsch was extremely disappointed when she met Hitler and "locked herself in her room and cried for three days" (88). Again, there is no mention of a source, not even the name of the "friend" to whom Reitsch confessed her disappointment.
100. "Meine Gedanken gehörten dem Wind, den Wolken und den Sternen. Dort hinauf aber reichte das politische Ränkespiel der Welt nicht" (Reitsch, *Fliegen*, 228).
101. See Reitsch, *Fliegen*, 188.
102. See Piszkiewicz, *From Nazi Test Pilot to Hitler's Bunker*, 125.
103. "Völlig schuldlos" (Reitsch, *Unzerstörbare*, 100).
104. "Ohne es zu wissen und ohne mich wehren zu können, auf eine politische Bühne gezogen … auf die ich nie gehörte" (Reitsch, *Unzerstörbare*, 97; see also *Fliegen*, 8).
105. See Reitsch, *Unzerstörbare*, 126; *Fliegen*, 9 and 193.
106. "Deutscher Kulturboden" (Reitsch, *Unzerstörbare*, 11); see also her comments on "östliche Unberührtheit" and "westliche Zivilisation" (Reitsch, *Fliegen*, 131). On her father's suicide, see Piszkiewicz, *From Nazi Test Pilot to Hitler's Bunker*, 118, and Reitsch, *Unzerstörbare*, 11.
107. "Gott zurückgeben" (Reitsch, *Unzerstörbare*, 92).
108. See Reitsch, *Unzerstörbare*, 93.
109. Reitsch, *Unzerstörbare*, 104.
110. "Herr vergib ihnen, denn sie wissen nicht, was sie tun" (Reitsch, *Unzerstörbare*, 57).
111. Reitsch, *Fliegen*, 226 and 331.
112. Reitsch, *Fliegen*, 38, 104, 137–138, 194; Reitsch, *Unzerstörbare*, 80; see also Römer, who reports that Reitsch was universally disliked by German soldiers (*Kameraden*, 119).
113. "Die den tapferen Soldaten an der Front, die ihre Väter, Männer, Söhne und Brüder waren, auf ihre Weise halfen" (Reitsch, *Unzerstörbare*, 88); see also Reitsch, *Fliegen*, 257.
114. Piszkiewicz, *From Nazi Test Pilot to Hitler's Bunker*, 86.
115. Gartmann is not the only female author who fictionalized her experiences during the war. Annemarie Heinz's *Anna, die Soldatin* is also based on the

author's experiences. Unlike *Blitzmädchen, Anna* features a third-person narrator.

116. See Moeller, "What Did You Do," 564.

117. On the text's strategy of turning serious concerns into jokes, see also the comment about the girls' fear of partisans: "Pap sagt immer, wer uns bei Dunkelheit wegholt und dann bei Hellem sieht, bringt uns sofort zurück" ("Pap always says that whoever takes us in the dark and then sees us in daylight will bring us right back") (Gartmann, *Blitzmädchen*, 60).

118. "Kein Kino, kein Tanz, nicht einmal Ausgang" (Gartmann, *Blitzmädchen*, 17).

119. "Lehmann hat für ihr Hurenleben bezahlt, das ist alles" (Gartmann, *Blitzmädchen*, 113).

120. See Gartmann, *Blitzmädchen*, 35.

121. "Wir scheinen Parolen gegenüber immun zu sein; die Worte bleiben an der Oberfläche unserer Gedanken hängen" (Gartmann, *Blitzmädchen*, 24; see also 22).

122. "Viele Polen werden sich rächen wollen . . . Und genaugenommen haben sie recht" (Gartmann, *Blitzmädchen*, 235). See also 244 and 109.

123. "Die Bonzen saufen und wir verrecken" (Gartmann, *Blitzmädchen*, 207).

124. Harvey, *Women and the Nazi East*, 301.

125. "Man alle Juden umgebracht hatte. Doch wir glaubten es nicht. Warum sollte man die Juden umbringen? Sie hatten uns ja nichts getan" (Gartmann, *Blitzmädchen*, 68).

126. For information on the expulsion of the Polish population and women's roles in this colonization effort, see Harvey, *Women and the Nazi East*.

127. See Gartmann, *Blitzmädchen*, 22, 42, 254.

128. "Bandenbekämpfung" (Gartmann, *Blitzmädchen*, 83).

129. "Wir dürfen uns nicht einmischen. Es würde doch nichts nützen. Sie würden uns alle einsperren" (Gartmann, Blitzmädchen, 199).

130. See Gartmann, *Blitzmädchen*, 276.

131. See also references to soldiers' brothels with Russian women (Gartmann, *Blitzmädchen*, 44).

132. In fact, the auxiliaries' own sexual adventures may have been included precisely because fictionalization allows the author to narrate her experiences without violating her need for privacy.

133. See "mir ist jetzt klar, dass wir von einer ganzen Reihe krankhafter Naturen regiert werden" ("it is clear to me now that we are being ruled by a whole series of sick characters") (Gartmann, *Blitzmädchen*, 202); and on Keil: "er ist also krank" ("therefore he is ill") (Gartmann, *Blitzmädchen*, 202).

134. "Es ist Krieg, da gelten andere Gesetze . . . Morgen können wir tot sein" (Gartmann, *Blitzmädchen*, 95). See also "Wer weiss, was morgen ist? Ich jedenfalls will nicht, wenn es sein muss, als Jungfrau krepieren" ("Who knows what will happen tomorrow? I for one, if it has to be, do not want to die a virgin") (Gartmann, *Blitzmädchen*, 165). Sexual mores were also undermined by the dire material circumstances of the war. Constantly

hungry because of their meager rations, Vera's friend Margot sleeps with the local butcher to get meat. She then lies to the butcher about being pregnant to be able to blackmail him into giving her even more meat.

135. Army auxiliary did not receive permission to disband until April 1945 (Seidler, *Blitzmädchen*, 28).

136. "Hilflose Flüchtlinge … kaltblütig niederzumetzeln" (Gartmann, *Blitzmädchen*, 266).

137. "Keil, das Vieh, ich hasse ihn. Für seine Schandtaten an den Polen büssen wir" (Gartmann, *Blitzmädchen*, 302); "begnadeter Künstler" (Gartmann, *Blitzmädchen*, 90); "im Bett wie am Flügel" (Gartmann, *Blitzmädchen*, 302).

138. "Sie stehen Wache, erfüllen ihre Pflicht wie Soldaten. Nur des Nachts, wenn sie sich alleine wissen, sind sie keine Soldaten mehr, sondern ängstliche junge Mädchen" (Gartmann, *Blitzmädchen*, 62).

139. See Gartmann, *Blitzmädchen*, 28, 49, 57.

140. "Wir bezweifeln langsam, ob sie wirklich weiblichen Geschlechtes ist" (Gartmann, *Blitzmädchen*, 44).

141. "Dieser elende, beschissene Krieg! Wir haben ihn nicht gewollt! Warum lässt man uns hier verrecken?" (Gartmann, *Blitzmädchen*, 269).

142. "Der ganze Kommiss müsste aus Frauen bestehen, sagt Beate, dann wäre jeder Krieg schnell zu Ende … Ihr habt Potter vergessen" (Gartmann, *Blitzmädchen*, 26).

143. "Gestrüpp der Erinnerung" (Schmidt, *Die Mitläuferin*, 13).

144. See Maubach, *Stellung* 164.

145. "Ich führe ein angenehmes Leben" ("I lead a pleasant life") (Schmidt, *Die Mitläuferin*, 23); "Paris ist doch zum Amüsieren da" ("Paris is made for amusement") (Schmidt, *Die Mitläuferin*, 22).

146. "Herrlich sorglose Zeit" (Schmidt, *Die Mitläuferin*, 24).

147. See Schmidt, *Die Mitläuferin*, 48, and "fick sie, die alte Sau" (Schmidt, *Die Mitläuferin*, 98).

148. "Was ich eigentlich damals genau gemacht habe, weiß ich heute nicht mehr" (Schmidt, *Die Mitläuferin*, 63).

149. See Schmidt, *Die Mitläuferin*, 63.

150. "Mich läßt das Gefühl nicht los, ich ließe es mir gutgehen, und die anderen liegen im Dreck" ("I cannot shake the feeling that I am enjoying myself and the others are lying in the dirt") (Schmidt, *Die Mitläuferin*, 109).

151. See Maubach, *Stellung*, 195.

152. Huyssen, *Twilight Memories*, 3.

153. "Um des lieben Friedens willen sei still" (Schmidt, *Die Mitläuferin*, 16); "Mich gegen meinen Vater aufzulehnen wäre mir nicht in den Sinn gekommen" ("It would not have occurred to me to rebel against my father") (Schmidt, *Die Mitläuferin*, 18). See also Schmidt, *Die Mitläuferin*, 33.

154. "Wo alles sich abspielt zwischen Nachrichten, über die niemand zu reden wagt, und Propagandalügen, an die niemand glaubt" (Arendt, *Elemente und Ursprünge totaler Herrschaft*, 882–883).

155. See Schmidt, *Die Mitläuferin*, 65.

156. "Da Menschen für Wissen wie Erfahrungen der Mitmenschen bedürfen, die das Gewußte und Erfahrene mitverstehen und bestätigen können, verliert das, was jeder irgendwie weiß, aber nie laut werden lassen darf, alle greifbare Wirklichkeit" (Arendt, *Elemente und Ursprünge totaler Herrschaft,* 902).

157. "Selbst das unbedeutendste Rädchen eine Funktion hat und viele dieser Rädchen die ganze große Maschine ergeben" (Schmidt, *Die Mitläuferin,* 46).

158. "Was mache ich in diesem Männerkrieg? Männer machen Krieg. Männer töten. Und sie brauchen Frauen als Handlangerinnen in ihrem Krieg" (Schmidt, *Die Mitläuferin,* 81).

159. When she happens upon a former Jewish professor who is reduced to ironing her friend's underwear, she is ashamed (Schmidt, *Die Mitläuferin,* 73). In the early years of the Third Reich, she appears to have been genuinely ignorant of the plight of the Jews. For example, she remembers being angry at a Jewish classmate who disappeared one day without saying goodbye (Schmidt, *Die Mitläuferin,* 74).

160. Kuhn 9; see also von Chamier and Eschebach, "Ilse Schmidt," 67.

161. Maubach, *Stellung,* 166.

162. Schwarz, "We Girls," 134.

163. "Tut mehr! Das ist nicht genug! Wehrt euch!" (Schmidt, *Die Mitläuferin,* 74).

164. "Wer bin ich, was hätte ich tun müssen, warum habe ich nichts getan?" (Schmidt, *Die Mitläuferin,* 164). See also Schmidt, *Die Mitläuferin,* 165.

165. See von Chamier and Eschebach, "Ilse Schmidt," 68.

166. Christiansen's statement about the total absence of a critical perspective with respect to Nazi terror in Schmidt's memoir fails to take account of this aspect of Schmidt's text.

167. See Kompisch, *Täterinnen,* 7 and 243.

168. "Soldatenglück, das wir trotz allem gehabt haben" (Vogt, "Bericht über den Einsatz als Flakwaffenhelferin," 76).

169. "Daß ich das erste Mal selbständig in mein Leben eingegriffen, allein über meine Zukunft entschieden und unabhängig reagiert habe" (Schmidt, *Die Mitläuferin,* 106).

CHAPTER 3

Cropped Vision
Nursing in the Second World War

Today, when we think of nurses in the Second World War, the image that comes to mind is that of an angel in white. Numerous films and novels of the Second World War and the postwar period have glorified army nurses as self-sacrificing, ethereal mother figures. Nurses function as symbols of home and peace. They are idolized as embodiments of purity and morality, who remain miraculously untouched by the moral morass of war and genocide.[1] If women as a gender are often seen to embody the antithesis of war, the stereotype of the selfless nurse takes this notion to its extreme: army nurses are "a miracle, the only one in this time that did not dissolve in disillusionment . . . They had an effect simply by being there, members of the gender that symbolizes resistance to destruction."[2] In other words, we have been habituated to think of nurses as incapable of complicity with the Third Reich.

As I show in the following analyses, there is a striking contrast between the literary and cultural glorification of nurses and the brutal reality of nursing near the front lines. Indeed, such mythifications of the angel in white have frequently served to obscure the fact that nurses were also employees and agents of a murderous regime. Although many nurses provided invaluable care for soldiers, they were witnesses of and, in some cases, complicit with Nazi atrocities. In his study *The Birth of the Clinic*, Foucault speaks of "a spontaneous and deeply rooted convergence between the requirements of political ideology and those of medical technology."[3] Such a convergence characterizes the role of medicine in the Third Reich in the most disturbing manner. It is visible in the "early and active support of the German medical profession for National Socialism" and in the fact that "the Nazis found biology and medicine a suitable language in which to articulate their goals."[4] In the German army, medical care was reserved for those defined as racially fit, and nurses, just like doctors, had to comply with Nazi policy.

Since the literary glorification of German medicine in the Second World War has shaped our understanding of nurses and has made it difficult to perceive nurses as complicitous in the Nazi regime, I begin with a brief examination of texts that exemplify the exaltation of Nazi medicine: Peter Bamm's *The Invisible Flag: A Report* (1952); Heinz G. Konsalik's *The Doctor of Stalingrad* (1956); and Hertha Cabanis's novel *Das Licht in den Händen* (1951), which depicts the stereotype of the angel in white in its purest form. I then problematize the cultural fascination with the angel in white by contrasting it with the reality of frontline nursing and of caregiving in the Nazi camp system. I argue that the obsession with the angel in white has promoted a form of cropped vision that erases the trauma of nursing on the front line and severs the nurse from the political and military objectives of the regime that these nurses served. Thus, it is not only the authors of memoirs but also readers who have trouble reconciling the figure of the nurse with the notion of complicity.

This brief historical survey of nursing in the Second World War is then followed by an analysis of two memoirs by German army nurses which I have chosen because they occupy the middle ground between enthusiasm for and opposition to the regime and are thus particularly suited for an analysis of the structure of complicity: Erika Summ's *Shepherd's Daughter* (*Schäfers Tochter*) (2006) and Ilse Ochsenknecht's *As if the Snow Covered Everything: A Nurse Remembers Her Deployment on the Eastern Front* (*Als ob der Schnee alles zudeckte: Eine Krankenschwester erinnert sich an ihren Kriegseinsatz an der Ostfront*) (2004). I argue that, in order to cope with their role in the war, many nurses edited out experiences that were too difficult to reconcile with their self-image as benevolent caregivers. In other words, they developed their own form of cropped vision, evident not only in the text but also in the photographs included in these memoirs. Finally, the last section shows that while Summ's and Ochsenknecht's cropped vision highlights German victimization but fails to take account of German complicity and of the suffering inflicted by Germans, nurses in Nazi concentration camps were forced to confront the full extent of the Nazi genocide. Drawing on a number of memoirs by inmate nurses and physicians, including Olga Lengyel's *Five Chimneys: A Woman Survivor's True Story of Auschwitz* (1946), Lucie Adelsberger's *Auschwitz: A Doctor's Story* (1945), and *Als Krankenschwester im KZ Theresienstadt: Erinnerungen einer Ulmer Jüdin* written in 1945 by German Jewish nurse Resi Weglein, this section deals with the paradox of care in the concentration camps. I argue that in order to cope with the immensity of suffering in the camps and with a complicity that was forced upon them, inmate nurses such as

Weglein refocused their gaze and ultimately redefined the very meaning of care. As inmate nurses were caught in a system in which all too many of their choices ultimately served the ends of the Nazi regime, they resisted by redefining caregiving as spiritual solace, emotional comfort, and commemoration after death.

The Glorification of Nazi Medicine

While many fictional treatments of soldiers on the front lines, such as Erich Maria Remarque's *All Quiet on the Western Front* (1929) or Henri Barbusse's *Le Feu* (1916) do not shy away from the sordidness of war, many novelistic and even some autobiographically based portrayals of army nurses and physicians offer a mythicized version of wartime medicine. Consider, for example, Peter Bamm's frequently cited *The Invisible Flag: A Report* (*Die unsichtbare Flagge: Ein Bericht*) (1952), in which medicine emerges as a shining alternative to Nazi corruption. Told from the perspective of an army surgeon, Bamm's autobiographically inspired "report" casts medicine as a realm apart from politics and surgeons as soldiers who fight a different kind of battle.[5] Although the text acknowledges both the pervasive influence of Nazi ideology and the reality of the Nazi genocide – with detailed references to massacres in Sewastopol and Nikolajew – it also insists that medical officers serve under an invisible flag, the "flag of humanity," which upholds the values of Western civilization and remains untainted by Nazi policy.[6]

Even more so than Bamm, Heinz G. Konsalik's bestseller *The Doctor of Stalingrad* (*Der Arzt von Stalingrad*) glorifies its physician protagonist, Dr. Fritz Böhler, and German medicine along with him. Böhler, a prisoner of war in a Russian camp, selflessly sacrifices himself for the good of his fellow inmates and even stays behind to help them when he is offered a chance to return to Germany. While the state of Russian medicine is deplorable, Böhler is a medical genius who performs miracles heretofore unknown in Russian medical history: "With the most primitive tools, he saved the lives of thousands."[7] Böhler operates on a POW with a perforated appendix with an old pocketknife and performs brain surgery with a chisel, drill, and spoon. While it glorifies medicine, *The Doctor of Stalingrad* is pervaded with racist stereotypes of servile Jews, uncivilized Mongolians, and nymphomaniac Russian women who are slaves to their own sexuality, and Konsalik even has the gall to defend SS medical experiments in concentration camps as necessary sacrifices for scientific progress.[8] Clearly, in these texts from the 1950s, the deification of doctors is designed to preclude any thought of a complicity of Nazi medical personnel.

Konsalik prefaces his novel with the claim that it is based on actual events, which he gleaned from reports of returned POWs. Similarly, Bamm's text is filled with precise historical information even if the text does not call the Nazis by name but consistently refers to them as "the Others" and to Hitler as "the primitive man."[9] In contrast, Hertha Cabanis's novel *Das Licht in den Händen*, published in 1951, is infused with metaphysical murmurings that overlay the visible world with transcendent laws and immaterial essences, but remains devoid of any concrete political or social references: There is the "whispering of the blood" and the "mystery of the silent creature," and there are landscapes that are "filled with essences."[10] Much like Bamm, Cabanis casts medicine as fundamentally untouched by National Socialist ideology. Unlike Bamm, however, she never references specific political events explicitly, but limits herself to vague allusions. For example, in a memorable passage, Cabanis discusses the emigration of Jewish intellectuals and professionals without a single mention of the word "Jew" and without any references to the laws and policies that caused the emigration.[11] She cryptically refers to the political circumstances of the time as chaos and a "cramp of separation," only to conclude that this is nationalism's last stand and the beginning of a united Europe.[12] Repeatedly, Cabanis hints at the war and Germany's imminent defeat with the phrase "it's crackling in the woodwork."[13]

As these citations and the title itself suggest, Cabanis's text stages a cosmic battle between the realms of darkness and light, between the demonic and the forces of good without burdening its readers with insalubrious details. The world of light and of nature is dedicated to healing and self-realization, but such self-realization must unfold within the confines of a higher law.[14] In the hospital setting of *Das Licht*, much like in Vicky Baum's *Menschen im Hotel*, the life stories of individuals from different segments of society – patients, nurses, and doctors – intersect and touch one another. But this intricately woven net serves only to show that all life follows a preordained rhythm, and that all individuals are beholden to their destiny, which they can accept or reject but never escape.[15] It stands to reason that such a notion of destiny, which absolves the individual of responsibility and offers assurance that everything is exactly as it is meant to be,[16] must have appealed to readers who experienced the Third Reich.

Cabanis's protagonist, Bettina, is an exponent of the light, free of any selfish impulses. She is presented as a saint and Joan of Arc figure.[17] When readers first meet her, she is a young nurse who has feelings for

Dr. Christiansen, a tall, young, and radiant demigod.[18] But when Bettina learns that he is married, she renounces every thought of personal happiness and lives only for suffering humanity, proclaiming that she finds fulfillment tending to the sick.[19] Bettina is the perfect embodiment of the mythicized angel in white who cares for others with no thought for her own needs: "She had no more thoughts, no wishes for herself. She spent herself in caregiving."[20] Cabanis emphasizes that Bettina's selflessness is not imposed from the outside, but innate, an imperative embedded in her own nature.[21] Glossing over the reality of racialized medicine in the Third Reich, the text insists that, in this elevated devotion to healing, there are no races or social classes.[22] Consequently, Bettina does not discriminate between different kinds of patients, but rather bestows loving care on every human being: "She loved her homeland, her language, but she also would have helped and cared for a Negro ... the language of the heart, did it not tower above those of the nations, resistant to conscious acquisition, innate."[23] In short, Cabanis combines reactionary gender politics, manifest in the myth of the naturally selfless woman, with a radically sanitized representation of National Socialist medicine.

When Bettina becomes an army nurse, the narrative abandons its strict chronological order and presents a jumbled retrospective motivated by Bettina's injury and resultant fever dream. Here too, references to contemporary events as well as descriptions of the war and life on the front remain vague. There are hints of horror and abuse – "Not to mention the other things we see, have to see, even though one would have preferred to look the other way"[24] – but no explanations or specific information. The war is presented in a mythological frame and overlaid with nature metaphors. Battles are likened to natural events, particularly thunderstorms, guns are beasts of prey, and artillery metallic birds.[25] Unsurprisingly, the mythological sheen that characterizes Cabanis's portrayal of the war also extends to her only passing mention of the Holocaust. Evoking "entire processions of prisoners, of Jews, in whose dark eyes the pain of the past is awakened in the agony of the present,"[26] the text casts the suffering of Jews as a timeless condition divorced from political circumstance.

If there is a point of convergence between Cabanis's novel and the memoirs of army nurses, such as Erika Summ and Ilse Ochsenknecht, it lies not only in the reluctance to engage with female complicity but also in the focus on German victimization. Tellingly, the only act of war that the novel describes in great detail highlights German suffering, namely an attack on a German city. This air raid, which Bettina experiences in a shelter in a church, is presented in unusually graphic terms. Bettina, who cares for the wounded, is faced with a "picture of such overwhelming suffering."[27] It would appear that in Cabanis's novel vagueness is reserved for crimes committed by Germans whereas there is much specific information about the suffering Germans experience. The description of the air raid is topped off by an episode in an army hospital in which an American prisoner of war asks a German officer who lost his family in an air raid for forgiveness: "I had to conduct many air raids on your country, many terrible raids."[28]

Cabanis's novel does not try to make sense of history. Rather, history, and along with it notions of responsibility and guilt, give way to an all-encompassing sense of destiny as the text embarks on a metaphysical quest for the greater meaning of suffering and death, ultimately defining death as a transition into a higher form of life – "nothing can perish unless it changes" – and suffering as a gateway toward catharsis: "pain is bridge, teacher and catharsis."[29] And yet, in spite of the text's intense interrogation of suffering, it is concerned almost exclusively with German victimization, but fails to account for the pain and death inflicted by Germans and for the role and contributions of a young nurse to the Nazi reign of terror. Cabanis's nurse emerges as a creature of light whose radical selflessness forecloses even the possibility of political entanglement. But while Cabanis's fictional nurse remains at a distance from the Nazi genocide, real German army nurses were very much caught in the moral morass of war.

Nursing in the German Army

While the experiences recorded in nurses' memoirs do not correspond to the portrayal of nursing in *The Light in One's Hands*, the ideology that justified the exploitation of professional nurses was very much in line with the image of the angel in white. In the early twentieth century, any form of caregiving was considered an emanation of woman's true nature, and nursing in particular, as nurse and historian Liselotte Katscher summarizes, was seen as "the most feminine of all professions: Everything one expects from a nurse: helpfulness, kindness, motherliness and true femininity are the essential qualities of a true woman. And thus, other than being a mother, there is hardly a profession more dignified for a woman than nursing."[30] Consequently, there is also hardly a profession whose image stands in starker contrast to the very notion of complicity in war and genocide.

Although the characterization of nursing as an innate capability of female nature is meant to defend women's employment, it also suggests that nursing is not really a profession at all. Thus, it is hardly surprising that, by the beginning of the Second World War, the professionalization of nursing had only just begun, although the status and reputation of nurses had improved drastically during the past two decades.[31] In the early twentieth century, nurses had no right to time off or vacations. Typically, a nurse worked a sixty-hour week and instead of a proper salary, she received a modest allowance. As McFarland-Icke points out, "emotional compensation (i.e., gratitude) was proffered as an appropriate complement to inadequate financial compensation."[32] In short, "*dienen statt verdienen*" ("serving instead of earning") was the operative motto for nurses, and hospitals followed the maxim that nurses' "rights must end where higher duties toward patients begin."[33]

As doctor's assistants, nurses remained in a vulnerable and highly exploitable situation, exacerbated greatly by gender stereotypes. Nurses had to obey doctors and were discouraged from independent decision-making. As McFarland-Icke points out in her study of nurses in Nazi Germany, their "professional socialization . . . dictated obedience, practical and intellectual subordination to doctors."[34] Needless to add that such discipline and the ethos of selfless service suited the purposes of the Nazi regime extremely well. Still, it would be wrong to assume that nurses lacked all measure of autonomy. Indeed, the reformation of nursing associated with Florence Nightingale has as much to do with introducing standards of care as it does with a professional revaluation that puts nurses in charge. As Nightingale writes, "To be 'in charge' is certainly not only to carry out the proper measures yourself but to see that every one else does so too."[35]

Efforts to improve the status of nurses and redefine their roles are visible even in Nazi Germany, if only for pragmatic reasons. Initially, nurses were considered unfit for service in the army or near the front lines, but such delicate objections were quickly put aside when Germany's military needs ran roughshod over traditional gender roles.[36] The same relaxation of requirements applied to nurses' marital status. Before the First World War and even at the beginning of the Second World War, nurses were forced to quit when they married.[37] But as the German army started losing and the need for qualified nurses increased, married women were allowed to serve. During the war, properly trained nurses, so-called *Vollschwestern*, were granted the rank of officer,[38] and many nurses were acutely aware of their power and used it to its full extent. While Nightingale implemented reforms to strengthen the authority of nurses in the hospital, the chaos of war achieved the same effect: as traditional hierarchies crumbled near the front lines, nurses were forced to work independently. Personnel shortages were often so acute that nurses were forced to proceed without the guidance of a superior and were even in a position to give orders to helpers, particularly foreign orderlies. Army nurse Brigitte Penkert, for example, writes: "If I were not such a natural at organizing, directing and employing people, this could not have been done."[39] According to Wilma Ruediger, who herself held a leadership position in the Red Cross, nursing offered a haven for women who were looking for responsibility and who were "dissatisfied with the narrow daily life of women, who wanted to help others, who wanted to rule and organize."[40] Clearly, even more so than in the hospital, fully trained nurses in the army enjoyed a degree of autonomy and authority.

While the stereotype of the woman in white casts the nurse as a selfless angel, the memoirs of army nurses suggest that they chose this life because it offered many perks: service in the army allowed women to escape the strictures of family and the narrowly defined gender code of a petty-bourgeois environment. Many women enjoyed the increase in power that a professional situation afforded. Consider, for example, the following comments by Ruediger, who availed herself of the career opportunities in the Red Cross and rose to a supervisory position: "As *Frau Generalführerin* I mostly met people to whom I gave orders, who had to adjust to me. . . . But the life of a wife and homemaker is determined by the dispositions and wishes of the husband."[41] In addition to being free of parental and marital authority, nurses, like army auxiliaries, were relieved of common household chores, which were typically handled by female members of the occupied nations.[42] Particularly during the first years of the war, nurses also enjoyed a vibrant social life with parties, dances, and outings, and their deployment frequently offered opportunities for sightseeing and tourism. On or near the front lines, a small cadre of women interacted with a surplus of men who lavished attention on them. Ruediger comments disdainfully that "women to whom no man paid attention at home now were the life of the party."[43] Others report that nurses, through their sheer presence, had a morale-building function: "If you angels can take it, we can take it."[44] This, however, was not a universally shared feeling. In his analysis of records obtained during the clandestine surveillance of German prisoners of war, Felix Römer shows that many soldiers resented the presence of women near the front lines. Moreover, there is substantial evidence that, while some women basked in admiration, others reported instances of sexual harassment and even rape.[45]

While some women chose nursing because it offered many tangible benefits, others responded to National Socialist appeals to women's idealism and to the deft mobilization of women's desire to work for a cause larger than themselves. The letters of German nurse Brigitte Penkert, for example, show that she, along with many others, appreciated the opportunity to "be at home with bigger things, to venture beyond their own little lives."[46] National Socialist propaganda actively promoted the "myth of the frontline nurse" (*Mythos der Frontschwester*), which cast the nurse as the female equivalent of the soldier.[47] In Nazi ideology, nurses were subject to the same code of honor that governed the conduct of the soldier and were inspired by the same sense of camaraderie and patriotism. Indeed, the similarities between soldier and nurse are striking. For both soldiers and nurses, periods of boredom alternated with phases of overwhelming exertion. Especially in the early years of the war, there were times of relative calm. But once a battle intensified, the perks of life in the army gave way to grueling labor. During an active battle, nurses typically worked for several days without rest or sleep.[48] Frequently suffering from lack of sleep, malnutrition, extreme climates, and stress, many nurses developed health problems. Moreover, just like soldiers, nurses were often traumatized by the severity and frequency of the military injuries they treated. In fact, it is reasonable to assume that, because of her occupation, a nurse witnessed far more and more brutal injuries than the average soldier. Such intimate familiarity with the carnage of war put them in an ideal position to see through the lies of political propaganda.[49] But even though army nurses knew when the Germans were winning or losing based on the demand placed on their services, their memoirs show that they were not always willing to acknowledge the impending defeat.

In addition to witnessing and treating injuries, many nurses found themselves exposed to enemy fire. Although the Geneva Conventions of 1929 "stipulated that, in time of war, hospitals were not legitimate military targets,"[50] opposing armies did not always adhere to this noble ideal. Again and again, medical personnel were subject to shelling and numerous nurses died as a result of such attacks. In dealing with such intense stress, nurses, like many soldiers, self-medicated with alcohol. Furthermore, many nurses were prepared to defend themselves and carried a gun for this purpose. Penkert, for example, had a Browning and knew how to use it. Finally, nurses, like soldiers, experienced difficulties when they returned to civilian life. Unlike soldiers, however, nurses lacked the official recognition of veterans, a fact that frequently exacerbated the difficulty of dealing with the trauma of war.

Although the angel in white is clearly imagined as an apolitical figure, the Third Reich thoroughly politicized the profession of the nurse. Under the Nazis, the employment of nurses was guided by the *"Berufsbeamtengesetz,"* which sorted nurses into categories based on their racial and political profiles: Jewish nurses were restricted to caring for Jewish patients in Jewish hospitals while nurse candidates who could prove Aryan descent, were in good health, and were either party members or could proffer a police certificate of good conduct were free to seek employment with a variety of regime-approved organizations. Only one group of nurses, the so-called *Braune Schwestern,* who made up 9.2 percent of all nurses, was directly subordinate to the NSDAP.[51] These "brown nurses," who were recruited from the younger generation, were primarily assigned to SS hospitals and concentration camps as well as health care on the communal level as *Gemeindeschwester* and in the occupied territories. Although they tended to be particularly fanatical in their support for National Socialism, all nurses were ultimately affiliated with the Nazis. In a process of *Selbstgleichschaltung,* the Red Cross had hastened to embrace the new regime. In its new incarnation, it was highly militarized and no longer obeyed the guiding principle of neutrality.[52] Similarly, the Protestant welfare organizations of the *evangelische Diakonie* welcomed the Third Reich, at least initially.[53] Many Protestant nurses as well as nurses from other denominational organizations were politically conservative. To them, the Nazi state represented a bulwark against Marxist ideology, itself seen as the embodiment of atheism.[54] Thus, there was but little resistance when nurses were integrated into the Reich Association of Nurses (*Reichsfachschaft Deutscher Schwestern und Pflegerinnen*), which was founded in July 1933 and beholden to the Reichs Ministry of the Interior. As of January 1, 1938, all Red Cross nurses were required to swear an oath to the *Führer*: "I swear unconditional loyalty and obedience to my *Führer* Adolf Hitler. I commit to fulfill my duties as a National Socialist nurse faithfully and diligently wherever I am assigned. So help me God."[55]

By the time a nurse swore loyalty to the *Führer*, she had already undergone intense political training. The education of nurses, which was funneled through National Socialist organizations such as the BDM and the Labor Service, included instruction in human genetics and racial hygiene.[56] Although the law that regulated nursing ("*Gesetz zur Ordnung der Krankenpflege*" of September 28, 1938) shortened the training of nurses from two years to eighteen months, ideologically tainted subjects took up 20 percent of the curriculum.[57] It is perhaps because of such thorough politicization that many German nurses do not seem to have felt conflicted about their role in the war.[58] To be sure, the activities of frontline nurses saved numerous lives and, as such, are ethically valuable. But at the same time they cannot be separated from the political and military objectives of the regime that these nurses served. In particular, the selectivity of care that forms the foundation of Nazi medicine is highly problematic, and yet many German nurses and doctors did not seem concerned with this moral dilemma. While Jewish socialist intellectual Käte Frankenthal, who served as a doctor in the Austrian army in the First World War, characterized the military policy that German soldiers had to be treated first as "almost unbearable for doctors,"[59] many German nurses and doctors in the Second World War appear to have internalized the racial standards of the regime. Penkert, for example, declares with conviction that "one only pampers proletarian instincts with the doctrine of the equality of all who bear a human countenance, with the demand for brotherly love at all cost across the boundaries of blood, value and honor."[60] Similarly, many German nurses in the Second World War did not reflect on the ethical dilemma that restoring a soldier to good health may lead directly to his death, a fact that someone like Frankenthal was acutely aware of: "Of course, I could not answer the question how healthy a person has to be before he can perish in the trenches. . . . One had to wonder if it would not be more correct to think of perfect health as a reason that qualified for use as cannon fodder."[61] In fact, it is precisely such considerations that motivated pacifist feminist Lida Gustava Heymann's categorical refusal to work in an army hospital: "To bring half dead human beings back to life and health only to expose them to the same and even worse torture. No, we would not participate in such madness."[62]

In her study of the participation of nurses in the Nazi euthanasia program, McFarland-Icke notes the "self-imposed ignorance" of many nurses who chose to turn a blind eye to the systematic killing of psychiatric patients.[63] A similar "self-imposed ignorance" also characterizes many accounts of frontline nurses who had firsthand knowledge of the Nazi genocide. In a general climate of what Zygmunt Baumann describes as "free-floating responsibility," many nurses "distanced themselves, both physically and psychologically, from their roles as accomplices."[64] In his study of medical practitioners in the Third Reich, Robert Jay Lifton points out that "meaning came to lie in the performance of one's daily tasks rather than in the nature or impact of those tasks,"[65] and this is certainly true of many army nurses. Typically, nurses who served in Russia had ample opportunity to witness the Nazi genocide. As bedside companions, nurses were often the first contacts when soldiers felt the need to talk about their experiences. Nurse Magdalena Wortmann, for example, mentions a soldier who confessed his participation in an execution commando.[66] In spite of this proximity to mass murder, however, few nurses' memoirs mention ghettos or the Holocaust. Moreover, while there are precious few comments on the Nazi policy of conquering living space (*Lebensraum*) in Russia, there is a great deal of affinity with Nazi racial ideology. Penkert, for example, cannot help but feel disgust when Russian women touch her bedding: "Our Germany is a dream of pure beauty and warmth and love. How bestial those Asians can be! In Russia, more so than at other fronts, one knows what one is fighting for, what one dies for."[67]

Clearly, much as the figure of the angel in white propagates an image of nurses as ethereal, selfless creatures, Second World War nurses were political agents who were caught in the moral morass of the Nazi war of aggression and its accompanying program of mass extermination. In order to cope with their role in the war, many nurses edited out experiences that were too difficult to reconcile with their self-image as benevolent caregivers. In other words, they developed a form of perception that is best described as cropped vision. This cropped vision that brackets perceptions that touch on one's own complicity is evident not only in the narrative strategies employed in these texts, but also in the many photographs included in their memoirs.

Erika Summ's *Shepherd's Daughter* (*Schäfers Tochter*)

The memoir *Shepherd's Daughter* by army nurse Erika Summ was written many years after the war and after the death of her husband. The decision to tell her story was motivated by the prompting of friends and relatives who all showed an interest in her wartime experiences, and Summ reports that the process of writing helped her recover much that she had forgotten. Summ had not originally intended to publish her manuscript, but when her son told her about Birgit Panke-Kochinke's book project *Frontschwestern und Friedensengel*, she contacted Panke-Kochinke and, after some hesitation, made her manuscript available. Summ supplemented the text with images to make it "more lively,"[68] and also with some notes and poems that she had received from soldiers. It was published in 2006.

In her foreword, Panke-Kochinke praises Summ's story as an example of how "one can remain humane and alive in the face of death and destruction."[69] To Panke-Kochinke, Summ is an innocent victim who sacrificed her youth to a criminal regime while her story, whose can-do spirit leaves no room for the kind of self-pity that informs many similar memoirs, represents a "counterweight to violence and destruction."[70] Throughout, Summ comes across as a kind and competent professional. And yet, in spite of Panke-Kochinke's enthusiastic endorsement and even though Summ is not a Nazi, there would seem to be affinities to National Socialist ideology. These points of contact between the young Summ and National Socialist politics, however, are less disturbing than the complete absence of a retrospective discussion of the murderous crimes the Nazis inflicted on the Jews and the occupied nations. Although Summ's memoir was written many years after the war and published in 2006, that is, after decades of highly public debates on *Vergangenheitsbewältigung*, it shows little awareness of the horrendous nature of the Nazi war of extermination.

Erika Summ was born on August 8, 1921 in Stachenhausen in Baden-Württemberg into a hardworking but poor family. In spite of material hardship and the lack of modern amenities, Summ has fond memories of her childhood. Her parents were kind, and the children enjoyed a lot of freedom.[71] Summ emphasizes that her family lived in harmony with nature and with God. She characterizes her father as pious and loyal and points out that prayer was important in her family. Regardless of these positive notes, however, there is a dark undertone: both Summ's family and her local community are steeped in violence and death.[72] As Summ draws a vivid picture of her community, readers begin to understand why certain aspects of National Socialism might have appealed to Summ's family and neighbors. For example, even young children frequently had to run errands and walk home alone at night, and Summ remembers being afraid of the homeless and unemployed during such outings. In such a milieu, the National Socialist crackdown on "asocial" individuals promised relief. Later on, when Summ works in labor and delivery, she is tormented by the sight of newborn babies with physical malformations.[73] Here too, one cannot help but wonder how Summ responded to the Nazi euthanasia program. Faced with hardship, decease, and death, the National Socialist pseudo-solutions of contemporary problems may have been welcome.

In entitling her memoir *Shepherd's Daughter*, Summ turns her father's profession into a leitmotif. She further emphasizes the motif of the good shepherd by choosing a photo of her father for the cover of her book. In it, her father is a lone figure who walks calmly and upright next to a large flock of sheep along a country road whose embankment is framed by a line of trees. Some sheep graze next to the road; most follow her father. The horizon is framed by a faint trace of wooded mountains. This picture of a mountain idyll sets the tone for the story. Indeed, of the thirty-eight

pictures of Summ's prewar life, no fewer than eight centrally feature
activities related to shepherding. They evoke innocence, but also hark
back to the Christian concept of a sacrificial lamb, slaughtered to atone
for the sins of the world. The motif is clearly chosen because it creates a safe
distance between the narrator and the political arena, echoing Summ's
efforts to portray her family as cut off from village life and removed from
the political fray of the time.[74] And yet, the theme of shepherding also
unwittingly reintroduces the political realm and the theme of complicity.
With its emphasis on leaders and followers, on a "leader whom the other
sheep follow unconditionally,"[75] it mirrors the political reality of the time.
Summ sees herself as an innocent who is corralled into formation: she feels
pressured to join the BDM amidst a general atmosphere of support for the
regime, evident in the palpable increase in SA presence in the village and
also in her parents' decision to sport the "yes sticker" that attested to
support for the NSDAP.

In the beginning, Summ's family experiences National Socialism primarily as socialism: their farm is divided into seven smaller farms and
administered by a Nazi-appointed official. They now live for rent in their
own home and are paid a small hourly wage for their labor. In 1934, Summ
joined the *Landdienst* (service in agriculture). In 1937, she started working
as a maid and cook for a priest, whose responsibilities included Nazi-
mandated investigations into the Aryan descent of members of his con-
gregation. The idea to become a nurse arose when Summ met two Red
Cross nurses at a country dance. She was unhappy with her status as
a common maid and nursing offered a way out.

Summ received her training at the Katharinenhospital in Stuttgart
in October 1940, followed by an apprenticeship in a labor and delivery
station. A big part of her work consisted in cleaning so that she felt like
a "municipal cleaning woman" for the meager remuneration of 5
Reichsmark per month.[76] Her day was frequently disrupted by air raids,
and Summ remembers vividly how the nurses frantically carried baskets
with newborns down several flights of stairs to a shelter. When she passed
her exam in March 1942, she was transferred to a hospital in Marbach. Her
service for the army started abruptly when her hospital was taken over by
the military and repurposed for wounded soldiers from the eastern front.

In October 1942, at age twenty-one, Summ was sent to the eastern front,
an experience that she describes as depressing and frightening.[77] She traveled
solo on a train of soldiers first to Warsaw, then via Brest to Shitomir in the
Ukraine. Since nurses with professional training (*Vollschwestern*) enjoyed
officer rank, Summ was invited to sit in the officers' compartment. During

the trip, she was exposed, for the first time, to the sight of destroyed villages and to what the Nazis referred to as "partisan activity," including attempts to sabotage the train tracks. In such surroundings, fear of partisans became her constant companion.[78]

A siege mentality and constant fear also characterized the atmosphere at the field hospital where she was stationed. And yet, none of this is evident in the photos included in her memoir. Summ's narrative mentions moments of normality, such as snowball fights, card games, the planting of a vegetable and flower garden, and even sightseeing,[79] but she is clear that, for the most part, her days consisted of grueling labor. Summ worked for hours on end in rooms that reeked of blood and pus amidst the screaming of the wounded, and was exposed to horrifying burns and disfigurations.[80] Tellingly, frontline nurses often referred to the room for surgery as a "battlefield," thus poignantly expressing the similarity between the experiences of nurses and those of soldiers. In contrast to Summ's narrative, however, the photographic record from her time on the eastern front does not venture inside the hospital. The only image that features wounded soldiers, captioned "Transport of the Wounded," shows a seemingly able-bodied group smiling happily at the viewer from atop a horse-drawn cart.

While several of Summ's prewar images feature sheep, three of the eight photos from the eastern front show Summ as a gardener, planting vegetables and harvesting grapes. There is no sense of location – the gardens could be anywhere – and not a trace of the war. The first of these garden scenes is a long shot showing Summ and a doctor planting barren soil in spring while the second zooms in on Summ and two soldiers amidst lush vegetation in summer. Thus, while the narrative paints a clear picture of decline and escalating violence, the photos suggest progression and growth. Summ never comments on the glaring discrepancy between the content of her narrative and the motifs that dominate her photos.

As the front moves closer, the number of casualties increases drastically, Summ's hospital is bombed, and the chaos of the retreat begins. Army regulations differentiate between the main hospital (*Hauptlazarett*), which is closest to the front, the field hospital (*Feldlazarett*), which is further removed, and the war hospital (*Kriegslazarett*), where nurses such as Erika Summ work. Even under normal conditions, there is constant coming and going in these hospitals since all patients whose injuries are not life threatening are immediately moved. However, once the Germans started losing and embarked on a frantic retreat, the neat differentiation into different types of hospitals became meaningless as all hospitals were flooded with newly injured soldiers. Erika's unit was moved to Poland, then Hungary and the Czech Republic. Toward the end of the war, Summ and her fellow nurses cared not only for soldiers but also for refugees, including many children.[81] When Summ finally joined the trek herself, she was sick with measles, her train was attacked, and she and her fellow nurses continued on foot until they were taken prisoner by the Americans.[82]

Like many German Second World War memoirists, Summ is acutely aware of German suffering, including the plight of the refugees, and this focus is evident in the photographic record. While two of the eight photos from the eastern front showcase German fatalities, none is devoted to non-German victims. The first of these two photos of German victimization shows a military funeral, the second depicts the makeshift grave of a fellow nurse. The photo of the funeral centers on several coffins already lowered into the ground and a group of soldiers who stand at attention in a barren wasteland that contains no hint of human habitation or vegetation. Although both coffins and soldiers are organized in a line, the effort to create order is foiled by a coffin that sits askew on top of the others and an officer who turns his back to the grave. While nature itself seems to repel the human actors, the viewer's eyes are anchored by a large flag draped over one of the coffins. This flag, which prominently displays the swastika, functions as the only source of orientation in a starkly inhospitable environment.

Unlike the military funeral, which gives the impression of a formal and semi-dignified affair, the photo of the grave of nurse Martha Weller shows but few signs of planning. It appears to be situated at the side of a road and is dwarfed by a large, nondescript truck in the background. Perhaps unwittingly, this image speaks to the situation of women near the front lines. While the soldiers are embedded in a group and their actions governed by ritual, the nurse's grave is framed as a solitary and marginal site. And yet, it too is linked to the National Socialist army through the iconography of the Iron Cross, which is plainly visible on the improvised crucifix that marks the site of the grave. The Iron Cross, which was typically decorated with the swastika at the center of the cross, offers the only familiar frame of reference and lends stability and meaning in an otherwise disorienting environment.

While Summ highlights German victimization, she does not acknowledge crimes committed by Germans nor does she reflect on her own role in the war. Consequently, her narrative is truncated and even incoherent. Summ reports being afraid of the Czechs but provides no context that could explain why the Czechs might want to hurt the Germans. Similarly, she claims that many American soldiers took revenge because they were the children of emigrated Jews,[83] but this desire to take revenge also remains unmotivated since the Holocaust does not feature in her narrative, except for passing references to the deportation of Jews near Pecs and to a nearby ghetto, which she mentions in order to explain why the nurses' toothbrushes were stolen.[84] In comparison, readers learn much about a strip search for SS tattoos to which American soldiers submitted German nurses and soldiers alike and that Summ experienced as particularly humiliating. Summ also shares that she felt much sympathy for people who had to vacate their houses for American troops and for fellow nurses who lost their employment because of their NSDAP membership, but does not even mention the millions who died at German hands. And since there is no mention of genocide, there can be no discussion of complicity either.

Although Summ's memoir was written many years after the war had ended, it contains next to no criticism of the Nazis. Summ comments on the horror of the war and remembers particularly gruesome sights, such as a dead man hanging from a balcony or public executions in Shitomir.[85] Although the experience was clearly traumatizing, she provides no context and no information about the victims. Summ wonders where people live in this Eastern landscape of ruins and remarks on the absence of children, but there is no thought about who caused the war and to what end. Furthermore, her description of life in an occupied territory is similarly devoid of context. Summ does not criticize or even acknowledge the imperialist agenda that informed the Nazi pursuit of *Lebensraum*. Instead, she shows appreciation for the German colonization of the East, particularly for the *Volksdeutsche* who had "helped to transform the villages into pretty places."[86] When she does take note of the existentially precarious situation of the Ukrainian women, she attributes their poverty to the Bolsheviks who deported their husbands. In general, Summ likes to think of the relationship to the occupied population as a form of commerce between equals,[87] although she admits that theft is a problem. The encounters that stand out in her memory are characterized by kindness and care.[88] And yet, it is plain that, in spite of such occasional friendliness, the nurses' relationship to the local population is marked by suspicion and mistrust. Summ meets Ukrainian women with caution since there is always a possibility that they might work with partisan groups and spy on the Germans. She remembers Ukrainians who were arrested for partisan activities and a Polish partisan who shot at a male nurse and was shot in turn. To Summ, all these events are part of the general moral murkiness of war: "In this war there were so many uncertainties on both sides."[89] There is no acknowledgment of cause and effect, no narrative of guilt and responsibility, and no reflection on her own role. Rather, war is portrayed as an all-encompassing devastation that inflicts damage on all parties.[90]

In spite of witnessing many events that can only be described as horrifying, Summ, who turned twenty-four in 1945, appears to have emerged if not unscathed then at least reasonably intact from a series of experiences that would have devastated a less resilient person: the physical exhaustion that results from prolonged periods of overwork and sleep deprivation, the constant exposure to air raids and to the sight of traumatic injuries, along with Summ's own illnesses, including measles, appendicitis, and a bad case of influenza. And yet, when Summ claims "I was able to save my cheerful temperament over the course of the war,"[91] one cannot help but wonder if her resilience is linked to her innate optimism or to her refusal to engage with the moral dimension of the Nazi war of extermination.

Inge Ochsenknecht: *Als ob der Schnee alles zudeckte: Eine Krankenschwester erinnert sich an ihren Kriegseinsatz an der Ostfront*

Inge Ochsenknecht's memoir *As if the Snow Covered Everything: A Nurse Remembers Her Deployment on the Eastern Front* was recorded by Fabienne Pakleppa and published in 2004 by Ullstein with a foreword by Dr. Martha Schad. Like Summ, Ochsenknecht, the mother of German actor Uwe Ochsenknecht, claims to have been motivated to tell her story by the promptings of friends and relatives, in particular her grandchildren. In addition, she reports that the renewed interest in the war and the Third Reich in the German media, particularly television, brought back memories.[92] Her prologue, however, offers another story of origin that frames Ochsenknecht's experience as deeply traumatizing. Ochsenknecht reports that in 1965 she considered contributing to the meager family income by resuming her former work as a nurse. But on the morning of her job interview, she felt sick and during the trolley ride to the interview she experienced flashbacks that transported her back in time to the war and the many train rides to the front. In the hospital elevator she was haunted by visions of the soldiers she treated. Simply by stepping into a hospital, Ochsenknecht had opened the floodgates to the memories she had worked so hard to forget. The experience was so terrifying that she decided to find another form of employment. As she explains, she had seen enough injuries and deaths to last her a lifetime. But while she could not go back to nursing, Ochsenknecht realized that the past would not be shut out and that she would have to tell her story.

Although both women were German nurses on the eastern front, Ochsenknecht's memoir is different from Summ's both stylistically and politically. While Summ prefers matter-of-fact statements, Ochsenknecht offers descriptive details and enlivens her narrative with dialogue. Such heightened realism is likely due to the fact that, unlike Summ, Ochsenknecht consulted the diary that she kept during the war and even places excerpts from it at the beginning of each chapter. Through this technique, she is able to jump back and forth in time, thus creating a dialogue between her present and past selves that explores her own ideological conformity. For example, her diary entry on her first visit to Krakow reads: "It is a beautiful city, but unfortunately it suffered much under Polish rule."[93] In contrast, the older Ochsenknecht notices the political provenance of this statement and comments: "When I read these sentences, I realize how Nazi propaganda had blinded me. This is exactly what we were told all the time – that the Poles have only themselves to blame for their misery. But it was the Germans who had started the war and had starved the population."[94] As these passages show, the juxtaposition of past and present holds the potential for a radical reevaluation of Ochsenknecht's experience during the war.[95] And yet, although the memoir makes an effort to work through the past, it does not fully realize this ambition. Throughout, important insights stand side by side with regurgitated Nazi platitudes, and it is not always clear if Ochsenknecht seeks to convey her former state of mind or if the author is still beholden to the worldview of her younger self. Moreover, especially toward the end of the book when we most expect a summary rejection of National Socialist politics, the narrative fizzles out into a series of anecdotes and rare moments of reflection are dwarfed by long passages that recount pranks and "fun" adventures.

Ochsenknecht's life before the war resembles that of Summ to some extent. Like Summ's family, Ochsenknecht's mother and father were in dire financial straits in the 1920s and 1930s. They had to sell their house and young Inge was not allowed to go to the Lyzeum because the family could not afford it. Like Summ, Ochsenknecht joined the BDM. She applied for the Labor Service (*Arbeitsdienst*), but was rejected for health reasons and started a year of domestic service (*hauswirtschaftliches Volljahr*) in her hometown of Arnstadt instead. When the war began, she was excited.[96] Like many others, she was convinced that the war would be over in a couple of weeks, and she welcomed the opportunity to serve her country:

"The feeling of 'being needed' gave my life meaning."[97] Even later when she was exposed to numerous hardships on the eastern front, she reported feeling happy because she was part of something bigger than herself – an opportunity that was only rarely afforded to women in her time.[98]

The excitement of the early years of the war is clearly visible in the photographs included in the memoir. The first image that readers behold, and the only one of the thirty-four photos in the book that occupies an entire page, features a young, smiling Ochsenknecht in a nurse's uniform, a blinding vision in white, standing in front of a large gate. The caption informs us that this is the gate of the hospital in Arnheim, but nothing in the picture indicates a specific location or institutional affiliation. Like many of the pictures that follow, this photo foregrounds a human figure while occluding the viewer's sense of location. Ochsenknecht's photos tend to be closely cropped around the figures they depict and frequently offer only the most general sense of the surroundings. There are no pictures of recognizable tourist attractions or characteristic features of a city or land-scape. Rather, the viewer's vision is limited to the small cadre of characters who form Ochsenknecht's social circle.

This focus on colleagues and friends is mirrored in Ochsenknecht's narrative. Ochsenknecht draws a picture of herself as a young girl who shows great interest in boys but none whatsoever in politics. For example, she remembers the first time she attended an event by the NSDAP, but cannot recall any of the speeches. Rather, what stuck in her mind is the company of her blond cousin whom she adored. The same perspective characterizes her time on the eastern front, where German women were a rare sight and were consequently showered with attention.[99] To Ochsenknecht, the war is an adventure that allows her to explore romantic relationships, escape the strictures of the family home and experience a previously unknown freedom.

Ochsenknecht started caring for wounded soldiers in April 1940 when her former school was turned into a reserve hospital (*Reservelazarett*). She found her work fulfilling and volunteered to be moved closer to the front lines.[100] In preparation for the attack on Russia, her unit was stationed in Tschenstochau near the Russian border. Here, Ochsenknecht learned quickly that the experience of the nurse, much like that of the soldier, is marked by extremes. Several weeks of bored inaction ended abruptly when the first transports of wounded soldiers arrived, and Ochsenknecht got a taste of the severity of wounds incurred in battle. From now on, weeks of backbreaking labor with nineteen-hour shifts alternated with periods of relaxation and fun.[101] Although the injuries she saw were far worse than expected, Ochsenknecht, like many a male soldier, became addicted to the adrenaline rush of war and had difficulties adjusting to civilian life after the end of the war.[102]

Although the photos that correspond to this period of Ochsenknecht's life do not convey the horror of the time, they are more open to the reality of the war than the images in Summ's memoir. Unlike Summ, Ochsenknecht includes several images of wounded soldiers, one of whom appears to be in critical condition, and two photos that situate their subjects geographically. Similarly, while there are no photos of Russian towns or civilians, there is one long shot of Russian refugees with the rather vague caption "Summer 1942: Russian Refugees." In contrast, there are numerous pictures that show Ochsenknecht and her fellow nurses out for walks, frolicking in the snow (one chapter is entitled "Downtime in the Snow Paradise"),[103] and smiling into the camera while riding astride on the turret of a tank or sticking their heads out of the hatch after soldiers took them for a ride.

Interestingly, among these images of fun in snow and sun are two whose cropped view of reality opens up as we read Ochsenknecht's narrative. Both photos show Ochsenknecht and her fellow nurses in bikinis during a trip to the sea. In one picture, Ochsenknecht and a female friend face the camera as they let the surf wash over their feet. In the other, Ochsenknecht and two men sit on beach towels, getting a tan. Since both images are medium close-ups of the figures, they do not convey a sense of the surroundings. Looked at in isolation, they, like many of the other images, suggest carefree fun and adventure. Yet, when the events they depict are re-embedded in the narrative, it becomes clear that such fun required a great deal of repression and blindness. In the verbal description of this mini vacation, Ochsenknecht informs us that she was warned not to swim too far since there were bodies floating in the water.[104] As it turns out, this beach had recently seen military action and had been cleared of corpses, but not of the debris of war or of the dead horses killed in the battle. (Later on, Ochsenknecht swims in the Don but stops abruptly when she realizes that the pile of Russian uniforms on the bank of the river is the remnant of a mass execution.) Clearly, "fun" activities on the eastern front require a psychic splitting that makes it possible for Ochsenknecht to remain blind to much of what is going on around her, and the photos replicate this repression. Ochsenknecht lived in a cropped reality, and her postwar breakdown suggests that a great effort was involved in keeping the edges of this frame from fraying. Taking in the whole picture, however, would have been a fraught endeavor since it necessarily involved a reflection of one's own role in the war. On the eastern front, ignorance was not bliss, but it did help to prevent or, at the very least, postpone psychic breakdown.

As the war progressed, Ochsenknecht's situation and state of mind became increasingly schizophrenic. As nurses, Ochsenknecht and her colleagues were in an excellent position to see through the regime's propaganda. After all, they had firsthand experiences of the severity and number of injuries and casualties, which so clearly disproved the lies propagated on the radio. But Ochsenknecht did not criticize the Nazi regime, choosing instead to continue to believe in the *Endsieg* and to identify with the soldiers she cared for.[105] Conversely, while Ochsenknecht admired the heroism of her fellow Germans, those who were oppressed and murdered by the Nazis disappear from view in spite of Ochsenknecht's explicit acknowledgment that the relation between the German occupiers and the occupied nation was inherently problematic. Ochsenknecht is aware that the Poles do not like the Germans and that her own relationship with the Russian prisoner who is assigned to be her assistant cannot develop into a friendship because it unfolds within the context of conquest.[106] She also witnessed how German soldiers "requisitioned" food at gunpoint even though the Russians were starving. At the same time, however, the myth of the Germans as liberators continues to frame her experience of the eastern front.[107]

Even more so than her relationship with the Russians, Ochsenknecht's attitude toward the Jews is characterized by a blindness that is baffling. Thus, she recounts that to her the Star of David was simply another kind of uniform. Similarly, she claims that the local ghetto was created to prevent the spread of typhus. The most disturbing event, however, is her visit to the Krakow ghetto, which is not featured in any of her photographs. Most likely, the lack of photos in this context is due to official regulations: although the Nazis eagerly documented the atrocities they committed, they were savvy enough to forbid anybody else from taking photos that might serve as evidence of genocide. Even so, however, Nazi policies regarding photos do not account for the cropped vision of Ochsenknecht's textual account. Ochsenknecht reports that, upon arrival at the ghetto, she and her friend begin to flirt with the guards, who refuse to let them enter. Oblivious to the suffering behind the gates, nurses and guards discuss an exchange of kisses as entrance fee to the ghetto. When the nurses finally gain admission, they are unable to integrate what they see into their conceptual framework. Ochsenknecht feels "terribly ill at ease" and also greatly pities the inhabitants of the ghetto, but she cannot verbalize what is wrong here: "Nobody seemed sick or particularly thin, but the faces were somber and sad."[108]

Ochsenknecht's visit to the ghetto, more than any other aspect of the memoir, exemplifies drastically how average Germans knew but did not want to know because such knowledge would have cast a light on their own complicity with Nazi politics and thus would have made conformity and inaction inherently problematic.[109] Even though Ochsenknecht witnessed *Reichskristallnacht*, visited the Krakow ghetto, and served on the eastern front for extended periods of time, she claims to have been completely unaware of the fate of the Jews. But, to her credit, the older Ochsenknecht does wonder about this failure to notice what was going on around her during the war: "Were we blind then, did we not understand which crimes Germans committed on the Eastern front right in front of our eyes? Sometimes people ask me that, and in writing this book I myself ask these questions."[110] The impression one is left with is that of a very young woman – Ochsenknecht was nineteen when the war started – who, overwhelmed with the trauma of the war and the genocidal horror of her time, dealt with it by becoming blind and deaf to everything that was bound to upset her equilibrium. Tellingly, Ochsenknecht's motto is "Do not think, live."[111]

It would seem that both Summ and Ochsenknecht had learned to turn a blind eye to any and all experiences that were likely to disturb their emotional and cognitive equilibrium. In other words, they habituated themselves to a form of cropped vision that highlighted German victimization but failed to take account of suffering that Germans inflicted. In contrast, inmate nurses in Nazi concentration camps bore the full brunt of Nazi atrocities. Drawing on memoirs by inmate nurses and physicians, including Olga Lengyel's *Five Chimneys: A Woman Survivor's True Story of Auschwitz* (1946) and Lucie Adelsberger's *Auschwitz: A Doctor's Story* (1945), the following section deals with the paradox of care and the trauma of enforced complicity in the concentration camps. It then offers a reading of the memoir *Als Krankenschwester im KZ Theresienstadt: Erinnerungen einer Ulmer Jüdin* by German Jewish nurse Resi Weglein. I have chosen to include Weglein's text because it deals with the dilemma of enforced complicity in an intriguing way: faced with the impossibility of offering medical relief for the immense suffering around her, Weglein trained herself to refocus her gaze and ultimately redefined the meaning of care.

Nursing in Nazi Concentration Camps

It is painfully obvious that the care offered in Nazi concentration camp infirmaries was fundamentally different from that provided by army nurses such as Ochsenknecht and Summ. While a sick German soldier can expect the best care available, a sick Jewish inmate is a target for extermination. While frontline ambulances take the wounded to hospitals, Auschwitz ambulances were used to cart inmates to the crematoria. Where army nurses dealt primarily with battle wounds, inmate nurses sought to ameliorate the short- and long-term effects of intentionally inflicted malnutrition, neglect, and SS cruelty, including brutal beatings and dog bites. Where army nurses faced occasional shortages of equipment and medication, concentration camp nurses provided care without access to the most basic supplies, including disinfectants, bedpans, and even hot water.[112] Typically, several patients had to share one mattress or lie on the cold stone floor,[113] and surgeries were performed without anesthetics. Amidst all this horror, however, the experience that stands out as particularly traumatic in many memoirs is that of forcefully inflicted complicity: all too often, medical personnel faced impossible choices, such as whether to kill a newborn in order to save the mother, or let the baby live and thus condemn both child and mother to the gas chamber, or whether to release a critically ill patient or keep her in the hospital, which would brand her as too sick to work and would thus make her a target for extermination. As non-Jewish Auschwitz camp physician Ella Lingens Reiner writes, "in the case of those enfeebled women, a release was sometimes nothing short of murder." She comments on this paradox: "In our situation normal principles of human and professional ethics broke down."[114] At times the work of a nurse even resembled that of a Kapo. For example, massage therapist and Auschwitz survivor Simha Naor reports that, upon her arrival in Bergen-Belsen, she was given a stick and told to beat those who refused to get up, that is, those who were too sick to stand or walk. When she explained that she was a nurse, she was told: "That's why, what kind of nurse are you if you don't want to hit them?"[115] While army nurses were able to turn a blind eye to their own complicity, inmate nurses had to confront their enforced cooperation head-on. And even though the alternative they faced was death or compliance, many memoirs are plagued by a lingering sense of guilt.

As this brief survey shows, the very existence of medical care in the camps constitutes a paradox.[116] Why offer care to those whom you intend to kill? Concentration camp nurses were painfully aware that much of their work merely postponed the inevitable. Thus, after taking care of sick children, Ellen Loeb, a nurse in the Westerbork transit camp, writes, "it was thankful and wonderful work, but I knew that in the end they would be taken to Auschwitz."[117] And Olga Lengyel, who worked in the infirmary in Auschwitz-Birkenau, comments: "The doctors saved many of the inmates through their surgery, and the Germans sent the patients straight to the gas chamber."[118] Thus, attempts to counteract the goals of the Nazis were often accompanied by a sense of absurdity. In the camp, sickness was a black mark that predestined an inmate for extermination. As Magda Herzberger, an Auschwitz survivor, writes, "becoming ill in Auschwitz was like a death sentence."[119] Consequently, many tried to hide an illness at all cost. However, the appearance of health offered no protection either since anyone could be selected for extermination at any time, and the criteria for selection changed constantly: "For a while one category of sick would automatically be selected. Then one day it would all change, and those who had the same affliction, say diphtheria, would be put under treatment in an isolated room under the care of deportee doctors."[120] Finally, camp infirmaries were not only way stations to the gas chamber but killing sites themselves where patients succumbed to injuries inflicted during medical experiments or received lethal injections, including shots of phenol directly into the heart.

Being a nurse in a concentration camp was both a privilege and a crushing burden. The living conditions of nurses and physicians were often somewhat better than those of other inmates. For example, nurses sometimes had a bed of their own, access to washing facilities, and somewhat improved nutrition.[121] Naor reports that, as a nurse, she did not have to participate in the ordeal of the daily roll call.[122] This was no small advantage since the roll call, which Lucie Adelsberger, an inmate doctor in Auschwitz, calls "the horror of the camp,"[123] required that prisoners stand still for hours in sweltering heat, pouring rain, or freezing cold. Similarly, in Theresienstadt, long-serving nurses were protected from deportation to Auschwitz.[124] Typically, however, such benefits were offset by the great danger of being exposed to numerous contagious illnesses, by an unsustainable workload as a small number of nurses treated thousands of patients, and by the knowledge that, no matter what they did, their actions might ultimately serve the ends of the Nazi regime. Olga Lengyel's description of her experience in Auschwitz-Birkenau summarizes the catastrophic conditions of care in a camp: "The internees in our camp totaled from thirty to forty thousand. And the entire personnel in our infirmary consisted of five women . . . we became so fatigued that we staggered about as though we were drunk. However, we had an infirmary; and we were doing good, useful work."[125] In such dire circumstances and in the absence of medication, the best a doctor could do might be to offer the illusion of care. Thus, Ruth Reiser, who worked in the Theresienstadt hospital, speaks of a physician who, in the absence of proper medication, started to administer drops of water because she realized that her patients desperately needed to believe that they were being cared for.[126]

While extermination camps such as Auschwitz made a mockery of the very idea of care – tellingly, the Nazis used the German words for care (*betreuen* and *behandlen*) as euphemisms for murder – the so-called model camp Theresienstadt was invested in projecting the illusion of tending to the sick. Originally a garrison town founded by Joseph II in the second half of the eighteenth century, Theresienstadt, located 60 km northwest of Prague, was turned into a concentration camp in November 1941. To this day, Theresienstadt is often characterized as a relatively "tolerable" camp. Ernst Nolte, for example, calls it a camp where "a number of old and privileged Jews led an isolated but tolerable life."[127] The statistics, however, belie this assumption. Of the 141,000 Jews who were deported to Theresienstadt, 20,000 survived.[128] For most inmates, Theresienstadt was not the final destination but a stop on the way to extermination camps such as Auschwitz-Birkenau. In other words, Theresienstadt was a transit camp, and the responsibility for selecting who had to go and who got to stay fell to the council of Jewish elders who were coopted into the Nazi killing machine.[129]

The Nazis advertised Theresienstadt as a model camp, an *Altersghetto* for Jews of sixty-five years and older and for Jewish veterans of the First World War. Theresienstadt was also the infamous site of the Nazi propaganda movie *The Führer Gives a City to the Jews* (*Der Führer schenkt den Juden eine Stadt*). Because of its use as a propaganda tool, living in Theresienstadt meant living with a double reality: the pretense of a functional community with self-government was designed to obscure the horrendous suffering and planned starvation of thousands of Jewish men and women. Theresienstadt was a veritable Potemkin village. There were benches on which Jews were not allowed to sit, playgrounds where children were not allowed to play, bank-issued money that wasn't worth anything, and shops where inmates could buy items that the Nazis had stolen from their suitcases upon arrival. The particular perfidy of the Nazis consisted in creating a presentable façade for visitors. When inspectors came to the camp, the children were allowed to use the playground and the elderly were allowed to sit on the benches – for the duration of the visit. All the while and as the camp was being beautified for visitors, the transports to Auschwitz continued.[130] There was, however, one aspect that was not a Nazi-engineered deception. Theresienstadt was the site of a vibrant cultural life organized by the inmates that included scientific and literary presentations, book clubs, and performances of plays and operas.[131]

In his magisterial work on Theresienstadt, H. G. Adler, who spent thirty-two months in Hitler's model camp, notes that the camp's "forced community was a sick community."[132] Theresienstadt had a designated hospital, the Hohenelber Kaserne, and every barrack had sickrooms, but the conditions of care were appalling. In the beginning, there were no mattresses or even sacks of straw. Because there was no water in the sick station, it had to be carried in in buckets. In the absence of proper sanitary facilities, buckets also served as toilets. Although many patients were afflicted with diarrhea, the linen could only be changed every two to four months because the laundry facilities could not handle the volume.[133] There were no towels, only one piece of soap every six or seven weeks, one thermometer for fifty-eight patients, and a two-month wait to take a bath.[134] Since there were no disinfectants, contaminated clothes had to be burned. In addition to fighting a multitude of chronic diseases and epidemics, including tuberculosis, scarlet fever, enteritis, and typhus, nurses also had to combat hordes of rats and mice. And there was a chronic shortage of personnel: "In the hospitals patients fell out of their beds and remained lying on the floor for the entire night because there were not enough nurses."[135]

The memoir of German Jewish nurse Resi Weglein (1894–1977) offers a wealth of information about the conditions of care in Theresienstadt. During the first years of the Third Reich, Weglein had felt safe from deportation because she was married to a highly decorated First World War veteran. However, the protection extended to Jewish army veterans was short-lived. On August 20, 1942, the Wegleins were arrested in their apartment and deported to Theresienstadt. Of the 1,076 people who were sent to Theresienstadt with the Wegleins, fourteen survived. Weglein's status as an army veteran shielded the couple from deportation to Auschwitz, but it did not include special treatment in Theresienstadt, where Weglein spent the following three years.

Weglein began to write her memoir on July 14, 1945, barely two months after the liberation of the camp on May 9, 1945, but her report remained unpublished until 1988. The editors, Silvester Lechner and Alfred Moos, preface the text with an introduction stating that they corrected typos and added titles, but otherwise left the manuscript unchanged. Weglein hoped to find solace and healing in the process of writing,[136] but she also had an altruistic motive. Weglein wanted to provide information for the relatives of people who had died in the camp, hoping that "perhaps one or the other of my fellow sufferers all over the world might find the name of one of his relatives about whom he was worried."[137] Her text is both deeply spiritual and infused with an acute sense of irony. And indeed, in light of the sustained lie inherent in the concept of the model camp, what Adler calls the "paradoxical contradiction between impotence and the semblance of freedom,"[138] irony would seem to be a highly appropriate tool. Thus, Weglein speaks of "the sumptuous meal" that she enjoyed and refers to the callous remark of an SS officer, "well, another Jew kicks the bucket," as "the lovely address of the gentlemen."[139]

Weglein comes across as a nurse who thinks of her chosen profession as a calling. She begins to take care of her fellow inmates on the train to the camp, continues after the liberation of Theresienstadt, and never shies away from treating highly contagious patients. Weglein's memoir offers a wealth of detailed information about the conditions of care in a camp. At the same time, however, she repeatedly refuses to dwell on the medical aspect of her work, begging that the reader may spare her the ordeal of describing specific cases.[140] Instead, Weglein seeks to redefine the meaning of care itself. In the absence of proper equipment, the notion of care shifts from providing medical assistance to offering emotional comfort. It would appear that Weglein was motivated by the conviction that such comfort cannot be coopted for the Nazi machinery of death. And Weglein is not the only inmate nurse who redefines the concept of care. Hanna Muller Bruml, another inmate nurse in Theresienstadt, explains, "we didn't have any disinfectants. All we had was us, kindness." Similarly, Lucie Adelsberger writes that "the only thing the doctors could do for their patients . . . was to comfort and encourage them."[141] While medical care remained imbricated in the camp system, kindness and interpersonal relations offered a way out of the system of enforced complicity.

Throughout, Weglein highlights the spiritual aspect of her work. Weglein sees nursing in the camp as a challenge that, if met, offers the hope of self-improvement. She interprets her personal suffering as an experience that allows her to develop empathy for the sick and to become a true *Krankenschwester*, that is a sister to the sick:

> During those days I have doubted divine justice and was desperate in the truest sense of the word. . . . Very soon I came to realize that I have to go through all these trials to be free in my inner self. I had to bear all need, all misery, all illnesses myself in order to be able to be for others what I imagined to be the meaning of "sister."[142]

Because Weglein redefines care as a spiritual and emotional task, she is able to extend it to the dead. Weglein's memoir is filled with long lists of the names of men, women, and children who died in Theresienstadt.[143]

Through these lists, Weglein succeeds in offering a modicum of care to those whom she could not help in life. In Weglein's memoir, commemoration emerges as the final and only possible service to the dead and as a clear and direct rejection of complicity.

Conclusion

It should be clear by now that the motivations and daily routines of army nurses bear little resemblance to those implied in the idealized image of the "angel in white." Indeed, the social and political conditions of nursing in the Second World War are designed to prevent the kind of care associated with this glorification of female caregiving. While many fictional representations of the Second World War portray frontline nursing, and army medicine in general, as a world apart from politics, untainted by the demands of a murderous regime, the memoirs of German army nurses such as Summ and Ochsenknecht show that, willingly or unconsciously, these women were caught in the vortex of Nazi politics and frequently complicit with it. Many joined a highly politicized profession out of a desire to escape the authority of their families and the social strictures of their upbringing. They take pleasure in the authority (*regieren*) and status of being a nurse. However, if they were to enjoy the perks of their profession, army nurses needed to develop a form of cropped vision that allowed them to remain blind to the atrocities committed by the regime they served and to their own complicity in it. At the very least, they needed to acquiesce in the Nazi vision of the medical professions that reserved care for those deemed racially fit while patients outside of the Aryan community were marked for extermination. They entered an implicit compact based on the refusal to perceive or speak about German crimes.

Unlike army nurses who could look the other way if they chose to, inmate nurses were forced to confront not only the full extent of the Nazi genocide but also their enforced cooperation in the camp system. In order to cope, they too needed to refocus their gaze. In the absence of viable choices, they redefined caregiving as providing solace and emotional comfort. Instead of medical assistance, they offered consolation, spiritual support, and a commitment to commemorate after death those whom they could not help in life.

Notes

1. During the World Wars, the image of the woman in white as both comrade and helper replaced the turn-of-the-century image of nurses as drunkards and prostitutes (Grundhewer, "Von der freiwilligen Kriegskrankenpflege bis zur Einbindung des Roten Kreuzes in das Heeressanitätswesen," 138).
2. "Ein Wunder, das einzige jener Zeit, das sich nicht in Ernüchterung auflöst . . . Sie wirkten durch ihr Da-Sein, Angehörige des Geschlechtes, das Widerspruch gegen die Vernichtung verkörpert" (Panke-Kochinke and Schaidhammer-Placke, *Frontschwestern und Friedensengel*, 167).
3. Foucault, *The Birth of the Clinic*, 38.
4. Proctor, *Racial Hygiene*, 7 and 45. See also "In 1929, at the Nuremberg Nazi Party Congress, a group of German physicians (forty-two men and two women) formed the National Socialist Physicians' League (*Nationalsozialistischer Deutscher Ärztebund* – NSDÄB) . . . Doctors in fact joined the Nazi party earlier and in greater numbers than any other professional group" (Proctor, *Racial Hygiene*, 65). Lifton points out that "doctors had one of the highest ratios of Party members of any profession" (Lifton, *The Nazi Doctors*, 34).
5. See Bamm, *Die unsichtbare Flagge*, 12.
6. "Flagge der Humanitas" (Bamm, *Die unsichtbare Flagge*, 19). For references to massacres, see 152 and 74; for the impact of ideology, see "Der Traum von der Weltherrschaft fing an, auch auf besonnenere Gemüter seine faszinierende Wirkung auszuüben" ("The dream of world domination began to fascinate even level-headed minds") (154). Bamm's statements are often contradictory. In the same breath, he speaks of the general outrage about the "massacres," but then continues that this outrage was not very pronounced since anti-Semitism in the army was too strong: "Zweifellos war die Empörung über die Massaker in der Armee allgemein. . . . Aber es war keine lodernde Empörung der Humanitas. Das Gift des Antisemitismus hatte sich schon zu tief eingefressen" ("Without a doubt, the outrage about the massacres in the army was strong. . . . But it was not the flaming outrage of humanitas. The poison of anti-Semitism had already grown deep roots") (Bamm, *Die unsichtbare Flagge*, 75); similarly, he acknowledges the problematic role of medicine, "Für die erfolgreiche Anwendung der Wissenschaft in der Vernichtung sowohl wie in der Errettung von Leben wurden die gleichen Orden verliehen" ("the same medals were awarded for the successful application of science for the extermination and the saving of lives") (12), but does not qualify his statements about the "flag of humanity."
7. "Der deutsche Arzt habe eine Operation gewagt, die es in der russischen Medizingeschichte noch nicht gegeben habe" (Konsalik, *Der Arzt von Stalingrad*, 252); "Mit den primitivsten Mitteln hat er das Leben von Tausenden gerettet" (Konsalik, *Der Arzt von Stalingrad*, 152).
8. "Wir hätten Tausende nach Abschluß der Forschung retten können" (Konsalik, *Der Arzt von Stalingrad*, 227).

9. "Die Anderen" (Bamm, *Die unsichtbare Flagge*, 58); "der primitive Mann" (Bamm, *Die unsichtbare Flagge*, 124).

10. "Raunen des Blutes" and "Rätsel der stummen Kreatur" (Cabanis, *Das Licht in den Händen*, 8); "wie erfüllt von Wesenheiten" (Cabanis, *Das Licht in den Händen*, 22).

11. See Cabanis, *Das Licht in den Händen*, 120.

12. "Krampf der Vereinzelung" (Cabanis, *Das Licht in den Händen*, 120). See also 121.

13. "Es knisterte schon im Gebälk" (Cabanis, *Das Licht in den Händen*, 215).

14. "Die dämonische Gewalt der ganzen Welt" (Cabanis, *Das Licht in den Händen*, 11) and "Höherentfaltung" (81).

15. See Cabanis, *Das Licht in den Händen*, 81.

16. "Erzwingen läßt sich nichts in der Natur" ("Nothing can be forced in nature") (Cabanis, *Das Licht in den Händen*, 78); "es nichts Zufälliges gibt in ihrem Leben" ("There is nothing coincidental in life") (239).

17. "Kleine, holzgeschnitzte Heilige" (Cabanis, *Das Licht in den Händen*, 18); see also 32.

18. "Halbgott" (Cabanis, *Das Licht in den Händen*, 104), who is "groß, jung, strahlend" ("tall, young, radiant") (10).

19. "Am Krankenbett finde ich meine Erfüllung" (Cabanis, *Das Licht in den Händen*, 59).

20. "Sie hatte keine Gedanken, keine Wünsche mehr für sich selbst, sie verströmte sich in der Pflege" (Cabanis, *Das Licht in den Händen*, 176).

21. "[Bettina's] Gabe zu pflegen war angeboren, war naturhaft" (Cabanis, *Das Licht in den Händen*, 117).

22. See Cabanis, *Das Licht in den Händen*, 211.

23. "Sie liebte ihre Heimat, ihre Sprache, doch auch über einen Neger hätte sie sich helfend, pflegend gebeugt ... die Sprache des Herzens, stand sie nicht über denen der Nationen, unerlernbar, eingeboren" (Cabanis, *Das Licht in den Händen*, 212).

24. "Ganz zu schweigen von dem, was man sonst noch sieht, sehen muß, denn lieber hätte man weggeblickt" (Cabanis, *Das Licht in den Händen*, 229).

25. "Das Auge des Mars" (Cabanis, *Das Licht in den Händen*, 227); "Raubtiere" (235); "metallenes Geschwader" (236).

26. "Ganze Züge von Gefangenen, von Juden auch, in deren dunklen Augen das Leid der Vergangenheit aufwacht in der Qual der Gegenwart" (Cabanis, *Das Licht in den Händen*, 253).

27. "Bild eines so überwältigenden Leides" (Cabanis, *Das Licht in den Händen*, 266).

28. "Viele Luftangriffe habe ich auf euer Land ausüben müssen, viele schreckliche Angriffe" (Cabanis, *Das Licht in den Händen*, 285).

29. "Vergehen kann nichts, es sei denn, dass es sich wandele" (Cabanis, *Das Licht in den Händen*, 286); "Schmerz ist Brücke, Lehrmeister und Läuterer" (238) see also 88. Although the text concedes that, at times, changes brought about by suffering do not outlast the pain (112), it also insists that suffering raises our consciousness and awakens empathy for others (175).

30. "[Er ist] der fraulichste aller Berufe. Alles, was man von einer Schwester erwartet: Hilfsbereitschaft, Güte, Mütterlichkeit und wahres Frauentum sind die Wesenszüge einer echten Frau an sich. Und so gibt es für die Frau kaum einen würdigeren Beruf neben dem der Mutter als den Schwesternberuf" (Katscher, *Krankenpflege und Drittes Reich*, 139).

31. "The first widespread implementation of wage contracts in nursing (1919–1921), the legal restriction of work time to a ten-hour-day, sixty-hour week (1924), the introduction of accident insurance (1928) and social security, and a gradual expansion of training programs" (McFarland-Icke, *Nurses in Nazi Germany*, 25), see also Panke-Kochinke and Schaidhammer-Placke, *Frontschwestern und Friedensengel*, 18 and Grundhewer, "Von der freiwilligen Kriegskrankenpflege bis zur Einbindung des Roten Kreuzes in das Heeressanitätswesen," 140.

32. McFarland-Icke, *Nurses in Nazi Germany*, 51.

33. McFarland-Icke, *Nurses in Nazi Germany*, 26; see also Gaida, *Zwischen Pflegen und Töten*, 11.

34. McFarland-Icke, *Nurses in Nazi Germany*, 12.

35. Nightingale, *Notes on Nursing*, 30.

36. Even in the First World War, more than 10,000 nurses had served in European armies (Burke Fessler, *No Time for Fear*, 4–5).

37. See McFarland-Icke, *Nurses in Nazi Germany*, 20.

38. See Ebert, "Mein Schmuck ist im Krieg die Tracht und mein Leben der Dienst," 46.

39. "Wenn ich nicht so selbstverständlich organisieren, regieren u. Menschen anstellen könnte, wär es gar nicht zu schaffen gewesen" (Penkert, *Briefe einer Rotkreuzschwester von der Ostfront*, 222).

40. "Das Rote Kreuz war hier ein Sammelpunkt von Menschen, denen im allgemeinen der enge Frauenalltag nicht genügte, denen das Regieren und Organisieren lag" (Ruediger, *Frauen im Dienst der Menschlichkeit*, 44).

41. "Als 'Frau Generalführerin' hatte ich eigentlich hauptsächlich Menschen erlebt, über die ich zu bestimmen hatte, die sich nach mir richteten und die ihren Stimmungen in meiner Gegenwart nicht nachgaben. Das Leben einer Ehe- und Hausfrau wird aber von den Dispositionen des Mannes und seinen Wünschen bestimmt. ... Diese zwei so verschiedenen Welten habe ich damals sehr deutlich empfunden" (Ruediger, *Frauen im Dienst der Menschlichkeit*, 152). See also "Die Frauen liebten die Selbständigkeit und Freiheit ihrer Arbeit und die geachtete Stellung" ("the women loved the independence and freedom of their work and the honored position") (179) and "einer Frau wird das Geschenk solchen Wirkens nur selten oder nur in besonderen Zeiten und Lebensumständen zuteil" ("a woman is only rarely granted the gift of such work or only in special times and circum-stances") (280).

42. "Zimmer scheuern u.s.w. Schuhe putzen, Wäsche waschen, eben alle Nebenarbeit machen Russenfrauen für uns" (Penkert, *Briefe einer Rotkreuzschwester von der Ostfront*, 111).

43. "Frauen, die der Mann in der Heimat kaum ansah, wurden plötzlich Mittelpunkt" (Ruediger, *Frauen im Dienst der Menschlichkeit*, 128). See also the comments of an American nurse who was interviewed by Burke Fessler: "Looking back it was a wonderful time. Never had so many boyfriends and so much fun, despite the seriousness of why we were there" (Burke Fessler, *No Time for Fear*, 185).
44. Burke Fessler, *No Time for Fear*, 90.
45. See Schorer, *A Half Acre of Hell*, 30, 230.
46. "Ich werde eben noch ein wenig mehr in den größeren Dingen zu Hause sein müssen, werde noch ein wenig weiter aus dem eigenen, kleinen Leben herausgehen" (Penkert, *Briefe einer Rotkreuzschwester von der Ostfront*, 70). See also "stehst du auf dem Platz für den Du geschaffen bist, dienst dem Sinn, der über Deinem Leben steht, bist ein winziger Teil, ein Steinchen in dem Wall von Leibern, der das Leben schützt" ("you are at the place for which you were created, serve the meaning that determines your life, you are a tiny part, a brick in the wall of bodies that protects life") (77).
47. See Panke-Kochinke and Schaidhammer-Placke, *Frontschwestern und Friedensengel*, 25. See also Breiding, who points out that nurses were often referred to as the "female soldiers of the Führer" (Breiding, *Die Braunen Schwestern*, 30 and 257). In this, the Nazis could rely on a well-established tradition that reached back to Henry Dunant, the founder of the Red Cross, who noted that nurses "confront the same dangers as the warrior, of their own free will, in a spirit of peace, for a purpose of comfort, from a motive of self-sacrifice" (Dunant, *A Memory of Solferino*, 58).
48. See, for example, "Wir arbeiteten von morgens früh 8 Uhr bis nachts 2 oder 3 Uhr durch" ("we work without interruption from 8 in the morning to 2 or 3 at night") (cited in Panke-Kochinke and Schaidhammer-Placke, *Frontschwestern und Friedensengel*, 52).
49. Note, for example, the incisive criticism of the German press by female doctor Käte Frankenthal, who served in the First World War: "Alle Zeitungen brachten rührende Geschichten von Verwundeten, die, kaum verbunden, verlangten, in den Schützengraben zurückgeschickt zu werden. ... Ich habe in den drei Jahren, die ich draußen war, keinen derartigen Fall gesehen. Andere Fälle habe ich massenhaft gesehen, und zwar alle Grade von Simulation, Angstneurosen, Hysterie und Selbstverstümmelung" ("All newspapers brought touching stories of wounded men who, barely bandaged, demanded to be sent back to the trenches. ... During the three years that I was at the front I have not seen one such case. I saw hundreds of other cases, namely all kinds of simulation, anxiety disorders, hysteria and self-mutilation") (*Der dreifache Fluch*, 59).
50. See Monahan and Neidel-Greenlee, *And If I Perish*, 18.
51. For more information, see Panke-Kochinke and Schaidhammer-Placke, *Frontschwestern und Friedensengel*, 18; Gaida, *Zwischen Pflegen und Töten*, 19.
52. See Seithe and Hagemann, who point out that the German Red Cross (*Deutsches Rotes Kreuz*) (DRK) sided with the Nazis. It was concerned with "'German heroes,' that is, wounded soldiers, not with the victims of the

regime" (Seithe and Hagemann, *Das Deutsche Rote Kreuz im Dritten Reich (1933–1939)*, 90; see also 10, 58, 191). On September 1, 1934, Hitler became *Schirmherr* (patron) of the DRK (Seithe and Hagemann, *Das Deutsche Rote Kreuz im Dritten Reich (1933–1939)*, 97). Gertrud Scholtz-Klink, in her role as leader of the National Socialist women's organization, was put in charge of the DRK *Reichsfrauenbund* (Seithe and Hagemann, *Das Deutsche Rote Kreuz im Dritten Reich (1933–1939)*, 99).

53. See Katscher, *Krankenpflege und Drittes Reich*, 12.

54. Panke-Kochinke and Schaidhammer-Placke provide detailed information about the number of nurses who worked for different organizations: for 1941, they count 6,745 Red Cross nurses with the army and SS, 12,497 assistants (*Schwesternhelferinnen*), 4,619 DRK auxiliary nurses (*Hilfsschwestern*), 35,472 DRK helpers, 4,784 Catholic nurses, 2,482 deaconesses, 1,054 National Socialist nurses, and 827 other nurses (Panke-Kochinke and Schaidhammer-Placke, *Frontschwestern und Friedensengel*, 155). For June 25, 1944, they list 5,230 nurses and 5,543 assistant nurses on the front lines; in Germany, there were 5,374 DRK nurses, 8,728 Catholic nurses, 2,751 Protestant nurses, 3,409 National Socialist nurses, 1,339 other nurses, and 43,260 assistant nurses (Panke-Kochinke and Schaidhammer-Placke, *Frontschwestern und Friedensengel*, 155).

55. "Ich schwöre Adolf Hitler, meinem Führer, unverbrüchliche Treue und Gehorsam. Ich verpflichte mich, an jedem Platz, an den ich gestellt werde, meine Berufsaufgaben als nationalsozialistische Schwester treu und gewissenhaft im Dienste der Volksgemeinschaft zu erfüllen, so wahr mir Gott helfe" (cited in Steppe and Ulmer, *Ich war von jeher mit Leib und Seele gerne Pflegerin*, 7).

56. For more information, see Gaida, *Zwischen Pflegen und Töten*, 30; Seithe and Hagemann, *Das Deutsche Rote Kreuz im Dritten Reich (1933–1939)*, 128–129.

57. See Gaida, *Zwischen Pflegen und Töten*, 33. The training of *Samariterinnen* and "helpers" was more rudimentary, limited to only twenty to thirty lessons (Seithe and Hagemann, *Das Deutsche Rote Kreuz im Dritten Reich (1933–1939)*, 170). The reduced training was one of several attempts to remedy the pervasive shortage of nurses during the Second World War. Another directive, implemented in October 1936, required that all female students of medicine had to have training as an assistant nurse to be admitted to the exam. In 1942, when the needs of the army were dire, nurses were no longer allowed to enter a different profession (Panke-Kochinke and Schaidhammer-Placke, *Frontschwestern und Friedensengel*, 19).

58. On the nature of such conflicts, see Bleker and Schmiedebach, who argue that medicine and war are ethically incompatible ("Vorwort," 7–8). When a doctor heals a soldier, he may save his life, but he also helps to send him back to the battlefield where he may be killed. Furthermore, providing care for individual soldiers effectively prolongs the war. According to Bleker, this creates a dilemma between the duty to the fatherland and the obligation toward one's fellow beings (Bleker, "Medizin im Dienst des Krieges," 15).

59. "Die militärische Anordnung erst für die eigenen Leute zu sorgen, ist wohl verständlich. Für Ärzte ist es aber fast unerträglich" (Frankenthal, *Der drei-fache Fluch*, 72). Frankenthal's memoir was written in response to a competition organized by Harvard University when she was in exile in the United States in 1940.

60. "Man zieht nur pöbelhafte Instinkte groß mit der Lehre von der Gleichheit all dessen, was Menschenantlitz trägt, mit der Forderung nach Nächstenliebe um jeden Preis, über die Schranken des Blutes, des Wertes, der Ehre hinweg" (Penkert, *Briefe einer Rotkreuzschwester von der Ostfront*, 159).

61. "Die Frage freilich, wie gesund ein Mensch werden muß, bevor er im Schützengraben umkommen kann, konnte ich mir selbst nicht beantworten. . . . Man mußte zweifeln, ob es nicht richtiger wäre, vollwertige Gesundheit einen Grund zu nennen, der zur Verwendung als Kanonenfutter untauglich macht" (Frankenthal, *Der dreifache Fluch*, 63).

62. "Wir würden keine Arbeit für direkte Kriegszwecke leisten, wie Hospitaldienst, Verwundentenpflege. Halbtot geschundene Menschen wie-der lebendig und gesund machen, um sie abermals den gleichen und noch schlimmeren Qualen auszusetzen? Nein, für solchen Wahnsinn würden wir uns nicht hergeben" (cited in Meiners, 19).

63. McFarland-Icke, *Nurses in Nazi Germany*, 238.

64. Zygmunt Baumann, cited in McFarland-Icke, *Nurses in Nazi Germany*, 241 and 246.

65. Lifton, *The Nazi Doctors*, 459.

66. "Seine Kompanie mußte einmal Menschen erschießen . . . Und er war froh, sich einmal dieses Entsetzliche von der Seele geredet zu haben" (Panke-Kochinke and Schaidhammer-Placke, *Frontschwestern und Friedensengel*, 195). See also "In diesen Tagen sind alle Juden aus Borrissow auf dem Flugplatz erschossen worden" ("in those days all Jews from Borrissow were shot on the airfield") (227) and "Von einem Landser bekam ich ein Foto, da war eine ganze Grube angefüllt mit Leichen zu sehen, ausgemergelte Menschen. Das sei ein russisches Altenheim gewesen" ("I got a photo from a Landser, it showed a pit filled completely with corpses, emaciated people. That had been a Russian nursing home") (238).

67. "Ich werde nur ein ekelhaftes Gefühl nicht los, wenn sie meine Waschschüssel u. mein Bettzeug anfassen. Für uns ist bestimmt schon das Beste rausgesucht, aber es ist eben alles dreckig u. elend, was hier rumläuft. Der Zustand, in dem dieses Volk existiert ist wahrlich unbeschreiblich. Was ich bisher hörte u. sah hat mir nur den Glauben gestärkt, den ich immer hatte: daß unser Deutschland ein Traum ist aus lauter Schönheit u. Wärme u. Liebe. Wie bestialisch können diese Asiaten sein! . . . In Rußland weiß man wohl noch besser als an anderen Fronten worum man kämpft, wofür man fällt" (Penkert, *Briefe einer Rotkreuzschwester von der Ostfront*, 111).

68. See Summ, *Schäfers Tochter*, 9.

69. "Man auch im Angesicht von Tod und Zerstörung menschlich und lebendig bleiben kann" (Panke-Kochinke, "Vorwort," 8).

70. "Gegengewicht zu Gewalt und Zerstörung" ("Vorwort," 8). To Panke-Kochinke, the blame for the war lies with those in power who would rather destroy than negotiate.

71. "Für uns Kinder war es einfach schön, dort aufzuwachsen" ("for us kids it was simply beautiful to grow up there") (Summ, *Schäfers Tochter*, 24).

72. Her father is one of seven brothers, six of whom fought in the First World War; two died. Summ's mother also lost a brother in the war. Other family members fell victim to disease and accidents, including Summ's two brothers. Summ's teacher is a former officer who beats the children on a regular basis, and the husband of the local pharmacist suffered a head injury in the First World War that caused fits of uncontrolled anger.

73. "Bedrückend waren für mich Missgeburten. . . . Für mich waren es schreckliche Erlebnisse, wenn die Mütter zum ersten Mal das behinderte Kind im Arm hielten und bitter weinten" ("Malformations were depressing to me. . . . To me, these were horrible experiences when the mothers held their handicapped child for the first time and cried bitterly") (Summ, *Schäfers Tochter*, 99).

74. See also "wir lebten ziemlich abseits" (Summ, *Schäfers Tochter*, 67).

75. "Leittier, dem die anderen Schafe bedingungslos folgen" (Summ, *Schäfers Tochter*, 13).

76. See Summ, *Schäfers Tochter*, 97.

77. See Summ, *Schäfers Tochter*, 115.

78. "Wenn es dunkel wurde, kam wieder die Angst . . . Dunkelheit bedeutete, dass man ausgeliefert war – den Partisanen, die uns überall und jederzeit verfolgen konnten" ("When it got dark, fear returned . . . darkness meant that one was exposed – to the partisans who could follow us everywhere and at all times") (Summ, *Schäfers Tochter*, 119).

79. Summ went sightseeing in Hungary and reports that, in general, "verbrachten wir in Dombovar einen sehr schönen Sommer" ("we spent a very beautiful summer in Dombovar") (Summ, *Schäfers Tochter*, 154).

80. See "Die Belastung ging manchmal bis an die Grenzen dessen, was man ertragen konnte" ("the workload sometimes reached the limits of what one could bear") (Summ, *Schäfers Tochter*, 126). Summ singles out the burns and disfigurations suffered by soldiers in tanks as particularly difficult to bear. See also 109.

81. See "Diese Einzelschicksale lasteten sehr auf mir" ("these individual destinies weighed heavily on me") (Summ, *Schäfers Tochter*, 165).

82. Before she is herself taken to a camp in Pilsen, Summ helps hide two German army doctors from the Americans.

83. See "Viele der Amerikaner sprachen deutsch. Oft waren ihre Eltern ausge-wanderte Juden und nun rächte sich mancher" ("many of the Americans spoke German. Often their parents were emigrated Jews and some took revenge") (Summ, *Schäfers Tochter*, 176).

84. Summ and her fellow nurses were stationed in the houses that had belonged to the deported Jews, a situation she finds "belastend" ("depressing") (Summ, *Schäfers Tochter*, 153).

85. "Wenn wir durch Shitomir liefen, sahen wir oft Entsetzliches" ("When we walked through Shitomir, we often saw horrible things") (Summ, *Schäfers Tochter*, 132).
86. "Mitgeholfen, die Dörfer in hübsche Ortschaften zu verwandeln" (Summ, *Schäfers Tochter*, 154).
87. "Richtiger Tauschhandel" ("true exchange") (Summ, *Schäfers Tochter*, 131).
88. She remembers that she gave some Ukrainian workers medicine when they contracted dysentery even though such help was illegal. She also reports that her unit returned a cow to its rightful (Ukrainian) owner: "Das war ein nettes Erlebnis in dieser sonst schrecklichen Zeit" ("that was a nice experience in this otherwise horrible time") (Summ, *Schäfers Tochter*, 129).
89. "In diesem Krieg gab es so viele Unklarheiten auf beiden Seiten" (Summ, *Schäfers Tochter*, 152).
90. "Was auf allen Seiten und in allen Ländern zerstört wurde, wie viele Menschen getötet wurden, war unfassbar" ("what was destroyed on all sides and in all countries, how many people were killed, was incomprehensible") (Summ, *Schäfers Tochter*, 152).
91. "Dennoch konnte ich mir mein fröhliches Wesen durch den Krieg hindurch retten" (Summ, *Schäfers Tochter*, 126).
92. Interestingly, like Summ, Ochsenknecht did not record her story until after her husband's death, though neither author offers an explanation for this.
93. "Es ist eine schöne Stadt, doch leider hat sie unter den polnischen Zuständen sehr gelitten" (Ochsenknecht, *Als ob der Schnee alles zudeckte*, 57).
94. "Wenn ich diese Sätze nachlese, wird mir klar, wie verblendet ich von der Nazi-Propaganda war. Genau das redete man uns damals permanent ein – dass die Polen selbst schuld an ihrer ganzen Misere waren! Dabei waren es die Deutschen, die den Krieg begonnen hatten und die Bevölkerung aushungern ließen" (Ochsenknecht, *Als ob der Schnee alles zudeckte*, 57).
95. For example, Ochsenknecht reports honestly that she was a Hitler devotee even though her father, a First World War veteran, was highly critical of Hitler. When her father tells her that Germany is going to lose the war, she counters: "Der Führer weiß, was er tut" ("The Führer knows what he is doing") (Ochsenknecht, *Als ob der Schnee alles zudeckte*, 49).
96. She remembers feeling safe ("geborgen") in the crowd at the train station (Ochsenknecht, *Als ob der Schnee alles zudeckte*, 21).
97. "Das Gefühl 'gebraucht zu werden' verlieh meinem Leben einen Sinn" (Ochsenknecht, *Als ob der Schnee alles zudeckte*, 24). Later, she writes, "Ich fühlte mich nützlich, und das beglückte mich" ("I felt useful and that made me happy") (45).
98. See "In diesem Augenblick verspürte ich nur Glück und Stolz. Ich durfte dabei sein" ("In this moment I felt happiness and pride. I was allowed to be a part of it") (Ochsenknecht, *Als ob der Schnee alles zudeckte*, 127).
99. See "so lernten wir ständig neue Männer kennen und wußten, wie man sie dazu brachte, unsere Wünsche zu erfüllen" ("thus, we got to know new men

all the time and knew how to get them to fulfill our wishes") (Ochsenknecht, *Als ob der Schnee alles zudeckte*, 83; see also 96 and 130).

100. When her unit, which comprised twenty nurses (six *Vollschwestern* and fourteen helpers), boarded a train to Krakow in June 1941, she was giddy with excitement.

101. "Ich schuftete in jenen Tagen wie eine Maschine" ("in those days I worked like a machine") (Ochsenknecht, *Als ob der Schnee alles zudeckte*, 87).

102. "Als sei ich nach neuen Herausforderungen süchtig geworden" ("as though I had become addicted to new challenges") (Ochsenknecht, *Als ob der Schnee alles zudeckte*, 184). After a brief vacation at home, she cannot wait to get back to the front, and toward the end of the war she declares: "Genauso stark wie ich mir wünsche, dass der Krieg aufhört, wünsche ich mich zurück an die Front" ("Just as much as I wish that the war would stop, I want to return to the front") (Ochsenknecht, *Als ob der Schnee alles zudeckte*, 218). About the injuries, she says: "Dass es so schlimm sein würde, hatte ich nicht erwartet" ("I had not expected that it would be so bad") (68).

103. Here, Ochsenknecht remembers feeling like a princess during sleigh rides in a fairy tale forest (Ochsenknecht, *Als ob der Schnee alles zudeckte*, 109).

104. See Ochsenknecht, *Als ob der Schnee alles zudeckte*, 161.

105. See Ochsenknecht, *Als ob der Schnee alles zudeckte*, 163. Even when Ochsenknecht began to doubt the wisdom of the *Führer*, she fulfilled her responsibility to uphold the morale of the soldiers: "unsere Aufgabe war es auch, sie auf andere Gedanken zu bringen. Wir durften nicht nach ihren grauenvollen Erlebnissen fragen. Wenn sie davon zu berichten begannen, sollten wir ihnen sagen, dass es jetzt vorbei sei" ("It was our job to get them to think of other things. We were not allowed to ask about their horrible experiences. When they started talking about them, we were supposed to say to them that it is all over now") (98–99).

106. See Ochsenknecht, *Als ob der Schnee alles zudeckte*, 138.

107. "Wie viele Ukrainer wünschten sich nichts mehr als die Befreiung ihres Landes von der russischen Herrschaft" ("How many Ukrainians wished for nothing more than the liberation of their country from Russian rule") (Ochsenknecht, *Als ob der Schnee alles zudeckte*, 165).

108. "Niemand schien krank oder besonders mager zu sein, doch die Gesichter waren duster und traurig . . . ich fühlte mich schrecklich fehl am Platz . . . Mir taten diese Menschen unendlich leid" (Ochsenknecht, *Als ob der Schnee alles zudeckte*, 84–85).

109. This inability to notice extends not only to the suffering of the Jews and the occupied nations but also to all arenas of Ochsenknecht's life in the army. E.g., Ochsenknecht remembers a pile of amputated limbs behind a hospital, but remarks that at the time the horrible stench and ghastly sight did not bother her at all. After the war, however, she had nightmares about it. Similarly, toward the end of the war, Ochsenknecht had an affair with a married doctor who was addicted to morphine. Even though as a nurse she should be familiar with the signs, she remains unaware of his addiction

for the entire duration of the affair. At the same time, her memoir contains critical remarks about the widespread use of drugs and uppers in the army and about the oversupply of alcohol to keep soldiers and nurses from thinking too much – "haben sie ihre Gefühle mit Alkohol zugeschüttet" ("they drowned their feelings in alcohol") (Ochsenknecht, *Als ob der Schnee alles zudeckte*, 104).

110. "Ob wir damals blind waren, ob wir nicht verstanden, welche Verbrechen die Deutschen an der Ostfront vor unseren Augen begingen? Das werde ich manchmal gefragt, und beim Schreiben dieses Buches stelle ich mir selbst diese Fragen. Von den Todeslagern habe ich erst nach dem Krieg erfahren. Ich habe weder Vergasungswagen noch Massengräber, noch Menschen am Galgen baumeln gesehen. Aber ich wusste von den Hinrichtungen, die als Vergeltung für die Anschläge der Partisanen stattfanden ... Damals dachte ich, das sei in jedem Kriege so" (Ochsenknecht, *Als ob der Schnee alles zudeckte*, 171).

111. "Denke nicht, lebe" (Ochsenknecht, *Als ob der Schnee alles zudeckte*, 144).

112. See Ritvo and Plotkin, *Sisters in Sorrow*: "wir in den Krankenstuben ja ohne alle Hilfsmittel waren" ("We were without any equipment in the hospital") (30; see also xii). See also Adler's study of Theresienstadt, supposedly a "model camp": "In der ersten Zeit herrschte ein katastrophaler Mangel an Medikamenten und allen therapeutischen und klinischen Behelfen" ("In the beginning there was a catastrophic lack of medication and all therapeutic and clinical devices") (*Theresienstadt 1941–1945*, 496). According to Adler, the situation improved somewhat over time.

113. See Weglein, *Als Krankenschwester im KZ Theresienstadt*, 28; Lengyel, *Five Chimneys*, 134.

114. See Lingens Reiner, *Prisoners of Fear*, 61–62, 77, and 83.

115. "Eben deswegen, was bist Du für eine Krankenschwester, wenn Du nicht schlagen willst?" (Naor, *Krankengymnastin in Auschwitz*, 113).

116. As Heinrich Himmler stated, "in a camp, there are only the able-bodied or the dead. The sick don't exist" (cited in Ritvo and Plotkin, *Sisters in Sorrow*, 9).

117. Cited in Ritvo and Plotkin, *Sisters in Sorrow*, III.

118. Lengyel, *Five Chimneys*, 172.

119. Herzberger, *Eyewitness to Holocaust*, 15.

120. Lengyel, *Five Chimneys*, 75.

121. See Adler, *Theresienstadt 1941–1945*, 364; Naor, *Krankengymnastin in Auschwitz*, 82; Lingens Reiner, *Prisoners of Fear*.

122. Naor, *Krankengymnastin in Auschwitz*, 79; see also Lingens Reiner, *Prisoners of Fear*.

123. Adelsberger, *Auschwitz*, 46.

124. See Weglein, *Als Krankenschwester im KZ Theresienstadt*, 39.

125. Lengyel, *Five Chimneys*, 70.

126. Ritvo and Plotkin, *Sisters in Sorrow*, 87.

127. "Eine Anzahl von alten und privilegierten Juden ein zwar abgesondertes, aber doch erträgliches Dasein führte" (cited in Moos, "Vorwort," 5).

128. See Lechner and Moos, "Ulm – Theresienstadt – Ulm," 11.

129. Adler lists the criteria for contesting selection, including age over sixty-five years, medals awarded for bravery in the First World War, mixed marriage with an Aryan, and foreign citizenship (Adler, *Theresienstadt 1941–1945*, 90).

130. See Weglein, *Als Krankenschwester im KZ Theresienstadt*, 63, and Adler *Theresienstadt 1941–1945*, 180.

131. See Schwertfeger, *Women of Theresienstadt*, 72–75.

132. "Die Zwangsgemeinschaft stellte eine kranke Gesellschaft dar" (Adler, *Theresienstadt 1941–1945*, 492).

133. Weglein reports that they had three sets of fresh linen for eighty-four patients (*Als Krankenschwester im KZ Theresienstadt*, 82).

134. Adler, *Theresienstadt 1941–1945*, 97.

135. "In den Krankenhäusern fielen Patienten aus den Betten und blieben nächtelang auf dem Fußboden, da es an Pflegepersonal mangelte" (Adler, *Theresienstadt 1941–1945*, 194). According to Adler, the nursing staff was, with some exceptions, below average in terms of training and conduct; some nurses accepted bribes and/or were negligent (Adler, *Theresienstadt 1941–1945*, 500). He further points out that some became nurses because nursing promised protection from transports. See also Ellen Loeb, who writes: "I knew absolutely nothing [about being a nurse], but I acted as if I knew everything" (Ritvo and Plotkin, *Sisters in Sorrow*, 109). See also Lengyel, who writes that the most rudimentary knowledge of medicine "was enough in surroundings where proper medical care and treatment was impossible anyway" (*Five Chimneys*, 145).

136. "Heilung von der Haftpsychose" (Weglein, *Als Krankenschwester im KZ Theresienstadt*, 14).

137. "Vielleicht findet der eine oder andere meiner Leidensgenossen in der Welt den Namen eines seiner Angehörigen, um den er gebangt hat" (Weglein, *Als Krankenschwester im KZ Theresienstadt*, 14).

138. "Paradoxe Widerspruch von Ohnmacht und Scheinfreiheit" (Adler, *Theresienstadt 1941–1945*, 630).

139. "Das üppige Mahl" (Weglein, *Als Krankenschwester im KZ Theresienstadt*, 49); "So, ist wieder ein Jude verreckt!" "die schöne Anrede der Herren" (55).

140. "Die Pflege und die Arbeit bei diesen Fällen zu beschreiben, erlasse man mir" (Weglein, *Als Krankenschwester im KZ Theresienstadt*, 60).

141. Muller Bruml, cited in Ritvo and Plotkin, *Sisters in Sorrow*, 30, and Adelsberger, *Auschwitz*, 40.

142. "In diesen Tagen habe ich an der göttlichen Gerechtigkeit gezweifelt und war im wahrsten Sinne des Wortes verzweifelt. . . . Ich habe sehr bald eingesehen, daß ich durch alle diese Prüfungen mußte, um innerlich frei zu werden. Alle Not, alles Elend, auch Krankheit, mußte ich am eigenen Leibe ertragen, um anderen das sein zu können, was ich mir unter 'Schwester' vorgestellt habe" (Weglein, *Als Krankenschwester im KZ Theresienstadt*, 30).

143. See Weglein, *Als Krankenschwester im KZ Theresienstadt*, 15 and 17.

Interrupted Silences
German Victims of Rape

In the two preceding chapters, the focus has been on women who actively participated in the Nazi war effort, either as army auxiliaries or as nurses. Consequently, these chapters highlighted women's political agency and their various contributions to the National Socialist regime of terror. In contrast, Chapters 4 and 5 deal with narratives by and about women who held no official functions in the Third Reich that mandated direct contributions to the war effort. Moreover, they differ from the texts discussed so far because the authors' complicity is offset by the magnitude of their own victimization. Specifically, Chapter 4 asks if and how German women who were raped toward the end of the war can talk about their suffering in light of the enormous suffering Germans had inflicted. In other words, what is at stake is a representation of victimization that is not built on the presumption of innocence but rather allows for an accounting of complicity.

During the past two decades, the German book market was flooded with publications that highlight the victimization of Germans in the wake of the Second World War. According to Bill Niven, the interest in German suffering "has taken on an obsessive dimension,"[1] though one should add that such increased attention does not imply that these works have lost their controversial character. In particular, the representation of the rape of German women by Russian soldiers remains an ethical and aesthetic minefield. To be sure, even in civilian life, rape is a crime associated with shame and silence. In the German Second World War context, however, the taboo that adheres to all forms of sexual violence is exacerbated by the politically explosive nature of these rapes: told from the perspective of the perpetrator, these stories turn coercion into consent and frame the rapes as well-deserved punishment for female Nazis. Told from the perspective of the victim, they are likely to recycle Nazi propaganda with its specific cast of national characters: the Russians are beasts; the Poles, murderers; the German soldiers, saviors, and the Jews are absent from this tale. Thus, the issue of complicity informs all narratives of Second World War rapes.

In the following, I discuss representations of the mass rape of German women during the end of the Second World War when the Russian army advanced west. So far, scholars have focused mostly on filmic representations, in particular on Helke Sander's controversial *Liberators Take Liberties* (*Befreier und Befreite*), and on a small number of memoirs, including the widely discussed *A Woman in Berlin* (*Eine Frau in Berlin*).[2] In contrast, I combine readings of memoirs that have received little or no critical attention with an analysis of the representation of rape in two recent novels. I have chosen to read fiction alongside memoir because the fictional texts seek to imagine solutions to the dilemmas that the memoirists fail to address. Moreover, unlike previous analyses, I juxtapose texts by Russian soldiers and German women because I believe that a binational perspective is best suited to illuminate the ethical complexity of the confluence of complicity and victimization.

As I show in what follows, stories of wartime rape do not fit the categories that define classic narratives of war, and no established discourse does justice to the stories of victims who are also members of a perpetrator nation.[3] All stories of wartime rape defy established power structures, they confound the assumption that all victims are innocent and thus blur the boundaries between victims and perpetrators, they undermine the dichotomy of silence and discourse, they are uneven and contradictory, and they are insolubly tied up with the body. Rape is, as Sabine Sielke maintains, "a dense transfer point for relations of power."[4] When wartime rape is made to serve an ideological agenda, as it often is, the experience of the victim, her trauma and pain, threaten to disappear amidst the noise of justifications, metaphors, and political deployments.

My reading of memoirs by rape victims suggests that there is a dilemma inherent to this form of victimization.[5] Typically, rape, a crime strongly associated with shame, is referred to and evoked in quasi-formulaic language, but not narrated extensively. Consequently, narratives of rape are often suspended halfway between silence and discourse. Although many rape victims consider public acknowledgment of the trauma of rape therapeutic, they often do not perceive elaborate narrations of rape as conducive to their healing process. But this partial and intermittent silence, intended to avoid a reinscription of the original trauma, also contributes to a corresponding silence in public discourse.

In order to elucidate the narrative and ethical complexity of wartime rape, the first section of the chapter introduces the historical context and theoretical framework of my analysis. In the second section, I discuss the fiction of "consensual" rape in *Germany Diary 1945–46* (*Deutschland*

Tagebuch 1945–46) by Red Army soldier Wladimir Gelfand, and contrast Gelfand's account with representations of rape in Alexander Solzhenitsyn's *Prussian Nights* (1974) and in Lev Kopelev's memoir *To Be Preserved Forever* (1976). As I show, both Gelfand and, in very different ways, Solzhenitsyn situate rape within an ideological discourse that makes it readable as just punishment for the complicity of Nazi women. In the third section, I focus on memoirs of German rape victims, in particular on Gabi Köpp's *Why Was I a Girl? The Trauma of a Flight 1945* (*Warum war ich bloß ein Mädchen: Das Trauma einer Flucht 1945*), which I have chosen because to Köpp, the experience of (multiple) rape is not one of many traumatizing events but rather is front and center. Here, I show that, in these accounts of rape survivors, the trauma and shame of rape and the acute awareness of the victim's affiliation with the perpetrator nation obstruct the effort of narration in such a way that the experience of rape is often elided. Following the discussion of memoirs, I then analyze the political deployment of rape in Ingo Münch's historical study, *Come, Woman! The Mass Rapes of German Women and Girls 1944–45* (*Frau komm! Die Massenvergewaltigungen deutscher Frauen und Mädchen 1944–45*), and the tendency to downplay the suffering of rape victims in works by left-leaning historians. In all these accounts, rape is silenced, denied, or drowned out either because of the shame associated with the experience or because the authors fail to reconcile stories of victimization with those of complicity. Thus, rape becomes invisible even in texts that explicitly address the topic of wartime rape. Finally, I conclude with an interpretation of two fictional representations of rape that offer a potential solution to the dilemma outlined earlier: Julia Franck's *Blindness of the Heart* (*Die Mittagsfrau*) and Jenny Erpenbeck's *Visitation* (*Heimsuchung*). As I show in what follows, both writers skillfully avoid the discursive traps outlined earlier, and instead seek to find aesthetic solutions for a complex moral problem. Franck achieves this by focusing on a German Jewish protagonist, while Erpenbeck forecloses revisionist readings by juxtaposing the perspectives of multiple narrators.

Rape and Representation

Toward the end of the Second World War, Russian soldiers raped several hundred thousand German women. Some estimate that as many as 2 million women were victimized, many of whom were raped multiple times by several soldiers.[6] There was no target demographic.[7] Although children were often, though not always, spared, young girls were not. Nor were old women, pregnant women, nuns, or Holocaust survivors. Frequently, women who refused were beaten brutally or killed while husbands or parents who tried to protect them might be shot. Rapes were committed in private bedrooms, in ditches by the side of the road, and in full view of family members or even entire communities. Many women did not survive the ordeal. Some succumbed to injuries incurred during the rape; some were killed after the rape; many committed suicide. Some women entered an exclusive relationship with an officer who offered protection in exchange for sexual services. Others tried to hide, pretended to be sick, or cross-dressed to disguise their gender.[8] Some women betrayed others to save themselves. As a consequence of the rapes, many women were pregnant with the child of a Russian soldier, and many more contracted venereal diseases. In theory, rape was punishable by death. In actuality, most rapists acted with impunity.

In their edited collection *Rape and Representation*, Lynn Higgins and Brenda Silver claim that, in narrative, "rape exists as an absence or gap that is both product and source of textual anxiety."[9] This is certainly true, but in the German context these absences are of a peculiar nature. First, given the staggering scale of the rape crimes, the number of narratives is small indeed. Second, when rape features in victims' narratives, it tends to be referred to rather than described, evoked rather than presented. Thus, we are not dealing with an absence, but rather with a partial absence. Third, rape is subject to a taboo, but a taboo that is, as Laurel Cohen-Pfister has shown, "repeatedly broken and then reinstituted."[10] Consider a story recounted by Eichhorn and Kuwert. Here, a rape victim from the Second World War wins an essay prize for a narrative about her traumatic experience. When she is handed the prize, however, she is instructed never to mention "that" again.[11] Clearly, a simple dichotomy of silence versus narration does not adequately describe discourses on rape.[12]

In the German discourse, the taboo and shame associated with all forms of rape are exacerbated by the politically charged nature of these rapes, since many of the victims in question were citizens of Nazi Germany who actively supported or were passively complicit in Nazi policies. Thus, it is hardly surprising that, until recently, many writers on the left steered clear of this topic because they were concerned that any acknowledgment of crimes committed against members of the perpetrator nation would relativize German war crimes and the Holocaust and indicate "tacit approval of the anti-Bolshevik program of the Nazis."[13] In other words, there was concern that any effort to shine a compassionate glimmer on German rape victims would constitute an attempt to turn the spotlight away from the average German as a perpetrator, by effecting a reversal in which the Russians – who constituted the largest group of victims of the Nazis[14] – appear primarily as perpetrators. Seen in this light, knowledge about German crimes against Russians mandated silence about Russian crimes against Germans, including the crime of rape. Even feminists toed the party line. In her landmark study of rape, *Against our Will*, Susan Brownmiller proclaims "that a noticeable difference in attitude and behavior toward women existed on the part of the armies of liberation as opposed to the armies of conquest and subjugation in World War II."[15] Here, the victimization of German women is minimized in favor of a narrative of liberation. Such silencing was taken to extremes in the German Democratic Republic (GDR), where any memory of the rapes was banished, lest it tarnish the reputation of the Soviet "brothers."[16]

Conversely, on the right end of the political spectrum, the suffering of Germans takes center stage while German crimes recede into the background. Here, the rapes are reinterpreted to signify the violation of the entire German nation. Consequently, stories of wartime rape present a dual challenge: if we fail to acknowledge the suffering of the victims, thus replicating the silence attached to this crime, we are in danger of aligning with the perpetrators and reactivating the trauma of rape. Conversely, if we ignore the moral quandaries and the stain of complicity inherent in many of these stories, we erase the political and historical context in which these rapes occurred and thus fail to do justice to those who were victimized by National Socialist Germany. But the answer to this dilemma does not lie in silence or evasion. Rather, the question is how "to address German suffering in light of the suffering caused by Germans or whether German victimhood can even be addressed without simultaneously calling into remembrance the millions harmed or killed by Germans."[17] In other words, the challenge consists in the integration of stories of complicity into the narrative of victimization.

It is hardly accidental that the classic victim of rape, Philomela, is violated in two distinct ways: first she is raped, then her tongue is cut out. Philomela, however, does not remain silent but weaves a tapestry that illustrates her experience. The story of Philomela teaches us an important lesson. It shows that the discourse of rape is not simply one of silence, but a complicated transaction where an irresistible desire to express oneself exists alongside different forms of silence, repression, and redeployment. Because rape hinges on the question of consent and thus on "the primacy of psychological states,"[18] it is a crime that does not exist without narrative.

Consequently, in analyzing the representation of rape, we must attend not only to "the rhetoric of rape,"[19] to the various silences that undergird these narratives, to the white noise that hides the silence, but also to the many discourses in which rape is detached from individual suffering and made to perform the work of ideology.[20] Even amidst a proliferation of texts about rape, the voice of the victim – what Cathy Caruth calls the "voice that cries out from the wound" inflicted on body and mind[21] – may still be missing. Moreover, as we listen to the voices of rape victims, we must remember that their victimization is intricately interwoven with the suffering of those who were persecuted by the Nazi regime.

Finally, we must attend to our own discomfort with these stories, to our unease about how these stories defy conventional moral categories, and to the fact that we as readers enjoy the luxury of detachment because, unlike the memoirist, we are not trapped in a body that bears the trauma of this history. As Tanner reminds us, the "reader's freedom parallels the auton-omy of the violator . . . Insofar as the reader's imagination manipulates the victim's body as a purely textual entity, the reality of pain and the vulner-ability of that body may be obscured by the participation of a reading subject who perpetuates the dynamics of violation."[22] If we as readers fail to do justice to the dual challenge of these texts, that is, if we fail to acknowl-edge either the suffering of the victims or the political complexity and the burden of complicity inherent in these stories – we are likely to reactivate the trauma of rape or to replicate the silence that obstructs the representa-tion of rape in the first place.

"Consensual Rape":
Wladimir Gelfand's *Germany Diary 1945–46*

While only a few stories focus on German victims of wartime rape, even fewer accounts of rape are told from the perspective of Red Army soldiers.[23] In spite of the relative absence of firsthand documents, historians have sought to understand the motivations that underlay the orgies of destruc-tion and rape on the way to Berlin. Many point to the role of alcohol in unleashing violence and also to the fact that the soldiers had been brutal-ized through the constant exposure to violence and death during four years of war.[24] Others make mention of the *shtrafniki*, members of punishment units, some of whom had been in prison for political reasons, others for violent crimes.

Then there was the impact of German wealth on Soviet soldiers. Three-quarters of the Red Army came from villages, and many had never seen an electric light or been on a train before the war.[25] To these soldiers, German wealth (or what was left of it) was exotic and came to symbolize the German claim to national superiority even without overt reminders of Nazi racial ideology. Most importantly, perhaps, all these impulses that fostered violence were stoked by relentless propaganda. According to historian Catherine Merridale, "there is no doubt that the men's activities were encouraged, if not orchestrated, by Moscow."[26] As the Russians closed in on Germany, many soldiers were exhausted and wished to go home. In response, the political officers intensified their propaganda efforts. Ilya Ehrenburg's saying, "if you have not killed at least one German a day, you have wasted that day,"[27] is perhaps the most prominent, but by no means the only example of a propaganda of hate. Exhortations to rouse the Fascist beast from its lair were accompanied by pictures of the horror of Majdanek, the first concentration camp discovered by the Red Army, and sweetened by the prospect of plunder. Finally, Red Army soldiers were acutely aware of their inferior status in the Nazi racial hierarchy. "Break with force the racial arrogance of Germanic women! Take them as legitimate spoils of war,"[28] a slogan attributed to Ilya Ehrenburg, poignantly refers to Nazi claims of superiority and casts rape as just punishment for women's ideological complicity with the regime. Taken together, these motivations amounted to a volatile mix that led to the rape of hundreds of thousands of women.

In the memoirs of Russian Second World War veterans, as well as in the reports of the People's Commissariat for Internal Affairs (*Narodnyy Komissariat Vnutrennikh Del*) (NKVD), rape simply does not exist.[29] When Russian veterans do speak about wartime rape, they frequently insist that the women had participated willingly. In ways both subtle and crass, a narrative of violence and coercion is replaced by one of consensual intercourse.[30] This discursive shift is evident in interviews with Red Army veterans conducted by German filmmaker Helke Sander. There were no rapes, one veteran suggests. Rather, the women followed their own needs.[31] Similarly, Ingeborg Jacobs reports that the Red Army veterans she talked to invariably claimed that German women had not resisted for a long time and that some had even lifted their skirts.[32] Statements such as these accord with Merridale's finding that misogyny was rampant in the Red Army,[33] though it should be pointed out that the Red Army was not the only army afflicted with misogyny nor were Red Army soldiers the only soldiers guilty of rape.[34] In *The Fall of Berlin*, Beevor cites a British journalist who reports that the Russians "often raped old women of sixty, seventy or even eighty – much to these grandmothers' surprise, if not downright delight."³⁵ This statement is in line with a boast by American servicemen that "German soldiers fought for six years, the German women for only five minutes."³⁶ Moreover, the same attitude prevailed among parts of the German population, as evidenced by an issue of the German journal *Der Stern* from 1948 entitled "Has the German Woman Failed?," thus suggesting not only that German women were eager participants in the crimes committed against them, but that being raped constituted a moral failure, a betrayal of their husbands and fathers.

The pattern that transforms coercion into consent while toying with the idea of rape as just punishment for Nazi women also informs Wladimir Gelfand's *Germany Diary 1945–46*, which was published in Sweden and Germany in 2005, but not in Russia. In light of the general dearth of accounts of rape told from the perspective of Russians soldiers, Gelfand's memoir is a highly unusual document, even more so since Gelfand, a native Ukrainian, was of Jewish descent. Gelfand had planned to write a novel based on his notes, but died before he could execute his plan. In its present form, *Germany Diary*, a collection of letters and diary entries, is based on Gelfand's extensive literary estate and edited by Elke Scherstjanoi. The book offers vivid descriptions of everyday life on the front and in occupied Berlin. Gelfand discusses battles and politics, but he also dwells on trips to the movies, his amorous designs, personal gripes, and encounters with German civilians.

For the most part, Gelfand's notes, in which sexual violence is largely absent, suggest that we are dealing with a ladies' man, not a rapist. Gelfand portrays himself as a man who does not so much pursue women, as he is pursued by them.³⁷ And yet, though cruel violence is absent in his account, coercion is not. Gelfand's amorous gestures are interlaced with intimations of various forms of strong-arming, bullying, and compulsion. Convinced that German women "do not refuse tender gestures, as they generally do not refuse anything,"³⁸ Gelfand sees himself as a sheep among wolves, a gentleman who helps damsels in distress. He is the type of soldier who is approached with offers of an exclusive relationship in exchange for protection. But, as such an offer suggests, under the dire circumstances of the immediate postwar period, *consent* is a troubled concept.³⁹ Gelfand is fully aware that both protection and food can be traded for sex and uses his buying power quite consciously. In the following episode, for example, Gelfand proclaims with utter confidence that the proffered victuals should buy him the right to all kinds of intimacy:

I put down food, sweets, and butter, sausage and expensive German cigar-
ettes on the altar of trusted and well-meaning relationships. Half of this
would have been enough to be allowed to do as I wish with the daughter
right in front of the mother's eyes. . . . Today food is more precious than
life.[40]

Where starvation is a real and immediate threat, the line between prostitution and rape is thin, indeed.

While this episode blurs the boundary between prostitution and coercion, the memoir also contains several explicit references to rape.
Curiously, though, what starts out as an account of rape invariably turns
into a narrative of consensual sex. In particular, Gelfand relates a bizarre
incident during which he and his men take several members of a German
women's battalion prisoner. Since there never was a German women's
battalion, Gelfand is either confusing female army auxiliaries with women
soldiers, or he is simply making this up. Gelfand explains that these
captured female soldiers are divided into three groups: native Russians
(presumably forced labor), who are shot as traitors; married women; and
"girls." The last group is then "*verteilt*":

> From the third group, the spoils were distributed to the houses and beds,
> and experiments, which cannot be rendered on paper, were conducted with
> them for several days. The Germans were afraid; they did not resist the
> young ones, but rather implored them to sleep with them in order to escape
> rape by older soldiers. Andropow was a member of this happy age group. He
> chose the youngest and took her along to sleep with her. But when he urged
> her to satisfy his basic desire, she shook her head and whispered ashamedly:
> This is not good, I am a virgin. . . . She refused for a while longer until he
> pulled his pistol. Then she was silent and pulled her underwear down. . . .
> Then with a nod to his pistol he advised her: do well. . . . Thus, they worked
> in unison and arrived at their goal. He felt that something tore, the girl
> screamed and moaned. . . . Soon, however, she forced a smile. He gave her
> civilian clothing, a dress to put on, and she went outside to her fellow
> sufferers, happy and innocent.[41]

This account is quite remarkable. What starts out as a clear reference to
rape turns into a tryst of young lovers, topped off by the claim that the rape
victim left the scene of the crime "happy and innocent." At several points,
the narrator alternates between an open acknowledgment of violence and
coercion, even of atrocity, and an emphasis on the willing cooperation of
the victims. Although Gelfand is aware that the women seek young lovers
in order to avoid older men, he still refers to the young men as a "happy
group." Similarly, although Gelfand knows that the young woman who is

raped by Antropov resists until threatened at gunpoint, he describes the two lovers as acting in unison toward a common goal. Thus, even as he describes the crime of rape, Gelfand erases it.

There is a casualness and irony to Gelfand's accounts of rape that is deeply troubling. And yet, his diary entries are also uniquely qualified to illustrate the ethical complexities of sexual encounters between Russian soldiers and German women rooted in the insoluble mesh of victimization and complicity. Note, for example, the following episode in which Gelfand invites a German woman to his room. The woman follows him willingly at first, or so he claims, but has second thoughts and wants to leave. Again, an encounter that appears consensual in the beginning becomes coercive as Gelfand refuses to let her go because it would undermine his masculinity.[42] Finally, the situation reaches an absurd climax when the German woman, munching on food Gelfand has provided her, starts to share her opinions on Jews: "she spoke with disgust about the Jews, explained to me racial theory, talked rubbish about white, red, and blue blood."[43] Gelfand, who had survived the battle of Stalingrad and had lost almost all relatives on his father's side in the Holocaust, is angered and determined to set her right about the "obscurantism of amateurish fascist theorists."[44] When his efforts fail, he decides to defer the political lesson until after intercourse. Here, sexual violence, Fascist ideology, and anger at the arrogance of the "master race" are intertwined in a most problematic way. Gelfand astutely withholds narrative closure. We do not know whether that which he claims had to happen did, in fact, happen,[45] though we may assume that he did not succeed in convincing his Fascist guest/victim of the error of her racist ways. What we do know, however, is that any simple binary of victim and perpetrator fails to capture all facets of the Russian soldier's ill-fated seduction/rape and of the German woman's racist ideology.

Although Gelfand appears to flirt with the idea of rape as punishment, his explicit calls for revenge typically relate to death in battle, pillage, and plunder. In contrast, in *Prussian Nights*, composed in the Gulag in the 1950s but not published until 1974, Alexander Solzhenitsyn both summons and critiques the assumption that the rape of German women is an adequate response to German atrocities in Russia and to German women's complicity in these crimes. *Prussian Nights* introduces a narrative voice in the plural, the collective "we" of the advancing Red Army. In the eyes of this "we," Germany is a feminine fiend, a "foul witch,"[46] whose excessive riches make the invasion of Russia even more incomprehensible. The "we" of Solzhenitsyn's epic poem contrasts with an "I," who, at least initially, refuses to participate in the orgy of destruction, but who is also unwilling to stop it. The "I" expresses both empathy for the Russian soldiers who burn and kill mercilessly[47] and shock at the crimes they commit. This shock, however, never translates into a willingness to put a halt to the violence: "I'll be off / Like Pilate when he washed his hands. . . . Between us many a cross there stands / Of whitened Russian bones."[48]

The unwillingness to intervene on behalf of the German enemy is particularly pronounced when the "I" is confronted with the victims of rape:

> The mother's wounded, still alive.
> The little daughter's on the mattress,
> Dead. How many have been on it?
> A platoon, a company perhaps?
> A girl's been turned into a woman,
> A woman turned into a corpse.
> It's all come down to simple phrases:
> *Do not forget! Do not forgive!*
> *Blood for blood!* A tooth for a tooth!
> The mother begs, "Töte mich, Soldat!"
> Her eyes are hazy and bloodshot.
> The dark's upon her. She can't see.
> Am I one of theirs? Or whose? . . .[49]

Here, the sight of rape prompts the "I" to question his loyalties. The line "Am I one of theirs? Or whose?" refers literally to the impaired vision of the mother, who does not know whether she is dealing with a Russian or German soldier. But it also signals an uncertainty about the moral obligations demanded of the "I" in light of the crimes he witnesses. Still, although the "I" experiences a conflict, he remains passive when he is again confronted with rape, in this case the rape of a Polish woman:

> "I'm not German! I'm not German!
> No! I'm – Polish! I'm a Pole! . . . "
> Grabbing what comes handy, those
> Like-minded lads get in and start –
> "And, oh, what heart
> Could well oppose?"[50]

The Polish woman's protestations that she is not German imply that, while German women may deserve rape, she does not. And yet, although this rape victim is not a member of the perpetrator nation, the "I" shows no desire to help her.

The stakes of this ethical dilemma become clear in the next scene, which deals explicitly with the racial arrogance attributed to German women. The narrator describes a proud German woman, the fiancée of a member of the SS and the very image of the blond Aryan, who "looked a little askance at the Untermenschen":[51]

> And then we see One, blond and magnificent,
> Stride erect and quite unshyly
> Along the path beside the highway,
> Keeping her proud heart unbent . . .
> Sergeant Baturin, flower of crime,
> Ex-convict who had served his time
> In labor camp on the Amur
> Strode unspeaking up to her.[52]

The blond German escapes the threat of rape posed by Baturin, only to be shot when the Russian soldiers discover a letter from her SS fiancé. Again, the "I" is conflicted about his complicity in a crime that he could have prevented with a mere wave of the hand. What stops him is the memory of how one of the soldiers who shoots the German girl "found the graves of his family" who had been murdered by German soldiers.[53] The "I" is resigned to inaction because he knows that, as Caruth puts it, "history, like trauma, is never simply one's own, that history is precisely the way we are implicated in each other's trauma."[54] Confronted with crimes on both sides, the "I" wonders: "Who knows who's guilty? Who can tell?"[55]

While Solzhenitsyn depicts a narrating "I" who is paralyzed by the complex entanglement of crime, complicity, and victimization, Lev Kopelev, in his memoir, *To Be Preserved Forever* (1976), describes not only his attempts to prevent rape but also the consequences that resulted from it. Because he intervened on behalf of Germans, Kopelev was charged with "anti-Soviet agitation and propaganda," as well as "bourgeois humanism" and "pity for the enemy";[56] his loyalty to the party is questioned; and he is sentenced to spend ten years of his life in Stalin's labor camps.

Although rape plays a prominent role in the memoir, Kopelev never describes the act of rape, but tends to represent it through metonymy, by portraying the weapons used and the wounds that result from it. Upon entering the city of Neidenburg, for example, the author comes across a victim of rape: "On a side street, by a garden fence, lay a dead old woman. Her dress was ripped; a telephone receiver reposed between her scrawny thighs. They had apparently tried to ram it into her vagina."[57] Later, Kopelev conveys the trauma of rape through references to the victim's wounds and the guilty conscience of the perpetrator: "The palms of her hands were scratched and bloody. Belyaev bustled about, avoiding looking at me." Shortly thereafter, he describes a girl with "blond pigtails, a tear-stained face and blood on her stockings."[58] The focus on the visible signs of rape turns our gaze away from the perpetrator and his motivations, and toward the suffering of the victim. Kopelev does not engage in a discussion of the possible motivations and justifications of such crimes. Rather, he insists that indiscriminate violence comes back to haunt the perpetrators: "Senseless destruction does more damage to us than to them."[59]

Unlike Gelfand's diary, where consent and coercion are confused and rape is situated in close proximity to female complicity, and unlike Solzhenitsyn's poem, which presents an extended reflection on the confluence of victimization, crime, and complicity, *To Be Preserved Forever* displays a moral clarity that made Kopelev an outsider in his own nation. To be sure, there is a certain unfairness in such a comparison. Due to his early death, Gelfand never had the opportunity to transform his diary into a work of art or to revise it in light of postwar discourses. *Germany Diary* is a compilation of letters and notes, not a carefully crafted poem or memoir. And yet, such a comparison is not only necessary in light of the scarcity of texts on the subject of wartime rape from the Russian perspective, but also highly instructive. In addition to illustrating the impossibility of consent in the struggle for survival in the postwar period, Gelfand directly juxtaposes rape and racism. While Gelfand does not reflect on this juxtaposition, Solzhenitsyn develops its ethical complexity and points to a danger: as long as the conflicted narrator seeks to do justice to both sides, the suffering of the rape victims and the motivations of the rapists, he remains condemned to inaction. In contrast, Kopelev refuses to engage in a discussion of the motivations that lead to rape and thus allows for a moral clarity that facilitates his admirable intervention on behalf of the victims. Kopelev is able to offer such an unequivocal condemnation of rape because he himself is not entangled in a web of complicity. The question then is: how to read a similar absence of references to the rationale of the perpetrators and to German racism and atrocities in the memoirs of German rape victims?

Rape and Complicity: Lacunae in Rape Memoirs

While Gelfand runs the risk of erasing rape by substituting consent for coercion but remains acutely aware of German complicity, the memoirs of German rape victims often feature both rape and complicity as narrative lacunae.[60] Like their mythical ancestor Philomela, rape victims are silenced by their experience, but this silence takes many different forms. We know that, in some cases, it was all-encompassing. In his memoir, *Peeling the Onion* (2006), Günter Grass reports that "repeatedly suffered violence had silenced my mother."[61] Interestingly, Grass replicates his mother's silence by referring to nonspecific "violence," rather than calling rape by its name. In many other cases, though, rape victims wish to talk about their traumatic experience, but shy away from describing the act of rape: "I spoke about it again and again, but never about the act itself, that was unspeakable."[62] Most memoirs of wartime rape victims do not contain elaborate descriptions of the violence inflicted on their bodies. They tend to offer little context and avoid metaphors. Instead of detailed accounts, readers find generic references such as "what had to happen, happened."[63] The anonymous author of *A Woman in Berlin* offers a number of details regarding the rape, but she also wields a whole arsenal of periphrasis, including: "having to endure it," "dying," and "getting it." At times, she uses hyphens or ellipses for the act of rape.[64] Similarly, Gabi Köpp, the author of *Why Was I a Girl*, employs the phrase "again there is no mercy."[65] In her memoir *"Come, Woman, raboti": I Was Spoils of War* (*"Komm, Frau, raboti": Ich war Kriegsbeute*), Leonie Biallas comments on this fact: "Strangely enough nobody uses the word rape. They say 'taken.'"[66]

Indirect and circumlocutory expressions also characterize the description of rape in interviews. For example, the women who spoke with Helke Sander employed terms such as "sacrificed," "attacked," "being fetched," or "to have to get involved."[67] The women interviewed by Jacobs often referred to the rape as being fetched or taken by Russians.[68] It is likely that the reluctance to verbalize the bodily experience of rape is rooted in the shame and trauma associated with this particular form of violence. The fact that victims want to talk about rape, but address it primarily through periphrasis and circumlocution, suggests that they do not perceive full verbalization as helpful to their healing process. In addition to these psychological considerations, the political implications of wartime rape also reduced the willingness of rape victims to narrate their experience. For example, Köpp's hope that her memoir would be published "in a time when the civil victims of the end of war are no longer unjustly stamped as perpetrators"[69] implies that the author is acutely aware of the controversial nature of German discourses of victimhood.

In her memoir, *Why Was I a Girl? The Trauma of a Flight 1945*, published sixty-five years after the war in 2010, Köpp relates her experiences on the trek west from Schneidemühl, West Prussia. Köpp fled together with her sister, but without her mother, who sent the girls ahead because she believed that an early escape was safer. Unfortunately, this was not the case, and Köpp was raped multiple times. When the young Köpp tried to talk to her mother about her experiences, the latter refused to listen, but encouraged her to write about it. Köpp initially followed her mother's advice, but stopped writing when the process of remembering brought on recurring nightmares. Overwhelmed, Köpp locked her notes away in a safe and did not touch them for several decades.

Interestingly, the event that prompted her to open the safe and resume writing was the sixtieth anniversary of the liberation of Auschwitz, January 27, 2005. Thus, in Köpp's memoir, the Holocaust is not only a frame of reference, but a point of origin. Köpp looked at her notes because she wanted to know what she had reported in her diary on the date of the anniversary. As it turns out, January 27, 1945 was the darkest day of Köpp's life, the day when she was raped multiple times. Clearly, even though Köpp's personal story stands in stark contrast to the history of Europe's persecuted Jews, Köpp constructs it in parallel to their suffering. When Köpp boarded a west-bound train on January 26, 1945, she noticed showerheads and a sign reading: "delousing car." Köpp relates that she was unaware of the Holocaust at the time and did not link this experience to the mass murder of Jews until years later. Still, her description of her journey on the train cannot but evoke Holocaust imagery: officials bolt the doors, and the passengers are trapped when the train is bombed. Because Köpp does not develop these parallels, it is unclear whether she intends to compare her trauma to that of Jewish victims or whether the juxtaposition is circumstantial. What is clear, however, is that, in their conception and composition, narratives of the wartime rape of German women are inextricably linked to the German crimes that preceded them and that this link is often presented as a form of shared suffering rather than a chain of cause and effect.

While Köpp presents the rape as an omission, she offers descriptions of the selection process. In particular, Köpp cites the imperative, "*Frau, komm,*" with which Russian soldiers designated their specific victims. She also describes various attempts to hide from the Russians, to duck behind others, to crouch under tables, or to pretend to have a contagious illness. Furthermore, Köpp details threats and acts of violence against German rape victims. The rape itself, however, is unmentionable to the point that, several times in Köpp's memoir, the reader does not know whether she was raped or whether she resisted successfully.[70] Instead of a description of the rape, Köpp offers confirmation of the crime through references to tattered clothes and through italicized citations from the original diary that speak to her desolate emotional condition.[71]

In Köpp's memoir, rape and the threats of violence associated with it are by far the most traumatizing experiences. In spite of its overwhelming impact on its victims, however, rape is not an isolated trauma, but occurs in a general atmosphere of loss, betrayal, and deprivation. Several times, Köpp teams up with a companion who is killed shortly thereafter. Köpp also relates how she is repeatedly victimized by other women. From the start, her relation to her mother is deeply troubled. Köpp not only feels rebuffed by a mother who does not want to hear about the violence inflicted on her daughter, she also feels abandoned because her mother left her two daughters to fend for themselves: "In a certain way, she let me run into an open blade."[72] We know from similar accounts that Köpp's accusations are well-founded. The fact that she lacked the protection of a parent made Köpp an easy victim, not because her parents could have stopped the Russians, but because her isolation made her a convenient scapegoat when other mothers sought to protect themselves and their own daughters. Thus, when Russian soldiers threatened to shoot everybody unless some girls "volunteered," one of the women in the shelter promptly dragged the young Köpp out from underneath the table where she was hiding: "Out of icecold selfishness they sent a fifteen-year old girl to her doom through their betrayal."[73] The ethical and emotional challenges of the time are brought home when we learn later that the woman who betrayed Köpp becomes her closest friend in the group.

Throughout, Köpp interweaves citations from her original diary entries into her narrative. These citations are visually marked through italicization and form part of a dialogue between Köpp the fifteen-year-old diarist and Köpp the eighty-year-old professor of physics. Since the italicization marks these citations as foreign bodies in the text, readers expect an interplay of immediate experience and retrospective insights. And yet, much that is reported is left uncommented. For example, Köpp relates that the Russians justify their actions with references to German atrocities in their home-land. She continues by stating that she did not believe them because she thought of her father, whom she deemed incapable of such atrocities. No comment from the older Köpp follows to contextualize or relativize this account. Similarly, although Köpp avoids generalizations about Russian soldiers,[74] her descriptions of the Russian rapists, whom she calls "inhuman" and "beasts," cannot but echo Nazi jargon of "bestial subhumans."[75] To ask for political correctness from someone so brutally victimized at such an early age is a tall order. And yet, it is references such as these that have contributed to a silence about the suffering of German rape victims: the jarring presence of racist stereotypes in narratives of rape victims troubled the notion of innocent suffering and thus could not be integrated into our culturally available scripts of sexual victimization.[76]

The absence of retrospective contextualizations and explanations leaves readers in an uncomfortable position. In light of what Köpp experienced, it is not surprising that she wonders, "are these still humans?"[77] No reader of Köpp's memoir will fail to be moved by the enormous suffering and brutality inflicted on a fifteen-year-old girl, and Köpp's youth at the time certainly accounts for the lack of *Ideologiekritik*. And yet, we are not dealing with the young Köpp's diary, but with a memoir that was published after decades of highly publicized *Vergangenheitsbewältigung*. At the same time, some readers might be troubled not only by the absence of acknowledgments of German culpability but also by a discomfort with their own discomfort. After all, the reader's concern with a politically balanced account is afforded by what Tanner calls "the gap between intellectual relativity and physical absoluteness."[78] Readers can afford to be detached because, unlike the memoirist, they have not experienced the trauma of wartime rape. (To this day, Köpp is plagued by PTSD.) If readers are reluctant to engage in a political critique, it is because their "freedom parallels the autonomy of the violator."[79] But before we as readers succumb to silence, we might do well to remember Philomela's story in its entirety. In this myth, the mute victim overcomes the silence imposed on her as she expresses her trauma through weaving, and, as we know, the Latin verb for "weave" is *textere*. However, it is often forgotten that Philomela's creation serves to incite further violence. Philomela gives her tapestry to her sister Procne, who is married to the rapist, Tereus. Responding to this message, Procne kills their son, Itys. Importantly, the second victim here is not the perpetrator, but an innocent child. The perpetuation of violence in Philomela's story suggests that we should take great care when reading stories of rape: we should not hesitate to critique the ideological blind spots that inform the accounts of victims even if, in formulating such a critique, we are liable to reinhabit the position of the violator.

The Politicization of Rape

Rape is not only a crime, but also a powerful trope that lends itself to political appropriation. Indeed, in cases of wartime rape, the translation of sexual into national politics is seamless. In countless myths and stories, the rape of a woman stands metonymically for the conquest of a nation, so that woman's supposed vulnerability is made to signify a weakness in the body politic. Where women are raped, the husbands and fathers, who failed to protect them, are stripped of their authority and power. As Anonyma explains, "at the end of this war the defeat of men as a gender stands alongside many other defeats."[80]

The Nazis were acutely aware of this link and skillfully used it to further their political agenda. Hitler himself repeatedly invoked the specter of rape to encourage fierce resistance: "You soldiers from the East know to a large extent what destiny awaits German women, girls, and children. While old men and children will be killed, women and girls will be barrack whores."[81] Such rhetoric reached its climax when the Nazis elevated the atrocities of Nemmersdorf, the first ethnically German village taken by Russian soldiers, into a massacre of mythic proportions. In Günter Grass's *Crabwalk*, first published in 2002, *Nemmersdorf* is a code word that evokes the National Socialist instrumentalization of German suffering for the purpose of propaganda.

The politicization of rape narratives did not end with the Nazis, but extends into the present. Ingo Münch's book about the mass rapes is a case in point. Münch, a politician and professor emeritus of constitutional and international law, uses the plight of German women to highlight the immensity of German suffering and eclipse both German atrocities and female complicity. Because other national narratives fail in the context of the Holocaust, the rape of German women comes to signify the violation and rape of the entire German nation. In Münch's "pseudoscience of comparative victimology,"[82] the suffering of German women is "unparalleled": "never before have foreign soldiers abused so many women and girls in one country and within such a short period of time as the Red Army did in 1944/45 after the invasion of Germany."[83] Münch's desire to claim first rank in a competition of victims is highly problematic for a number of reasons. First, Münch's assertion that the German rapes are unique is based on his problematic reliance on statistics that remain "colored, to the last, by Goebbels's pen."[84] After all, as Anonyma reminds us, who was keeping count? Second, wartime rape has occurred in numerous cultures throughout history. During the past two decades, the rape of Muslim women in Bosnia-Herzegovina was widely discussed in Western media, but this too is not an isolated atrocity. Rather, rape and warfare frequently go hand in hand. Mass rapes took place in Pakistan, Guatemala, Nanking, Bosnia, Rwanda, Indonesia, Congo, Peru, Liberia, Haiti, Sudan, Myanmar, El Salvador, East Timor, Kuwait, Cambodia, Vietnam, Bangladesh, Afghanistan, Algeria, Somalia, and Sierra Leone. Rapes were part of almost every major military conflict, including the Thirty-Years' War, the First and Second World Wars,[85] the Vietnam War, and the Persian Gulf War, though they varied in scope and nature. Wartime rape may be chaotic or systematic, even strategic. Some armies institute rape camps and impregnation policies. Sometimes, the victims are forcibly abducted and kept in sexual slavery, as were the comfort women of the Japanese army during the Second World War. Other theaters of war involved rape-and-kill practices and forced incest. Of course, the number of victims is crucially important, but so is the suffering of every individual woman. Finally, it should not surprise us that Münch does not dwell on the fact that German women were not the only victims of rape during the Second World War. And yet, we know that Polish and Hungarian women, forced laborers from Ukraine and Poland, as well as Jewish survivors, were victimized along with non-Jewish German women.

In addition to his specious claim for German women's exceptional suffering, Münch relies on a problematic association of victimization and innocence. In Münch's version of events, victim and perpetrator are mutually exclusive and highly gendered categories. By definition, women and girls are innocent victims who were not complicit in Nazi crimes. Münch denies women political agency, and, in so doing, uses their supposed "innocence" to rehabilitate unspecified segments of the German population: "the nation of perpetrators . . . Those who consider this often used formula – by now a stereotype – appropriate and correct cannot entertain the thought that there were victims alongside the perpetrators."[86] As Heinemann has shown, the generalization of stories of female victimhood is a discursive maneuver that emerged in the immediate postwar period: Because "women's narratives emphasize their sufferings and losses and downplay their contributions to and rewards from the Nazi regime," they are easily appropriated in the formation of a national identity that emphasizes German victimhood.[87] As Heinemann points out, such appropriations have traditionally not served women well: "as rape became a powerful metaphor for German victimization, the government declined to recognize real rape by the enemy or occupier as a form of wartime injury deserving compensation."[88]

Furthermore, Münch maintains that the rape of German women cannot be interpreted as retaliation for the rape of Russian women, since the German army did not rape. He argues that German soldiers felt no desire for revenge. After all, their homeland had not been attacked, and they thus behaved in a more civilized manner. Finally, Münch, drawing on the trope of the romance of conquest, asserts that German soldiers did not need to rape, because Russian women were attracted to them.[89] As recent research has shown, however, Münch's assertion that German soldiers did not rape is simply wrong. Mühlhäuser offers detailed evidence that sexual violence was common on the eastern front.[90] She also reminds us that, whenever starvation is a clear and present threat, coercion and prostitution are all but indistinguishable.

Whereas Münch claims that German women, whom he lumps together with children, are collectively innocent, many Russian soldiers were convinced of the opposite. Naimark reminds us that Soviet newspapers portrayed German women as eager Nazis.[91] The often-quoted Russian slogan "break the racial arrogance of Germanic women with force" implies the support of German women for Nazi ideology that Münch denies. Moreover, Münch's focus on retaliatory rape obscures the fact that the revenge that Russian soldiers sought was not necessarily revenge for rape, but for other, nonsexual crimes. After all, 27 million citizens of the Soviet Union lost their lives in this war, two-thirds of whom were civilians. As Atina Grossmann points out, the image that Russian soldiers evoked in their quest for revenge is not that of a German raping a Russian woman, but that of a German soldier dashing a baby's head against a wall.[92]

While Münch's revisionist account hypertrophizes rape and denies women agency, historian Atina Grossmann has presented important work that highlights the racism and complicity of German women. Grossmann rightly points out that the figure of the Russian rapist reinforced German women's "preexisting convictions of cultural superiority,"[93] but she tends to downplay the suffering of the victims. Although she grants that, in some cases, rape may have been experienced as the worst of many horrible deprivations, she also assumes that, because rape was so common, its sting was not felt as acutely. According to Grossmann, women commented on the rapes with "unsentimental directness." She attributes this "sangfroid" to a "self-preserving sexual cynicism" that originated in "the modernist *Sachlichkeit* of Weimar culture and . . . the loosened mores of the Nazis' war."[94]

Grossmann's reference to sangfroid stands in a long tradition that reaches back to Erich Kuby's 1965 study *The Russians and Berlin, 1945,* which also minimizes the suffering of rape victims. According to Kuby, "it is a fact that many of the victims emerged from their unsavory experiences with a quiet, very feminine, grin."[95] Kuby, who sought to debunk anti-Russian stereotypes, introduced a number of highly problematic rape myths, including the assumption that "whoever had the inner strength and intelligence to show neither distrust nor fear, and made the right move at the right moment . . . usually managed to escape unmolested."[96]

To be sure, Kuby's and Grossmann's point that German racism did not end with the war is well taken. Such racism is plainly visible in the government directives that promoted abortion if a woman was raped by a Russian, but forbade it if the rapist was American.[97] Grossmann correctly points out that rape victims are not immune to racism. As Mardorossian explains, "there is no guarantee that being raped makes an individual more sensitive to the workings of the discursive context through which experience is given meaning. Victims are as likely to reproduce rape 'myths' as other members of society."[98] While Grossmann does well to remind us that rape was one of many traumatizing experiences, it does not follow that multiple sufferings reduce the weight of each individual trauma. In fact, a recent study by Eichhorn and Kuwert suggests that the trauma of rape was felt more acutely than other forms of brutalization and loss. According to Eichhorn and Kuwert, 74 percent of the female interviewees who had experienced multiple forms of traumatization during the war list rape as the most traumatic experience.[99] More importantly, though, quantitative rape comparisons run the risk of missing a crucial point: rape accounts do not present a uniform picture, but are riddled with unevenness and inconsistencies. Grossmann insightfully claims that *A Woman in Berlin* contains passages that are marked by unsentimental directness, but she fails to mention that, alongside these matter-of-fact passages, its author also reports pervasive depression, vomiting after the rape, feeling disgusted with her own skin, and being dead to all feelings.[100] Similarly, texts by Margret Boveri and Ruth Andreas-Friedrich contain matter-of-fact references to rape, but they also report numerous suicides and the intense suffering of rape victims.[101]

While Grossmann's research is largely based on written accounts, German historian Regina Mühlhäuser draws on interviews with rape survivors. Based on the conversations she conducted between 1995 and 1999, Mühlhäuser concludes that the laconic acceptance of rape that Grossmann perceives was not evident in any of these interviews. Interestingly, though, Mühlhäuser then suggests that the original experience of rape did not necessarily induce feelings of shame.[102] According to Mühlhäuser, the feelings of desperation and shame expressed in the interviews are a later ingredient, added because of the discursive exigencies of the postwar period. Again, it is undoubtedly true that memories of rape, like all memories, are shaped by dominant discourses and that such discourses may exacerbate or ameliorate the primary trauma. But to conclude from this premise that no desperation and shame was involved in the experience of rape is as questionable as it is epistemologically unfounded.

The fact that the effects of trauma change over time and may even intensify with age does not imply that the initial trauma did not cause suffering.

Dual Narratives of Complicity and Victimization in Recent Fiction

As the discussion of Münch's work shows, the topic of rape remains vulnerable to political appropriation. But while reactionary deployments of female victimization persist, recent fictionalizations of wartime rape experiment with new discursive strategies that no longer mandate silence about rape but also steer clear of emplotments that minimize female complicity. As I show in what follows, contemporary German women writers Julia Franck and Jenny Erpenbeck have both presented new narrative strategies for the representation of rape.

Franck and Erpenbeck are highly decorated authors: Erpenbeck is the recipient of the Ingeborg Bachmann Prize and the Heimito von Doderer Literaturpreis, while Franck was awarded the German Book Prize in 2007. Both are sometimes counted among the writers of the so-called *Fräuleinwunder*,[103] both were born in East Berlin – Franck in 1970 and Erpenbeck in 1967 – and both belong to a generation that was, as Janzen puts it, no longer directly affected by the Second World War and yet burdened with its legacy.[104] Indeed, it is precisely their position as "Nachgeborene," as Köhler calls it,[105] that may have facilitated their innovative approach to the fraught topic of rape. Published in 2007 and 2008, respectively, Franck's and Erpenbeck's novels mark the threshold, defined by the lifespan of three generations, at which the communicative memory of the witness gives way to objectified and symbolic forms of cultural memory.[106] In other words, the transition to a different generational cohort is accompanied by discursive shifts as emerging social and political frameworks of the present leave their imprint on individual recollections of the past.[107] Thus, it is hardly accidental that fictional representations of rape became possible in the wake of discourses on *Vergangenheitsbewältigung* and German victimization in the 1990s and 2000s. Some scholars, such as Berger, have even suggested that "the full acceptance of the extent of German crimes and German guilt was, in fact, the precondition for the emergence of the German victims' discourse in the second half of the 1990s."[108] Whereas Christa Wolf's 1976 *Patterns of Childhood* bracketed the trauma of rape because Wolf was convinced that any account of German suffering would necessarily participate in a revisionist discourse, Franck and Erpenbeck are no longer plagued by such fears. While Wolf was concerned that no amount of explaining could prevent the instrumentalization of rape,[109] Franck and Erpenbeck's novels attest to the authors' confidence that such misreadings can be prevented by framing the representation of rape within the larger discursive framework of National Socialist war crimes and female complicity.

Franck's *Blindness of the Heart* and Erpenbeck's *Visitation* are frequently characterized as family novels, a highly popular contemporary genre that tells "big history" in the form of family history and that tends to amalgamate fiction and fact.[110] As this definition suggests, family novels are ideally positioned to explore the tension between official, national history on the one hand and individual and family experiences on the other precisely because they are frequently situated across a tension of "fictionality and referentiality."[111] Both Franck and Erpenbeck integrated autobiographical elements by drawing on their parents' and grandparents' experiences.[112] In Franck's case, one of the characters, the young Peter Sehmisch, bears the name of the author's father. Like his fictional counterpart, Franck's father was abandoned at a train station in Vorpommern in 1945 while the family fled from Stettin. Like Peter, he was seven years old. Erpenbeck also mixes fictional elements with actual experiences of her parents and grandparents. Like the writer in *Visitation*, Erpenbeck's grandmother, communist Hedda Zinner, spent the Second World War in exile in Russia, where Erpenbeck's father was born. Another character in *Visitation*, a guest of the writer, was part of the trek, much like Erpenbeck's mother, who fled from Masuria to Berlin in 1945. Finally, like the granddaughter of the writer, Erpenbeck's family was faced with a restitution claim following German reunification.

In her study of contemporary family novels, Friederike Eigler claims that the children and grandchildren of family members who were actively involved in, or complicit with, Nazi crimes are more likely to minimize their parents' or grandparents' culpability than is the older generation itself. Drawing on Harald Welzer's work on family memory, Eigler attributes this to feelings of family loyalty.[113] Similarly, Rosenthal has shown that "in the families of perpetrators, the victim role of family members is heavily stressed."[114] This well-documented trend, however, is not evident in Franck's and Erpenbeck's novels. Neither *Blindness of the Heart* nor *Visitation* seeks to obfuscate the guilt of their fictionalized forebears: Franck highlights her fictionalized grandfather's involvement with National Socialism; conversely, Erpenbeck portrays a rape victim who is herself complicit with the National Socialist regime.[115] Their novels combine accounts of German culpability with the representation of the trauma of rape: Franck sidesteps some of the ethical challenges associated with the wartime rape of German women by choosing a Jewish protagonist rather than a non-Jewish German woman, while Erpenbeck combines the experience of the rape victim with the perspective of the rapist.

Julia Franck's novel *Blindness of the Heart*, published in 2007 and a recipient of the Deutscher Buchpreis, features a protagonist who is victimized by Russian soldiers and who herself victimizes her son. In the prologue, readers are introduced to Alice, a nurse, who is raped several weeks after the official end of the war and who subsequently abandons her son at a train station on the way west. The main sections of the book then explain the psychological motivations and historical forces that led to the abandonment. Through this narrative structure, *Blindness* invites us to empathize with the female protagonist and to understand an act that is likely to elicit condemnation and contempt.

After the prologue, which prominently features the rape scene as well as the abandonment, the text seemingly shifts gears. Under the header "The World Is Open to Us," it introduces us to young Helene, an exceptionally talented girl, who lives with her father, her mother, Selma Würsich, and her lesbian sister Martha in Stettin. Helene's family life is anything but idyllic. Her mother, a social outcast because she is Jewish, is mentally ill, and abuses Helene to the point of attacking her physically. In addition to her family troubles, Helene is a victim of racial and gender discrimination. She is a baptized Jew and an exceptionally gifted girl in a society without professional options for women. Both of Helene's parents ignore her outstanding performance in school. When she works as a nurse, the supervising professor insists that women can be assistants, but should not be allowed to attend university.[116]

In the next section of the book, entitled "No Moment More Beautiful Than This One," Helene's already troubled family disintegrates further when the father dies from injuries incurred in the First World War and the family's wealth is wiped out by the Great Depression. Helene and Martha move to Berlin, where Martha is reunited with her now married lover Leontine and becomes a morphine addict. Helene falls in love with Carl Wertheimer, a student of philosophy, aborts his child, but wishes to marry him. When he is killed in a bicycle accident, Helene's dream of a future with Carl and her plan to study medicine die with him. Alone in the city, Helene is left to grieve the loss of her fiancé.

In the last section, titled "Night Trap," a grieving, apathetic Helene meets the blond and blue-eyed Wilhelm Hanussen, who pursues her until she agrees to marry him – "one day resistance was too cumbersome for her."[117] Unlike the artistic and literary Carl, Wilhelm is an engineer and an enthusiastic National Socialist. When he learns that Helene is half Jewish, he procures fake papers for her under the name Alice Schulze. But Wilhelm's love for Alice is short-lived, and the marriage falls apart quickly. Because Helene/Alice had to cut off all contact to relatives and friends to maintain her fake identity, she is now completely alone. Selma is institutionalized at Schloss Sonnenstein, Martha is in a labor camp, and her Aunt Fanny has been deported.

Although readers will have realized that Helene is Alice, the text withholds confirmation for some 300 pages. Once the identity is confirmed, though, Helene's rape by Russian soldiers emerges as the endpoint in a long history of victimization: in her aunt's house, Helene is a victim of sexual harassment: her aunt's lover Erich "kissed her wherever and however he liked."[118] The most drastic form of sexual exploitation, however, occurs in her relationship with her husband. Sex with Wilhelm is characterized by one principle: "the less she wanted to the better he appeared to like it."[119] Alternating between professorial instructions in sexual matters – "it doesn't work like this"; "that is love, Alice" – and insults, Wilhelm is titillated by resistance: "She resisted, this aroused him."[120] Throughout, the textual descriptions of their sexual encounters evoke (marital) rape: "He drove his member into her, stroke by regular stroke, as a hammer drives a nail into the wall."[121] Wilhelm's interest in Helene does not survive her defloration. Once his sexual curiosity is satisfied, he begins to find fault with her "*Rasse*" and soon abandons both Helene and their son, Peter. As a final blow, Helene, who must keep her real identity hidden, is alienated from her own son, who, unaware of his Jewish heritage, apes Nazi propaganda and even sings anti-Semitic ditties.

It is significant that the main sections of the novel are told by a third-person narrator, but from Helene's perspective. In contrast, both the prologue and the epilogue about the failed reconciliation of mother and son are told from the perspective of Helene's son, Peter. Peter is an eyewitness to the rape of his mother by Russian soldiers, but fails to comprehend the significance of the event:[122]

> The door to the apartment was left ajar, Peter opened it. He saw three men around the kitchen table, on which his mother was half sitting, half lying. The naked bottom of a man moved back and forth at Peter's eye level, his flesh wobbled with such force that Peter wanted to laugh. But the soldiers held his mother tight. Her skirt was torn, her eyes opened wide, Peter did not know whether she saw him or saw through him. Her mouth was gaping open – but she remained silent. . . . His mother had been visited by soldiers once before.[123]

Whereas other sections of the text are highly attuned to Helene's bodily sensations and quite eloquent in their rendering of premarital and marital sex, pregnancy, abortion, and breastfeeding, the prologue does not dwell on Helene's experience of the rape, but rather chooses to stay at a distance. Readers witness the rape through Peter's distorted testimony, and deduce Helene's traumatization from her compulsive cleaning, from her icy manner toward Peter, and from her sudden revulsion at Peter's emerging sexuality, which includes her decision to ban Peter from her bed.[124] In addition, the text conveys the pervasiveness of rape from snippets of conversation about a woman who was speared to death[125] and a woman who bled to death after a rape, and from Helene's encounter with a wounded nurse who was infected with syphilis.

In choosing to narrate the rape from the perspective of a young child, who fails to comprehend the emotional and political significance of rape, and by focusing on a German Jewish victim, *Blindness* sidesteps some of the ethical pitfalls involved in discussing the wartime rape of non-Jewish German women. If the text had featured a non-Jewish German woman, it would have had to address her potential involvement in National Socialist crimes. Even so, however, Franck does not eschew the topics of complicity and guilt altogether. As a Jew, Helene is first and foremost a victim of Nazi racial politics, but the text highlights her agency and complicates our perception of her by portraying her as a victim in one context and a perpetrator in another. Readers learn that, in her Aryan guise, Helene/Alice is an active participant in the Nazi sterilization program,[126] and that her maternal duties are the only reason that prevents her transfer to Meseritz-Obrawalde, one of the Nazi euthanasia centers. Most importantly, Helene is not only involved in the execution of Nazi policy, but also becomes a perpetrator in relation to her son – although the text is clear that this occurs after, and possibly as a result of, the rape.[127]

Because the terse and distanced description of the rape by Russian soldiers is preceded by lengthy passages that dwell on Helene's sexual victimization by Wilhelm, the rape by Russians is almost an afterthought, a final confirmation or master metaphor for the "Night Trap" that Helene's life has become, that is, for her multiple victimizations in a sexist and racist society. By the time the Russians arrive, irreparable damage has already been done to Helene's spirit. Thus, Franck tells a story of wartime rape that does not invert historical parameters by casting Germans as victims and Russians as aggressors. Rather, in *Blindness*, Helene's Nazi husband remains the primary culprit, and the target of his violence is Jewish.

Franck's novel is at its best when the text traces subtle ambiguities. The madness of Helene's mother, Selma, for example, is presented as both a degenerative disease and a form of radical resistance.[128] However, while Franck's female figures are complex and intriguing,[129] many of the male characters in the novel appear flat. Helene's father, for example, is a pale creature compared to the female family members. The doctor in the Stettin clinic and the men in Fanny's house are sexually aggressive chauvinists. Wilhelm has no redeeming quality of any kind, and the Russian soldiers who rape Helene are presented as carousing brutes – "they were in a good mood."[130] Interestingly, though, while the representation of almost all male characters in the novel – with the exception of Peter – lacks nuance, the rape scene hints at a story that is not being told and that has the potential to complicate our perception of this event. In passing, Peter notices a crying soldier: "head in his hands, the man sat on the floor sobbing."[131] Unlike Erpenbeck, however, Franck, whose feminist agenda is more pronounced, does not develop this motif: the motivations and background of the rapists remain unexplored.

The genre of the family novel in general and *Blindness* in particular have been accused of ignoring politics in favor of family dynamics. In her discussion of contemporary fiction since 1989, Eigler, for example, is concerned about the "privatization and trivialization of historical relations . . . so that the Germans appear as the real victims of the ideological aberrations and catastrophes of the 20th century."[132] Similarly, in her reading of Franck's novel, Eidukeviciene claims that "instead of the historical guilt of the war generation, personal guilt becomes the center of interest (e.g., the lack of maternal feeling) . . . the emphasis on gender conflicts (abuse of a wife by her husband, rape by Russian soldiers)."[133] Along the same lines, Janzen, who, rather problematically, posits a one-to-one identity between Franck's grandfather and the character of Wilhelm – laments that "although Franck's grandfather is portrayed as a Nazi, this is less important than the fact that he abused her grandmother."[134] To be sure, such a critique is not without foundation: in *Blindness* historical and political events function as little more than a distant roar in the background. Because the characters are uninformed about politics – "what did they know about world events?"[135] – these world events are not discussed in detail but are mentioned only in passing. There is a quick reference to mobilization when the First World War is about to start, and later on readers casually learn about the boycott of Jewish businesses. And yet, it does not follow that Franck's novel is apolitical. On the contrary, precisely because grand historical events are relegated to the background, *Blindness* illustrates that political decisions have pervasive and violent consequences for everyone, including those who do not concern themselves with world affairs. Similarly, Wilhelm may be the most visible representative of National Socialism, but the text does not reduce Nazi racial politics to sexual politics. Rather, the political becomes visible because it is intertwined with the personal: Helene agrees to marry Wilhelm partly because she is depressed and no longer has the energy to resist him, but also, and most importantly, because she is left without other options: fired from the hospital when she cannot provide proof of Aryan descent, Helene can no longer provide for herself, and so is forced to enter into a marriage of convenience with a man she does not love.

Just as *Blindness* circumvents the discursive traps inherent in the representation of wartime rape, it also redefines the meaning of the much-cited taboos and silences regarding German suffering. The German title contains a reference to the Slavic (in this case, Sorbian) folk legend of the "*Mittagsfrau*," which is designed to illustrate the harmful consequences of silence. "Lady Midday," otherwise known as the Noon Woman or Noon Demon, is a mythical character, originally a personification of sunstroke, who haunts workers laboring in the field. Carrying a scythe or shears, she attempts to engage the workers in conversation and kills anyone who fails to talk to her. Clearly, in this legend, salvation lies in narration: only those who can talk about their labors will survive unharmed. This maxim certainly applies to Franck's novel. However, unlike in recent public debates, where the concept of silence tends to refer to the victimization of Germans and to the rape of German women in particular, in Franck's novel the silence in question is that of a Jewish character who survives by hiding her true identity. With all her friends and relatives either dead or persecuted by the Nazis, Helene has no one left to talk to. And because her young son cannot be trusted to keep her secret, Helene cannot tell him the truth.[136] Because she cannot communicate openly, Helene, a victim of rape and Nazi racial politics, becomes herself a victimizer in relation to her son. One may fault Franck for choosing an atypical victim, a Jewish woman in hiding, and thus skirting the confluence of complicity and victimization that adheres to the rape of a Nazi woman by a Russian soldier. But one might also commend her for creating a narrative that portrays wartime rape without recycling Nazi narratives or obfuscating German guilt.

Like *Blindness, Visitation* (2008) is frequently assigned to the much-discussed genre of the family or generational novel that seeks to negotiate the "relationship between private and public memory."[137] However, as

Probst points out, in Erpenbeck's case this categorization is not entirely accurate.[138] *Visitation* does not tell the story of a family. Rather, it chronicles the history of a house and its various inhabitants.[139] In so doing, the text includes a variety of perspectives of different third-person narrators, who are not related to each other. These perspectives are in turn framed by a prologue and an epilogue, and are separated by brief interludes that focus on a gardener who takes care of the house and yard. While the activities of the gardener, who bears "traits of a mythical figure,"[140] are repetitive, and as cyclical as the recurrence of the seasons, all other characters in Erpenbeck's novel are deeply affected by the course of history. They include: the farmer who originally owned the land; the architect who built the house; his Jewish neighbor who emigrated to South Africa while his family was killed in the Holocaust; the wife of the architect; the niece of the Jewish neighbor who hid in a ghetto but was discovered and killed; the Soviet soldier who raped the architect's wife; a female writer who was in exile in the Soviet Union; a female refugee from Poland and guest in the house of the writer; a tenant who lives in the shed, having tried to flee the GDR; the childhood friend of the writer's granddaughter; and the writer's granddaughter. As this cast of characters with vastly different backgrounds and stories indicates, Erpenbeck's "discontinuous, multi-voiced narrative"[141] is ideally suited to the representation of a complex event from multiple angles.

Like *Blindness, Visitation* portrays the rape of a German woman by a Russian soldier. Here, the victim is the wife of a National Socialist architect who was a member of the *Gruppe Albert Speer Germania Projekt*, a group charged with rebuilding Berlin after Hitler's projected *Endsieg*. Erpenbeck characterizes the architect as an opportunist with highly flexible morals who benefits from his alliance with the Nazi regime.[142] Readers learn that the architect's application to the *Reichskulturkammer* was accepted because he omitted information about his Jewish great-grandparents, and that he subsequently bought the property of his Jewish neighbors for half its value. The exploitative nature of this transaction is revealed in Erpenbeck's rendering of the architect's self-justifications: "After all, he had paid half the current market value. And even that was quite a bit."[143] Far from recognizing the injustice of the expropriation of Jewish property, the architect casts himself as a savior who helps his neighbors escape by financing their emigration.

Like her husband, the architect's wife leads a comfortable life during the Nazi regime. Her husband laughingly teases her about her "resistance" to the regime, which consists in her refusal to give the *Führer* children.[144]

Clearly, in this home, resistance is a joke. The picture that emerges is one of complete indifference to the plight of the Jews in the Third Reich, illustrated by a conversation in which a friend of the family, a film director, talks about the difficulty of making Aryan actors look like "annoying Jewish hustlers."[145] By highlighting the Nazi affiliation of the architect and his wife, Erpenbeck insists that the victim of rape is not an innocent, but one of the many Germans who made the regime possible through their indifference and determination to look the other way: "Humor is when you laugh anyway."[146]

Like Franck, Erpenbeck does not depict the rape through the eyes of the victim. Instead, it is told from the perspective of the perpetrator. In so doing, Erpenbeck provides information that contextualizes the crime. When the Red Army soldier is introduced, readers learn that his entire family was murdered by the Germans: "He volunteered when he was fifteen after his mother, his father and his sisters had been killed by the Germans."[147] Thus, Erpenbeck situates the rape in the larger context of German war crimes in the East. Second, Erpenbeck shows us a Russian soldier who is overwhelmed by the immensity of German material wealth. Consequently, from his perspective, the German desire to conquer a country that is so much poorer than Germany appears all the more gratuitous: "The more German houses they entered, the more painfully they wondered why the Germans could not have stayed there, where they lacked nothing, really not the tiniest little thing."[148] This emphasis on German wealth is designed to highlight the criminal nature of the Nazi war of conquest, which is further underlined by the parallel between the wife's hiding place and the hidden nature of the Nazi genocide: When *der Rotarmist*, who has slept in the architect's bedroom for several days before he notices anything untoward, finds the architect's wife hidden in a closet, he comments: "Perhaps the Germans had hidden too much before."[149]

In addition to creating a historical context for the representation of rape, *Visitation* emphasizes the youth and inexperience of the soldier who, before the rape, has never even kissed a woman, and who calls his victim "mama." The rape itself is presented as a disturbing mixture of coercion and tenderness: "Then he releases her arms and caresses the woman's head, she no longer defends herself, but he hears her begin to cry, he caresses her head as if to comfort her."[150] Tellingly, the metaphor that dominates the subsequent narration of the rape is warfare, and it is not clear who is attacking whom:

Maybe war consists only in the shift of the front lines, because now that she
pushes his head between her legs, perhaps only pushes it between her legs
because she knows that the soldier has a weapon and it is smarter not to
defend oneself, she takes control. . . . And when the young soldier now,
perhaps only because he is afraid of the woman, pushes his tongue between
her curly hair . . . a hot stream, first gingerly, then more forcefully, gushes
over his face, the woman pees in his face . . . so she is waging a war after all, or
is this love, the soldier does not know. . . . Amidst the silence the woman
attacks again . . . grabs his dick through his pants and pushes the boy to the
ground . . . he no longer defends himself.[151]

The narrative of the rape as told from the perspective of the *Rotarmist* raises
doubts whether we are dealing with an act of violence or of seduction.[152]
Interestingly, this is typical of rape narratives told from the perspective of
the perpetrator.[153] When seen through the eyes of the victim, though,
a different picture emerges. From the perspective of the architect's wife,
the rape is a traumatic experience that separates her life into a before and
after and robs her of her laughter:

And then the Russian came. She does not want to think the word, the word
with which he called her, the unthinkable word with which he drilled a hole
in her eternity for all eternity. Her body, already barren at the time, had
pulled him, who had known the word that disempowered her, toward her
with great force, and had suffocated her laughter that had been in his way for
so long, for approximately the time it takes to give birth, during this night –
in the hidden closet that her husband had built just for her, because she had
wanted it then, when she still was a circus princess – she had finally defected
to the enemy.[154]

While the Russian soldier is confused about the meaning of the rape, the
victim experiences it as a life-shattering event that irreparably damages her
relation to the other sex. We learn that she bequeaths the house to her
nieces, and "definitely not to any man."[155]

In addition to juxtaposing the perspectives of the architect's wife and the
Rotarmist as well as the war against an enemy and that against a menopausal
body,[156] *Visitation* further refracts our perception of rape by creating
parallels to two more stories. First, the motif of hiding from an enemy
reappears in the story of *Das Mädchen*, who also takes refuge in a closet in
the dark. Unlike the architect's wife who hides from the Russians,
das Mädchen, the niece of the architect's neighbors, hides from the
Nazis.[157] She is the last inhabitant of a ghetto from which everybody else
has already been deported. Like the architect's wife, she is found, but in her
case the consequences of being found are fatal: she is shot.

While the story of *das Mädchen*, which is situated between that of the architect's wife and that of the *Rotarmist*, serves to put the experience of the architect's wife in perspective – she survives her victimization, *das Mädchen* does not – the story of the *Kinderfreund* reminds readers of the horror of rape. The writer's granddaughter and her childhood friend witness the rape of a twelve-year-old girl in the woodshed. Here, however, it is not the victim who hides, but rather the witnesses, who secretly observe the rape from behind a stack of wood. Interestingly, even for the witnesses, rape is presented as a traumatic and lasting experience: "The seeing from back then still continues."[158] Here, too, the rape ruptures the sense of time as the *Kinderfreund* reflects that "they never got out, but remain sitting under the roof of the shed even today ... that one is more firmly tied to a place through shared greed and shame than through shared happiness, he wishes he had never learned this."[159] By relying on a multi-voiced narrative, Erpenbeck succeeds in contextualizing the rape historically, while at the same time conveying its traumatic impact on its victims and witnesses. Because we are dealing with a multiplicity of nonrelated narrators, whose stories are organized around common motifs, the representation of German suffering does not serve to minimize female complicity.

In *Geschichte im Gedächtnis*, Aleida Assmann suggests that the "father literature" of the 1970s and 1980s tends to emphasize the distance from the previous generation, and is intent on uncovering the hidden guilt of family members – "their thematic center is the confrontation, the argument, the reckoning with the father"[160] – whereas family novels highlight continuities. Similarly, Eigler suggests that the new family novels are characterized by "a high degree of distance and reflection" on the one hand, and "the propensity to empathy and affective intimacy with one's ancestors" on the other.[161] Although both Assmann's and Eigler's observations are astute characterizations of a large number of texts, they do not fully describe *Blindness* and *Visitation*. To be sure, neither Franck nor Erpenbeck seeks to uncover hidden crimes – but only because the guilt of the Nazi generation is plain for all to see. Similarly, there are signs of an "affective intimacy" in Franck's novel, but this only applies to some characters, not to others: while Franck's representation of Helene is characterized by compassion and sympathy, her portrait of Wilhelm remains distant. In contrast, Erpenbeck's novel shows no sign of an emotional intimacy, even though it traces the motivations and intentions of all her characters, rapist and rape victim alike. Finally, neither Franck nor Erpenbeck's novels create a sense of continuity, but rather emphasize ruptures and irreconcilable differences between the generations. And yet, perhaps it is precisely because they do not fulfill genre expectations that *Blindness* and *Visitation* succeed in portraying rape without falling into the trap of highlighting German suffering while minimizing female complicity. By introducing multiple perspectives and juxtaposing multiple forms of traumatization, Franck and Erpenbeck have created texts in which suffering and guilt stand side by side without canceling each other out.

Conclusion

Undoubtedly, complicity is at the heart of the silence that attends narratives of rape: a sense of complicity may motivate the victim to remain silent about her experience, but it may also prevent others from listening to her story. There is a danger in privileging decontextualized accounts of individual rape victims that work strenuously to maintain an intimate link between victimization and innocence. If we listen to these accounts exclusively, we may indeed "exchange history for emotion."[162] But there is also a price to be paid if we exclude these stories from the canon. The literature of war abounds with descriptions of the trauma of the front, of the physical and psychological wounds of war. As Ann Cahill points out, "as a society, we laud war heroes, listen intently to their suffering (and the sufferings they imposed on others). We do not wish to hear the sufferings of rape victims."[163] And yet, if we are to understand the repercussions of war, then it is vital that every form of wartime victimization enter the official record and form part of our concepts and imaginations of war. At the same time, if we want to explore the complexities of female complicity in the Second World War and the Holocaust, we need to approach stories of rape with a critical perspective. In other words, we should heed the stories of rape victims but also reject the legacy of racism that they may imply, not least because such stories, and their interrupted silences, teach us to question pat dichotomies of victims and perpetrators and of silence and discourse. And as we recognize the ambivalent legacy of stories of rape, embodied in the myth of Philomela, we may also remember another rape victim in classic mythology who did not write her story: the beautiful maiden Medusa, who was raped by Poseidon in Athena's temple and then turned into a monster by the goddess, who was enraged over the defilation of her sacred space. Clearly, there is a legacy of violence in both silence and in narrative, but there is also an ethics of reading and writing that allows one to pay tribute to the victims' suffering even as one negotiates and recontextualizes their stories.

Notes

1. Niven, "Introduction," 8. Anne Fuchs points out that these works are often presented as a "triumphant recovery of unofficial private memories of the Nazi period" (*Phantoms of War in Contemporary German Literature, Films and Discourse*, 7).
2. There are a number of excellent analyses of rape discourses in films such as *Deutschland, Bleiche Mutter*, and *BeFreier und Befreite*: see McCormick, "Rape and War, Gender and Nation, Victims and Victimizers"; Grossmann; Koch, "Blut, Sperma, Tränen"; Bos; Dahlke; Prager, "Occupation as the Face of War"; and Smith, "Sounds of Silence," 180–181.
3. See Rogoff, "Von Ruinen zu Trümmern," 265; Dahlke, "Tagebuch des Überlebens," 212.
4. Sielke, *Reading Rape*, 2.
5. A discussion of feminist discourses on rape would exceed the scope of this chapter. Suffice it to say that I agree with Seifert that "rape is not an aggressive manifestation of sexuality, but rather a sexual manifestation of aggression" ("War and Rape," 55) and with Cahill, who states, "it *matters* that sexuality is the medium of the power and violence" inflicted on the victim (*Rethinking Rape*, 27).
6. See Jacobs, *Freiwild*, 10; Naimark, *The Russians in Germany*, 133; Sander, "Zuwort zum Vorwort," 5.
7. Petö suggests a link between the force of German resistance to the Russian army and the number of rapes in a given area ("Stimmen des Schweigens," 894).
8. For example, Hildegard Knef cross-dressed as a soldier to avoid being raped (*Der geschenkte Gaul*, 76).
9. Higgins and Silver, *Rape and Representation*, 3.
10. Cohen-Pfister, "Rape, War, and Outrage," 318.
11. Eichhorn and Kuwert, *Das Geheimnis unserer Großmütter*, 9.
12. The anonymous author of *Eine Frau in Berlin* is an excellent example of this dialectic of silence and discourse. For example, Anonyma declares that rape victims will have to remain silent about their experience (163) *and* that women come to terms with the rapes by talking about them (161).
13. Naimark, *The Russians in Germany*, 3. See also Garraio, who demonstrates that Cold War anticommunist discourses used the mass rapes to demonize the Soviet Union ("Hordes").
14. Niethammer, *Deutschland danach*, 562.
15. Brownmiller, *Against Our Will*, 64.
16. See Eichhorn and Kuwert, *Das Geheimnis unserer Großmütter*, 30, Poutrus, "Ein fixiertes Trauma," 121, and Dahlke, "Frau komm."
17. Cohen-Pfister, "Rape, War, and Outrage," 321; see also Taberner and Berger, "Introduction," 2.
18. Ferguson, "Rape and the Rise of the Novel," 99.
19. Sielke, *Reading Rape*, 1.

20. Linda Williams offers another perspective on the question of silence. She suggests that the rape scenario that is most conducive to reporting is characterized by the following factors: rape in public, rape by a stranger, high degree of force, serious injury, and physical and verbal resistance.

21. Caruth, *Unclaimed Experience*, 3.

22. Tanner, *Intimate Violence*, 10.

23. Alexijewitsch's monumental work on Russian women soldiers contains two references to the rape of German women by Russians; see *Der Krieg hat kein weibliches Gesicht*, 36 and 338.

24. Beevor believes that sexual repression under Stalin contributed to the excesses in Germany (*The Fall of Berlin 1945*, 45). Russian soldiers, unlike the Germans, did not have access to field brothels, nor were they granted home leaves (although officers routinely kept mistresses, so-called field wives).

25. See Merridale, *Ivan's War*, 14, 21.

26. Merridale, *Ivan's War*, 312.

27. Cited in Naimark, *The Russians in Germany*, 72.

28. Cited in Nawratil, *Schwarzbuch der Vertreibung 1945 bis 1948*, 228.

29. See Naimark, *The Russians in Germany*, 85.

30. According to Bourke, the fantasy of consent is typical of accounts of rape told from the perspective of the perpetrators, whose "recitals of consent . . . and pleasure . . . are attempts by sexual abusers to integrate their actions into a bearable narrative of the self" (*Rape*, 14). For an investigation of the motives of soldier-rapists, see Price, "Finding the Man in the Soldier-Rapist." For information on the structural conditions that facilitate wartime rape, see Morris, "By Force of Arms."

31. "Sie haben das aus eigenem Bedürfnis gemacht" (cited in Sander 119).

32. Jacobs, *Freiwild*, 8.

33. Merridale quotes from a letter written by a young soldier in 1943: "In the army they regard women like gramophone records. . . . You play it and play it and then throw it away" (*Ivan's War*, 239). See also Reeves Sanday, who concludes that "female power and authority is lower in rape-prone societies" ("Rape and the Silencing of the Feminine," 85).

34. There were 1,198 documented cases of rape by French soldiers in the city of Stuttgart alone (Lilly, *Taken by Force*, xvi); on the rape of German women by French soldiers, see Bechdolf, "Den Siegern gehört die Beute." Lilly estimates that "the United Kingdom had slightly less than 2,500 rapes, France more than 3,600, and Germany more than 11,000" by US soldiers (*Taken by Force*, 12). Gebhardt argues that the last number is far too low. She demonstrates that 190,000 German women were raped by American soldiers (see also Kardorff, *Berliner Aufzeichnungen 1942–45*, 321). In France, 152 American soldiers were tried for rape (Roberts, *What Soldiers Do*, 195). According to Roberts, many rape charges in France were motivated by racial prejudice: African Americans were more likely to be accused of rape and also far more likely to be executed for it than white soldiers (199–213).

35. Beevor, *The Fall of Berlin 1945*, 31.

36. Cited in Bourke, *Rape*, 373.

37. In her afterword, Elke Scherstjanoi assures readers that Gelfand's sexual interests were reciprocated by the German women he approached and notes that the war had led to promiscuity ("Ein Rotarmist in Deutschland," 328).

38. "Zärtlichkeiten nicht ab[lehnen], wie sie ja allgemein nichts ablehnen" (Gelfand, *Deutschland Tagebuch 1945–46*, 111).

39. On the troubled notion of consent when starvation is a real threat, see also Röger's analysis of occupied Poland ("Sexual Contact between German Occupiers and Polish Occupied in World War II Poland").

40. "Habe ich auf dem Altar für vertrauensvolle und wohlwollende Beziehungen Lebensmittel, Süssigkeiten und Butter, Wurst und teure deutsche Zigaretten niedergelegt. Bereits die Hälfte wäre genug, um mit Fug und Recht mit der Tochter vor den Augen der Mutter alles Erdenkliche anzustellen. . . . Lebensmittel sind heute wertvoller als das Leben" (Gelfand, *Deutschland Tagebuch 1945–46*, 157).

41. "Aus der dritten Gruppe wurde die 'Beute' über die Häuser und Betten verteilt, und dort wurden einige Tage lang mit ihnen Experimente angestellt, die auf Papier nicht wiederzugeben sind. Die Deutschen hatten Angst; den jüngeren widersetzten sie sich nicht, und sie flehten diese an, daß sie mit ihnen schlafen sollten, um bloß den Schändungen durch die älteren Soldaten zu entgehen. Zu dieser glücklichen Altersgruppe gehörte auch Andropow. Er wählte sich die Allerjüngste und nahm sie mit, um mit ihr zu schlafen. Doch als er sie bedrängte, sein grundlegendes Anliegen zu befriedigen, schüttelte sie den Kopf und flüsterte verschämt: {Das ist nix gut}, ich bin doch Jungfrau. . . . Sie weigerte sich noch eine ganze Zeit, bis er die Pistole zog. Da wurde sie still und zog zitternd ihre Gamaschenhose herunter. . . . Da gab er mit einem Nicken zur Pistole den Rat: nur {gut machen}. . . . So arbeiteten sie einmütig und kamen ans Ziel. Er spürte, daß etwas zerriß, das Mädchen schrie auf und stöhnte. . . . Sie konnte sich aber bald zu einem Lächeln zwingen. Er gab ihr Zivilkleidung, ein Kleid zum Anziehen, und sie ging nach draußen zu ihren Leidensgenossinnen, fröhlich und unschuldig" (Gelfand, *Deutschland Tagebuch 1945–46*, 62).

42. See "sie . . . versuchte mich zu überreden, sie gehenzulassen. Das konnte ich selbstverständlich nicht tun, denn was wäre ich dann für ein Mann" ("She tried to persuade me to let her go. I could not do this, of course. After all, what kind of man would I be" (Gelfand, *Deutschland Tagebuch 1945–46*, 186).

43. "Sie sprach mit Abscheu von den Juden, erklärte mir die Rassentheorie. Faselte von weißem, rotem und blauem Blut" (Gelfand, *Deutschland Tagebuch 1945–46*, 187).

44. "Obskurantismus stümperhafter faschistischer Theoretiker" (Gelfand, *Deutschland Tagebuch 1945–46*, 187).

45. He refers to intercourse as "dem, was meiner Vorstellung nach unbedingt passieren musste" ("that which, according to my notions, absolutely had to happen") (Gelfand, *Deutschland Tagebuch 1945–46*, 187).

46. Solzhenitsyn, *Prussian Nights*, 3.

47. See "we have ourselves to save" (Solzhenitsyn, *Prussian Nights*, 7).
48. Solzhenitsyn, *Prussian Nights*, 19.
49. Solzhenitsyn, *Prussian Nights*, 37–39.
50. Solzhenitsyn, *Prussian Nights*, 51.
51. Solzhenitsyn, *Prussian Nights*, 81.
52. Solzhenitsyn, *Prussian Nights*, 77–85.
53. Solzhenitsyn, *Prussian Nights*, 87.
54. Caruth, *Unclaimed Experience*, 24.
55. Solzhenitsyn, *Prussian Nights*, 87. Pointing to the last lines of the poem, in which the "I" himself engages in rape, Brostrom claims that Solzhenitsyn aims to show that we must "rise above passive distress over barbarism" (*"Prussian Nights,"* 241).
56. Kopelev, *To Be Preserved Forever*, 9 and 10.
57. Kopelev, *To Be Preserved Forever*, 39.
58. Kopelev, *To Be Preserved Forever*, 49 and 54.
59. Kopelev, *To Be Preserved Forever*, 38.
60. Like all memoirs, those of German rape victims are shaped by the discursive environment in which they are written and thus reflect the various phases of *Vergangenheitsbewältigung*. Even so, the preference for periphrasis characterizes memoirs of the immediate postwar period as well as recent memoirs. However, note that these texts are difficult to date: recent memoirs often build on diaries or letters that were written during or immediately after the Second World War.
61. "Mehrmals erlittene Gewalt hatte die Mutter verstummen lassen" (Grass, *Peeling the Onion*, 271).
62. "Ich habe immer wieder 'darüber' gesprochen, allerdings nie über den Akt an sich, das war unaussprechlich" (Jacobs, *Freiwild*, 47).
63. "Es geschah, was geschehen musste" (Böddeker, *Die Flüchtlinge*, 140).
64. "Es mehrfach aushalten müssen" (Anonyma, *Eine Frau in Berlin*, 69), "dran glauben müssen" (134), "es abbekommen" or "abkriegen," and "es hat sie erwischt" (140–149). For ellipses, see Anonyma, *Eine Frau in Berlin*, 57, 62, 178; see also Bletzer, "A Voice for Every Woman and the Travesties of War," 701, and Prager, "Occupation as the Face of War," 72–73.
65. "Wieder gibt es ... kein Erbarmen" (Köpp, *Warum war ich bloß ein Mädchen?*, 93).
66. "Eigenartigerweise spricht niemand das Wort Vergewaltigung aus. Sie sagen 'genommen'" (Biallas, *"Komm, Frau, raboti,"* 22). See also Tröger, who points out that Anonyma uses the "old-fashioned, biblical word defilement throughout, although rape was the more common word" ("Between Rape and Prostitution," 101). On the use of circumlocution when referring to rape, see also Garraio, "Schlüsselbegriff," 6–7.
67. "Geopfert," "überfallen" (Sander, "Frauen erzählen," 88), "herausgeholt" (92), or "sich einlassen müssen" (94).
68. "Geholt" and "genommen" (Jacobs, *Freiwild*, 22).

69. "Einer Zeit, in der den zivilen Opfern des Kriegsendes nicht mehr das Unrecht angetan wird, sie zu Tätern zu stempeln" (Köpp, *Warum war ich bloß ein Mädchen?*, 12).

70. This ambiguity also characterizes Biallas's description of rape. Biallas writes that a soldier threatened her with a knife, pulled her pants down, and threw himself upon her, but then reports that she was still a virgin afterwards (*"Komm, Frau, raboti,"* 20).

71. E.g., *"Mir ist schon bald alles egal. Wenn doch irgendwie Schluss wäre"* (*"I don't care about anything anymore. If only this were somehow over"*) (Köpp, *Warum war ich bloß ein Mädchen?*, 70).

72. "In gewisser Weise liess sie mich ins offene Messer laufen" (Köpp, *Warum war ich bloß ein Mädchen?*, 18).

73. "Aus eiskaltem Egoismus lieferten sie durch ihren Verrat ein fünfzehnjähriges Mädchen ans Messer. Im vollen Wissen, was sie mir antaten" (Köpp, *Warum war ich bloß ein Mädchen?*, 79).

74. See Beck-Heppner, "Frauen im Dienst der Wehrmacht," 141.

75. "Unmensch[en]" (Köpp, *Warum war ich bloß ein Mädchen?*, 53) and "Bestien" (74); see Grossmann, "Eine Frage," 19, and Sielke, who underscores the importance of racist rhetoric in the representation of rape in American literature (*Reading Rape*, 38). See also Bourke, who notes that the rape of a white woman by a black man was considered "an assault on the entire structure of white power and authority" (*Rape*, 105).

76. Other rape memoirs offer a different picture. Biallas, e.g., portrays the Russians as both rapists and friends and protectors (see *"Komm, Frau, raboti,"* 70). On Nazi stereotypes of the Russian "Untermenschen," see also Bonner, "Vielleicht besteht der Krieg nur in der Verwischung der Fronten," 27–30.

77. *"Sind das denn noch Menschen?"* (Köpp, *Warum war ich bloß ein Mädchen?*, 64).

78. Tanner, *Intimate Violence*, xi.

79. Tanner, *Intimate Violence*, 10.

80. "Am Ende dieses Krieges steht neben vielen anderen Niederlagen auch die Niederlage der Männer als Geschlecht" (Anonyma, *Eine Frau in Berlin*, 51).

81. "Ihr Soldaten aus dem Osten wisst zu einem hohen Teil heute bereits selbst, welches Schicksal vor allem den deutschen Frauen, Mädchen und Kindern droht. Während die alten Männer und Kinder ermordet werden, werden Frauen und Mädchen zu Kasernenhuren erniedrigt" (cited in Mühlhäuser, "Vergewaltigungen in Deutschland 1945," 366).

82. Naimark, *The Russians in Germany*, 7.

83. "Beispiellos," "nie zuvor sind in einem einzigen Land und innerhalb eines so kurzen Zeitraums so viele Frauen und Mädchen von fremden Soldaten missbraucht worden wie 1944/45 nach dem Einmarsch der Roten Armee in Deutschland" (Münch, *Frau komm!*, 15).

84. Merridale, *Ivan's War*, 318.

85. For an analysis of discourses relating to rapes of French women by German soldiers during the First World War, see Harris, "The 'Child of the

Barbarian.'" On wartime rape, see Frederick and the Aware Committee on Rape, *Rape*, 2–3; Morris, "By Force of Arms," 656; Barstow, *War's Dirty Secrets*, 2.

86. "Das Volk der Täter ... Wer diese unzählig oft gebrauchte Formel – inzwischen schon ein Stereotyp – für angemessen und richtig hält, kann sich nicht mit dem Gedanken anfreunden, dass es neben den Tätern eben auch Opfer gab" (Münch, *Frau komm!*, 26).

87. "The Hour," 359; see also Rogoff, "Von Ruinen zu Trümmern." When West Germany sought integration into NATO, the mass rapes no longer served a purpose in a newly re-masculinized national narrative, although, as Münch's book shows, discourses of national victimization never disappeared altogether.

88. "The Hour," 372.

89. See Münch, *Frau komm!*, 29.

90. According to Mühlhäuser, German soldiers forced women to undress and submitted them to sexual torture and rape, both as individuals and in groups (*Eroberungen*, 367). Among German crimes of a sexual nature, one might also list the forcible prostitution of female concentration camp inmates (see Eschebach and Mühlhäuser, *Krieg und Geschlecht*; Paul, *Zwangsprostitution*).

91. Naimark, *The Russians in Germany*, 108.

92. "Eine Frage", 20; see also Anonyma, *Eine Frau in Berlin*, 146.

93. Grossmann, *Jews*, 52.

94. Grossmann, *Jews*, 54. And yet, there is much to indicate that many rape victims, particularly young ones, lacked all sexual knowledge and were raised in a culture that considered sexuality shameful. Thus, one of the women interviewed by Hoerning thought that being raped meant being shot (Hoerning, "Frauen als Kriegsbeute," 333). See also Biallas, who recounts that many young girls panicked when they had their first period. Lacking all knowledge about the body's sexuality, they assumed that they would bleed to death (*"Komm, Frau, raboti,"* 90).

95. Kuby, *The Russians and Berlin, 1945*, 280. Kuby calls a woman who claimed that she had been raped twenty-four times "rather pedantic" (19). He cites the comment "better a Russian on the belly than an American overhead" (20) and believes that "genuine love relationships developed out of what began as rape" (274).

96. Kuby, *The Russians and Berlin, 1945*, 275.

97. See Schmidt-Harzbach, "Eine Woche im April, Berlin 1945," 61.

98. Mardorossian, "Toward a New Feminist Theory of Rape," 769.

99. Eichhorn and Kuwert, *Das Geheimnis unserer Großmütter*, 72.

100. See Anonyma, *Eine Frau in Berlin*, 90, 74, 70, 76.

101. See Andreas-Friedrich, *Schauplatz Berlin*, 23, 176 and Boveri, *Tage des Überlebens*, 84, 89, 109, 172, 179 181. See also Kardorff, *Berliner Aufzeichnungen 1942–45*, 358. For more information about long-term consequences, see also Gebhardt, *Als die Soldaten kamen*, 249–303, and Hoerning, "Frauen als

Kriegsbeute." For more reports of suicide following rape, see Knef, *Der geschenkte Gaul*, 111–112.

102. See "Vergewaltigungen," 390. In the German version of her article on rape, Grossmann also claimed that rape does not lead to feelings of shame, a statement that she omitted in the revised English version of her article ("A Question," 42).

103. On Erpenbeck's uneasy fit in the category of *Fräuleinwunder*, see Müller, *Das literarische Fräuleinwunder*. For a critique of the concept of *Fräuleinwunder*, see Franck's essay "The Wonder (of) Woman" and Biendarra, "Gen(d)eration Next," 211–212.

104. "Direkt von dieser Geschichte nicht mehr betroffen war und sie doch in ihren Biographien mit sich herumschleppt" (Janzen, "Erinnerungen der Dritten Generation," 115).

105. Köhler, "Große Form," 231.

106. For a detailed explanation of communicative and cultural memory, see Jan Assmann, *Das kulturelle Gedächtnis*. For a succinct summary of Assmann's theory in relation to contemporary German literature, see Braun, *Die deutsche Gegenwartsliteratur*, 109–122.

107. See the work of Halbwachs (*On Collective Memory*), Connerton (*How Societies Remember*), and Misztal (*Theories of Social Remembering*).

108. Berger, "On Taboos, Traumas and Other Myths," 218. See also Bartov (*Germany's War and the Holocaust*), Heer (*Vom Verschwinden der Täter*), and Frei (*1945 und wir*). Numerous scholars, including Moeller, Sichrovsky, Fuchs, Frahm, Niven, and Schmitz, claim that, far from being a taboo, perceptions of Germans as victims of the Second World War emerged in the 1950s, remained popular during the following decades, and gained in intensity in the 1990s. Other scholars have modified this thesis by pointing to the important difference between what Welzer, Moller, and Tschuggnall call the difference between album and lexicon, i.e., between "private memory and official remembrance" (Taberner and Berger, "Introduction," 4). Aleida Assmann, for example, argues that the shift toward official national perpetrator narratives occurred after the German reunification. She claims that, from this perspective, public recognition of experiences of victimization that dominated family narratives was not possible (*Unbehagen*, 145).

109. Her explanation is telling: Wolf was concerned that it would not be enough to write a balanced account. Rather, a writer's endeavor for truth is always in danger of being foiled by a reader: "Heute weisst du, dass es im Zeitalter des Argwohns das aufrichtige Wort nicht gibt, weil der aufrichtige Sprecher auf den angewiesen ist, der aufrichtig zuhören wollte, und weil dem, dem lange das verzerrte Echo seiner Worte zurückschlägt, die Aufrichtigkeit vergeht" ("Today you know that, in the age of suspicion, there are no sincere words because a sincere speaker relies upon a sincere listener, and he who is confronted with the distorted echo of his words for a long period of time, forgets how to be sincere") (*Kindheitsmuster*, 333).

110. Schmitz dates the "renaissance" of the family novel in German-language literature to the mid-1990s ("Family, Heritage," 70). He sees in these novels "a transition from a juristic to a therapeutic discourse, substituting the judgmental attitude of '68 for a position of listening and understanding" (71).

111. "Im Spannungsfeld zwischen Fiktionalität und Referenzialität" (Eigler, *Gedächtnis*, 101). See also Assmann, *Generationsidentitäten*, 25, and Franck's comment in an interview with Janzen: "Für diesen Roman habe ich sehr lange recherchiert, wobei nur ein verschwindend geringer Teil davon in das Buch eingeflossen ist" ("I conducted a lot of research for this novel, however, only a vanishingly small part of it entered the book" (Janzen, "Erinnerungen der Dritten Generation," 111).

112. See Gerstenberger, "Fictionalizations," 105, Brandt, "In der Verjüngungsmaschine," and Geu, "Schreiben zum Überleben." Franziska Meyer calls *Heimsuchung* "ein autobiographischer Text, der nicht autobiographisch erzählt" ("an autobiographical text that is not told autobiographically") ("Sommerhaus, früher," 325).

113. See Eigler, *Gedächtnis*, 23.

114. "In Familien von Tätern die Opferrolle der Familienangehörigen strapaziert wird" (Rosenthal, *Der Holocaust im Leben von drei Generationen*, 25).

115. The rape victim's complicity consists in her support for her Nazi husband. As Schlink explains, "the act of not renouncing, not judging and not repudiating carries its own guilt with it ... one becomes entangled in another's guilt if one maintains or establishes solidarity with that person" (*Guilt about the Past*, 15).

116. See Franck, *Mittagsfrau*, 158.

117. "Eines Tages war ihr der Widerstand zu mühsam" (Franck, *Mittagsfrau*, 315).

118. "Küßte sie, wo und wie es ihm gefiel" (Franck, *Mittagsfrau*, 301; see also 194).

119. "Je weniger sie selbst wollte, desto besser schien es ihm zu gefallen" (Franck, *Mittagsfrau*, 342).

120. "So geht das nicht" (Franck, *Mittagsfrau*, 343); "Das ist die Liebe, Alice" (342); "Sie sträubte sich, das reizte ihn" (956).

121. "Wie ein Hammer einen Nagel in die Wand trieb er sein Geschlecht Schlag um Schlag gleichförmig in sie" (Franck, *Mittagsfrau*, 342).

122. Dylewska calls him a "Reflektorfigur" ("Grenzen des Schweigens," 342).

123. "Die Wohnungstür war nur angelehnt, Peter öffnete sie. Er sah drei Männer um den Küchentisch, darauf seine Mutter, sie saß halb, halb lag sie. Der nackte Po eines Mannes bewegte sich auf Peters Augenhöhe vor und zurück, dabei wackelte das Fleisch so heftig, dass Peter lachen wollte. Doch die Soldaten hielten seine Mutter fest. Ihr Rock war zerrissen, ihre Augen weit geöffnet, Peter wusste nicht, ob sie ihn sah oder durch ihn hindurch blickte. Aufgesperrt war ihr Mund – aber sie blieb stumm. ... Schon einmal zuvor hatte seine Mutter Besuch von Soldaten gehabt" (Franck, *Mittagsfrau*, 18).

124. "Seit Tagen machte sie die Wohnung sauber" (Franck, *Mittagsfrau*, 18); "zeige sie mit einer gewissen Abscheu auf sein Geschlecht" (10).

125. "Aufgespießt wie Tiere, der ganze Unterleib zerfetzt" (Franck, *Mittagsfrau*, 23); see also 383.
126. See Franck, *Mittagsfrau*, 384 and 319.
127. Interestingly, the text mentions that Peter forgot to buy a lock for the door (Franck, *Mittagsfrau*, 20). Although it is unlikely that a lock would have kept the Russians out, this detail suggests that Helene might blame Peter for the rape.
128. Because she is Jewish, Selma is socially isolated, and the text suggests that this isolation, along with the deaths of four infant sons, may have contributed to her madness. But Selma's madness also manifests as an artistic appreciation for the beauty of everyday things: Selma collects objects that others consider trash. Unlike in the social world of Stettin, in Selma's world nothing is abject. Against a discourse that differentiates between the valuable and the worthless, Selma posits her "declaration of love for generally superfluous and seemingly worthless things" (Franck, *Mittagsfrau*, 68). She "recognized a soul in things" (119). In addition to appreciating what others throw away, Selma stands alone in her violent hatred of the war. When her husband enlists – with a heavy heart and only because he cannot legally stay home – she refuses all further contact with him. Her daughter reminds her that the father "went to war for all of us," but Selma replies: "not for me" (121). Clearly, Selma embodies a radical counter-discourse to the official narratives of war, fatherland, and the Nazi bifurcation of valuable and worthless lives. She insists on the primacy of her relationship to her husband over the demands of the state and on the beauty of what others consider abject.
129. The ambiguity evident in Selma's madness also characterizes the representation of Helene and Martha's incestuous relationship. Helene can be seen as a victim of sexual abuse by an older sister, but their relationship can also be read in a much more positive light as one of great intimacy and harmony.
130. "Sie waren guter Laune" (Franck, *Mittagsfrau*, 20).
131. "Den Kopf in die Hände gestützt, saß der Mann am Boden und schluchzte" (Franck, *Mittagsfrau*, 21).
132. "Privatisierung und Verharmlosung historischer Zusammenhänge ... so dass etwa die Deutschen als die eigentlichen Opfer der ideologischen Irrwege und Katastrophen des 20. Jahrhunderts erscheinen" (*Gedächtnis*, 9); See also Peitsch, who is concerned that family novels privilege empathy and identification over critical reflection of social and political conflicts (*Nachkriegsliteratur*, 355).
133. "An die Stelle der historischen Schuld der Kriegsgeneration rückt hier die persönliche Schuld ins Zentrum des Interesses (z.B. fehlende Muttergefühle) ... die Betonung der Geschlechterkonflikte (Misshandlung der Frau durch den Ehemann, Vergewaltigung durch russische Soldaten)" (Eidukeviciene, "(Re)konstruktion der Vergangenheit," 44).

134. "Der Großvater Francks wird zwar als Nazi dargestellt, doch ist diese Tatsache weniger wichtig, als dass er ihre Großmutter misshandelte" (Janzen, "Erinnerungen der Dritten Generation," 110).
135. "Was wussten sie schon über das Weltgeschehen?" (Franck, *Mittagsfrau*, 168).
136. See "and how could he be *her* Peter, if she could not be anything to him, couldn't talk with him, or tell him stories, if she simply couldn't say anything" (Franck, *Mittagsfrau*, 397).
137. Pye, "Jenny Erpenbeck and the Life of Things," 112.
138. Probst, "Auf märkischen Sand gebaut," 68.
139. Several critics have focused on the novel's exploration of space and of the notion of *Heimat*; see Cosgrove, "*Heimat* as Nonplace," Schuchmann, "Die Zeit scheint ihr zur Verfügung zu stehen wie ein Haus," and Goodbody, "*Heimat* and the Place of Humans in the World."
140. "Züge einer mythischen Figur" (Köhler, "Große Form," 237).
141. Eigler, "Critical Approaches to *Heimat* and the Spatial Turn," 46. See also Probst, who points out that such "plural narratives" resist the focus on German suffering and concomitant omission of Jewish victims ("Auf märkischen Sand gebaut," 78), and Bobinac, who discusses multi-perspectival narration with unreliable and traumatized narrators ("Am Herzen erblindet," 147).
142. Pye speaks of the architect's "failure to recognize the suffering of another, and his willful privileging of the self, veiled as the universal entitlement to the material comforts of home" (Pye, "Jenny Erpenbeck and the Life of Things," 124).
143. "Immerhin die Hälfte des Verkehrswerts hatte er den Juden gezahlt. Und das war schon nicht wenig gewesen" (Erpenbeck, *Heimsuchung*, 43–44).
144. See Erpenbeck, *Heimsuchung*, 75.
145. "Lästige jüdische Schieber" (Erpenbeck, *Heimsuchung*, 71).
146. "Humor ist, wenn man trotzdem lacht" (Erpenbeck, *Heimsuchung*, 71). Nobile points out that Erpenbeck employs intertextual references to critique the architect and his wife ("'Ihr Erbteil,'" 69).
147. "Freiwillig hat er sich gemeldet mit fünfzehn, nachdem seine Mutter, sein Vater und seine Schwestern von den Deutschen umgebracht worden waren" (Erpenbeck, *Heimsuchung*, 95).
148. "Je mehr deutsche Häuser sie betraten, desto schmerzhafter stellte sich ihnen die Frage, warum die Deutschen nicht hatten dort bleiben können, wo ihnen zum Bleiben nichts, aber auch wirklich nicht das Allergeringste fehlte" (Erpenbeck, *Heimsuchung*, 95).
149. "Vielleicht haben die Deutschen vorher zuviel verborgen" (Erpenbeck, *Heimsuchung*, 98).
150. "Dann gibt er die Arme frei und streicht der Frau über den Kopf, sie wehrt sich nicht mehr, aber er hört, wie sie zu weinen beginnt, er streicht ihr über den Kopf, wie um sie zu trösten" (Erpenbeck, *Heimsuchung*, 99–100).

151. "Vielleicht besteht der Krieg nur in der Verschiebung der Fronten, denn jetzt, da sie seinen Kopf zwischen ihre Beine schiebt, vielleicht nur deswegen zwischen ihre Beine schiebt, weil sie weiß, daß der Soldat eine Waffe hat, und es klüger ist, sich nicht zu wehren, übernimmt sie die Führung. . . . Und als jetzt der junge Soldat, vielleicht nur aus Angst vor der Frau, seine Zunge zwischen die krausen Haare schiebt . . . ergießt sich, erst sanft, dann heftiger, ein heißer Schwall über sein Gesicht, die Frau pinkelt ihm aufs Gesicht . . . also führt sie doch Krieg, oder ist das die Liebe, der Soldat weiß es nicht" (Erpenbeck, *Visitation*, 100). "In die Stille hinein greift die Frau nun wieder an . . . packt durch die Hose hindurch seinen Schwanz und drückt den Jungen zu Boden . . . er wehrt sich nicht mehr" (Erpenbeck, *Heimsuchung*, 103).

152. See also "then she slowly pulls her dress up" (Erpenbeck, *Heimsuchung*, 100).

153. See Jacobs, *Freiwild*, 8.

154. "Und dann war der Russe gekommen. Sie will das Wort nicht denken, das Wort, mit dem er sie rief, das undenkbare Wort, mit dem er für alle Ewigkeit ein Loch in ihre Ewigkeit bohrte. Ihr zu der Zeit schon unfruchtbarer Körper hatte ihn, der das Wort gewußt hatte, das sie entmachtete, mit aller Gewalt an sich gerissen und ungefähr für die Dauer einer Geburt ihr Lachen, das ihm so lange im Weg gestanden hatte, erstickt, in dieser Nacht in dem verborgenen Schrank, den ihr Mann eigens für sie gebaut hatte, weil sie es sich damals, als sie noch eine Zirkusprinzessin war, so wünschte, war sie endlich zum Feind übergelaufen" (Erpenbeck, *Heimsuchung*, 73–74).

155. "Jedenfalls keinem Mann" (Erpenbeck, *Heimsuchung*, 76).

156. Although the experience of rape is undoubtedly portrayed as traumatic, Erpenbeck further complicates matters by highlighting the wife's menopausal body. In Erpenbeck's rendering, the attack by a foreign soldier and the experience of menopause ("already barren") work together to effect the wife's permanent alienation from her own body: the wife is victimized both by the Russian soldier and by her own body. Repeatedly, the wife's body is portrayed as a subject and agent to whose every whim the wife submits passively (see Erpenbeck, *Heimsuchung*, 64 and 65). *Visitation* even compares Germany's war against the Allies to the war that the wife's own body wages against her (see 72). Thus, when the rape is characterized as a form of surrender to the enemy (74), the capitulation in question is as much to the Russian as to her own body and the process of aging, and one might wonder if the word that disempowered her is "mama"/mother. The text repeatedly refers to the infertility of the architect's wife, who is portrayed as a female Peter Pan figure who does not want to grow up, and whose refusal to have children appears to be related to her desire to remain a child herself. For most of her life, she revels in the experience of time-lessness: "Today could be today, but also yesterday or twenty years ago" (70). Thus, when the young soldier rapes her, he not only pins her into her aging body, but also forces a maternity on her (by calling her "mama") against which she fought her whole life.

157. In an interview, Erpenbeck noted that she wrote this story last because she perceived it as the most difficult (see Schubert, "Kein Zivilisationsbruch," 98).

158. "Das Sehen von damals dauert ja immer noch an" (Erpenbeck, *Heimsuchung*, 163).

159. "Sie niemals hinausgelangt sind, sondern bis heute unter dem Schuppendach hocken ... Daß man an einen Ort durch gemeinsame Gier und Scham gründlicher festgeknüpft wird als durch gemeinsames Glück, das hätte er gern niemals gelernt" (Erpenbeck, *Heimsuchung*, 165).

160. "Ihr thematisches Zentrum ist die Konfrontation, die Auseinandersetzung, die Abrechnung mit dem Vater" (Assmann, *Geschichte im Gedächtnis*, 26).

161. "Einem hohen Grad an Distanz und Reflexion ... einer Bereitschaft zur Empathie und zur affektiven Annäherung an die eigenen Vorfahren" (Eigler, *Gedächtnis*, 25).

162. Cohen-Pfister, "Rape, War, and Outrage," 327.

163. Cahill, *Rethinking Rape*, 120.

CHAPTER 5

Parallel Stories
Women Refugees

Much like "Interrupted Silences," Chapter 5 focuses on the life writing of women who did not contribute to the functioning of the regime in any official capacity. Caught up in the chaos of the German retreat during the last months of the war, these women experienced a form of wartime violence that is often considered peripheral even though it forms a crucial aspect of modern warfare: the plight of the refugee.[1] As members of the perpetrator nation who were fleeing from the advancing Russian army, the writers discussed in what follows all struggle to negotiate three conflicting discourses: the suffering inflicted by Germans, the suffering experienced by Germans, and their own complicity in the Third Reich; they rarely manage to do so successfully. All too often, one of these three strands is highlighted while the other two are repressed or sidelined. Indeed, the impression that arises is one of parallel stories that remain intricately interwoven but do not overlap.[2] As in the stories of rape victims, emplotments of victimization are not easily reconciled with narratives of complicity.

Much like stories of wartime rape, representations of the trek, that is, of the flight west from the Russian army toward the end of the Second World War, are intensely political documents.[3] As stories of German victimization in a context of the German war of conquest and the Holocaust, narrative accounts of the trek negotiate the gaps and overlaps between subjectivity and history, between individual and national suffering and accountability. In the following, I parse the narrative and conceptual difficulties that arise when female memoirists seek to reconcile the divergent perspectives of complicity and victimization. My goal is twofold: first, although recent scholarship has acknowledged that victimization does not signal innocence, the dichotomy of German suffering and German atrocities continues to define our understanding of these texts. In contrast, I would like to propose that such a binary approach does not do justice to the complexity of discourses that shape life writing about the trek.

In particular, I ask not only how these authors offer testimonies of their own suffering and whether or not they acknowledge German guilt but also whether they reflect on their own complicity in the national endeavor. Second, although the experience of the trek, much like that of the refugee in general, is highly gendered,[4] gender is frequently not a defining category in the reception of these texts. In contrast, I seek to contribute to the critical discourse on German victimization not only by including texts by female memoirists that have largely been ignored but also by highlighting how the author's gender affected her experience of the trek and her attempts to narrative this experience. More often than not, the trauma of the trek is intricately interwoven with the partial or total failure of maternal care. Memoirs of the trek, if they discuss the issue of complicity at all, cast it not as a female, but as a human condition. In contrast, the trek itself is portrayed as a female and, specifically, maternal experience.

In order to contextualize the life writing discussed here both historically and discursively, I begin this chapter with a brief overview of the trek along with a discussion of the controversies surrounding its representation. I then focus on five texts by female writers, which I have chosen because they represent different strategies of dealing with the thorny issue of complicity: the essay "Nobody Went East Anymore" (*"Nach Osten fuhr keiner mehr"*) (1962) by Marion Gräfin Dönhoff; the memoir *Trek: An American Woman, Two Small Children and Survival in World War II Germany* by Mary Hunt Jentsch, published in 2008, but written in 1959; the novel *Patterns of Childhood* (*Kindheitsmuster*) (1976) by Christa Wolf; and the memoirs *Surviving Was More Difficult Than Dying* (*Überleben war schwerer als Sterben* (2004) by Erika Morgenstern, and *And Deep in the Soul the Distance: The Story of a Displacement from Silesia* (*Und tief in der Seele das Ferne: Die Geschichte einer Vertreibung aus Schlesien*) (2004) by Katharina Elliger.

Dönhoff, Hunt Jentsch, Wolf, Morgenstern, and Elliger were all part of the trek west, and they all published their accounts decades after the experience, but they are divided by social class, age, politics, and, in Hunt Jentsch's case, nationality. In 1939, Dönhoff was a young woman from a privileged family who took over the management of her parents' estate. Although the family lost the estate, she came to support Brandt's *Ostpolitik* in the postwar period. In her writing, Dönhoff acknowledges German guilt, but does not dwell on the suffering of the trek. Moreover, because she was involved in the resistance, she enjoys the luxury of not having to reflect on her own complicity.

Unlike Dönhoff, Hunt Jentsch was not a member of the Prussian elite, but an American woman, who was married to a German official in the Foreign Office. While Dönhoff never married and laid claim to a male lifestyle, Hunt Jentsch's experience of the trek was profoundly affected by the fact that she was the mother of two children. And yet, Dönhoff and Hunt Jentsch also have much in common. Unlike Wolf, both belong to elite groups, both cast themselves as resourceful agents, and their writing is infused with a can-do spirit. Like Dönhoff, Hunt Jentsch is untroubled by feelings of guilt and complicity in National Socialist crimes, not because she resisted but because of the outsider status afforded by her nationality. Unlike Dönhoff and Wolf, however, who could not integrate accounts of German victimization into narratives of German guilt, Hunt Jentsch paints a vivid picture of the suffering of German refugees.

Even more so than Dönhoff's text, Christa Wolf's *Patterns of Childhood* is marked by a deep commitment to acknowledge German crimes. Although Wolf's autobiographically inspired novel was published in the 1970s and thus precedes much of the public discourse on *Vergangenheitsbewältigung*, its analysis of the complicity of average Germans is far more sophisticated than that presented in many memoirs published after 2000. And yet, much like Dönhoff, Wolf shies away from the representation of German suffering because she cannot conceive of a narrative of German victimization that would not immediately relativize or even erase the awareness of German guilt.[5]

Unlike Dönhoff and Hunt Jentsch, who were adult members of the upper class, Morgenstern, like Wolf, hailed from a lower-middle-class family and joined the trek as a four-year-old child. Both Morgenstern and Elliger, who was fourteen years old at the time, convey a vivid picture of the horror of the trek, but while Morgenstern dwells on idyllic descriptions of a paradise lost, Elliger makes an effort to contextualize her experience in a larger political context. She seeks to come to terms with her own and her family's complicity, but ultimately fails to reconcile stories of victimization, guilt, and complicity and thus feels silenced.

The Trek

During the last months of the war and the postwar period, Germany experienced an enormous influx of refugees. In addition to the so-called displaced persons (DPs), that is, some 200,000 Jewish concentration camp survivors and forced laborers from Russia, France, Belgium, Italy, and other countries, 12 to 14 million ethnic Germans fled to the German heartland from East Brandenburg, East Prussia (Memelland, Danzig), West Prussia (Posen), Pomerania, Silesia, the Czech Republic (Sudetenland, Bohemia, Moravia), Estonia, and Latvia. There were the Danube Swabians (*Donauschwaben*), including the Banater Swabians, who were dispersed across Romania, Hungary, and Yugoslavia; and the *Siebenbürger Sachsen*, who were forced to leave Romania. Of these 12 to 14 million refugees, some 2 million died of cold, hunger, and exhaustion, or were killed by Russian artillery.[6]

While these numbers are well known, it is often forgotten that being a refugee in the Second World War was a largely female experience. Indeed, many memoirs of the trek are told from the perspective of a mother or a child. Since all able-bodied men had been drafted, the population that fled from the advancing Russian troops consisted of women, children under sixteen, and old people. They moved in treks as long as sixteen kilometers through ice and snow in subzero temperatures, frequently pushed off the main roads to make way for military convoys.[7] They walked, pushed handcarts and strollers, or rode on bicycles, horse-drawn carriages, and wagons on clogged roads while exposed to strafing bombers, whose attacks catapulted people into the air "as though they were dolls."[8] When East Prussia was cut off from Germany, many perished while crossing the ice of the Vistula Lagoon (Frisches Haff) to get to the ports of Danzig and Pillau.

For the refugee, the texture of everyday life unravels. The constant threat to one's survival and property eroded family bonds. Children who were used to look to their parents for support realized that their caregivers had become powerless. Many families were torn apart by the vagaries of the trek, many children orphaned or separated from their mothers.[9] Old people and infants, whose diapers and nourishment were frozen, were among the first victims. Those who survived faced an ever shrinking world. They had to cope with the loss of all objects that once defined home and personal identity: valuables, linen, silver, and porcelain were left behind; everything a family holds dear, symbols of a vibrant cultural life, pianos and books, had to be abandoned; children relinquished their dolls and pets; farmers left land that many had held for generations, knowing that their livestock was unlikely to survive.

Many German women and children who either stayed behind in spite of the advancing Russian army or returned after an initial retreat were expelled in the postwar years when the geopolitical and ethnic reorganization of Eastern Europe was completed.[10] Typically, "these expulsions were accomplished with and accompanied by great violence."[11] Much like the

Poles who had been expelled by the Germans in the early years of the war, German expellees were given very little time to gather their belongings: "30 MINUTES – WITH NO MORE THAN 8 KILOGRAMS OF LUGGAGE PER PERSON,"[12] so the official pronouncement, cited in Jirgl's powerful historical novel *The Unfinished* (*Die Unvollendeten*) (2003). The expelling countries often held back employable males for compulsory labor, while women and children were packed into unheated boxcars – a fact that produced numerous and often decontextualized comparisons to the deportation of Jews.[13] Once in Germany, the refugees were likely to find unwelcoming communities as Protestants were often assigned to predominantly Catholic areas, while urban middle-class refugees might be relocated to rural farms. Since Allied policy sought to disperse ethnic groups for fear that keeping them together might lead to unrest, refugees could not even seek comfort with compatriots.[14] More often than not, the newcomers were greeted with hostility and blamed for their fate. If they were decent people, they would not have been expelled, so they were told.[15]

It is clear that the experiences of many German refugees were horrifying, but it is also clear that they were intimately related to the war of conquest and racial policy of the Nazi regime; in particular, they can be seen as a response to the large-scale effort to repatriate or resettle ethnic Germans from Latvia, Lithuania, Estonia, Bukovina, Bessarabia, Volhynia, and Galicia to Poland or the *Altreich*.[16] To make room for these German "colonists" in the western part of Poland, the National Socialist "*Generalplan Ost*" decreed a corresponding ethnic reorganization of German-occupied Poland that forcibly moved 1.2 million Polish citizens to the "*Generalgouvernment*."[17] And yet, although National Socialist "resettlement" policies pioneered the displacement and systematic killing of large segments of the Eastern European population, many accounts of the trek and the expulsion sideline considerations of cause and effect in favor of a pervasive sense of victimization and injustice. Indeed, the enormous difficulty of joining narratives of national guilt, individual complicity, and personal suffering shapes this discourse even today. Revisionist accounts frequently equate the trek with the Holocaust, claiming simply that "the Germans now suffered the same fate as the Jews."[18] Along the same lines, historian Hubertus Knabe calls the expulsion of the German population east of Oder and Neisse a genocide and tops this assertion off with the claim that the disciplined Nazi concentration camp guards were superior to the lawless Soviet guards: "The Soviet guards were mentally different from National Socialist guards. Corruption, black market trade, and excessive consumption of alcohol were common."[19]

Similarly, German lawyer and author Nawratil claims that the suffering of Germans exceeded that of the victims of National Socialism by far: "Never before in history was such a large population liquidated and exterminated from maps and history books with one stroke of the pen."[20] Much like Knabe, Nawratil maintains that the suffering of Germans was particularly acute because the Russian perpetrators lacked civilized moderation and acted with a cruelty "that went beyond anything Western Europeans can imagine."[21] Clearly, such claims and comparisons are highly problematic not only because they constitute a gross distortion of facts but also because they erase crucially important differences: while the Germans actively pursued a whole array of extermination programs, ranging from the organized murder of mentally ill people to that of Jews and other ethnic minorities, there never was an organized extermination program that targeted Germans.

Revisionist discourses such as these have led to concern, particularly on the left end of the political spectrum, that a focus on German suffering "undermines awareness of German perpetration."[22] As Taberner puts it, "a concentration on 'ordinary' Germans may engender a sentimentalisation of their fates which excises the bigger picture of complicity."[23] Even though German cruelty cannot serve as carte blanche for crimes against Germans, it is the context within which the plight of German refugees must be understood. Thus, historian Norman Naimark shows great empathy for the suffering of German refugees, but also insists that "the nature of the German occupation of Poland, in which the Poles were exploited, brutalized, humiliated, and subjected to mass murder, puts their lust for revenge and their fearsome attacks on the Germans in a more understandable context."[24] Similarly, Douglas points out that many Germans, who were "themselves the beneficiaries of a *Herrenvolk* status that even in the midst of war surrounded them in a cocoon of relative privilege ... were unaware of how much resentment their taken-for-granted advantages ... generated among those they had usurped."[25] Such a lack of awareness is undoubtedly evident in many memoirs of the trek. Curiously though, while scholars such as Heinemann have drawn attention to the instrumentalization of gender in public discourses of wartime rape, the stories of refugees are often discussed as though they were gender-neutral. And yet, the large majority of memoirs of the trek was written by women. Again, a gender-inflected experience, that of the refugee, serves to anchor revisionist readings of the Second World War.

Much like accounts of wartime rape, revisionist accounts of the trek tend to establish the bifurcation of German victimization and complicity qua gender. Guido Knopp, for example, who produced numerous popular television documentaries about the Nazis and the Second World War, insists that the refugees "were no perpetrators ... they were defenseless people. Mostly women, children, old people."[26] To be sure, the advancing Russian army did not discriminate between loyal Nazis, resistance fighters, and even victims of National Socialist racial policy. But again, to conclude from this that all German women (and old people) are necessarily victims of and never political agents in the Nazi regime is highly problematic. Much recent scholarship has proven beyond a doubt that women were not only complicit with but, in many cases, actively supportive of Nazi policies.

Another commonplace in contemporary discourses about the trek is the assumption that a public taboo enforced silence about German victimization. Thus, Nawratil laments that the "crimes of displacement are among the best documented but worst published mass crimes of history."[27] However, even a cursory survey of the numerous studies, literary representations, and memoirs dedicated to the trek quickly puts paid to the claim that the stories of the refugees were not published.[28] Rather, as Moeller has shown, postwar discourses frequently highlighted German suffering. And while the interest in German suffering dwindled in the 1980s, it "has taken on an obsessive dimension" in recent decades.[29] But again, to say that there was no blanket taboo is not to say that those who wrote about the trek did not face discursive restrictions.[30] Rather, in representations of the trek as in accounts of rape, a simple dichotomy of silence and discourse fails to capture the challenges inherent in narratives of German victimization and complicity.

Self-censorship is visible in some, but not all, memoirs of the trek. Indeed, a survey of narratives of the trek reveals a multifaceted picture, occasioned by differences in personality and ideology but also by the historical distance that separates the composition of the memoir from the events of the Second World War and postwar period. Some report that they remained silent for decades out of a sense of shame.[31] Some, such as East Prussian Anneliese Panzer, see no rhyme or reason to the suffering the Polish victors inflicted on Germans. They do not connect their own experience to the Nazi war and genocide but rather, in an inversion of National Socialist rhetoric, see themselves as the victims of an extermination program, claiming that they wanted to "destroy us like vermin."[32] Others acknowledge, however indirectly, a connection between German suffering, Nazi crimes, and their own or their family's complicity.[33] Pomeranian Renate Meinhof, for example, wonders, "what did my brothers do in Russia that caused them to attack us like this?"[34] Some, like

Pomeranian Ingrid Hesse-Werner, developed a new perspective after gaining some historical distance: "At the time I was shocked, but today, sixty years later and after obtaining much information about this hellish war, I can understand the occupations. They were a response to the immense suffering that had been inflicted on them and their families at the beginning of the war."[35] Similarly, Monika Taubitz, who grew up in Silesia, declares in her memoir *Flotsam* (*Treibgut*) that "the Polish desire for revenge ... the Russian orgies of victory were somehow understandable because the Nazis had committed grave crimes against both nations in the name of the German people."[36] (Note that Taubitz creates two separate categories: Nazis and the German people.)

In addition to ideological differences between authors, the memoirs themselves are often riven with contradictions. Many refugees blame the Russian army for their suffering but admit that it was aggravated by Nazi officials who refused to evacuate cities and entire regions in a timely fashion. Furthermore, even those who speak of "the Russians" as a collective entity often made friends with individual Russians and remember spontaneous gestures of affection and kindness. Finally, more than any other issue, representations of the author's or her family's complicity in the National Socialist dictatorship are likely to be uneven and contradictory. Thus, Panzer admits freely that her father was a fanatical National Socialist even as she constructs a familial "we" that is positioned in opposition to the state.[37]

In his study of "*Vertriebenenliteratur*," Helbig claims that texts about the trek do not display "nationalist tendencies," but rather are marked by a "strong component of humanitarianism and the desire for reconciliation."[38] In propagating a "community of suffering"[39] that includes Holocaust survivors and German refugees alike, Helbig decontextualizes German suffering, levels crucial differences, and, in doing so, displays exculpatory tendencies. It is true that the "memory of German suffering need not always be a strategy of guilt avoidance; it can serve to sensitize to expulsions and bombing wars in the present."[40] At the same time, many texts about the trek are marked by omissions and it is left to readers to negotiate conflicting moral imperatives: while a political critique of a text that foregrounds questions of complicity and guilt could be seen to deny the enormous suffering described in these texts, a reading that focuses exclusively on individual suffering or that conflates femininity with a lack of agency runs the risk of ignoring the historical framework and the myriad forms of individual complicity that made the war and genocide possible to begin with.

Marion Gräfin von Dönhoff: "Nobody Went East Anymore"

Few memoirs are as apt to dispel the identification of women and victim-hood as Marion Gräfin von Dönhoff's account of her trek west on horse-back. Indeed, Dönhoff's experience is highly atypical for her gender: she occupied a position of authority and she traveled by herself without children or elderly parents. To be sure, Dönhoff's strong sense of agency has much to do with her socially privileged heritage: for Dönhoff, class overwrites gender. The descendant of an old and wealthy aristocratic East Prussian dynasty, the Countess, as she was known in the postwar period, describes the world in which she was raised as one of honor and obligation, and her memoirs are infused with pride of tradition and family. For centuries, the Dönhoffs belonged to the political and cultural elite of the German empire. Dönhoff's memoir *Childhood in East Prussia* (*Kindheit in Ostpreussen*), published in 1988, begins with the statement "only three handshakes separated me from Humboldt, Schadow, Rauch or Goethe."[41] Castle Friedrichstein where she grew up had rooms specially designated for visiting Prussian royalty.[42] Where other memoirs feature pictures of sundry aunts and cousins, Dönhoff includes photos of *Feldmarschall* von Hindenburg and Empress Auguste Viktoria. After the war, Dönhoff, building on her family's tradition of leadership, shaped German public discourse as a columnist and editor of the weekly *Die Zeit*.

In her account of the trek, first published in 1962 but drawing on a contribution to *Die Zeit* from 1946,[43] Dönhoff, who was born in 1909, casts herself as a woman in charge. She was acquainted with the local authorities and, due to family connections, extremely well informed about the goings-on on the front and among Hitler's leading staff. Consequently, Dönhoff was aware of the Russian approach and well prepared for the trek. Even though the local Gauleiter threatened her with severe punishment, she had maps drawn up in secret and instructed her men to build light straw covers for the wagons according to her designs. Before she set out on horseback herself, she gave detailed orders about the time of departure and quantity of luggage. On route, she solved unexpected difficulties with aplomb.[44] With the Russians in hot pursuit, Dönhoff still found time to stay at Bismarck's manor home, Varzin, and drink wine with Bismarck's daughter-in-law, who, like the captain of a sinking ship, refused to leave her estate. The despair that characterizes so many accounts of refugees is absent in Dönhoff's narrative. Aided by her socially privileged position, her extensive network, and substantial resources, Dönhoff faced all challenges with resolve and can-do spirit.

Clearly, Dönhoff's experience of the trek is shaped by her elevated status in society. Her resources, including a horse, "worth a kingdom in those times,"[45] and easy access to estates such as Varzin may have insulated her against some of the dangers of the trek.[46] More importantly, unlike many female refugees, Dönhoff was not burdened with the responsibility for children or aging parents. But if Dönhoff's account is not as harrowing and conflicted as many others, it is not only because she was an unmarried member of an elite circle, but also because she enjoyed the luxury of a guilt-free conscience. Along with many of her friends and acquaintances – among them those who attempted a coup against Hitler on July 20, 1944 – Dönhoff opposed the *Führer* and actively worked to rid the country of its tyrant. She helped prepare the planned assassination by recruiting leaders for a future Germany and by maintaining contact between East Prussia and Berlin. Consequently, unlike Elliger and Wolf, Dönhoff is not burdened with the memory of her own complicity.

Throughout her life, Dönhoff emphasized the importance of the German resistance to the regime. At the same time – and even though in her essay of the trek she repeatedly appears to blame Hitler alone for the loss of her homeland[47] – she did not simply assign all responsibility to the upper echelons of the Nazi hierarchy but remained aware of pro-Nazi sentiments in all social classes.[48] Consequently, she is careful to situate the Second World War refugee crisis within a larger political context. To Dönhoff, the trek is the result of National Socialist imperialism and of a war designed to enslave all conquered territory. But while Dönhoff is acutely aware of the repercussions of Nazi policy and though her own conscience is clear, she does not discuss the role played by her own family. To the end, Dönhoff remained silent about her brother's involvement with the Nazis.

Dönhoff's narrative of the trek was published as part of the essay collection *Names that Nobody Knows Anymore* (*Namen, die keiner mehr kennt*) that is characterized by a deep sense of rootedness, a great love for her *Heimat*, and an acute sense of loss. To Dönhoff, East Prussia is a "lost paradise," a "sunken world in which the seasons still determined the rhythm of life."[49] Dönhoff, whose ancestors settled in the East in the fourteenth century, describes her flight from the advancing Russian army as the reversal of 600 years of history.[50] And yet, although Dönhoff's text commemorates her homeland, she insists that "those who stayed at home, no longer are at home," a slogan that also serves as the title of one of her essays.[51] This acknowledgment of the loss of home comprises several different aspects: there is a loss of life as many who stayed behind were shot by the Russians or deported to forced labor camps in Siberia or the Urals; there are irreversible changes as many buildings were destroyed, including Friedrichstein Castle, which burnt to the ground, and those who survived thus lived in radically new circumstances; last but not least, Dönhoff's acknowledgment of the loss of home also includes a willingness to let go in the interest of peace in Europe: "Perhaps this is the highest degree of love: to love without possessing."[52]

Dönhoff, who in 1971 received the *Friedenspreis des Deutschen Buchhandels* for her efforts to effect a reconciliation between East and West, did not obfuscate German guilt for the war – but it took some time before she listed the Holocaust among the crimes committed by Germans. She was quick to admit that the loss of her homeland was a direct consequence of Germany's conduct in the war and acknowledged the enormous suffering caused by the occupation: "Who could blame the Poles? Never before has so much pain been inflicted on a nation as on them during the Third Reich."[53] Her memoir of the trek highlights Eastern colonization and the war of aggression, but, unlike her later journalistic work, it does not reference the Holocaust explicitly,[54] which remains subsumed under the greater heading of German war crimes. Conversely, Dönhoff also does not dwell on German suffering. Many of the horrifying details that feature in almost every other memoir of the trek are left out, and while German suffering including her own is not completely absent, it is reduced to spare comments about the biting cold and terse references to dead bodies along the way.[55] It would appear that, in an essay written as early as 1946 and expanded and published in 1962, Dönhoff can account for German guilt but she cannot yet afford to offer graphic details of German crimes or suffering. Rather, she shines a light only on those pieces of her past that help her build a future. The rest is history.

Mary Hunt Jentsch: *Trek: An American Woman, Two Small Children and Survival in World War II Germany*

Mary Hunt Jentsch's memoir is not the only account of the trek written in English, but it is, to my knowledge, the only one by an American-born citizen while texts such as Regina Maria Shelton's *To Lose a War: Memories of a German Girl* (1982) and Bärbel Probert-Wright's *Little Girl Lost* (2006) were penned by German natives who emigrated after the war. Hunt Jentsch spent the war years in Germany and wrote *Trek* in 1959 after she had returned to the United States. The book, which was published posthumously in 2008 by Hunt Jentsch's descendants, contains short introductions to every chapter that situate the author's experiences in the larger historical context. A foreword and an epilogue by Steve Mumford, Hunt Jentsch's grandson, further contextualize the account and provide information about the author's life before and after the war.

Although not a wealthy aristocrat like Dönhoff, Hunt Jentsch was a member of a privileged class. Born in Louisville, Kentucky, in 1898, Hunt Jentsch attended Simmons College in Boston. After graduation, she worked at Houghton Mifflin, where she befriended Esther Forbes, the author of the classic children's novel *Johnny Tremain*, and fell in love with Gerhart Jentsch, a young German who studied at Harvard. The couple moved to Paris and married. (One of the witnesses at the ceremony was Eleanor Lansing Dulles, the sister of future secretary of state John Foster Dulles.) After ten years in Paris, where Gerhart set up an international exchange program, the couple moved to Geneva. Here, their children Erika and Jerry were born. In 1940, the family relocated to Berlin, where Gerhart directed the America department of the Reich's Foreign Office. Much like Dönhoff, who refused to engage with her brother's involvement with the regime, Hunt Jentsch is strangely silent on the matter of her husband's politics. According to a letter by Gerhart's friend John Rothschild, Gerhart was critical of the invasion of Czechoslovakia and of the Reich's treatment of the Jews – and yet, he told his grandson after the war that he did not know about the death camps. The picture that emerges is that of an all too dedicated, though perhaps conflicted state official. Gerhart's publications at the time conformed to Nazi politics and essentially constituted Nazi propaganda.[56] And while he eventually left the Foreign Office because of his opposition to the war with Russia, he volunteered for active service during the last months of the war.

Much like Dönhoff's writings, Hunt Jentsch's memoir emphasizes her agency. Even before the war tested her resilience, Hunt Jentsch was an independent spirit. When she married in France, she refused to accept the inferior legal status assigned to French wives and had special documents drafted that specified that her marriage was to follow the laws of her native Kentucky. During the war, Hunt Jentsch was separated from her husband and left to fend for herself. Although Gerhart's absence was motivated by the war, it is striking that Hunt Jentsch never comments on it: there is not one reference to an exchange of letters, and she never mentions being worried about Gerhart or waiting for news from him. Much of this reticence may be due to a highly developed sense of privacy, a refusal to lay bare one's innermost thoughts and feelings, but it may also mirror the state of her marriage. Either way, Hunt Jentsch's independence reflects a typically female experience at the time: Since many husbands, fathers, and older sons were either dead or away, a woman's social circle consisted mostly of other women. Indeed, the reason Hunt Jentsch is able to cope as well as she does can in large part be attributed to her ability to forge strong bonds of friendship, some of which were to last beyond the end of the war. Much has been made of male frontline camaraderie, a staple in war novels by male authors, but little critical attention has been devoted to the communities of women that feature so prominently in refugee memoirs.

In many ways, *Trek* offers a unique perspective: as an American married to a German, Hunt Jentsch is both an insider who shares the plight of ordinary Germans and an outsider with a keen eye for the peculiarities of German everyday life. In fact, some parts of her account read like a travelogue. When the British began to bomb Berlin, Hunt Jentsch and her children sought refuge in Langenbielau in Silesia with Gerhart's parents. Here, she describes the beauty of the Silesian countryside, inserts snippets of historical information, and offers up her views of local habits and customs. Hunt Jentsch enlightens her readers about the quasi feudal hierarchy in the eastern farming provinces, the wartime rationing system, the grueling labor on wash day, staples of German food such as potato dumpling and "*Streusselkuchen*," and even German bedding, which she finds "monstrous."[57] Later on, after Goebbels had ordered the evacuation of women and children from Berlin, Hunt Jentsch found temporary shelter in Pomerania as a paying guest in the house of *Frau* Pastor Schwarz in Barnimskunow. Again, she offers fascinating insights into the social life of the village and describes the daily labor involved in feeding a thirteen-person household. There are expressive vignettes that illustrate the manifold ordeals of life in Second World War Germany, including an episode when Hunt Jentsch left a ten-pound sack of sugar, the ration allotted to thirteen members of her household, in the lap of her young son and came back to find him and the surrounding snow covered by rapidly melting sugar.

As the war progresses, news of native sons of Barnimskunow who died in battle becomes more frequent, more and more children are killed in bombing raids, and the first refugees pass through town. When Russian artillery fire moves closer, Hunt Jentsch decides to join the trek west, first on the wagon of the proprietor of the local estate, then by train. Her acute powers of observation allow Jentsch to chronicle life as a refugee in vivid detail. She describes the painful process of packing and choosing the most useful of her possessions. Once en route, progress is slow. Whenever a wagon breaks down or is passed by military vehicles, the entire trek comes to a halt: "To be fleeing for one's life at the pace of farm horses was a strain on us all," she comments.⁵⁸ When passage across the Oder River is cut off by Russian tanks, Hunt Jentsch and her friend Dora split off from the trek. Soldiers take them to Stettin, where they board the last train west. The scene at the railway station is familiar from numerous memoirs of fleeing Germans. Repeatedly squeezed onto the tracks by the crowd and braving the threat of air raids on the platform, Hunt Jentsch and her party are finally pulled through the train's windows by amputee soldiers and end up in a hospital car so packed that Hunt Jentsch stands on one foot for the entire ride. During the trip, children who need to pee are passed overhead and held out the window. After many detours, traveling on trucks and trains, hiding from dive bombers, Hunt Jentsch and her family finally end up in East Holstein.

Although Hunt Jentsch describes her life as one in which "taking risks became normal,"⁵⁹ she relates her experiences in the same matter-of-fact style that characterizes Dönhoff's essay. Thus, in three short paragraphs, Hunt Jentsch informs us that, due to the poor wartime diet sorely lacking in vitamins and minerals, a wound on her finger got infected so badly that the flesh had to be cut down to the bone without the benefit of an anesthetic. Throughout, Hunt Jentsch does not dwell on feelings and refuses to express self-pity or parse her suffering. Like Dönhoff, she never portrays herself as a victim but rather as a resourceful survivor with a great capacity for coping with adversity. What fear she does admit to usually relates to her children, such as when she describes the anguish she felt during air raids in Berlin when she left her children in the basement while she herself climbed to the roof to put out fires. Similarly, when Erika and Jerry contracted scarlet fever, terse statements inform us of Hunt Jentsch's fearful daily trips to the children's hospital not knowing whether this hospital, which was located in an industrial area and hence a prime target in air raids, would still be there. Again, the experience of the war and the trek is intricately interwoven with and inflected by that of motherhood.

Both Dönhoff and Hunt Jentsch evince a preference for curt matter-of-fact statements, but while Dönhoff refers to the horrors of the trek in the most general terms, Hunt Jentsch is more willing to provide detailed information, all of which highlights the victimization of women in this war. She relates that "the tales of rape were bad enough – any female between eight and sixty – and I still have no reason to believe they were exaggerated, as I saw evidence."⁶⁰ She also expresses her horror about the many children who froze to death: "Most of those under a year hadn't sufficient body warmth and vitality to withstand the prolonged cold. It was a sight I hope never to see again: these young girls wresting a score of dead babies from their frantic mothers."[61] A mother herself, Hunt Jentsch calls the lost children the "most tragic aspect of this great migration."[62] In spite of these gruesome details, however, Hunt Jentsch's book is easier to read than many other memoirs of the trek, not only because its author proves so resilient but also because some of the worst horrors that befell other refugees did not affect her. Hunt Jentsch was not raped or beaten; her children and best friends were not killed; and she left behind a town where she stayed for eighteen months, not a home where her family had lived for generations. Hunt Jentsch reports the horrors of the trek truthfully, but she does not dwell on them and, for the most part, they are not her horrors. Consequently, her memoir differs not only from Dönhoff's essay and Wolf's novel, which do not engage with German suffering, but also from the recollections of refugees like Morgenstern and Elliger whose descriptions of hardships tend to be extensive, not laconic. Unlike Morgenstern and Elliger, Hunt Jentsch includes moments of joy, whose intensity is magnified in contrast with the deprivations of war: the visit of a circus in her Pomeranian town; an evening of song and conversation with other refugees; and, most importantly, the intense friendships and solidarity with other women and mothers. Thus, the most lasting impression readers take away from this memoir is perhaps Hunt Jentsch's admirable ability to enjoy life, her talent for friendship, and her inspiring resilience and good cheer even as the front moves closer and death intrudes in the village's daily life.

Unlike the life writing of many German refugees, *Trek* does not exhibit a nagging sense of guilt or a lurking feeling that the Germans deserved what they got. Although Hunt Jentsch lived among Germans, she retained a strong sense of her American citizenship and defined herself as a foreigner. Indeed, one wonders if her outsider status and the attendant freedom from complicity made it possible for her to form strong bonds of friendship untainted by mutual suspicion and a shared, if unacknowledged, sense of guilt. As an outsider, Hunt Jentsch conveys an impression of distance to the regime – in spite of her husband's work in the Foreign Office. Hunt Jentsch admits that her daughter Erika joined the *Kinderschar*, which she describes as Nazi Cub Scouts, but insists that she was able to avoid participation in other Nazi organizations. She also reports being shocked when she first realized that there were separate benches assigned to Jews.[63] It is not clear if such blindness is willful ignorance or truly a form of misapprehension caused by cultural differences.

Hunt Jentsch's self-presentation as an outsider precludes a discussion of any form of complicity in the actions of the regime on her part. Moreover, she is quite forgiving when it comes to the complicity of ordinary Germans. Hunt Jentsch is convinced that the Germans did not know what they were getting themselves into and, adopting a communal "we," professes to have shared in the general lack of knowledge: "We knew they had been taken to concentration camps, but we didn't know then what happened there."[64] Later on, she claims that the Germans knew that Jews were being imprisoned and shot but not that the government committed genocide.[65] Overall, Hunt Jentsch's account is conciliatory to the point of downplaying the involvement of ordinary Germans in Nazi politics. According to Hunt Jentsch, there was only one Nazi Party member in the Pomeranian village where she stayed. Similarly, she is aware of the miserable life of the forced laborers in the village, but simultaneously claims that most villagers were kind to them.[66] Certainly, Hunt Jentsch's view was colored by the fact that she gravitated toward the anti-Nazi villagers, but at times her view of the Nazi government is disturbingly positive. In a passage that is quite singular in a refugee memoir, Hunt Jentsch proclaims that the local Nazi authorities "had planned and hoped to carry through an orderly exodus."[67] When it is finally clear that the Germans are losing, Hunt Jentsch remains convinced that her personal sense of relief was widely shared: everyone was "awed and overjoyed" when Hitler died. "There may have been some who were sorry, though I doubt it."[68] Still, there are moments when her moral optimism is less pronounced: she admits that some Germans saw in Hitler a savior and that there was "a good deal of anti-Semitic feeling in Germany before World War II."[69] Indeed, it would have been surprising if the perceptive Hunt Jentsch had missed German complicity entirely. Rather, it appears likely that her willingness to overlook guilt and moral failings is the flipside of her survivor spirit, her ability to put a good face on terrible circumstances. Like Dönhoff, she focused only on those aspects of the past that helped her build a future.

Christa Wolf: *Patterns of Childhood*

Unlike the other texts discussed in this chapter, Christa Wolf's *Patterns of Childhood*, published in 1976, is not a memoir, but a novel in the tradition of the *Bildungsroman*. In a preface to her work, Wolf insists on its fictional character: "All characters in this book are inventions of the narrator. No character is identical with a living or dead person. Similarly, the episodes portrayed here are not identical with real events."[70] In spite of this assertion, however, it is widely acknowledged that Wolf's novel is, to a large extent, inspired by autobiographical events and thus is among the "limit cases that sit on the fence between life writing and fiction."[71] If Wolf categorizes her work as fiction, it may be less because of a desire to deny its autobiographical roots but rather because she shares the postmodern conviction that all autobiographies are fictions of the self.

Although it is aesthetically and theoretically more sophisticated than the other memoirs discussed in this chapter, Wolf's text, which she initially referred to as "my book about 1945,"[72] also seeks to come to terms with the experience of the trek: Wolf fled from Landsberg an der Warthe in January 1945. Unlike Morgenstern, however, Wolf does not share fond memories of an idyllic childhood. Instead, she offers a trenchant analysis of family dysfunction, of first lessons in shame, deception, and betrayal, and of complicity with the Nazi regime.

Just as it straddles genre categories, *Patterns of Childhood* also juggles different chronologies. Specifically, Wolf introduces three distinct layers: the protagonist's childhood during the Third Reich from 1932 to 1947, a visit to the protagonist's hometown in 1971, and the time of writing from 1972 to 1975. Wolf's child protagonist Nelly grows up in a town profoundly shaped by National Socialist politics. Its inhabitants are enthusiastic or, at the very least, obedient citizens of the Third Reich, who celebrate the electoral triumphs of the NSDAP, boycott the office of the Jewish doctor Leitner, and take advantage of the plight of the Jews.[73] The narrator's research – there are excerpts of newspaper articles, scientific treatises, schoolbooks, political speeches, and Nazi propaganda[74] – reveals that Nazi crimes were plainly visible for all who cared to notice them: transports to concentration camps passed through town and the local newspapers printed reports about the opening of new camps.[75] At the time, however, Nelly's family and neighbors looked the other way: "That seemed easy for us: overhear, overlook, neglect, deny, forget."[76]

Patterns of Childhood fascinates precisely because Wolf does not delegate the responsibility for the war and Holocaust to a small elite of Nazi functionaries, but explores the passive acceptance and quiet complicity of an entire community.[77] Wolf's narrator is not primarily concerned with horrifying atrocities and excessive cruelty, but rather with the willingness to tolerate such aberrations and with the "small" sins of betrayal and indifference: "Only this beast does not remotely interest you as much as the masses of half humans-half beasts about whom, generally speaking, you know much more because of what is inside you."[78] *Patterns of Childhood* suggests that as long as we would rather enjoy "the bliss of conformity" than oppose injustice and oppression, the past is still with us.[79] Wolf tries to live up to this insight by linking her reflections on the Second World War with an analysis of her attitude toward the wars in Vietnam, Chile, Greece, and the Middle East that unfolded at the time of writing.[80]

Much like the other texts discussed in this chapter – and like some of the most famous West German novels about the Third Reich and the postwar period, such as Günter Grass's *The Tin Drum* (1959) – *Patterns of Childhood* is marked by the inability to reconcile stories of German victimization with those of German complicity. Inevitably, one of the two is either lost or reduced in importance. But while *The Tin Drum* elides the trek entirely even though Grass was a native of Danzig, Wolf chooses to include it, but relativizes its importance by confining it to three chapters, chapters 13, 14, and 15 (out of eighteen), which themselves do not so much represent the trek as discuss the impossibility of doing so, and by linking it closely to the Holocaust.[81] It bears mention that Wolf's decision not to omit the flight west entirely goes against GDR denials of the reality of the trek and the expulsions, which were officially referred to as "resettlements."[82]

Interestingly, Wolf had originally started her novel with the trek,[83] but decided against such an opening. While this decision indicates a realignment of priorities, it also reflects an impasse: in *Patterns of Childhood*, the experience of the trek resists representation; it is a "black box" or "black hole."[84] The reasons for this are twofold: first, the trauma of death and suffering in ice and snow emotionally numbed its victims, and this numbness impedes the attempt to narrate the events of the trek. As Wolf explains, Nelly "pretends to be deaf and ignorant. Then she became deaf and ignorant."[85] Wolf suggests that those who cannot afford to open their eyes to the trauma they are experiencing are not in a position to record it later. Second, Wolf's reluctance to narrate the trek is motivated by a fear that any such account will unwittingly participate in a revisionist discourse that employs German suffering to erase German guilt and complicity. Wolf suggests that this concern is all the more pressing since it is not enough to write a balanced account. Rather, a writer's search for truth is always in danger of being foiled by her readers: "Today you know that in an age of suspicion there is no sincere word because a sincere speaker depends on someone who wants to listen sincerely, and because whoever is confronted with a distorted echo of his words for a long time loses his sincerity."[86] In essence, Wolf suggests that the German public is not, or not yet, ready for a discussion of German victimhood.

As the introductory survey of discourses of the trek has shown, Wolf's concerns are not unfounded. The comparative victimology propagated by scholars such as Nawratil and Knabe distorts and falsifies the historical record. And yet, when Wolf herself attempts to lay bare the shortcomings of revisionist accounts, she too marshals precisely such comparisons. *Patterns of Childhood* recounts a conversation between the narrator and a taxi driver whose wife was raped by Russians and wanted to commit suicide afterward.[87] The taxi driver claims that German soldiers would never have done such a thing, and the narrator finds herself in the strange position of "having to prove German war guilt in a taxi."[88] Pressed to defend herself, she seeks to settle matters with a quantitative reckoning: "he does not want to acknowledge that the tally on the other side, if there is to be a tally, would be bigger,"[89] an argument that strikes me as profoundly unsatisfactory. To be sure, quantity matters. Whether we are dealing with tens, hundreds, thousands, or millions of victims is of the utmost importance. But at the same time, quantitative deliberations cannot do justice to the complex relation between subjective experience and political context, between individual suffering and national accountability. Every victim matters.

Still, one might argue that Wolf's novel succeeds where the narrator's rational explanation in the taxi falls short. Unlike *The Tin Drum*, which highlights German anti-Semitism but does not concern itself with German suffering, and unlike memoirs such as Morgenstern's, which largely fail to address German complicity, *Patterns of Childhood* seeks to strike a balance between subjective authenticity and national accountability. Because her writing draws on her own experience, Wolf was accused of a "fascination with the I," or, in Reich-Ranicki's words, of "annoying us with family history" much like "retired teachers, older priests and demure housewives."[90] But it is precisely this insistence on the gaps and overlaps between individual experience and national history that allows Wolf to live up to an ideal of the author as a "transfer station between object and subject and back to the object."[91]

Chapter 13, the first to introduce the flight from the advancing Russian troops, does not actually represent it. Although the second sentence of the chapter points to the life-defining importance of the trek – "Flight against one's will – also one of the keywords that could determine a life"[92] – the chapter fails to portray the trek; in fact, it barely touches on the topic until the very end but rather meanders from a discussion of recent murders in Chile to thoughts on the work experience in the GDR and the concept of *Heimat*. Scholars have criticized such jumbling of chronologies and discourses as impressionistic and confusing, but, as an analysis of chapter 13 shows, the juxtapositions are in fact quite purposeful. Instead of portraying Nelly's loss of her home, Wolf offers a discussion of the meaning of *Heimat*, which both relativizes and contextualizes Nelly's experience.[93]

The motivations for Wolf's reluctance to depict the trek are complex. First, Wolf is acutely aware that her personal experience offers a highly perspectival picture of the trek that cannot do justice to all its horrors. Consequently, she acknowledges that there were other forms of trauma, but calls upon others to represent them: "The scenes that happened at the station should be described by someone who experienced them."[94] Second, the politically motivated hesitation to represent German suffering expressed at the beginning of chapter 13 reappears toward the end. Tellingly, the recollection of the trek is cut short by the memory of a racist song: "All of a sudden the interest in describing how some people – Germans – experienced the end of the war has disappeared. These people can go to hell. One song sung in summer of 74 by Germans has robbed you of all empathy."[95] Rather than concluding with a description of German suffering, the chapter ends with a discussion of medical experiments on Polish women in Ravensbrück.

Although Wolf refuses to narrativize the trek, she does not omit its horrors entirely but rather compresses them into cameos, such as the memory of a frozen baby handed to Nelly from one of the wagons and of Nelly's mother, who stays behind while Nelly and her brother are carted away.[96] Here too, the experience of the trek is gender-specific, funneled through the lens of motherhood and told from the perspective of a daughter. Wolf's narrative reliance on flashbulb memories reflects the structure of traumatic experience, which resurfaces through graphic but isolated images that take the place of sustained narrative. Chapter 15, in which the family, after a stay in Grünheide, sets out on foot and then in a horse-drawn carriage, also refrains from lengthy descriptions of suffering and instead interjects nightmarish snippets of horror: Nelly is shot at from low-flying planes; one of the men in her group is killed by a projectile; the trek encounters concentration camp survivors; female prisoners defecate along the side of the road and Nelly realizes that extreme cruelty can reduce humans to an animal state. In addition to these flashbulb memories, Wolf conveys the long-term effects of the trek through indirection and allusions. Thus, before the text proceeds to describe how the strain of the trek lead to family quarrels, to a "corruption of morals,"[97] it introduces a Goethe poem whose last line, "we bid you hope,"[98] the narrator cannot remember.

Wolf pairs the story of the trek with the narrative of Nelly's development from complicity and denial to a gradual realization of the criminal nature of the Third Reich. Although it is true, as Stone maintains, that Wolf does at times "fall back on idealized gender stereotypes" that associate women with "empathetic (albeit limited) acts of resistance,"[99] the text does not simply present women as "beacons of moral hope"[100] but remains attuned to Nelly and her mother's problematic complicity in the Third Reich. Readers learn that the fourteen-year-old Nelly, an eager member of the BDM, remains convinced that Hitler will win the war even as her grandparents succumb to the strain of the trek. Indeed, denial is portrayed as a family trait shared by mother and daughter. Wolf inserts a jarring conversation that takes place after American soldiers had taken the trek to a refugee center. Here, a German Jew who had joined the American troops seeks to comfort Nelly and her mother only to be rebuffed by the latter: "Our fatherland is in ruins. . . . You are the victors."[101] The chapter concludes with an encounter with a communist concentration camp survivor. When Nelly's mother refuses to believe that he was in a camp simply because he was a communist, he responds: "Where have you all been living?"[102] In Wolf's text, female complicity and willful ignorance are not abstract constructs, but rather situated in the heart of her own family.

Like all accounts of the trek, this one too contains both typical motifs and idiosyncratic experiences. In some respects, the Jordans are lucky. Unlike most refugees, they escape on a truck, if only for the first part of the trip, and as a coherent, though dysfunctional, family unit. Moreover, neither Nelly nor her close female relatives were victims of rape though other women in the now Russian-administered village were less fortunate. In other respects, however, Nelly's experience is arguably worse than that of many contemporaries. In particular, her mother's decision to send the children ahead while she stayed behind aggravated the trauma of the trek. To young Nelly, this means that her mother would rather abandon her children than her house. Clearly, the experience of the trek is intimately tied to notions of motherhood, and the vulnerability of children in the chaos of the war is often conflated with maternal failure.

Many scholars have remarked on one of the most striking features of *Patterns of Childhood*: the text's "substitution of the second and third person for the first."[103] Wolf uses this device to signal a crucial insight about the Third Reich. Unlike other narratives of the trek, which identify the trek as the origin of all suffering, Wolf suggests that the foundational trauma – the alienation from the "I," or more precisely from the childhood self – was not caused by the trek, but rather predates it. It is Nelly's childhood, the inculcation of complicity in a dictatorship, that led to a rift between internal feelings and external events.[104] The novel has as its desired endpoint the moment "when second and third person meet again in the first, or rather become identical."¹⁰⁵ If it fails to reach this point – the "I" does not appear until the last two pages and then only tentatively – it is not because the personal trauma of the trek places too great a burden on the "I." Rather, it is because "it is unbearable to have to think the small word I along with the word Auschwitz."¹⁰⁶ In Wolf, the root cause of Nelly's alienation from the self is not trauma but complicity.¹⁰⁷ *Patterns of Childhood* has been criticized as individualistic and acquiescent. Some have argued that, by focusing on personal guilt, Wolf avoids an exploration and criticism of political structures.¹⁰⁸ And yet, while it is true that social and political mechanisms transcend the sphere of the individual, Wolf's interrogation of personal complicity not only differentiates her text from many other autobiographical texts, it is also mindful of the fact that, in many ways, the Third Reich relied on and elicited popular consent. The various experimental strategies that Wolf employs – her decision to write in the second and third persons, the self-reflective passages on the process of writing, the juxtaposition of different temporal layers – offer an extended meditation on the impossibility of intertwining stories that, although interconnected, run parallel to each other: the suffering of the trek, the complicity of average Germans, and the atrocity of genocide.

Erika Morgenstern: *Surviving Was More Difficult Than Dying: East Prussia 1944–48*

Unlike Dönhoff's, Hunt Jentsch's and Wolf's accounts, Erika Morgenstern's memoir paints a drastic picture of the suffering of an East Prussian mother and her children. The hunger, fear, and violence experienced by the six-year-old Erika and the heroic efforts of her mother to keep the family alive are deeply moving. And yet, *Surviving Was More Difficult Than Dying* is a difficult read not only because of the immense trauma inflicted on a child, but also because the bulk of the narrative refuses to engage with German crimes and complicity. Of course, since Morgenstern, who was born in 1939, was only a child at the time, any such complicity would not be hers, but would be transmitted through the "unconscious power of transgenerational legacies"¹⁰⁹ via her family, friends, and neighbors. And yet, Morgenstern's text is not the diary of a young girl, but the memoir of an adult – likely drawing not only on her own recollections but also on those of her mother and published decades after the war, in 2004. Although she clearly conducted research for the book and had the benefit of hindsight,[110] she does little to contextualize the experiences of her six-year-old self.

Morgenstern opens her story with the fairy tale formula "once upon a time."[111] To her, East Prussia is a beautiful land of cotton ball clouds, crystal clear lakes, white beaches, the singsong of old fir trees, and flaming fields of poppies. The doors are never locked, neighborliness is paramount, and the people are as open and uncomplicated as the land itself.[112] In short, East Prussia is a lost paradise where "everything was surrounded by love, peace, harmony and safety."[113] Morgenstern's memoir is infused with nostalgia for a happy childhood with sleigh rides, baked apples, and beach days and with longing for a land that she believes died twice: once in the war and a second time in the postwar period when memories of East Prussia were taboo.[114]

Morgenstern's romantic idealization of her homeland is typical of German discourses of *Heimat*.[115] As Blickle points out, this hypertrophic notion of *Heimat* frequently unfolded as "an act of celebrating one's own good moral qualities." *Heimat* is constructed as "the utopian antithesis to the experience of alienation in general" and inspired by the "persistent German longing for a space of innocence."[116] In Morgenstern's memoir, this innocence implies that East Prussia remained untouched by National Socialism. Morgenstern's *Heimat* is a highly stylized parallel universe where everyone was pious, respectful, and kind and where hospitality and a helping hand were extended to all without regard for social class, race, or politics. Morgenstern sharply contrasts the strict education she enjoyed with the lax pedagogy of the postwar era which, she believes, lacked "values and standards for a healthy development of soul and mind."[117] In doing so, she conveniently glosses over the fact that the "superior values" of an education in the 1930s propagated the Nazi world-view. In Morgenstern's memoir, neither the Holocaust nor National Socialism existed in her community.

The war first intrudes in Morgenstern's life in the summer of 1944, when young Erika and her family are evacuated from Königsberg but then ordered to return to the destroyed city.[118] Since their house was bombed, they move into a shabby apartment in which they live like "prisoners in a death cell."[119] To fend off starvation, Erika's mother ventured outside for food while her three- and seven-year-old daughters waited at home terrified that she would not return. In order to escape this daily horror, the family moved to the grandparents in Hindenburg near Labiau. Shortly thereafter, on January 28, 1945, the Russians approached, and they had to flee again. With the land route now cut off, they were forced to cross the ice of the

Haff, and young Erika watched in horror as wagons broke through the ice and low-flying planes shot at anything that moved.[120] Worst of all, her mother realized that the refugees were moving in circles and decided to go back to Königsberg. In Königsberg, now a "burning, smoking, stinking, whistling hell of death,"[121] they climbed over rubble amidst constant artillery fire accompanied by the incessant screaming of the wounded and dying. Eventually, they made their way to the harbor, caught a ship to Pillau, boarded a train to Rauschen, and then hitched a ride on a truck, which, because of an expected major attack, took them back to Königsberg.

Once the attack was over and the fires were extinguished, the Russians entered the city and the mass rapes began. Erika's heart-wrenching scream-ing protected her mother at first, but soon she too was raped. Women and children were taken from their basement hideouts to camps (*Sammellager*), and Erika's mother was chosen to bury young soldiers in mass graves. To avoid deportation to Russian work camps, they fled again, and, after several more harrowing days, found refuge with an old lady, *Frau* Schubert, with whom they formed a strong bond. During the next couple of months, Erika's life was determined by hunger (she reports rumors of cannibalism), fear of death and of being separated from her mother. Erika worried about being easy prey for deportation when her mother was out looking for food, and she was terrified when her mother contracted typhoid. Miraculously, however, her mother returned from the makeshift hospital, one of very few patients to survive in spite of inadequate medication and food.

Morgenstern refers to the next stop on her journey, the town of Blöcken where her mother is forcefully recruited for farm work, as the time that robbed her of her ability to laugh.[122] In the labor camp of Blöcken, a woman must show up for work for ten days in a row in order to receive her ration of food. No rations are allotted to dependents, that is, children and old people. Since one ten-day ration consisted of a quarter loaf of bread, one spoonful each of white beans, sugar, and fat, those who did not want to starve had to steal food from heavily guarded fields. Even the smallest accident was a matter of life and death.[123] For three years, her mother set out on nocturnal foraging expeditions after a day of back-breaking labor while Erika sought to make a contribution by gathering firewood, berries, and herbs.[124] For Erika, life is characterized by hunger, fear of the Russian authorities and of being denounced by German neigh-bors, and worry about her mother during the latter's nightly forays. When her beloved Tante Schubert succumbs to blood poisoning, Erika has to take over all household duties. Although she longs to go to school, she grows up like a feral child, clinging to a book that she found but cannot read and trying to draw letters in the sand. In spite of everything, Erika, her mother, and her sister survive and are released on April 1, 1948. When they leave for Germany, Erika is fifteen years old. She finally learns to read, and, for the first time in years, she eats eggs and cheese.

There is no doubt that Morgenstern's experiences were traumatizing. Even before she was confined to the Blöcken camp, she was surrounded by death and pain. On the trek, dead bodies were ubiquitous: rape victims, bodies lined up by the side of the road, burnt to a crisp or floating in the water of the harbor: "Wherever I looked, always only bestially mutilated corpses."[125] Moreover, Morgenstern's traumatizing experiences are not isolated incidents but unfold in a context of hundreds of similar tragedies, to which she alludes in terse references.[126] And yet, while Morgenstern's narrative of the trek is an important contribution to our knowledge of the Second World War, her account of the root cause of all this terror is conveniently narrow. Morgenstern lays the blame for her fate squarely on Hitler's shoulders and his alone. In a manner reminiscent of Andreas Hillgruber's theory of "two kinds of ruin" (*zweierlei Untergang*), Morgenstern sees the Germans as victims of Hitler much like the Jews: "The injustice that he had inflicted on his own and other nations . . . found its completion with us" as the Germans "followed their fellow Jewish citizens and many others who had been murdered by the Nazis."[127] In assigning Hitler, or a small group of Nazi functionaries,[128] sole blame for both the Holocaust and the expulsion, Morgenstern elides the complicity of ordinary Germans in the Third Reich. To be sure, it is true that the obstinate refusal of the regime to acknowledge defeat contributed significantly to the suffering of German civilians. It is also true that Morgenstern was far too young to be accused of complicity herself. Hers is indeed a "life tragedy through no fault of her own."[129] And yet, in equating Jewish and German suffering, Morgenstern plays into revisionist interpretations of the trek.

Morgenstern's insistence that the Nazi elite is to blame for the war is complemented by the blanket assumption that women did not participate in the Nazi regime and are thus innocent qua gender.[130] Again, this too is a highly problematic claim. Women and children pay a steep price in war, but transferring the innocence of children onto all adult women glosses over the fact that, in spite of the structural discrimination against women in the Nazi regime, women were citizens and as such responsible for the political decisions they made. Some women were opposed to National Socialist ideology and innocent of all involvement in Nazi crimes, many others were not. If there is a lesson in these texts, it is not only that we must strive to avoid war at all cost, but also that we should be wary of any easy identification of women and victimization. Woman's agency comprised a plethora of possibilities: some were resourceful survivors, some resisted the regime, others were complicit with it.

In spite of ideological resonances with Nawratil and Knabe, however, Morgenstern's memoir offers a call for reconciliation and friendship that is not evident in these revisionist accounts. She strives earnestly to present a differentiated picture of the Russians, fondly recalls her friendship with a Polish prisoner of war, and refers to many kind acts of Russian soldiers who gave her bread or offered a ride.[131] She even empathizes with the Russian occupiers who were forced to leave their homes to resettle in the now devastated East Prussia and feels pity for a homesick Russian soldier: "Basically, he did not do any better than we did."[132] Although Morgenstern could never reconcile herself to the losses inflicted on her by the war,[133] she started to read history books and to comprehend that her story unfolded in a larger context: "The more I read, the more I was able to understand the atrocities of the Russian nation against us."[134] Tellingly, though, this insight is presented on the last two pages of the book, cut off from the main narrative. In Morgenstern's memoir, German crimes and suffering remain parallel stories while German complicity is nowhere in sight.

Katharina Elliger: *And Deep in the Soul the Distance: The Story of a Displacement from Silesia*

Much like Morgenstern, Elliger, a native of Bauerwitz in upper Silesia, experienced the trek and expulsion as deeply traumatizing. Like Morgenstern's memoir, her account, which was also published in 2004, renders the horror of the trek in graphic detail. But unlike Morgenstern, Elliger, who also fled with her mother, interrogates her own and her family's role in the National Socialist regime. Undoubtedly, her willingness to engage with the issue of complicity is a factor of age – born in 1929, Elliger was ten years older than Morgenstern and thus possessed more agency at the time – but it may also have to do with her political background. Unlike Morgenstern, who is silent about her family's politics, Elliger describes parents who remained at a distance to the regime.

For Elliger, the coming ordeal announced itself in December 1944, when treks began to move through town. In spite of rumors about the approaching Russian army, Elliger's mother trusted the assurances of the local authorities that the *Führer* would never let the enemy penetrate German soil and decided to stay. When the civilian population was finally instructed to evacuate, Elliger and her mother – she had lost her father to illness – missed the last train to Dresden, a mishap that turned out to be a blessing in disguise since almost all passengers of this train died in the Dresden inferno of February 13 and 14, 1945. On February 16, Bauerwitz experienced the first of many air raids, and the young Elliger found herself a target of low-flying bombers. In the chaos of an unorganized evacuation, those desperate to leave Bauerwitz were impeded by refugees who were returning because of a lack of nourishment or shelter on route. Elliger and her mother were again stranded when a farmer who had promised to take them in his wagon clandestinely left without them. After a frantic search for a means of transportation, they joined the trek west with their luggage on a wheelbarrow.

Throughout, Elliger's memoir is marked by the striking evocation of painfully intensified feelings. Much like Hunt Jentsch, Elliger juxtaposes moments of relative calm, intense pleasure, and even happiness – for example, when she sleeps on an open wagon gazing at the moon – with the enormous strain of the trek and its many horrors. When Elliger and her mother leave the trek to strike out on their own, they happen upon a farmer's family whose tongues had been nailed to the table. They also have several close encounters with enemy tanks. When the Russian army catches up with them, they decide to return to Bauerwitz, now completely destroyed. Elliger works for the Russians but makes every effort to minimize contact with them. Because she hides in potato cellars and piles of hay, she is not raped herself, but she does hear the screams of the many women who were less fortunate.

In the following months, Elliger's life was reduced to the bare essentials, and she had to expend tremendous effort to satisfy the most basic needs. In order to secure winter clothing for her daughter, Elliger's mother embarked on a 140-kilometer journey on foot. Much like procuring clothing, finding food for the family was a full-time job that involved long trips and painstaking labor. Elliger and her mother became hunter-gatherers whose diet consisted of dandelion, birch bark, elderberry, and rosehip. All the while, they had to fend off Russian and Polish soldiers, who shot at them and tried to rape them. When the Poles replaced the Russian occupiers, Elliger, whose familiarity with Polish culture extended no further than a passing acquaintance with Chopin, was elated and expected better treatment.[135] But to her surprise (she claims to have had no knowledge of German war crimes), the Polish occupiers proved far more cruel than the Russians. Elliger was imprisoned in a camp in a former brick factory where the lack of hygiene and food along with brutal treatment made her life miserable. During a typhoid epidemic, Elliger had to participate in the daily disposal of corpses. After a failed attempt to escape, Elliger and her mother were lined up against a wall for a mock execution. Eventually, they were able to purchase "exit permits" and left their hometown for good.

On route, they experienced yet more reversals in fortune.[136] They found refuge at an uncle's house, but were soon homeless again when Poles moved in. Elliger, recalling a day when the Polish farmer's wife for whom she worked forced her to lick up her own vomit, writes that she lost hope during this time: "There was nobody who could help me. My mother too could not help me. There were only people who wanted to destroy me and people who were as helpless as I."[137] At long last, Elliger and her mother were deported to the West German city of Ahlen. During this trip in an overcrowded train with eighty people per wagon and no provisions, they used every stop to look for grass to eat or puddles to drink from. In Ahlen, Elliger was accepted into a convent school after a humiliating time as a domestic servant on a farm. Both her brothers survived the war, but her sister died of tuberculosis in 1968. Elliger suffered from depression, but, unlike her brother Bernhard who never adjusted to his new life, she recovered and became a teacher and writer.

While Elliger illustrates her suffering in graphic detail, she also makes an effort to contextualize her experience. Unlike Morgenstern, Elliger does not open with stories of an idyllic childhood, cruelly disrupted by the war, but rather combines memories of her early years with the description of her first postwar trip to Bauerwitz in 1999 at the end of the book. As a point of entry into her story, Elliger chooses the march of German soldiers through Bauerwitz in 1939, noting that even as a little girl she doubted the official version of a German response to Polish aggression.

With great honesty, Elliger explores her own complicity in the regime. She recounts that she was taken in by the Nazis and consciously seeks to recover the perspective of the child she was then. Raised in a family that was critical of the Nazis and continued to shop in Jewish stores, Elliger experienced moments of critical distance and doubt.[138] She describes various forms of anti-Semitic discrimination and recalls that, as a child, she was puzzled by this and wondered what the Jews had done to merit such treatment. She also recalls keeping her doubts secret for fear of punishment. Elliger reports that she initially enjoyed participation in the Hitler Youth, but was soon disillusioned with it. She also remembers that she threw some bread out the window when Russian prisoners of war and concentration camp inmates from Auschwitz marched past her house and that she found dead bodies the next day.

Elliger's narrative of the trek is interwoven with a thought process that reflects the author's increasing awareness of German war crimes. Much like Morgenstern, Elliger compares the victimization of Germans to that of Jews – "What had we done to be so without rights? ... Now we were defamed and marked, just like we had branded the Jews with the Star of David"[139] – but she also points to a causal connection that acknowledges German guilt and complicity. Gradually, Elliger begins to question her own role in the war. Writing about a Russian cemetery, she asks: "What had they died for? Did I have something to do with it? I was a child of this town that liked to play, read, learn, and have fun. I had not wished for their death. And yet, I felt that this Russian cemetery was a threatening accusation, like a mirror held in front of us that revealed what we had done. After all, I too had marched with the Hitler Youth."[140]

Elliger takes great pains to contextualize the horror of the trek with references to German war crimes and with a reflection on her own complicity. While Morgenstern draws a clear line between average Germans and a small group of Nazis, Elliger locates National Socialism in the midst of German society. And yet, even though she makes an effort to offer a balanced account, she cannot reconcile her own story with her knowledge of the Holocaust and feels silenced. During her visit to Silesia in 1999,[141] she wonders: "I still always thought that I had to justify myself for what I had experienced. Wouldn't my experiences be relativized immediately? It still felt like my life was not worth anything. In any case, the fear of hurtful responses and the imcomprehension of others were still so big that I preferred not to say anything."[142] When she has trouble orienting herself in the changed landscape, she is gripped by a panic that her story is not real: "The old fear came over me again. What I am looking for does not exist. I've made it up."[143] In spite of her fears, Elliger emerges from her trip to the past not bitter, but proud of her homeland and firmly anchored in life. At the same time, the difficulty of doing justice to the suffering of Germans, her own complicity, and the victimization of Jews remains inscribed in Elliger's memoir to the very end. Although Elliger visits Auschwitz, she declares that she cannot write about it.[144] There is no room for the representation of both German suffering and the Holocaust in one memoir.

Conclusion

An analysis of autobiographically inspired texts about the trek offers a variety of valuable insights. To begin with, stories of the trek are highly gendered, frequently told by mothers or their daughters, and framed as a failure of or challenge to maternal care. It is notable that the formation of tightly knit communities of women, surrogate families of sorts, features so prominently in some of these memoirs. Much has been made of frontline camaraderie, a staple in war novels by male authors, but little critical attention has been devoted to these communities of women, even though they proved invaluable for survival. Second, it is evident that, even though the trek was defined by the loss of one's belongings, social differences continued to shape the world of the refugees. A comparison of the accounts of Dönhoff and Morgenstern shows that one's social class, and the availability or lack of resources that comes with it, directly impacted one's experience of the trek. Finally, it is instructive to observe how different authors embrace different forms of coming to terms with the past. While Morgenstern and Elliger struggle to make peace with their traumatic memories and Dönhoff and Hunt Jentsch build a future by repressing and turning a blind eye to some aspects of the past, Wolf seeks to account for German complicity. Clearly, narratives of the trek are not easily mapped onto a linear timeline of *Vergangenheitsbewältigung*. Although Morgenstern and Elliger published their memoirs in 2004, their texts are largely unmarked by public and scholarly discourses on the German past. In contrast, Wolf's text precedes much that has been written about the Holocaust, and yet it offers a highly sophisticated analysis of complicity of her former self, her own family, and her hometown.

The texts discussed here differ in many and important ways, but they are united by one common feature: all testify to the extreme difficulty of combining stories of suffering with both a depiction of the Holocaust and an exploration of one's complicity. Although it is often acknowledged that the categories of victim and perpetrator are not mutually exclusive, narrative accounts frequently resist attempts to merge them: authors who emphasize their agency omit or downplay their suffering while authors who perceive their suffering as overbearing struggle to integrate questions of complicity and guilt. Thus, albeit in different ways, all these texts are marked by the great difficulty of creating narratives that do justice to individual suffering while acknowledging not only Germany's immense burden of guilt but also one's own role in it.

Perhaps we would do better to think of a joint discourse of German complicity, crimes, and suffering as a multigenerational project. After all, the trek has not faded from memory but reemerges in recent fiction written by the grandchildren of refugees. In Tanja Dückers's *Himmelskörper* (2003), for example, the death of her grandmother Jo and her own pregnancy motivate the grandchild-protagonist Freia to investigate family secrets. When she was a child, all her questions about the war were fended off with half-baked explanations,[145] while the story of the trek was shared liberally but in a highly rehearsed, rigid form. Slowly, though, the carefully cultivated family narrative of a critical distance to the Nazis dissolves when the dying, delirious Jo reveals that she was a committed member of the NSDAP and gives free reign to racist slurs. Jo and Freia's mother, Renate, were admitted on board a ship and were thus able to save themselves because the four-year-old Renate denounced the political loyalty of another family and raised her arm in the Hitler salute.[146] Thus, Dückers's novel not only "balance[s] a largely empathetic identification with Germans as victims with an awareness of Germany's historical responsibility,"[147] but engages specifically with the complicity of female family members.

Clearly, the challenge to acknowledge both suffering and complicity constitutes one of the most important tasks in the writing and reception of these memoirs. But there is another important lesson to be learned. The memoirs of female refugees teach us that war is not fought exclusively on the battlefield, but has a tendency to pervade the entire web of society. And just as it affects all of society, war also emanates from the midst of society. Once we accept that suffering and complicity are not mutually exclusive categories, we also learn that the Holocaust did not begin in the concentration camps but originated much earlier in the gradual unraveling of civil life.

Notes

1. Note that the experience of being a refugee and of rape often go together. Not all rape victims were refugees, but most accounts of the trek mention rape (see, for example, Neary, *Frauen und Vertreibung*, 25, 35, 47).
2. On the difficulty of combining these stories, see also Boa, who notes that "the history of the millions of victims of National Socialist racial policies and that of German survivors of the war cannot be joined up; there is no integrated perspective on Germans as perpetrators and as victims, only jolting gear shifts ... the trauma of coming to know about the Holocaust overlies the child's trauma and changes its meaning" ("Wolf, *Kindheitsmuster*," 85).

3. Douglas calls them "a political hot potato" (*Orderly and Humane*, 3).
4. On refugees and gender, see Marfleet, *Refugees in a Global Era*, 198–199, and Callamard, "Refugee Women."
5. Here, I disagree with Jansen's readings of *Kindheitsmuster*. Although Wolf does integrate narratives of German suffering and German guilt, as Jansen argues, she achieves this not by representing the trek, but by discussing the impossibility of doing so. See also Schaal, who points out that very few critical discussions of *Kindheitsmuster* deal with the representation of the trek (*Jenseits von Oder und Lethe*, 197).
6. Estimates of the number of German refugee casualties range from 200,000 to 2.3 million (see Shephard, *The Long Road Home*, 125). Moeller lists 500,000 ("Politics of the Past," 27), while Naimark believes that as many as 2.5 million died in the process (*Fires of Hatred*, 14). On Jewish DPs, see Shephard, *The Long Road Home*, 102.
7. See Schwendemann, "Tod zwischen den Fronten," 72.
8. "Als seien sie Puppen" (Bienek cited in Helbig, Hoffmann, and Kraemer, *Verlorene Heimaten*, 36).
9. See Schenck, *Vom Massenelend der Frauen*, 92–93.
10. At the Potsdam conference in August 1945, the Allies approved the mass transfer of the German populations from Poland, Czechoslovakia, and Hungary (see Ahonen, Corni, Kochanowski, Schulze, Stark, and Stelzl-Marx, *People on the Move*. 82).
11. Douglas, *Orderly and Humane*, 1.
12. "30 MINUTEN ZEIT – MIT HÖCHSTENS 8 KILO GEPÄCK PRO PERSON" (Jirgl 5).
13. See Douglas, *Orderly and Humane*, 172.
14. Until 1948, the so-called *Koalitionsverbot* forbade the formation of interest groups. After 1948, the refugees organized in regional groups, the *Landsmannschaften* (Homeland Societies). The *Bund der Heimatvertriebenen und Entrechteten* (League of Expellees and Deprived of Rights) was founded in 1950, the *Bund der Vertriebenen* (League of Expellees), an umbrella organization, in 1957.
15. See Kossert, *Kalte Heimat*, 131.
16. See Ahonen, Corni, Kochanowski, Schulze, Stark, and Stelzl-Marx, *People on the Move*, 17–20; Brumlik, *Wer Sturm sät*, 20–29; Schlögel, "Bugwelle des Krieges," 179–181.
17. See Benz, "Fünfzig Jahre," 8, and "Generalplan," 46. Ahonen gives a higher number: 1.5 million Poles (37). All in all, the *Generalplan Ost* called for the removal or murder of up to 50 million people in Central and Eastern Europe (Douglas, *Orderly and Humane*, 41). See also Ahonen, Corni, Kochanowski, Schulze, Stark, and Stelzl-Marx, *People on the Move*, 33–42.
18. Neary and Schneider-Ricks, *Voices of Loss and Courage*, XXII. See also Nawratil, who presents the suffering of German refugees as the mirror image of the plight of Nazi victims (*Schwarzbuch der Vertreibung 1945 bis 1948*, 70). Others suggest that the suffering of the German refugees was the

worst suffering of civilians since the Thirty-Years' War (see Darnstädt and Wiegrefe, "Vater, erschieß mich!," 29).

19. "Das sowjetische Lagerpersonal unterschied sich auch mental von dem der Nationalsozialisten. Schiebereien, Schwarzhandel und Alkoholexzesse waren an der Tagesordnung" (Knabe, *Tag der Befreiung?*, 300). See also 70–71.

20. "Noch niemals in der Geschichte ist eine so grosse Bevölkerung liquidiert und mit einem einzigen Federstreich aus Atlanten und Geschichtsbüchern getilgt worden" (Nawratil, *Schwarzbuch der Vertreibung 1945 bis 1948*, 73).

21. "Die jedes westeuropäische Verfassungsvermögen überschritt" (Nawratil, *Schwarzbuch der Vertreibung 1945 bis 1948*, 161).

22. Niven, "Introduction," 5.

23. Taberner, "Representations," 173.

24. Naimark, *Fires of Hatred*, 122.

25. Douglas, *Orderly and Humane*, 63. While Naimark and Douglas take the connection between Nazi aggression and German suffering for granted, others consider such a causal link irrelevant. De Zayas, for example, does not contextualize the trek but rather insists that "all victims of injustice deserve our respect" (*A Terrible Revenge*, 3) regardless of nationality and circumstance. In some accounts, denying the link between Hitler's war and the plight of German refugees forms part of a larger anti-Soviet agenda. Thus, Nawratil maintains that the war was not the cause of the displacement, but simply a welcome opportunity (*Schwarzbuch der Vertreibung 1945 bis 1948*, 179); see also Knabe, who claims that the Soviet Union bears considerable responsibility for "Ausbruch und Verlauf des Krieges" ("the outbreak and course of the war") (*Tag der Befreiung?*, 24). Erika Steinbach, the controversial former president of the Federation of Expellees (*Vertriebenenverband*), makes a similar argument. Steinbach calls the mass expulsions a diplomatically arranged and systematically prepared "capital crime" ("Grossverbrechen") ("Vorwort," 10). In a baffling inversion, she accuses the Soviet Union of using its Second World War victory to implement dreams of a pan-Slavic empire. Furthermore, Steinbach emphasizes that the extent of the crimes against refugees in specific areas does not correlate to the severity of Nazi cruelty in these regions (see "Vorwort," 8–10). Steinbach's argument is not completely unfounded: there is some evidence that local populations who had collaborated with the Nazis were more prone to abusive behavior toward German refugees than anti-Nazi resistance fighters, even though the latter were more likely to have suffered from Nazi violence. However, even if it is not possible to posit a one-to-one correspondence, it is reasonable to assume that the sadistic behavior and policies of Germans during the war, including a war of aggression, genocide, and the abuse of forced laborers and prisoners of war, played a role in how Germans were treated after the war.

26. "Es waren keine Täter, an denen sich die Wut der Sieger austobte – es waren Wehrlose. Vor allem Frauen, Kinder, alte Menschen" (Knopp, *Die grosse Flucht*, 10).

27. "Die Vertreibungsverbrechen gehören zu den bestdokumentierten, aber am schlechtesten publizierten Massenverbrechen der Geschichte" (Nawratil, *Schwarzbuch der Vertreibung 1945 bis 1948*, 14).
28. In addition to individual documents such as memoirs, the *Ministerium für Vertriebene, Flüchtlinge und Kriegsgeschädigte* (Ministry of Expellees, Refugees and War-Damaged), abolished in 1969, commissioned the multivolume "Dokumentation der Vertreibung der Deutschen aus Ost-Mitteleuropa" ("Documentation of the Expulsions of Germans from Eastern and Middle Europe"), the archival records include the "Ostdokumentensammlung" ("Collection of Documents from the East") of the *Bundesarchiv* in Koblenz and the "Gesamterhebung zur Klärung des Schicksals der deutschen Bevölkerung in den Vertreibungsgebieten" ("Complete Survey Clarifying the Destiny of the German Population in the Displacement Areas") by the *Kirchliche Suchdienst*, Munich.
29. Niven, "Introduction," 8.
30. According to Austrian novelist Gertrud Fussenegger, "hatten wir als gute Demokraten die Pflicht, die eigenen Schmerzen und Verluste unter den Tisch zu wischen und nur der Vorteile zu gedenken, die uns der eigene Untergang gebracht hat" ("as good democrats, we were obligated to sweep our own pain and losses under the rug and think only of the advantages gained from our own downfall") (Fussenegger in Kroll, *Flucht und Vertreibung in der Literatur nach 1945*, 23).
31. See Malempré, *Flintenweib*, 9.
32. "Sie wollten uns alle ausrotten und vernichten wie Ungeziefer" (Elliger, *Und tief in der Seele das Ferne*, 142). Although Elliger relies on Nazi rhetoric here, her memoir, as I explain later in this volume, probes the issue of German complicity.
33. Berger argues that, contrary to expectations, "only a small minority of texts can be seen as genuinely revisionist or revanchist" ("Expulsion," 42).
34. "Was haben meine Brüder in Russland gemacht, dass die so über uns herfielen?" (Meinhof, *Das Tagebuch der Maria Meinhof*, 7).
35. "Damals war ich darüber geschockt, aber heute, sechzig Jahre später und nach Erhalt vieler Informationen über diesen höllischen Krieg, kann ich diese Besatzungen verstehen. Es war die Reaktion auf das viele Leid, was ihnen und ihren Familien zu Beginn des Krieges zugefügt worden ist" (Hesse-Werner, *Als Pommern brannte*, 17).
36. "Die Rachegelüste der Polen, . . . die Siegerorgien der Russen waren irgendwie verständlich gewesen, denn an beiden Völkern hatten die Nazis im Namen des Deutschen Volkes schwerste Verbrechen begangen" (Taubitz, *Treibgut*, 52).
37. See Panzer, *Ich war fünf und hatte das Leben noch vor mir*, 41.
38. "Völkische oder nationalistische Tendenzen" (Helbig, *Der ungeheure Verlust*, 264); "starke Komponente der Menschlichkeit und des Wunsches nach Versöhnung" (41).
39. "Gemeinschaft des Leidens" (Helbig, *Der ungeheure Verlust*, 262).

40. Niven, "Introduction," 20.
41. "Mich nur drei Händedrücke von Humboldt, Schadow, Rauch oder Goethe trennten" (Dönhoff, *Kindheit*, 7).
42. "Die Königsstuben" (Dönhoff, *Kindheit*, 10).
43. www.zeit.de/2002/12/Ritt_gen_Westen
44. When her fur gloves were stolen, Dönhoff fashioned substitutes from ski socks and requisitioned curtains.
45. "Ein Pferd war in diesen Zeiten ein Königreich wert" (Dönhoff, *Namen*, 39).
46. This is not clear, however. Malempré's memoir includes a reference to a Countess Dönhoff who was raped, but does not clarify if this refers to Marion von Dönhoff (*Flintenweib*, 64).
47. Cf. "Noch nie hat der Führer eines Volkes so gründlich das Geschäft des Gegners betrieben, noch nie hat ein oberster Kriegsherr seine Soldaten durch so dilettantisches Führen selbst zu Hunderttausenden in den Tod getrieben" ("Never has a leader of a people conducted the business of the opponent so thoroughly, never has a supreme commander driven hundreds of thousands of soldiers to their deaths through his dilettante leadership") (Dönhoff, *Namen*, 47) and "Was jener Wahnsinnige verspielt hat, lässt sich nicht zurückgewinnen" ("What this insane man gambled away, one cannot win back") (12).
48. See, for example, her comment that Secretary Fräulein Markowski is "eine begeisterte Anhängerin des Führers" ("an enthusiastic supporter of the Führer") (Dönhoff, *Namen*, 33).
49. "Verlorenen Paradies" (Dönhoff, *Namen*, 77); "versunkene[n] Welt, in der die Jahreszeiten den Rhythmus des Lebens noch ganz unmittelbar bestimmten" (11).
50. "600 Jahre Geschichte ausgelöscht" (Dönhoff, *Namen*, 19).
51. "Die zu Hause blieben, sind nicht mehr daheim" (Dönhoff, *Namen*, 75).
52. "Vielleicht ist dies der höchste Grad der Liebe: zu lieben ohne zu besitzen" (Dönhoff, *Kindheit*, 218).
53. "Wer könnte es den Polen verdenken? Nie zuvor war ja auch einem Volk soviel Leid zugefügt worden wie ihnen während des Dritten Reichs" (cited in Schwarzer, *Marion Dönhoff*, 335).
54. For example, Dönhoff's 1979 essay "Holocaust: A Lesson in German History."
55. See also Schwarzer, who notes Dönhoff's inability to use the first person (*Marion Dönhoff*, 27).
56. See Mumford's epilogue in Hunt Jentsch, *Trek*, 245.
57. Hunt Jentsch, *Trek*, 19.
58. Hunt Jentsch, *Trek*, 118.
59. Hunt Jentsch, *Trek*, 30.
60. Hunt Jentsch, *Trek*, 95.
61. Hunt Jentsch, *Trek*, 123.
62. Hunt Jentsch, *Trek*, 141.
63. See Hunt Jentsch, *Trek*, 25 and 27.
64. Hunt Jentsch, *Trek*, 27.

65. Hunt Jentsch, *Trek*, 167.
66. Hunt Jentsch, *Trek*, 51.
67. Hunt Jentsch, *Trek*, 95.
68. Hunt Jentsch, *Trek*, 97 and 162.
69. Hunt Jentsch, *Trek*, 166.
70. "Alle Figuren in diesem Buch sind Erfindungen der Erzählerin. Keine ist identisch mit einer lebenden oder toten Person. Ebensowenig decken sich beschriebene Episoden mit tatsächlichen Vorgängen" (Wolf, *Kindheitsmuster*, 6).
71. Rippl, Schweighauser, and Steffen, "Introduction," 7. According to Komar, "both Wolf and Nelly Jordan flee the approaching Russian troops in 1945; both serve as secretary to the mayor in the local principality. Both Wolf and Jordan recover from a mild case of lung disease in a sanatorium" ("The Difficulty of Saying 'I,'" 267). Furthermore, like Nelly, Wolf was a member of the Hitler Youth, and, as Hilzinger points out, Wolf's mother's sister had a child by a Jewish doctor; her uncle bought a candy factory from a Jewish owner; and Wolf's father was in charge of prisoners of war (*Christa Wolf, Kindheitsmuster*, 12–13). In light of such similarities, Ganguli notes "a certain hesitation in the minds of critics to apply to it the term 'novel'" ("Patterns of Childhood," 54).
72. "Mein Buch über 1945" (cited in Hilzinger, *Christa Wolf*, 90).
73. Nelly's uncle Alfons Radde, for example, acquires the candy factory of the Jew Geminder for very little money. For signs of resistance, scholars have pointed to Nelly's mother, who provides "rudimentary apprenticeship in political opposition" (Kraft, "Searching for a Motherland," 149).
74. On Wolf's research, see Camfield, "Das Zitat als narrative Struktur am Beispiel der Lieder in Christa Wolfs *Kindheitsmuster*," 24.
75. See Wolf, 219 and 42. To Holub, this is an example of "how information was not consciously absorbed even when it was published and available" ("Fact, Fantasy and Female Subjectivity," 219).
76. "Das scheint uns leichtzufallen. Überhören, übersehen, vernachlässigen, verleugnen, verlernen, verschwitzen, vergessen" (Wolf, *Kindheitsmuster*, 141).
77. Weedon points out that an interest in "the role played by ordinary people under the Nazis" was largely absent in GDR literature ("Childhood Memory and Moral Responsibility," 238).
78. "Bloss dass dieses Vieh dir nicht entfernt dasselbe Interesse abnötigt wie jene Masse von Halbmensch-Halbvieh, über die du, allgemein gesprochen, aus dir selber heraus besser Bescheid weisst" (Wolf, *Kindheitsmuster*, 39).
79. On the concept of conformity, see Marks, "The Alienation of I," 76. See also Wolf: "Das Vergangene ist nicht tot; es ist nicht einmal vergangen" ("The past is not dead; it is not even past") (Wolf, *Kindheitsmuster*, 9).
80. Wolf does not include Prague and Poland in her discussion of contemporary events, which several scholars interpret as a failure to take a stance against GDR politics (Fell, "Lenkas Traum," 247; Stephens, "Die Verführung der Worte," 130). In contrast, Boa argues that the novel "alludes to Stalinist persecution and criticizes the GDR for authoritarianism, inadequate

education about the Holocaust and popular racism" ("Labyrinths," 134). See also Hilzinger, who points out that the American translation of *Kindheitsmuster* omitted references to Vietnam (*Christa Wolf,* 94). Note also that Wolf did transgress taboos of a different nature: much GDR literature of the time portrayed "Helden, die sich schnell wandeln ... die eigentlich schon während des Faschismus zu ziemlich bedeutenden und richtigen Einsichten kommen, politisch, menschlich. Ich will keinem Autor sein Erlebnis bestreiten. Aber mein Erlebnis war anders" ("heroes who change quickly ... who gain relatively important and correct insights even during fascism, political, humane. I do not want to dispute the experience of any author. But my experience was different") (cited in Stephan, "Von Aufenthalten, Hosenknöpfen und Kindheitsmustern," 129). Wiesehan notes that, by focusing on bystanders, Wolf contradicted the GDR's "official theory of Fascism, according to which a 'criminal minority' of monopoly capitalist agents held the German people against their will" ("Christa Wolf Reconsidered," 80).

81. Here I disagree with Brangwen Stone, who notes that the narrative of the flight is fragmentary but argues that the narrator decides "that the story of German suffering can be told" ("Visiting the Hometown, Revisiting the Past," 604).

82. On *Umsiedler,* i.e., German refugees in the GDR, see Kossert, *Kalte Heimat*; see also Stone, "Visiting the Hometown, Revisiting the Past," 599; on the systematic denial of the experience of rape and the trek in GDR literature, see Dahlke, "Tagebuch des Überlebens," 200. For a representation of the expulsion in GDR literature, see also the novel *Wir Flüchtlingskinder* by Ursula Höntsch-Harendt. *Wir Flüchtlingskinder* offers a more detailed description of the trek than Wolf, but, compared with many contemporary reports, it too downplays the suffering of the refugees, particularly during the train ride west, which is condensed onto two pages (the second expulsion is somewhat longer and contains more grueling details). Höntsch-Harendt takes care not to denigrate the Russians ("so schlimm sind die Russen gar nicht") ("the Russians are not so bad") (87), and is careful to juxtapose German suffering with the suffering inflicted by Germans. However, unlike Wolf, she does not explore the complicity of average Germans and focuses instead on a couple of diehard Nazis.

83. See "Frühere Versuche fingen anders an: mit der Flucht" (Wolf, *Kindheitsmuster,* 10; earlier attempts started differently: with the trek).

84. Wolf, *Kindheitsmuster,* 262 and 273.

85. "Nelly weiss, was zu tun ist. Sie stellt sich taub und unwissend. Dann wurde sie es" (Wolf, *Kindheitsmuster,* 68).

86. "Heute weisst du, dass es im Zeitalter des Argwohns das aufrichtige Wort nicht gibt, weil der aufrichtige Sprecher auf den angewiesen ist, der aufrichtig zuhören wollte, und weil dem, dem lange das verzerrte Echo seiner Worte zurückschlägt, die Aufrichtigkeit vergeht" (333). See also Dwyer, who notes a reluctance "to concede control over her text to the reader" ("Runaway Texts," 622).

87. "Nach einer Woche den Strick nehmen" ("took the rope after a week") (Wolf, *Kindheitsmuster*, 331).
88. "Im Taxi die deutsche Kriegsschuld beweisen müssen" (Wolf, *Kindheitsmuster*, 331).
89. "Das will er nicht wahrhaben, dass die Rechnung der anderen Seite, wenn es ans Aufrechnen ginge, grösser wäre" (Wolf, *Kindheitsmuster*, 332).
90. "Ich Faszination" (Annemarie Auer cited in Pickerodt, "Christa Wolfs Roman *Kindheitsmuster*," 297); "so pflegen pensionierte Studienräte, ältere Pfarrer und brave Hausfrauen uns mit der Geschichte ihrer Familien zu belästigen" (cited on 297).
91. "Umschlagstelle vom Objekt zum Subjekt und wieder zum Objekt" (cited in Jackson and Saunders, "Christa Wolf's *Kindheitsmuster*," 324).
92. "Flucht wider Willen – auch eines der Stichworte, auf die ein Leben sich festlegen liesse" (Wolf, *Kindheitsmuster*, 251).
93. Similarly, throughout the book, the comments of the narrator's daughter Lenka offer a contrast to the feelings and thoughts of Nelly, who grew up in a dictatorship.
94. "Die Szenen, die sich auf dem Bahnhof abgespielt haben, mag der beschreiben, der sie miterlebt hat" (Wolf, *Kindheitsmuster*, 262).
95. "Mit einmal ist dir das Interesse dafür abhanden gekommen, zu beschreiben, wie einige Leute – Deutsche – das Ende dieses Krieges erlebt haben. Diese Leute können dir gestohlen bleiben. Ein Lied, in diesem Sommer 74 von Deutschen gesungen, hat dir jede Anteilnahme an ihnen genommen" (Wolf, *Kindheitsmuster*, 266).
96. The leitmotif of a baby that froze to death and was handed to a young woman haunts Wolf's prose like a ghostly affliction (see Didon, *Kassandrarufe*, 65).
97. "Verfall der Sitten" (Wolf, *Kindheitsmuster*, 270).
98. "Wir heissen euch hoffen" (Wolf, *Kindheitsmuster*, 268).
99. Stone, "The Pitfalls of Constructing a Female Genealogy," 50 and 56.
100. Stone, "The Pitfalls of Constructing a Female Genealogy," 57.
101. "Unser Vaterland ist kaputt . . . Sie sind die Sieger" (Wolf, *Kindheitsmuster*, 305).
102. "Wo habt ihr bloss alle gelebt" (Wolf, *Kindheitsmuster*, 306).
103. Levine, *Witness*, 107.
104. "Für immer dahin ist die schöne freie Entsprechung der Gefühle mit den Vorgängen" ("The beautiful free correspondence of feelings and events is gone forever") (Wolf, *Kindheitsmuster*, 151). See also Merkel ("Selbstreferenz und Selbsterschaffung aus dem Möglichkeitssinn," 87) and Voutta ("Figurationen des Unwiederholbaren," 187), who point out that the title *Patterns of Childhood* points to habituation through repetition.
105. "Wenn zweite und dritte Person wieder in der ersten zusammenträfen, mehr noch: zusammenfielen" (Wolf, *Kindheitsmuster*, 322). Gumpert interprets this goal as the end of the intentional separation and alienation from one's own history ("Noch einmal," 112). Lutz Köpnick sees the failure to achieve a first-person narrative stance as a strength because it acknowledges the

impossibility to ever come to terms with fascism ("Rettung und Destruktion," 85).

106. "Es nämlich unerträglich ist, bei dem Wort Auschwitz das kleine Wort ich mitdenken zu müssen" (Wolf, *Kindheitsmuster*, 215).

107. See also Mahr, who notes that female memoirists who dissolve the memoir's easy identification of author, narrator, and female protagonist are more likely to be critical of the Nazis (*Kriegsliteratur von Frauen?*, 451).

108. In her article "Pleasures of Fear," Anke Pinkert claims that Christa Wolf's form of dissidence ultimately serves to strengthen the GDR (34).

109. Stone, "Pitfalls," 58.

110. She offers information about East Prussia's history and economy, e.g., that East Prussia fed the entire Reich with its cornucopia of wheat, milk, and cheese; and that the borders of East Prussia had remained stable from 1422 to 1919.

111. "Es war einmal" (Morgenstern, *Überleben war schwerer als Sterben*, 6).

112. "Immer half man einander" ("One always helped each other") (Morgenstern, *Überleben war schwerer als Sterben*, 39); see also 6–7, 10.

113. "Alles war umhüllt von Liebe, Frieden, Harmonie und Geborgenheit" (Morgenstern, *Überleben war schwerer als Sterben*, 214).

114. "Man liess Ostpreussen ein zweites Mal sterben" ("They let East Prussia die a second time") (Morgenstern, *Überleben war schwerer als Sterben*, 14).

115. See Costagli, who notes that many responded to the loss of these territories with retrospective idealization of these landscapes ("Unverhofftes Wiedersehen," 282).

116. Blickle, *Heimat*, 20, 17 and IX.

117. "In der es keine Werte, Richtlinien und Massstäbe für eine gesunde Entwicklung von Seele und Geist gibt" (Morgenstern, *Überleben war schwerer als Sterben*, 26).

118. The reports of refugees from Königsberg and East Prussia included in the collection edited by Neary and Schneider-Ricks bear striking similarities to the events recounted in Morgenstern's memoir (see *Voices of Loss and Courage*, 70–91, particularly 87–88).

119. "Gefangene in einer Todeszelle" (Morgenstern, *Überleben war schwerer als Sterben*, 58).

120. "Sie machten keinen Unterschied, ob Soldat oder Zivilist, sie schossen auf alle Deutschen" ("They did not differentiate between soldiers and civilians, they shot at all Germans") (Morgenstern, *Überleben war schwerer als Sterben*, 65).

121. "Brennende, qualmende, stinkende, pfeifende Todeshölle" (Morgenstern, *Überleben war schwerer als Sterben*, 68).

122. "Raubte mir das Lachen" (Morgenstern, *Überleben war schwerer als Sterben*, 146).

123. When Erika loses the key to their room, the family can no longer protect their few belongings from theft and Erika herself can no longer venture outside. She survives festering boils on her legs because a traveling nun

treats her with penicillin and is almost shot by the Russians for stealing potatoes.

124. During this time, their diet included nettles, the only available source of vitamins, and meat from a frozen horse that the women had buried and secretly dug up again at night.

125. "Wohin auch mein Blick fiel, immer nur bestialisch verstümmelte Leichen" (Morgenstern, *Überleben war schwerer als Sterben*, 97).

126. One of her camp mates lost the youngest of her four children because she did not have the strength to push her two youngest in a wheelbarrow through the snow (Morgenstern, *Überleben war schwerer als Sterben*, 155). Another woman died when she tried to protect her daughter from rape.

127. "Das Unrecht, das er seinem eigenen Volk und den anderen Völkern zugefügt hatte ... erfüllte sich jetzt an uns" (Morgenstern, *Überleben war schwerer als Sterben*, 118). "Sie folgten ihren jüdischen Mitbürgern und vielen anderen von den Nazis Ermordeten in den Tod" (Morgenstern, *Überleben war schwerer als Sterben*, 15).

128. There is a reference to a small elite of Nazi functionaries whom she holds responsible for the war and she also highlights the Nazi refusal to evacuate Königsberg that led to the deaths of 85,000 Germans.

129. "Unverschuldete Lebenstragödie" (Morgenstern, *Überleben war schwerer als Sterben*, 18).

130. "Einmal mehr mussten arme, unschuldige Frauen für etwas büssen, das sie nicht angerichtet hatten" ("Once more poor, innocent women had to atone for what they had not caused (Morgenstern, *Überleben war schwerer als Sterben*, 134). See also "Wir fühlten uns ... zur Strafarbeit verurteilt für einen Krieg, den wir nicht verschuldet hatten. Aber müssen nach Kriegen nicht immer vor allem Mütter und Kinder dafür büssen?" ("We felt sentenced to forced labor for a war that we had not caused. But is it not always primarily mothers and children who have to pay after wars?") (Morgenstern, *Überleben war schwerer als Sterben*, 151).

131. She also comments that some Russians are highly educated and disciplined, a frequently recurring trope in memoirs of the trek.

132. "Im Grunde ging es ihm nicht besser als uns" (Morgenstern, *Überleben war schwerer als Sterben*, 188).

133. "Den Verlust unserer schönen Heimat Ostpreussen und die Zerrüttung unserer grossen, harmonischen Familienbande habe ich nie verwunden" ("I have never overcome the loss of our beautiful homeland East Prussia and the breakdown of our big, harmonious family ties") (Morgenstern, *Überleben war schwerer als Sterben*, 303).

134. "Je mehr ich las, desto mehr konnte ich die Greueltaten der russischen Bevölkerung an uns, der ostpreussischen Bevölkerung verstehen. Wenn man bedenkt, was die deutsche Armee beim Überfall auf die Sowjetunion im Jahre 1941 an Massakern unter der russischen Zivilbevölkerung angerichtet hat" (Morgenstern, *Überleben war schwerer als Sterben*, 302).

135. She writes that she assumed that, since Poles are Catholics, Polish culture is much like German culture.

136. Elliger was rounded up by a random soldier and almost ended up in a death camp, but escaped again.

137. "Es gab niemanden mehr, von dem ich Hilfe erwarten durfte. Auch meine Mutter konnte mir nicht helfen. Es gab nur Menschen, die mich vernichten wollten, und Menschen, die hilflos waren wie ich selbst" (Elliger, *Und tief in der Seele das Ferne*, 145).

138. For example, she reports being confused by the Nazi euphemism "shortening of the front line" ("*Frontverkürzungen*").

139. "Was hatten wir getan, um so rechtlos zu sein? . . . Wir waren nun verfemt und gekennzeichnet, wie wir die Juden mit dem Judenstern gebrandmarkt hatten" (Elliger, *Und tief in der Seele das Ferne*, 142–143).

140. "Wofür waren sie gefallen? Hatte ich etwas damit zu tun? Ich war ein Kind dieser Stadt, das gerne spielte, las, lernte und Spässe machte. Ich hatte ihren Tod nicht gewollt. Und doch empfand ich diesen Russenfriedhof wie eine bedrohliche Anklage, wie einen Spiegel, der uns vorgehalten und in dem offenbar wurde, was wir angerichtet hatten. Schliesslich war ich auch in der Hitlerjugend mitmarschiert" (Elliger, *Und tief in der Seele das Ferne*, 133–134).

141. This visit to the old homeland in the East is a common trope in memoirs of the trek. Gumpert considers it a genre in its own right: "Wiederbegegnungsliteratur" ("literature of re-encounters" ("Noch einmal," 111).

142. "Ich meinte immer noch, mich rechtfertigen zu müssen für das, was ich erlebt hatte . . . Würden meine Erlebnisse nicht sofort relativiert werden? Es kam mir immer noch so vor, als sei mein Schicksal nichts wert. Die Angst vor verletzenden Reaktionen und dem Unverständnis der anderen war jedenfalls nach wie vor so gross, dass auch ich es vorzog, nichts zu sagen" (Elliger, *Und tief in der Seele das Ferne*, 212).

143. "Mich überfiel wieder die alte Angst: Was ich suche, gibt es gar nicht, ich habe es mir nur eingebildet" (Elliger, *Und tief in der Seele das Ferne*, 241).

144. "Es wäre zu banal. Hier war alles vom Tode durchdrungen. . . . Wieder war ich entsetzt darüber, was Menschen Menschen antun können" ("It would be too banal. Everything here was permeated by death. . . . Again, I was horrified about what people do to people") (Elliger, *Und tief in der Seele das Ferne*, 231).

145. "Kinder, ihr fragt uns Löcher in den Bauch" ("Kids, you ask us holes in the stomach") (Dückers, *Himmelskörper*, 82).

146. While Dückers explores the family secret of complicity, Petra Reski's *Ein Land so weit* describes how the author gradually abandoned blanket suspicions of revanchist intentions (23–24) and comes to appreciate her East Prussian and Silesian roots. She offers details of the trek west, but does not elaborate on the National Socialist activities in her grandfather's family.

147. Berger, "Expulsion Novels of the 1950s," 19; see also Eigler, "Beyond the Victims Debate," 82.

CHAPTER 6

A View from the Outside In
Jewish Women and German Complicity

While the memoirs of non-Jewish German women tend to emphasize their reluctance to comply with the regime's policies and their endeavors not to cooperate any more than absolutely necessary, the life writing of Jewish women highlights the constant exposure to anti-Semitism in everyday life as well as numerous interactions and encounters with Germans of both genders who passively condoned or actively supported the regime.[1] All memoirs by Jewish women stress the increasing hostility of the non-Jewish social environment and the growing alienation from non-Jewish neighbors and former friends. As such, these memoirs not only remind us that "social death was the prerequisite for deportation and genocide," but also undermine "the myth of political innocence with which so many Germans today surround their accounts of 'daily life in Nazi Germany.'"[2] Although the vast majority of Nazi perpetrators was male, not female, a significant number of women was complicit with the regime while non-Jewish women who resisted or rescued Jews were "deplorably few."[3]

Again and again, memoirs by Jewish women detail their increasing isolation in German society. Jewish physician and Auschwitz survivor Lucie Adelsberger, for example, reports that, long before her deportation, she no longer felt at home in Berlin: "the people were different, too – no longer friends, but enemies."[4] Similarly, Eva Salier, a German-Dutch Jew and Holocaust survivor, writes that "it didn't take long for our friends and neighbors to shun us ... at school we were called *die Unkräuter*."[5] In addition to being shunned by former friends and neighbors, many Jews had to stand by as Germans stole their property. Thus, Czech Jewess Cecilie Klein recalls looking on as her neighbors carried silverware out of her sister's house while others "stood by and jeered, 'You Jews deserve this!'"[6] Hilde Huppert, whose Holocaust memoirs were edited by Arnold Zweig, even declares that greed provided the motivation for murder: "The Germans had murdered in order to rob."[7]

In light of these experiences, it is hardly surprising that memoirs by Jewish women emphasize that those who wanted to know about the plight of the Jews did know, whereas it required a great deal of effort and mental acrobatics to maintain one's willful ignorance. Scenes of Germans and Poles who either look on indifferently or cheer as Jews are marched through town are a staple in Holocaust memoirs. Thus, Simha Naor, an Auschwitz survivor, writes that "[we] were hunted again through fields and forests, occasionally saw people who indifferently hardly took note of our passing ... we are numbered and have yellow Stars of David. ... These Germans whom we had met must have known who we were, where we came from? And still? Or perhaps because of it this indifference?"[8] While Naor is shocked by the indifference of random bystanders, Rena Kornreich Gelissen, a Polish Jewess and Auschwitz survivor, remembers aggression and hostility: "We are marched through the middle of town to work. The townspeople come out of their shops and homes to spit at us as we pass. ... We are not human beings to them; we are lower than dogs."[9] Similarly, Ruth Klüger recalls being "loaned" to townspeople who stared at them "as though we were savages,"[10] and Sarah Miller, a young Polish woman who survived the occupation in France, recounts how "clusters of neighbors standing nearby on the street stopped to gawk at haggard men and women who were herded into trucks and suddenly whisked away."[11]

Another constant of memoirs by female Holocaust survivors is the view from the outside in. The crippling feeling of isolation and exclusion from an environment that used to be one's home finds expression in the image of the persecuted Jew peeking into the houses of Germans who are unperturbed by the violent persecution of their former neighbors. Thus, Czech Jewess Hana Muller Bruml writes: "We walked through the village at night. ... There were lit windows, and at Christmas people had Christmas trees. There were people living normal lives."[12] Similarly, Olga Lengyel, a Hungarian Jewess and camp physician at Auschwitz, declares that she "can never express the feelings which the sight of normal civilian life created in me. Homes with curtained windows behind which free people lived."[13] One of the most poignant expressions of this view from the outside in is contained in Rena Kornreich Gelissen's memoir *Rena's Promise: A Story of Sisters in Auschwitz*. In Kornreich Gelissen's eyes, an elegant woman on a passing train embodies everything that she has lost:

> [A] train passes us in the distance. I turn from my work to watch its journey, and for one moment my mind is transported beyond the walls and work fields of Auschwitz-Birkenau. There a woman bedecked in a white hat and

white gloves, her chin leaning on her pristine wrist, is looking out the window, looking at me, looking through me as if I were not there. She is clean and refined. She looks as if she might be going to visit somebody and the greatest burden on her mind is what to serve for dinner tonight . . . there is no stopping the tears pouring from the corners of my eyes. Where is she going? I ask myself. Why does she have a life and I have nothing?[14]

In memoirs by female Holocaust survivors, German women are not portrayed as innocent victims. Rather, they are indifferent onlookers at best and devoted Nazis at worst. They are also reminders of a normality from which Jewish women have been excluded. While memoirs by non-Jewish Germans tend to emphasize their inner distance to the regime, memoirs of Holocaust survivors portray the average German as an enthusiastic supporter of Hitler: "All Germans wore Nazi Party badges, and children were proud of their swastikas and were conscious of their importance as members of the master race."[15] Indeed, several Jewish survivors report that one of the most effective strategies of escaping Nazi persecution was to mimic the habitual anti-Semitism of one's environment. Thus, when Cecilie Klein tried to hide her Jewishness, she read an anti-Semitic newspaper and realized that she blended in perfectly.[16]

In the following, I discuss the representation of German women's complicity in the Holocaust memoirs of four Jewish women writers: Betty Lauer's memoir *Hiding in Plain Sight: The Incredible True Story of a German-Jewish Teenager's Struggle to Survive in Nazi-Occupied Poland*, composed in the 1950s, but published in 2004, details how the author survived the war in Nazi-occupied Poland by pretending to be a Polish Christian; Inge Deutschkron's *I Wore the Yellow Star* (*Ich trug den gelben Stern*) (1978) and Marie Simon Jalowicz's *Gone to Ground: One Woman's Extraordinary Account of Survival in the Heart of Nazi Germany* (*Untergetaucht: Eine junge Frau überlebt in Berlin 1940–1945*), published posthumously in 2014, both chronicle the author's life as a hidden Jew in wartime Berlin; finally, Ruth Klüger's *Still Alive: A Holocaust Girlhood Remembered* (*Weiter leben: Eine Jugend*) (1992) combines the narrative of the author's experiences in Hitler's death camps with sophisticated theoretical reflections on writing, memory, and discourses of *Vergangenheitsbewältigung*.

As this brief surveys shows, three of the four writers discussed here – Betty Lauer, Inge Deutschkron, and Marie Jalowicz – survived the war in hiding and/or by assuming an "Aryan" identity. I have chosen to focus on memoirs of women in hiding not only because I believe that their voices should be heard – as Sayner reminds us, women's memoirs about the Holocaust "have seldom become part of the canon of Holocaust literature"[17] and are cited less frequently in scholarly studies[18] – but also because the focus on women writers who "lived on the Aryan side" offers a particularly intimate look at the complicity of German women. While memoirs that focus on the author's experiences in concentration camps tend to portray Germans who worked in the camps and who can thus hardly be classified as bystanders, authors who survived in hiding encountered a wide range of personalities and moral choices. Moreover, because many Jews in hiding remained on the home front, they dealt with a larger number of German women and were thus in an ideal position to observe and evaluate their attitudes toward and behavior in the National Socialist reign of terror.

It is no accident that most memoirs of life in hiding are authored by women. As Weitzman has shown, 69 percent of all Jews who survived the war by passing as "Aryans" were women.[19] Those who chose a life in hiding were also more likely to be young, single, and from middle- or upper-middle-class families.[20] Conversely, "passing" presented a much greater challenge for men who were circumcised and could thus be identified as Jews.[21] In addition to this physical marker, adult Jewish men faced yet another obstacle: since almost every able-bodied German man was serving in the army, a healthy, middle-aged man without a Star of David immediately raised suspicions. In contrast, the presence of an adult woman in a German city did not call for an explanation. Finally, it is not accidental that two of the U-boats discussed here chose to stay in Berlin, the heart of the Nazi empire, while the third, Lauer, survived in Krakow and Warsaw. The anonymity of big cities offered the most propitious venue if one wanted to remain undetected. Deutschkron and Jalowicz were among the approximately 5,000 hidden Jews in wartime Berlin, the so-called U-boats who, like submarines, remained submerged but had to resurface every once in a while to make money or get provisions.[22] Of these 5,000, 1,400 survived the war.[23]

Although my analysis focuses on the concept of complicity, I do not mean to suggest that complicity is the only way in which German women cooperated with the Nazi regime. Many memoirs by female survivors include representations of women perpetrators. Nanda Herbermann, for example, who was imprisoned in Ravensbrück because of her work for the Catholic resistance in the circle of Bishop Clemens August Graf von Galen, writes about female guards who were accompanied by trained dogs and who took pleasure in inflicting untold suffering. She specifically remembers female guards who taunted inmates by challenging them "to end our lives at the electrically charged barbed wire."[24] Similarly, Grete Salus, a Jewish woman from Bohemia who survived Theresienstadt, Auschwitz, and Oederan, a satellite camp of Flossenbürg, notes that the female guards used the inmates as a "lightning rod for all their primitive instincts" and expresses her shock at "how much pleasure she [a guard] took in torturing human beings."[25]

Clearly, complicity is not the worst form of women's culpability portrayed in these memoirs nor are criminal sadism and compliant indifference the only forms of female behavior that these memoirs describe. Just as female Holocaust survivors record the cruelty of female concentration camp guards, they also remember German women who provided help and assistance, ranging from small gestures to significant sacrifices. Thus, Anita Lasker Wallfisch, who survived Bergen-Belsen and Auschwitz, where she was the cellist in the camp orchestra, recalls a Miss Neubert who worked for the manufacturer of toy soldiers that Lasker Wallfisch painted in prison. As part of her official duties, Miss Neubert had contact with the imprisoned Lasker Wallfisch and made a point of bringing cake, which the latter acknowledges gratefully: "It gave me a great lift at a time when I needed it most."[26] Similarly, when Betty Lauer's train was bombed and she found herself stranded in Germany with no money for public transportation, a young German girl saved the day by giving her 50 DMark: "The unsolicited offer, this act of kindness, brought tears to my eyes."[27] Clearly, although complicity forms the subject of this chapter, it is not the only form of interaction with German women portrayed in these memoirs.

While Lauer, Deutschkron, and Jalowicz were all in a position to witness the moral choices of German women from up close, their perspectives differed significantly. Unlike Deutschkron and Jalowicz, who spent the war years in Berlin, Lauer, a native German victim of the "*Polenaktion*," survived the war in Poland and thus experienced the Germans as an occupying force. Moreover, although Deutschkron and Jalowicz both hid in Berlin, their representations of German complicity differ markedly. While Deutschkron's memoir is particularly attuned to threats and humiliations by strangers, Jalowicz's most cruel suffering is inflicted by those who are her most important protectors and helpers. Finally, I have chosen to conclude this chapter with an analysis of Ruth Klüger's *Still Alive*. While Klüger did not go into hiding, her memoir includes recollections of numerous interactions with non-Jewish German women during her childhood in Vienna and in the postwar period as well as sophisticated reflections on the role of women in the Third Reich and on the nature of guilt and complicity.

Betty Lauer's *Hiding in Plain Sight: The Incredible True Story of a German-Jewish Teenager's Struggle to Survive in Nazi-Occupied Poland*

Betty Lauer, née Bertel Weissberger, started working on her manuscript in the 1950s, long before it was published in 2004. Entitled *Hiding in Plain Sight: The Incredible True Story of a German-Jewish Teenager's Struggle to Survive in Nazi-Occupied Poland*, Lauer's memoir, which comprises 550 pages, contains a great many details and vivid dialogues that testify to Lauer's talent as a writer. Although German is Lauer's native language, she, like many German Holocaust survivors, chose to write her story in English. She prefaces her account with an assurance that she portrayed her experiences truthfully, but notes that she changed some names to disguise the identity of some of the people mentioned in her text.

Her story begins in the German town of Hindenburg in April 1938, when her father received an expulsion order and emigrated to the United States. Betty, her mother, and her sister stayed on at first but fell victim to the *Polenaktion* on October 28, 1938, when the Nazis combed Germany for Jews of Polish nationality, loaded them onto trucks, and drove them to the Polish border. Since Poland refused to accept them, many were left stranded in No-Man's Land. Lauer and her mother managed to escape and spent the next couple of weeks with various Polish relatives.

Even before the expulsion, Lauer's family was confronted with growing hostility in their own hometown. Their neighbors stopped talking to them, the glass of their storefront window was broken, and the walls of their house were defaced with swastika graffiti. Gradually, their former friends and acquaintances turned from them. The superintendent of their house, a communist who owed his position to Lauer's father, no longer dared associate with them for fear that he would "once again wind up in prison."[28] *Frau* Pilne, the proprietress of the local bar, started to avoid them and no longer returned their greeting. Although she agreed to store their belongings, she "received the first package without saying a word."[29] Lauer further reports that the social experience of Jewish children was no different from that of their parents. Ursel Würfel, the daughter of the owner of the local hotel, "renounced all her Jewish friends" "when Herr Würfel joined the Nazi Party,"[30] and other non-Jewish girls who used to play with Lauer followed suit. They no longer wanted anything to do with Lauer and even began to taunt and chase her.

When the Germans invaded Poland, Lauer started working for Lutka Gomulka, a Polish dressmaker who relied on Lauer's German-language skills for communication with her many German clients. Unlike Deutschkron and Jalowicz, who hid among their countrymen in Berlin, Lauer, albeit born in Germany, spent the war years in Poland and thus experienced the Germans from an entirely different perspective: as an occupying force. She saw how German officers moved into the homes of forcibly removed Jews and witnessed firsthand their contempt for the local population. In her function as a dressmaker's assistant, most of Lauer's daily interactions were with German women who took full advantage of their supposed racial superiority: "The German women, who considered themselves members of the master race, were outraged by their dressmaker's lack of punctuality. Their common refrain was to complain about how sloppy Poles were and to disparage the Poles and their slave mentality."[31] In the colonial atmosphere of occupied Poland, the Nazi overlords and their female companions gave free reign to their disdain for the Polish and Jewish *Untermenschen*.

Repeatedly, Lauer suffered gross abuse at the hands of her German women customers. When she made a house call to the wife of a *Gestapo* official, the latter, upon noticing her armband, screamed at her and threatened to throw her down the stairs.[32] During her next house call, the wealthy wife of an employee of the Todt Company, "a woman in her fifties who suffered from a curvature of the spine," hurled insults at her. Lauer portrays *Frau* Heinrich as a crippled woman with a "venomous" temper,[33] who takes her unhappiness out on those who are in no position to defend themselves: "I heard *Frau* Heinrich shriek. She stood before me, her face an angry red, her finger pointing at my armband. 'How dare you!' She screamed. 'The effrontery to appear in my presence, you Jewish pig! A Jewess touching my garments. Fräulein Gomulka will soon learn that we won't tolerate this type of sabotage against the Reich.'"[34] Terrified by Heinrich's outburst, Lauer fled and fell down a flight of stairs, gravely injuring herself. But the episode does not end there. In her chauffeur-driven car, *Frau* Heinrich took it upon herself to call at Gomulka's house to demand the termination of Lauer's employment, to which Gomulka consented. *Frau* Heinrich's persecution of the young Lauer appears all the more vicious since Heinrich so clearly lived a life of luxury. Lauer's portrayal of her female Nazi customers suggests in no uncertain terms that their virulent anti-Semitism was not derivative. Rather, it was felt deeply and expressed violently. Both women customers displayed a great deal of aggression and, in *Frau* Heinrich's case, expended much effort and initiative to see a Jewish woman humiliated. In Lauer's memoir, non-Jewish German women in Poland fall in one of two categories: those who go out of their way to persecute and harm Jews and those who remain oblivious to Jewish suffering while they go about their business in the occupied city, shopping in the old town of Warsaw and enjoying the luxuries acquired in a criminal war.

When the Nazis started to deport Jews to concentration camps, Lauer and her mother quickly realized "that liquidation meant elimination."[35] Lauer, her mother and her sister Eva, who was arrested later on and deported, had the foresight to live outside of the Jewish ghetto, from whence deportations took place, and decided to go into hiding when the situation became untenable. They acquired false identity papers and assumed a Polish-Aryan identity. While her mother spoke Polish like a native, Lauer and her sister had a strong German accent. In order to hide this deficiency, they repeatedly pretended to be deaf. Even without such handicaps, life in hiding required constant vigilance and "nerves of steel"[36] since "the whole province is riddled with informers ... and one can't know who they are."[37] Passing as an Aryan also required considerable chutzpah since, as Weitzman explains, incongruous behavior was more likely to be overlooked and explained away "if one is confident and convincing in one's assumed identity."[38] At first, Lauer and her family lived on a farm in the village of Szczucin, and Lauer found work at the local magistrate's office. Soon, however, a disgruntled colleague grew suspicious and, fearing discovery, they moved to Krakow.

As Lauer's experience in Szczucin shows, Jews in hiding had to contend not only with the German enemy but also with Polish collaborators. Thus, every second spent in public was potentially life-threatening. Lauer notes that, while she herself was often able to pass unnoticed, her mother, who looked "Jewish," "was accosted, pursued and several times held by the arm, in an attempt to point her out to a policeman or a *Gestapo* agent."[39] Indeed, Polish collaboration was crucially important to the success of the Nazi persecution of Jews. According to Dr. Edith Kramer, an inmate physician in a camp in Posen, the Germans were unable to identify Polish Jews: "at first the Germans didn't know who was a Jew and who was not, but the Polish people began to point us out right away."[40] To expedite their genocidal policies, the Germans offered financial compensation to any Pole who informed on Jews. Conversely, ubiquitous posters warned that Christians who offered help to Jews would be severely punished. This two-pronged approach of enticement and punishment was highly effective. As Lauer notes, "it was beyond our comprehension that, in spite of lack of coal, inadequate clothing, and the continuous effort needed to get enough food, so many Poles were helping the Nazis round up Jews."[41]

In Krakow, Lauer worked as a nursemaid for *Frau* Ludwig, the wife of a highly placed official in the occupation authority. Like so many residences of career Nazis, *Frau* Ludwig's house was filled with art and Persian rugs stolen from deported Jews. *Frau* Ludwig moved in privileged circles and regularly attended receptions hosted by Governor Frank. In spite of her elevated social position, *Frau* Ludwig remains an unreadable character in Lauer's story. Before she hired Lauer, "she wanted to know if I was bitter and whether I hated all Germans."[42] *Frau* Ludwig's question evinces awareness of the German mistreatment of the Polish population, but it is not clear if her query is motivated by self-interest or by a guilty conscience. Similarly, when the *Gestapo* later came to the house to pick up another Jewish nursemaid who was also in hiding in the Ludwig residence, *Frau* Ludwig assured them that her employees were not Jewish and that "we have to hire some Poles to do the work. We can't live here and do all the work ourselves."[43] Again, it is not clear if *Frau* Ludwig was truly ignorant of her maid's identity, if she deemed racial concerns to be less important than effective help in the household, or if she was motivated by a genuine desire to help two Jewish girls – though it is curious that every other potential employer who interviewed Lauer immediately suspected her of being Jewish, just as it is notable that *Frau* Ludwig employed not one but two hidden Jews. In any case, Lauer, who likely never knew the answer to these questions herself, does not satisfy her reader's curiosity. Terrified by the arrival of the *Gestapo*, she left the house under a pretext and fled to Warsaw, where she found work in a garment factory. In Warsaw, she also made several Christian friends who remained unaware of her Jewish identity but whose company helped her maintain her cover.

When the Germans began to lose the war and the Polish Home Army fought to liberate Warsaw, Lauer took an active part in the struggle. She first worked at a first-aid station and then assisted her Gentile boyfriend Stefan, a photographer who documented the battle of Warsaw. (Later on, Stefan agreed to marry Lauer because it afforded her an additional layer of protection.) In spite of the initial Polish success, Lauer remained wary of her surroundings and did not disclose her Jewish identity, a decision that turned out to be prescient when the Germans retook the city. Along with many other Poles, Stefan and Lauer were marched to a train and taken to an internment camp in the German town of Spellen. There, they managed to secure a work permit for Katowitz in Silesia by bribing a camp official. During a layover in Berlin on route to Katowitz, Lauer was again confronted with German anti-Semitism: Much like her Nazi customers in Poland, the proprietress of a boarding house hurled insults at the couple and, refusing to rent them a room for the night, threw them out into the street: "We don't want you here. We'll take care of our own, and you go back to where you belong . . . we heard her shriek, 'Keine Juden und keine Ausländer.'"[44] When they finally found lodging, Lauer was taken aback by the level of luxury still available in German households: coffee from a china cup, fresh rolls, baths.

Against all odds, both Lauer and her mother survived the war. Even though they found it most difficult to abandon their search for Eva, whose final destiny remained unknown, they decided to join Lauer's father in the United States. Before she left Europe, however, Lauer visited her German hometown of Hindenburg one last time. During this visit, she ran into Fräulein Hedel, her former nanny and "once loyal family friend."[45] Although they used to share a deep bond, Lauer realizes immediately that their relationship is irreparably broken: "each of us knew that nothing would ever be as it had been, as it should have been. . . . The crimes committed against the Jewish people were too horrific to put into words. They were hovering between us, an insurmountable barrier."[46] Their differences emerge more clearly when Fräulein Hedel starts complaining about her own and her family's victimization at the hands of the Russians. While Lauer considered the Soviet soldiers her liberators and felt deep gratitude toward them, Hedel resented them because they deported her husband. Lauer concludes:

> [O]ur realities did not coincide. . . . She wanted me to understand that she and some members of her family, though not all, had also been victims of a war they did not want and of a regime they apparently had not embraced. . . . I knew that Hedel did not understand . . . I had not mentioned Eva, and I sensed that perhaps she did not really want to know the gruesome truth . . . I was not yet ready to sympathize with the victimization of German nationals who had been duped by Hitler, their elected leader.[47]

During this visit, Lauer was accompanied by Stefan, who did not speak German, while the Hedels did not speak Polish. As Lauer translated for Stefan and Hedel, she edited out Stefan's insulting comments about the Germans and Hedel's continuous references to her and her family's victimization. At the same time and even though the visit was clearly a strain on both parties, it is evident how much Fräulein Hedel valued her relationship to Lauer and how deeply she felt the loss. Fräulein Hedel taught her "Aryan" children Hebrew songs, which they now performed for Lauer, and presented photos from their time together, all of which she had kept as treasured possessions. Hedel insisted on giving Lauer her gold watch as a parting gift, but "there was an understanding that our paths would not cross again."[48] In return, Lauer bought expensive woolen leggings for Hedel's children and offered to intercede with the Polish authorities on Hedel's behalf. When Lauer decided to return the watch, Hedel told her, "I wanted to say something I could not put into words. ... 'I understand,' I responded. 'We are trying to say to each other what is important to both of us. We both won't forget.'"[49] It would appear that what remains unspoken in this exchange of gifts is Hedel's silent recognition of responsibility and an attempt at restitution, which Lauer rejected when she returned the watch, and Lauer's equally nonverbal attempt to acknowledge Hedel's suffering. However, the result is not reconciliation but rather a mutual understanding that there will be no further contact between the two. The rift runs too deep. For even when Hedel speaks about the plight of the Jews, she pivots back to her own victimization and consequently regards the Russians, not the National Socialists, as her true enemies: "'I will never really know what you endured. ... The Jews were powerless. ... We, however, did have an alternative. When the Russians invaded, we could have resisted. ... The wily Russians duped us.'... And we who thought we had nothing to fear, who never even belonged to the party, we have to pay the price."[50] Tellingly, in Hedel's account, it is the Russian invasion that the Germans should have resisted, not Nazi policies.

When Lauer and Stefan were deported to Germany, they received help from a young woman, and Lauer comments that "Stefan had to change his view about the German people. He had thought that all Germans were Nazis, and therefore all Germans were evil."[51] Implicit in this statement is a comparison in which Lauer herself is more balanced in her evaluation of the Germans than Stefan. And yet, the experiences she depicts in her memoir would seem to contradict this guarded judgment. Although Lauer is deeply touched by the German woman who gives them money when they needed it most, this female helper remains a lone figure in a mass of complicitous bystanders and vicious anti-Semites. The non-Jewish German women Lauer portrays are either virulently anti-Semitic, completely oblivious to the gross mistreatment of the Jews even when it occurs right in front of their eyes, or so preoccupied with their own suffering that there is little room for compassion with others.

Inge Deutschkron's *I Wore the Yellow Star*

Inge Deutschkron is one of the approximately 1,400 Jews who managed to elude their Nazi captors by hiding in wartime Berlin. Like so many others, Deutschkron and her mother failed to leave Germany in time because they initially believed that the Nazis would target men while sparing women and children. Since her father, an active socialist, was liable to persecution on both political and racial grounds, Deutschkron and her mother encouraged him to seek asylum in England.[52] When they attempted to join him, the war had started, the borders were closed, and they could not get out.

Although *I Wore the Yellow Star* was first published in 1978, Deutschkron started writing about her experiences in October 1945. The addressee of her account was her father. Since all contact to her father had broken off soon after his emigration, Deutschkron wanted to explain to him what she had gone through during her years in hiding. She completed her memoir three decades after the war when she lived in Israel. *I Wore the Yellow Star* offers a step-by-step account of how the noose gradually tightened. As the Nazis expanded their power, more and more civic arenas, including public transportation, parks, the cinema, and museums, were designated as off limits to Jews. Deutschkron was no longer permitted to attend public school, and was sent to a Jewish school instead. When isolation was followed by deportation, Deutschkron and her mother moved from one hiding place to another to escape the fate assigned to Jews. Survival under these circumstances required considerable skill and resourcefulness. While remaining under the Nazi radar was most easily accomplished if one stayed hidden, securing food and shelter required reemerging into the public sphere. U-boats, as hidden Jews were called, had to learn whom to trust, how to avoid the vicious denunciations of disgruntled acquaintances and the prying eyes of nosy neighbors, how to defend themselves against the abuses of problematic helpers, and how to make peace with their dependence on the kindness of others.

Through considerable efforts, Inge Deutschkron managed to secure employment, first in a workshop for the blind that remained exempt from Nazi persecution because its owner, Otto Weidt, who succeeded in saving fifty-six Jews,[53] manufactured goods for the army, and then in a bookstore. She obtained false papers under the name Gertrud Dereszewski, and, when this identity was no longer viable because the rightful bearer of the name was arrested, she became Inge Richter. Throughout her entire time in hiding, Deutschkron lived in constant fear of being identified as a Jew.

Like Lauer and Klüger, Deutschkron describes an increasingly hostile environment in which every neighbor was a potential enemy: "Could we be sure that such indifferent neighbors had not turned into convinced or opportunistic supporters of the new order over night?"[54] Since Deutschkron's parents were Jews and socialists, they experienced a form of double jeopardy. To protect themselves, they decided to burn all their political brochures and books in their kitchen oven because they dared not use the basement furnace where they would be exposed to their neighbors' prying eyes (they did not even dare open the windows to let out smoke for fear of arousing the suspicions of the neighbors). They then moved to a neighborhood where nobody knew about their political affiliation, but were denounced by a neighbor and subject to a search by the *Gestapo*.

Due to the Nazis' discriminatory laws designed to isolate Jews, Deutschkron's social world began to shrink until she moved in exclusively Jewish circles. When she did interact with Gentiles, contact was usually brief and fleeting. The anonymity of life in a city of millions both protected Deutschkron and made her vulnerable: she was surrounded by an anonymous mass of potential enemies whom she could not risk approaching and many of whom refused to become involved: "The Germans who did not want to know what happened around them did indeed not know how we lived in their midst."[55] Repeatedly, Deutschkron was taken aback by the attitude of willful ignorance that characterized her "Aryan" environment. The Berliners turned a blind eye to the deportations in their neighborhoods and wished to remain uninformed about the plight of Jewish citizens: "The war did not seem to exist for these people. I was very envious because they were so careless ... they knew nothing – or did not want to know anything – about the misery and distress of people who had been excluded from their society but who lived right next to them."[56]

Deutschkron's memoir is a powerful corrective to the myth of German innocence. The author describes how she came to accept anti-Semitic discrimination as a common fact of life.[57] The picture that emerges is not one of a few pro-Nazi outliers but of ubiquitous hostility toward Jews and widespread support for the *Führer*. And since women formed the majority of the population on the home front, they played a prominent role in the mistreatment of Jews like Deutschkron. At school, Deutschkron and her Jewish friends were teased and mobbed. In particular, she remembers Erika Seidel, "a true German girl with long blond braids" who flaunted her BDM membership and always greeted Deutschkron with raised hand and "*Heil Hitler.*"[58] And while she was mobbed by Hitler youth in school, in the building where she lived, she had to deal with a concierge who prominently displayed a photo of Hitler in her apartment.

Interestingly, while the confrontation with Nazi supporters in her everyday life offered an opportunity for small acts of resistance – Deutschkron poignantly countered Erika's "*Heil Hitler*" with a resounding "*Auf Wiedersehen*" – the most cutting encounters in Deutschkron's memoir are those with passing strangers. Deutschkron remembers a disconcerting experience at a subway station in which she defended herself against being objectified by a stranger:

> [T]he Star of David created a discriminating isolation. I had the feeling of carrying a mask in front of my face. There were people who looked at me with hatred. . . . I remember how this "being stared at" became intolerable once. It was at a subway station. We were waiting for the train. Again and again a woman walked past me and stared at me. Finally I could not take it any longer, approached her and asked: "Surely you have never seen a Jewess before?" She turned crimson. "Why don't you take your time to look at me very closely. I don't mind." She did not say a word and turned away.[59]

Tellingly, Deutschkron characterizes the Star of David as a mask, an objectifying mechanism that makes it impossible for others to see the person behind the forcefully imposed disguise. When Deutschkron literally talked back and thus resisted the role assigned to her, the female stranger who had stared at her blushed. In this blush lies the fleeting recognition of Deutschkron's humanity. If Deutschkron characterizes this particular encounter as "intolerable," it is perhaps because this glimmer of recognition was followed immediately by the failure to connect: the stranger did not respond and turned away. In its description of this and similar encounters, Deutschkron's memoir offers a powerful explanation why the Nazis' genocidal policies were preceded by isolating measures such as the Star of David. *I Wore the Yellow Star* paints a social world divided into two categories: Deutschkron's gentile helpers, who made her survival possible and who all emerge as well-drawn characters, and an amorphous mass of strangers who were indifferent at best and life-threatening at worst.

In her dealings with strangers, Deutschkron had to remain vigilant at all times. When Deutschkron and her mother went into hiding, the greatest threat to their safety was posed by nosy neighbors. In one hideout, a busybody neighbor forced her way into the kitchen to find out all she could about the suspicious visitors. In another hideout, Deutschkron's life was in danger because the man who helped her and her mother had an affair (with a third party) and his jealous wife sought to take revenge by denouncing his protégées to the *Gestapo*.[60] In addition to the peril of being denounced by an enterprising Nazi supporter, Deutschkron also perceived every anonymous crowd as a potential angry mob. Thus, when she worked in a milk shop, she lived in fear of her female customers: "The coming together of women was uncanny to me. They could have taken their impatience out on me. They could have denounced me. They also had a lot of time to look at me."[61]

Like many other Jews, Deutschkron also witnessed the avarice of Germans who greedily eyed Jewish belongings: "The buyers were like vultures,"[62] Deutschkron comments when her mother was forced to sell their belongings in preparation for emigration. Later on, Deutschkron witnessed how a *Gestapo* officer brought his wife along to the home of a deported Jew. Together, the couple chose linen and rugs from among the deported Jews' possessions: "The wife of the *Gestapo* official walked toward the beds, felt the down covers and said: 'Yes, good.' . . . And they took as much as they could carry."[63]

Clearly, in Deutschkron's memoir, complicity is the norm rather than the exception. Since many of Deutschkron's daily interactions involved other women, she was in an excellent position to observe the active and passive support of German women for the Nazi regime. Once the war was over, Deutschkron joined her father in England but returned to Germany in 1955 and was shocked to find so many former Nazis in positions of power. Thus, from Deutschkron's perspective, complicity with the regime did not end with the war but was plainly evident in postwar society. In response to her journalistic writings about the war and the persecution of Jews, she received threatening mail decorated with SS runes and anonymous phone calls peppered with insults. Again, the greatest threat to Deutschkron's safety emerged from an anonymous crowd of anti-Semitic strangers.

Marie Jalowicz Simon's *Underground in Berlin: A Young Woman's Extraordinary Tale of Survival in the Heart of Nazi Germany*

Unlike Lauer, Deutschkron, and Klüger, Marie Jalowicz Simon did not author her memoir herself. Although a professor of classics and devotee of the written word, Jalowicz refused to write about her experiences during the Nazi regime. On those rare occasions when she agreed to go on the record about the war, she used a pseudonym and invented cover identities for her various helpers and acquaintances. We owe the narrative of her experiences in wartime Berlin to her son's persistence. A historian himself, Hermann Simon coaxed his mother into telling her story and recorded the ensuing conversations. These joint sessions, which started in December 1997 and ended in September 1998, produced seventy-seven tapes. Jalowicz, who was born in 1922, died shortly after the completion of these interviews on September 16, 1998. Hermann Simon then tasked journalist Irene Stratenwerth with redacting the 900-page transcript. Both Simon and Stratenwerth conducted research to fill in missing dates or offer historical context and published the results as *Untergetaucht: Eine junge Frau überlebt in Berlin 1940–45* in 2014. The English translation *Underground in Berlin: A Young Woman's Extraordinary Tale of Survival in the Heart of Nazi Germany* was published in 2015.

Unlike Lauer, Deutschkron and Klüger, Marie Jalowicz Simon survived the war without the support of a close relative: her mother died of cancer in 1938 while her father succumbed to the strain and exhaustion caused by National Socialist anti-Semitic policies in 1941. An only child, most of whose relatives had been deported, Jalowicz was left to fend for herself and decided to attempt life as a U-boat in Berlin. After a period of forced labor for Siemens, she arranged for her disappearance by telling the mailman that Fräulein Jalowicz had been deported and then went underground. Since Jalowicz, the daughter of a lawyer, was highly educated, she experienced her life as a U-boat as an exile from her social class. Desperate for hiding quarters, Jalowicz was in no position to choose her helpers and frequently found refuge in socially disadvantaged, often communist neighborhoods. Expatriated from her habitual social sphere, Jalowicz saw the root cause for her situation in the failure of the German middle class: "It was primarily the German bourgeoisie that had failed."[64] While well-to-do Jews were targets of persecution themselves and thus severely limited in their capacity to offer help to other Jews, many non-Jewish members of Jalowicz's social class realized quickly that shunning Jews was a necessary prerequisite for maintaining their status. Thus, Jalowicz was forced into a milieu with which she had no previous contact: "I entered situations which I would never have dreamed of. I realized: This terrible apartment was entirely normal. There were more than a few people who lived like this."[65]

Jalowicz's decision not to author a memoir in spite of strong encouragement and publicly expressed interest is surprising not only because she was a professor of literature, but also because her commitment to the written word was so strong that even as a U-boat she took notes whenever her situation allowed for it and kept an "invisible diary" when it did not.[66] In this invisible diary, she experiments with different styles that reflect both her displacement from and her attempt to hold on to her familiar milieu: "I decided to write my inner diary in literary German for a certain period of time and in the crudest patois of whores for another period of time. I planned to think in hexameters for some time and to use older German, but had to abandon the latter."[67] In order to survive, Jalowicz had to become a social chameleon well-versed in elevated style and in the "patois of whores." Repeatedly, well-meaning acquaintances advised her to hide her education in order to blend in, but, again and again, she stood out because her level of education contrasted starkly with her poverty and social milieu. Thus, when she mentioned the name Fontane to a librarian, she was eyed suspiciously, and when she casually cited Kant, she was admonished to be more careful.

Although having to camouflage her intellectual interests and lifestyle weighed heavily upon her,[68] Jalowicz's refusal to author a memoir does not seem to be primarily motivated by the social alienation she experienced during the Third Reich. Rather, her insistence that "there is much about which one cannot talk until half a century later"[69] appears closely related to her deeply felt ambivalence toward some of the women and men who helped her survive the war. Indeed, one of the most interesting facets of Jalowicz's story consists in the representation of the various helpers who made her survival possible. Jalowicz's experiences not only show that the motivations of helpers were complex but rather necessitate a fundamental reconceptualization of the category of the "helper." To be sure, some of the men and women who came to Jalowicz's rescue acted altruistically, frequently in conformance with their religious or moral convictions. Others were prompted by friendship or spontaneous kindness. An example of such a selfless helper is the concierge at one of Jalowicz's hiding places who not only made it possible for her to use the air raid shelter but also arranged for a convenient escape route for her by convincing a dim-witted Nazi that connecting the attic of their apartment complex to that of the adjacent houses was a necessary precaution for future bombing raids. When Jalowicz thanked him, he responded: "We have to give thanks when we are allowed to help."[70] But there were also many helpers who took advantage of the plight of the Jews. Some demanded huge sums of money in exchange for shelter and food; others forced hidden Jews to work as domestic slaves, and some exploited them sexually.[71] Again and again in Jalowicz's memoir, the line between helper and perpetrator wears rather thin.

Unlike many other memoirs of U-boats, Jalowicz's account offers disturbing insights into the sexual vulnerability of persecuted Jews. Surprisingly, and contrary to conventional gender stereotypes, this vulnerability also affected Jewish men. Repeatedly, Jalowicz relied on the assistance of Jewish gynecologist Benno Heller, who helped place U-boats with his former patients. Later on, she found out that Heller had to pay for the services of Jalowicz's new landlady by sleeping with her: "'With my own virility I have to pay *Frau* Janicke for your lodgings!' I was unspeakably embarrassed, but what could I have done."[72] Similarly, Jalowicz's father did not dare refuse the advances of Hannelore Koch, who, later on, became one of Marie Jalowicz's most important, and most problematic, helpers. Without letting on why, he implored his daughter not to leave the house whenever Koch announced her visit. In addition, Jalowicz herself was not only forced to sell herself in exchange for protection but was raped repeatedly by the husbands of women who took her in. In one of her first hideouts, Willi, the communist husband of Tati Kupke, a distant relative, forced himself upon her while his wife looked the other way: "I could not raise hell nor send him away, so I let it wash over me. But I was sure that Tati was aware of everything."[73] When Willi raped her again the next night, she decided to find another shelter. Later on, Emil Koch, the husband of Hannelore Koch, raped Janowicz repeatedly, first out of revenge for her father's "affair" with his wife and later as payback when his wife was raped by a Russian soldier. In addition to these clear cases of rape, Janowicz was repeatedly in situations where she had no other option but to sell herself.[74] Thus, she agreed to marry a Chinese man in order to secure a visa to leave Germany, but abandoned her plan when she was unable to obtain the necessary permit. Later on, she entered a relationship with Dutchman Gerrit Burgers in exchange for shelter and food.

While rape offers a drastic example of the vulnerability of U-boats, it was not the only form of exploitation Jalowicz encountered. In the home of *Frau* Gerda Janicke, one of her helpers, Jalowicz was pressed into the role of a domestic slave. Jalowicz acknowledges that *Frau* Janicke risked her life for her but at the same time "she also enjoyed finally wielding power."[75] Jalowicz had to be available for housework at all times and was not allowed to leave the apartment. Because *Frau* Janicke did not share her food with Janowicz, this restriction was far more pernicious than it sounds. Janowicz's inability to leave the house cut her off from her only other source of food and led her to the brink of starvation.

Jalowicz's relationship with Luise Blase, her landlady during her time with Gerrit Burgers, is equally problematic. In particular, Blase's ongoing heated arguments with Gerrit Burgers proved dangerous to Jalowicz's safety. Again and again, banal domestic incidents devolved into angry fights followed by anti-Semitic insults and threats. Thus, when Gerrit forgot one of his boots in the kitchen, Blase called him a dirty foreigner and threatened to denounce Jalowicz "so that she would finally be killed. How she imagined this, she explained in great detail. Lust for murder and pornography were mixed together much like in the *Stürmer*."⁷⁶ And yet, when she does not heap anti-Semitic abuse upon her, Blase treats Jalowicz like the daughter she never had. Jalowicz comments: "I hated this disgusting, brown, filthy, criminal blackmailer. And I loved her like a mother figure. That's life, so complicated."⁷⁷ By far the most traumatic relationship with a helper is that with Frau Koch, who together with her husband bought the summer house of the Jalowicz family when they were no longer allowed to own property. Long after the war and indeed for the rest of her life, Jalowicz panicked at the mere thought that Hannelore Koch might come to call on her. When the Kochs bequeathed the house that had formerly belonged to her family to Jalowicz, she insisted on selling it right away and never set foot in it.⁷⁸ At the same time, Jalowicz also felt a strong sense of obligation toward Koch, who not only provided her with a fake identity by giving her her own *Kennkarte*, but repeatedly hid her in her own home and supplied her with food and money during weekly meetings. Clearly, Koch took great risks and endured personal hardships to ensure Jalowicz's survival, but she also continuously and insistently emphasized the magnitude of her sacrifice and expected eternal gratitude in return: "Promise me that you will never leave me, that you will always stay with me, and won't push me back into the misery from whence I came."⁷⁹ Repeatedly, Koch comes across as unhinged and her erratic behavior threatens Jalowicz's safety more than once.⁸⁰

In Jalowicz's account, Koch is a highly problematic helper figure. She thrived on Jalowicz's dependence and was jealous of other helpers, including her own husband, whom she did not want involved. To Koch, helping a hidden Jew was an adventure that enriched her life and gave it meaning. It also linked her to a social class to which she did not otherwise have access. Throughout, the class difference between Koch and Jalowicz was a source of conflict. Koch savored her affiliation with the upper classes, but she also felt overwhelmed by a lifestyle so different from her own and mocked Jalowicz for her bourgeois habits.⁸¹ Koch's biggest crisis occurred when Jalowicz asked her to borrow books from an uncle on her behalf but without revealing her identity. The uncle, who believed that Koch wanted to read the books herself, attempted to discuss them with her. Overwhelmed by the intellectual challenge and the pressure of making time in her already stressful schedule, Koch broke down crying, and the arrangement came to an end. In many ways, Koch is an almost tragic figure whose personal flaws were magnified by a criminal regime in which petty rivalries could have lethal effects. But from Jalowicz's perspective, the jealous, unstable disposition of her most important helper was not simply an annoyance that had to be borne but represented a grave threat to her survival.

In addition to the insightful portrayal of various helper figures, one of Jalowicz's most trenchant observations concerns the Germans' purported ignorance of Nazi crimes. In *Underground in Berlin*, "not knowing" is consistently shown to mean "not wanting to know." Thus, upon witnessing the arrest of her Jewish teacher, Jalowicz realized to her great dismay that she was supposedly the only child in her class who had seen the arrest even though it took place in broad daylight in the school building. Similarly, when she stayed in Hannelore Koch's house, she noticed that whenever one could hear loud screaming from the adjacent prisoner-of-war and forced labor camps, all the neighbors shut their windows as though on command: "That's how those people did it who claimed later on to have known nothing about it."[82]

Interestingly, Jalowicz contrasts the indifference of the German population, and of German women in particular,[83] with the active engagement on behalf of Jewish citizens that she experienced in Bulgaria. Jalowicz reports that Bulgarian girls rallied to support their Jewish schoolmates, that a Bulgarian policeman tore the Star of David off a jacket of a passerby and started insulting the Nazis, and an old Bulgarian man asked Jalowicz where he should go to protest against the deportation of Jewish citizens.[84] In contrast, Jalowicz portrays the citizens of Nazi Germany as not only fully cognizant of Nazi crimes but also fully committed to National Socialist ideals. Jalowicz perceived her fellow Germans not as innocent bystanders but as Hitler's devoted followers. In every one of her hideouts, she is confronted with fanatic party members: *Frau* Janicke's grandmother admires the *Führer*, as does her concierge; Trude Neuke's neighbor is a passionate Nazi; and the neighbor of another one of her helpers exhibits a quasi-religious adoration of Hitler: "When we happened to talk about politics and the name of the *Führer* was mentioned, this lonely and introverted old spinster smiled in a strangely delighted way and half closed her eyes. With her, I encountered for the first time the phenomenon of a passionate enthusiasm for Hitler bordering on religious mania."[85] All too frequently, Jalowicz is the object of vicious anti-Semitic abuse by these Hitler fanatics. Thus, the female overseer at the spinning factory where she is a forced laborer calls her a "*Judensau*" who is not even worth spitting at.[86] Even more disturbing is an encounter with a stranger: when Jalowicz was brought to the brink of despair and stood on a bridge over the Spree contemplating suicide, a random passerby noticed the Star of David and commented: "'Oh well there, then it does not matter.' This female Nazi did not feel obligated to offer assistance to a Jewess."[87] In spite of all these experiences, Jalowicz was determined not to condemn all Germans equally and reminded herself that the Nazis were not the only ones who harbored prejudices: "We too had prejudices against all non-Jews."[88]

While Jalowicz's exposure to public abuse and openly voiced anti-Semitism is in line with our knowledge of the Third Reich, it is much more difficult to make sense of her experiences with her helper enemies and Nazi friends. Indeed, in light of her experiences, it is not surprising that Jalowicz vacillates between welcoming the bombing raids on German cities because "those who voted for Hitler should pay the consequences"[89] and feeling compassion for the suffering of non-Jewish Germans.[90] To call Jalowicz's social network a cast of mixed characters is an understatement. *Underground in Berlin* paints a world in which the boundaries between friend and foe are so blurry as to become indistinguishable. *Frau* Koch, Jalowicz's most active helper, was also her greatest nemesis while Kurt, the Nazi son of landlady Blase, became one of her most loyal and reliable friends. Similarly, Trude Neuke, one of her most reliable helpers, happily bought the furniture of deported Jews.[91] The tenants in Blase's house worked together to protect her, but only because she was the beneficiary of a combination of racial and gender stereotypes. Jalowicz is sure that, although the neighbors were eager to help a young woman, they would not have hesitated to denounce someone who corresponded to the Nazi caricature of the fat rich (male) Jew.[92] Finally, the devoted non-Jewish wife of the Jewish doctor Heller did all she could to help her husband save as many Jews as possible but at the same time appeared to subscribe to "all traditional prejudices" against Jews.[93] And *Frau* Janicke, who had exploited Jalowicz as a domestic slave, worked tirelessly to provide food for all the Jews Heller had hidden when the latter was arrested. In *Underground in Berlin*, complicity is uncoupled from Nazi Party affiliation: the most unlikely suspects offer help while the strongest allies act cruelly and selfishly and actively inflict harm on the victims of Nazi persecution.

Ruth Klüger's *weiter leben*

Ruth Klüger grew up in Vienna. In 1942, at age eleven, she was deported to Theresienstadt, then Auschwitz and Christianstadt, a satellite camp of Groß-Rosen. After the war, she lived in a displaced persons' camp in Bavaria before emigrating to the United States in 1947. A professor of literature, Klüger began to research and publish on Holocaust literature in the mid-1980s.[94] Her memoir *weiter leben*, which she started to write in 1988 and published in 1992,[95] is exceptional in many ways: it stands out through its masterful "combination of autobiographical narration and essayistic commentary" and through what Rothberg calls its "interplay of the extreme and the everyday."[96] But Klüger's text is unusual not only because it joins narrative and critical reflection but also because Klüger clearly articulates her commitment to write the history of the Holocaust as women's history and, in doing so, to critique and redefine androcentric notions of war, fascism, and genocide: "The wars belong to men, therefore also the memories of war. And fascism even more so, whether one was for or against it: an exclusively male matter. Moreover: women have no past. Or should not have one. It's indelicate, almost improper."[97] While many scholars, writers, and survivors harshly criticized attempts to introduce a gender studies perspective to the topic of the Holocaust,[98] Klüger insists that her identity as both a woman and a Jew inflected her experience of the Holocaust.

Klüger's commitment to speak from a female perspective is paired with a critical reflection on the roles of non-Jewish German women in the Third Reich. Klüger distances herself critically from the demonization of individual female perpetrators. For example, she suggests that the average female concentration camp guard was less brutal than her male colleagues and superiors: "Much is being talked and little researched about the cruelty of female guards. To be sure, we should not make excuses for them, but they are being overestimated. ... I believe ... that on average they were less brutal than the men."[99] Klüger's refusal to make excuses for female guards shows that she does not wish to minimize the culpability of female perpetrators. Rather, this passage offers a critique of postwar and contemporary tendencies to single out and demonize individual female "furies" in order to exculpate "ordinary" Germans. Numerous scholars, including Wenk and Eschebach, have shown that the sensationalization and exoticization of female perpetrators often served to portray National Socialist atrocities as unnatural perversions and thus to define the Nazi genocide as a *crimen exceptum*, far removed from the everyday lives of average Germans.[100] In *unterwegs verloren*, the sequel to *weiter leben*, Klüger writes that some of her reviewers objected to the fact that Klüger "considers fascism and Nazism male conditions ... where women are and cannot be more than fellow travelers."[101] To Klüger, however, the claim that non-Jewish German women committed fewer crimes against Jews than German men is a "truism,"[102] a consequence of women's limited access to positions of power in the National Socialist regime. At the same time, the fact that women were not involved in the decision-making process does not mean that they were not instrumental in implementing National Socialist policies.[103]

Klüger continues her thoughts on women's involvement in the Third Reich in her appraisal of women's enthusiastic support of Hitler: "Certainly German women cheered for the *Führer*, just as loudly as the men. But as disgusting as such cheering may seem today, it is not a crime."[104] It would appear that the operative term here is the word "crime." Many readers will agree that cheering for Hitler did and does not rise to the level of criminal activity. However, to say that complicitous behavior is not criminal tells us little about its moral valence.

Klüger's representation of women as complicitous bystanders rather than perpetrators must be understood in light of her reflections on courage and cowardice. With a great deal of restraint and compassion, Klüger argues that one cannot expect people to be courageous under adverse conditions. Rather, such courage in the face of danger is exceptional, a form of heroism – "goodness is incomparable and also inexplicable because it has no real cause other than itself and also does not want anything other than itself" – whereas "cowardice is normal, and one should not condemn anyone for normal behavior."[105] Thus, Klüger continues, in a dictatorship, the morally salient question concerns the precise nature of one's compliance. In other words, we need to ask if we are dealing with a form of compliance that is necessary for one's survival or with a kind of compliance that exceeds "normal cowardice." As Klüger puts it: "If cowardice is the norm ... then one should disapprove only of that which is below cowardice, active participation, extra credit work for the bad cause."[106] Clearly, in reading memoirs of the Nazi era, it will not always be easy to differentiate between "extra credit work for the bad cause" and conformity to save one's own hide. And yet, judged by this standard, one might conclude that cheering for Hitler constitutes precisely the kind of active engagement that is not necessary for one's survival and thus offensive (*widerwärtig*) in both the aesthetic and moral sense of the word.

It is worth noting that Klüger's text is one of few Holocaust memoirs written in German. As Young points out, many survivors shied away from using the language of the perpetrators and instead "have chosen after the war to speak and to tell their stories only in English, which they regard as a neutral, uncorrupted, and ironically amnesiac language."[107] In contrast, Klüger's decision to write in German is directly linked to her desire to engage with a German audience.[108] Klüger states explicitly that she does not write for a Jewish audience, but rather for contemporary Germans: "In other words, I write this for Germans."[109] Her text is marked by an extraordinary and passionate desire to engage in a dialogue with its readers,[110] and, in line with the text's feminist commitment, these readers are conceived primarily as female: "The female reader (who expects male readers? They read only what other men have written)."[111] One might conclude that Klüger's generous characterization of non-Jewish German women is directly linked to her attempt to initiate a conversation with the German public. And yet, *weiter leben* is far more complicated than that. The text refuses to be tied down, frequently reverses itself and offers contradictory statements without subsuming them into a dialectic of reconciliation.[112] Throughout, Klüger engages her readers in a search for proper forms of representation by highlighting her own processes and quandaries: "Yesterday I wrote these sentences, today they seem wrong."[113] It is certainly true that Klüger's willingness to engage in a dialogue testifies to a "hope for community,"[114] but her conciliatory statements are not necessarily her last word. Rather, they compete and are partly refuted by her forceful rejection of any suggestion that she is offering reconciliation.

Tellingly, toward the end of *weiter leben*, Klüger rebuffs the admonishment of a friend not to bear grudges, "you should learn to forgive, yourself and others, you would feel better then," to which Klüger responds: "I am not an animal, I cannot forget. Forgiveness sucks."[115] Similarly, in *unterwegs verloren*, she takes exception to the notion that her book is an act of forgiveness or an offer of reconciliation: "Again and again they talked about reconciliation that I was supposed to have offered readers. That was wrong. I am not authorized to forgive the murder of other human beings."[116] Much as Klüger resists the demonization of female Nazis as a convenient strategy of exculpation, she also refuses to sell redemption on demand:[117] "I recognize myself only by my irreconcilabilities, to those I will hold fast."[118]

It would seem that Klüger's willingness to account for "normal cowardice" is related to an early experience of what she calls "moral ambivalence." In writing about her native Vienna, Klüger describes a social environment that was profoundly hostile: "The longer one's way the smaller the chance of avoiding spiteful glances and encounters. One stepped onto the street and was in hostile territory."[119] In spite of such ubiquitous threats, Klüger – much like Jalowicz, who writes about helpful Nazis and exploitative helpers – notes that her social world was not simply antagonistic but unpredictable: "It was not so easy to tell Nazis from non-

Nazis like cabbages and beets. Convictions were fluid, moods changed, today's sympathizers could become tomorrow's enemies and vice versa."[120] Klüger first experienced such moral ambivalence when she refused to eat the candy presented to her as a gift by a Christian maid who had been a mother figure for her. The child realized that her response had hurt the maid's feelings, but she cannot reconcile the maid's kindness with her affiliation with the world of "Aryan" perpetrators.[121]

While Klüger is acutely aware of the many shades of grey that make it difficult to tell friend from foe, she also remembers instances of victimization that were far less ambiguous. Interestingly, one such deeply felt humiliation that Klüger recounts in great detail was inflicted not by an official representative of the regime but by a young girl. When Klüger went to see *Snow White* even though Jews were not allowed to attend the cinema, the daughter of a local baker detected her and began to insult her.

> When it became bright in the room, I wanted to let the others exit first, but my female enemy stood and waited. . . . She spoke in a firm and self-righteous tone, in full awareness of her Aryan descent, as it behooved a BDM girl and even in her finest high German: "Do you know that your kind has no place here?"[122]

It is striking that this episode revolves around the author's victimization by another young girl. While the girl's age and her affiliation with the BDM suggest that she was influenced by Nazi indoctrination during her most formative years, everything in the girl's behavior – the fact that she went out of her way to wait for Klüger; her determination to prop up her "Aryan" status with a strained effort to speak standard German instead of the local dialect – characterizes the insult as "extra credit work." In order to make sense of the girl's cruelty, Klüger relates her humiliation to that of *Snow White*, thus casting the baker's daughter as the evil queen:

> She, in her own house, the mirror of her racial purity before her eyes, I, also at home here, but without permission, and in this moment excluded, humiliated, and exposed. . . . One sees oneself in the mirror of spiteful eyes, and one does not escape the image because the distortion affects one's own eyes until one believes it and considers oneself defaced. . . . If I had the audacity to come here one more time, she would report me, I should consider myself lucky that she didn't do so right now. . . . This afternoon, I experienced personally on my own turf and quite directly how it stood with us and the Nazis.[123]

Klüger's evocation of a mirror is telling. Feminist critics such as Sandra Gilbert and Susan Gubar have read the mirror in "Snow White" as the internalized voice of the king. Seen in this light, the fairy tale erases the agency of men as the queen is shown to be swayed not by the expectations of a patriarchal environment but rather by a seemingly gender-neutral object that purports to reflect her own innermost desires. Since the mirror in Klüger's account can be seen to represent National Socialist ideology, Klüger situates the girl's behavior in a larger context. And yet, even if the baker's daughter is not the originator but rather the vehicle of a racist value system, this does not diminish the danger to which Klüger was exposed as a result of the girl's actions nor does it change the fact that the agent who put Nazi theory into practice was not only female but a child.

While Klüger situates women's and girls' participation in the Third Reich in a larger context, her representation of postwar attitudes of German women toward the Third Reich is far less conciliatory. Klüger recounts several postwar conversations in which non-Jewish German women sought to downplay and trivialize the enormity of Klüger's suffering during the Third Reich. For example, there is the wife of a German veteran who all but accuses her of lying about her camp experience, claiming that Klüger was too young to have been in a camp.[124] Far more damning than this casual comment is the exchange with Gisela, the German wife of a colleague of Klüger's at Princeton University, who juxtaposes Klüger's experiences with those of non-Jewish German women and declares them to be rather tolerable in comparison: "Theresienstadt was not all that bad, the German wife of a colleague at Princeton informed me, herself a beneficiary of the mercy of a late birth." "Auschwitz, yes, according to everything she had heard, said Gisela, that must have been pretty bad, but I wasn't there for a long time, right? I did pretty well, I was able to go to America, and was spared the misery of the postwar period in Germany. Compared to her mother who lost her husband on the Russian front, my mother who married twice in America was pretty lucky."[125] Gisela's response would seem to be a prime example of what Trezise calls "the silencing of others entailed by the forgetting of ourselves."[126] But the conversation with Gisela also serves as a powerful reminder that complicity with the Holocaust is not limited to contemporaries. Rather, there is a complicity-after-the-fact that persists into the postwar period. If Klüger portrays this complicity-after-the-fact as far more vicious than female support for Hitler at Nazi rallies, it is perhaps because it is so clearly not necessitated by the life-threatening strictures of a dictatorship but plays out in the complacent safety of postwar American society and is motivated by an all too obvious need to whitewash a sordid past: "All experiences of the war were to be reduced to one single denominator, namely that of an acceptable German conscience with which one can sleep well."[127] In a time when compassion was cheap, Gisela's heartless and self-serving comments appear gratuitously cruel.

In *weiter leben*, Klüger writes repeatedly that she is not interested in the Nazi perpetrators but rather in the victims.[128] But while this statement expresses a clear alignment, her stance toward those who fall under the category of complicitous bystanders is more complicated. On the one hand, Klüger states that the war destroyed all bridges between her and Germans of the same generation. On the other hand, she notes that she often gets along fine with former Nazis because they share many experiences.[129] Klüger notes that, paradoxically, the average German is both oblivious to the suffering of the Jews – "What I had experienced had not even touched those on the outside. I discovered the secret of simultaneity"[130] – and in a unique position to understand the traumatization of Holocaust survivors. Thus, Klüger suggests that a German contemporary who lived through a bombing raid in a basement will have a better sense of what it is like to be transported in a cattle car than Americans who have no personal experience of war.[131] Moreover, Klüger's diverging statements about those who are neither victims nor perpetrators express not only her conflicted feelings of belonging to and being estranged from this group, but also reflect the moral ambivalence of complicitous behavior in a dictatorship: the fact that it can be very difficult to differentiate between "normal cowardice" and "extracurricular compliance." In Klüger's telling, perpetrators are a lost cause, but complicity unfolds in a grey zone and those who are guilty of it may yet respond to an urgent appeal. Consequently, it is the complicitous bystander for whom Klüger writes her book: "I write for those who do not want and are not able to feel with the perpetrators and the victims."[132] Comprising the vast majority of the population, complicitous bystanders are the ideal addressee: they were not only the ones whose compliance made the Nazi genocide possible, they are also democracy's greatest hope and thus well worth talking to.

Conclusion

Reading the memoirs of female Holocaust survivors offers a powerful counterargument to the myth of German innocence. I have not come across a single memoir whose author is willing to accept that the Germans did not know what was happening to the Jews. Rather, the picture that emerges is one of indifference, of complicity, and of a "social death" that

preceded and was a prerequisite for physical extermination. All memoirs by
Holocaust survivors discussed in this chapter paint a vivid picture of
a hostile environment; all authors recall being exposed to anti-Semitic
insults in public. In Lauer's memoir, for example, non-Jewish German
women are portrayed as either virulently anti-Semitic, oblivious to the
gross mistreatment of Jews even when it occurred right in front of their
eyes, or so preoccupied with their own suffering that there is little room for
compassion with others.

Much like Lauer, Deutschkron felt surrounded and threatened by an
anonymous crowd of potentially anti-Semitic strangers. Indeed, one might
be tempted to agree with Klüger, who argues that anti-Semites are by
definition strangers: "Anti-Semites did not socialize with Jews, or else they
would not have been anti-Semites."[133] However, while Deutschkron and
Klüger emphasize the danger posed by an amorphous mass of strangers,
Simon Jalowicz suffered the cruelest treatment at the hands of her most
important protectors and helpers. In her memoir, friend and enemy are at
times almost indistinguishable. Finally, Klüger's *weiter leben* not only
portrays the hostile attitudes and behavior of non-Jewish German
women, but also reflects on the link between war and gender and on the
nature of complicity.

In addition to portraying and reflecting on complicitious behavior
during the Third Reich, Deutschkron and Klüger also deal with what
one might call complicity-after-the-fact, that is, with the excuses, self-
exculpatory statements, and belittling of the suffering of Holocaust survivors in the postwar period. Lamentably, such complicity-after-the-fact is
a common experience portrayed in many survivor memoirs. Thus, Cecilie
Klein writes, "I returned to the world in great anticipation, to witness the
severe punishment the world would heap on the murderers. To my surprise, the world judged the victims."[134]

In light of so much complicity, it is hardly surprising that many
survivors believed that the Germans should pay for their participation in
Nazi crimes in some form.[135] What is perhaps surprising is that this is not
the only response. Many authors of Holocaust memoirs show amazing
generosity of spirit and even wonder if they themselves would have acted
differently.[136] Such generosity is exemplified by the willingness to consider
the motivations of average Germans and even more by the offer to engage
in a dialogue with those whose complicity contributed to the regime's war
and genocidal policies.

Notes

1. For a chronological overview over memoirs by Holocaust survivors, see Jaiser, "Die Zeugnisliteratur von Überlebenden der deutschen Konzentrationslager seit 1945."
2. Kaplan, *Dignity*, 5, and "Jewish Women in Nazi Germany," 189.
3. Bock, "Ordinary Women in Nazi Germany," 85.
4. Adelsberger, *Auschwitz*, 17.
5. Salier, *Survival of a Spirit*, 5.
6. Klein, *Sentenced to Live*, 67.
7. "Die Deutschen hatten gemordet, um rauben zu können" (Loeper, *Engpass zur Freiheit*, 95); see also "so hat die Bevölkerung die Früchte des Raubmordes genossen" ("in this way the population enjoyed the fruits of robbery and murder") (Loeper, *Engpass zur Freiheit*, 24).
8. "[Wir] sind wieder gejagt worden durch Felder und Wälder, haben auch manchmal Menschen gesehen, die unser Vorbeiziehen gleichgültig kaum zur Kenntnis genommen hatten. ... wir sind numeriert und haben gelbe Judendreiecke ... Diese Deutschen, welchen wir begegnet waren, mußten gewußt haben, wer wir sind, von wo wir kommen? Und trotzdem? Oder deshalb die Gleichgültigkeit?" (Naor, *Krankengymnastin in Auschwitz*, 112).
9. Kornreich Gelissen, *Rena's Promise*, 235.
10. "Als seien wir Wilde" (Klüger, *Weiter leben*, 152).
11. Miller and Lazarus, *Hiding in Plain Sight*, 58.
12. Muller Bruml, "I Was a Nurse in Theresienstadt," 45.
13. Lengyel, *Five Chimneys*, 217.
14. Kornreich Gelissen, *Rena's Promise*, 201.
15. Kramer, "Hell and Rebirth," 130. See also Lengyel's comments on German soldiers: "The soldiers of the Wehrmacht had an inflated morale. Whether drunk with victory or exasperated by defeat, these troops, both well and wounded, had nothing but ironic sneers for plague-ridden people like deportees in cattle care ... at no time did I see the slightest manifestation of sympathy or compassion" (*Five Chimneys*, 20).
16. Klein, *Sentenced to Live*, 64.
17. Sayner, *Women without a Past?*, 72.
18. Ofer and Weitzman, "Introduction," 16. See also Kremer, who points out that "significant books by women [Holocaust survivors] prematurely fall out of print" (*Women's Holocaust Writing*, 4).
19. Weitzman, "Living on the Aryan Side in Poland," 201.
20. See Weitzman, "Living on the Aryan Side in Poland," 200.
21. Examples of male Jews who passed as Aryans include notable historian Saul Friedländer, who survived in a Catholic school in France where he was baptized and given a French name, and German television entertainer Hans Rosenthal, who survived the war by hiding in the cottage of an old woman in the outskirts of Berlin.

22. In 1933, some 160,000 Jews were living in Berlin. Full-scale deportations began on October 18, 1941 (see Gross, *The Last Jews in Berlin*, xiii–xvi). According to Benz, in 1941, there were roughly 73,000 Jews in Berlin, many of whom were employed in the munitions industry. In 1945, this number had shrunk to approximately 12,000. Of these, many had been exempt from deportation because they were of mixed origin, so-called *Mischlinge*, or because they were married to "Aryans." The exact number of the U-boats is not known. Benz counts 5,000 Jews in hiding. Some believe that there were as many as 9,000 Jewish "submarines" in Berlin (Gross, *The Last Jews in Berlin*, 102) while Deutschkron lists 1,200 Jews (*Ich trug den gelben Stern*, 188).

23. Benz, *Überleben im Dritten Reich*, 23. According to Weitzman, 10 percent of Jews who survived the Holocaust lived on the Aryan side ("Living on the Aryan Side in Poland," 189). Weitzman lists the following factors as crucial to one's survival: self-confidence, no accent, non-Jewish friends, personal appearance, and good documents (211).

24. "Doch an dem elektrisch geladenen Stacheldraht unserm Leben ein Ende zu machen" (Herbermann, *Der gesegnete Abgrund*, 67).

25. "Blitzableiter für all ihre primitiven Instinkte" (Salus, *Ein Engel war nicht dort*, 72); "wieviel Vergnügen sie daran fand, Menschen zu quälen" (73).

26. Lasker-Wallfisch, *Inherit the Truth*, 60.

27. Lauer, *Hiding in Plain Sight*, 348.

28. Lauer, *Hiding in Plain Sight*, 5.

29. Lauer, *Hiding in Plain Sight*, 7.

30. Lauer, *Hiding in Plain Sight*, 366.

31. Lauer, *Hiding in Plain Sight*, 69.

32. See Lauer, *Hiding in Plain Sight*, 77.

33. Lauer, *Hiding in Plain Sight*, 80.

34. Lauer, *Hiding in Plain Sight*, 79.

35. Lauer, *Hiding in Plain Sight*, 94.

36. Weitzman, "Living on the Aryan Side in Poland," 188.

37. Lauer, *Hiding in Plain Sight*, 147.

38. Weitzman, "Living on the Aryan Side in Poland," 203.

39. Lauer, *Hiding in Plain Sight*, 229.

40. Kramer, "Hell and Rebirth," 174.

41. Lauer, *Hiding in Plain Sight*, 201. Later, during her employment in a garment factory, Lauer must deal with two coworkers who want to enlist her in their freelance detective work as they follow another colleague after work because they suspect her of being Jewish (265). Even when the Germans transport the inhabitants of the defeated Warsaw to Germany, she is not safe from Nazi collaborators: "Who would have thought that this inoffensive-looking house-wife, with children to care for, would be willing to become an instrument for the Nazis" (317).

42. Lauer, *Hiding in Plain Sight*, 178.

43. Lauer, *Hiding in Plain Sight*, 182.

44. Lauer, *Hiding in Plain Sight*, 358.

45. Lauer, *Hiding in Plain Sight*, 466.
46. Lauer, *Hiding in Plain Sight*, 466.
47. Lauer, *Hiding in Plain Sight*, 467.
48. Lauer, *Hiding in Plain Sight*, 470.
49. Lauer, *Hiding in Plain Sight*, 471.
50. Lauer, *Hiding in Plain Sight*, 467–468.
51. Lauer, *Hiding in Plain Sight*, 355.
52. In this case, as in many others, the precondition for a visa was the financial support of a relative who resided in the destination country. Deutschkron's father was able to emigrate to England because of a cousin who put up the required amount. But this relative did not have enough money to vouch for mother and daughter as well (Deutschkron, *Ich trug den gelben Stern*, 49).
53. For more information on Weidt, see Benz, *Überleben im Dritten Reich*, 37.
54. "Konnten wir sicher sein, daß aus so indifferenten Nachbarn über Nacht nicht überzeugte oder opportunistische Anhänger der neuen Ordnung geworden waren?" (Deutschkron, *Ich trug den gelben Stern*, 14).
55. "Die Deutschen, die nicht wissen wollten, was um sie vorging, hatten in der Tat keine Ahnung davon, wie wir in ihrer Mitte lebten" (Deutschkron, *Ich trug den gelben Stern*, 76).
56. "Der Krieg schien für diese Menschen gar nicht zu existieren. Ich war sehr neidisch, weil sie so sorglos waren … von dem Elend und der Not von Menschen, die zwar aus ihrer Gesellschaft ausgestoßen, aber neben ihnen lebten, wußten sie nichts – oder wollten nichts wissen" (Deutschkron, *Ich trug den gelben Stern*, 118). See also "Es war seltsam, wie die Berliner solchen Aktionen zu entgehen verstanden, die sich in ihrer Stadt zutrugen" ("It was strange how the Berliners managed to escape such actions that took place in their city") (Deutschkron, *Ich trug den gelben Stern*, 100).
57. "Man gewöhnte sich an die Tatsache, als Jude diskriminiert zu werden" ("One got used to being discriminated against as a Jew") (Deutschkron, *Ich trug den gelben Stern*, 18).
58. "Ein richtiges deutsches Mädchen mit langen blonden Zöpfen" (Deutschkron, *Ich trug den gelben Stern*, 23).
59. "Der 'Judenstern' schuf eine diskriminierende Isolation. Ich hatte das Gefühl, eine Maske vor dem Gesicht zu tragen. Es gab Menschen, die mich mit Haß ansahen. … Ich erinnere mich daran, wie unerträglich mir einmal dieses 'Angestarrtwerden' wurde. Es war auf einem U-Bahnhof. Wir warteten auf den Zug. Immer und immer wieder ging eine Frau an mir vorüber und starrte mich an. Schließlich hielt ich es nicht mehr aus, trat auf sie zu und fragte: 'Sie haben gewiß noch nie eine Jüdin gesehen?' Sie wurde knallrot. 'So sehen Sie mich doch ganz genau in aller Ruhe an. Ich habe nichts dagegen.' Die sagte kein Wort und wandte sich ab" (Deutschkron, *Ich trug den gelben Stern*, 83). Kaplan points out that discrimination by strangers was not uncommon: "Strangers on trams, in stores, and even on the street targeted those who 'looked' Jewish and mortified their victims by pronouncing their suspicions loudly" (*Dignity*, 34).

60. See Deutschkron, *Ich trug den gelben Stern*, 126, 113, 155.
61. "Die Ansammlung von Frauen war mir unheimlich. Sie hätten ihre Ungeduld an mir abreagieren können. Sie hätten mich anschwärzen können. Sie hatten auch viel Zeit, mich zu betrachten" (Deutschkron, *Ich trug den gelben Stern*, 161).
62. "Die Käufer waren wie Aasgeier" (Deutschkron, *Ich trug den gelben Stern*, 50).
63. "Die Frau des Gestapobeamten ging auf die Betten zu, befühlte die Daunendecken und sagte: 'Ja, gut.' ... Und sie nahmen, was sie tragen konnten" (Deutschkron, *Ich trug den gelben Stern*, 96).
64. "Es war vor allem das deutsche Bildungsbürgertum, das versagt hatte" (Jalowicz, *Untergetaucht*, 389).
65. "Ich kam in Verhältnisse, von denen ich mir nie hätte träumen lassen. Mir wurde klar: Diese entsetzliche Wohnung war etwas ganz Normales. Es gab nicht wenige Menschen, die so lebten" (Jalowicz, *Untergetaucht*, 122).
66. "Ich notierte in mein unsichtbares Tagebuch" (Jalowicz, *Untergetaucht*, 253). Unfortunately, her notebooks were lost during a bombing raid.
67. "Ich beschloss, mein inneres Tagebuch in einer bestimmten anderen Zeitspanne in literarischem Deutsch zu schreiben und in einer anderen Zeitspanne im gemeinsten Hurenjargon zu berlinern. Ich nahm mir vor, zeitweise in Hexametern zu denken und älteres Deutsch zu gebrauchen, doch Letzteres musste ich aufgeben" (Jalowicz, *Untergetaucht*, 275).
68. See "Oft sehnte ich mich nach Verhältnissen, in denen ich mich nicht taktisch verhalten musste. Ich wollte endlich wieder einmal so reden, wie mir der Schnabel gewachsen war, und nicht jede Vokabel daraufhin prüfen, ob sie zum Wortschatz meines Gesprächspartners passte oder deren Gefühle verletzte" ("Often I longed for circumstances in which I did not have to behave tactically. I wanted to finally talk as I was used to, and not examine every word whether it fit the vocabulary of my interlocutor or hurt their feelings") (Jalowicz, *Untergetaucht*, 251).
69. "Es gibt vieles, worüber man erst ein halbes Jahrhundert später berichten kann" (Jalowicz, *Untergetaucht*, 396).
70. "Wir haben zu danken, wenn wir helfen dürfen" (Jalowicz, *Untergetaucht*, 317).
71. See Benz, *Überleben im Dritten Reich*, 225ff. On the sexual abuse of Jewish women in hiding, see also Waxman, "Rape and Sexual Abuse in Hiding"; Ringelheim, "Women and the Holocaust," 377; Withuis, "Die verlorene Unschuld des Gedächtnisses," 87.
72. "'Mit meiner eigenen Potenz muss ich bei Frau Janicke für deine Beherbergung zahlen!' Mir war das unsagbar peinlich, aber was sollte ich machen" (Janowicz, *Untergetaucht*, 186).
73. "Ich konnte weder Krach schlagen noch ihn zurückschicken, also ließ ich es über mich ergehen. Aber ich war sicher, dass Tati alles mitbekam" (Janowicz, *Untergetaucht*, 117).
74. When her father fell in love with *Frau* Waldmann, the wife of their landlord, Jalowicz slept with Herrn Waldmann to avoid being thrown out of the apartment. One of her more bizarre sexual adventures concerns a Bulgarian

man named Todor Nedeltschwew. When she was once more out of options, she offered to sleep with him and even got engaged to him. He agreed, but when they could not find an apartment, their "relationship" ended without being consummated (Janowicz, *Untergetaucht*, 169).

75. "Sie genoss es auch, endlich einmal Macht auszuüben" (Jalowicz, *Untergetaucht*, 215). While a Jew in hiding faced certain death if discovered, the consequences for helpers were less clear. They might be let off with a warning, but they might also be sent to a concentration camp. Benz points out that punishments for women who helped Jews tended to be less severe than those for men. He also notes that in Germany nobody was put to death for helping Jews (Benz, *Überleben im Dritten Reich*, 40).

76. "Damit die endlich umgebracht würde. Wie sie sich das vorstellte, malte sie genauestens aus. Mordlust und Pornographie vermischten sich dabei miteinander wie beim 'Stürmer'" (Jalowicz, *Untergetaucht*, 269).

77. "Ich hasste diese widerliche, braune, zotige, kriminelle Erpresserin. Und ich liebte sie als eine Mutterfigur. So ist eben das Leben, so kompliziert" (Jalowicz, *Untergetaucht*, 286).

78. Jalowicz's son explains that his mother never got over her experiences with *Frau* Koch and lived in fear that *Frau* Koch would show up at her doorstep unexpectedly (Jalowicz 410).

79. "Versprich mir, dass du mich nie verlässt, dass du immer bei mir bleibst und mich nicht in das Elend zurückstößt, aus dem ich gekommen bin" (Jalowicz, *Untergetaucht*, 362). See also "Leider hatte sie die Tendenz, immer wieder zu betonen, wie mühsam sie diese Gaben von ihren eigenen Lebensmittelrationen abzweigte" ("Unfortunately, she tended to emphasize the great efforts it cost to save these offerings from her own ration") (*Untergetaucht*, 255) and "An mich klammerte sie sich in einer Weise, die mich sehr quälte" ("She clung to me in a manner that tortured me very much") (*Untergetaucht*, 362) or "Jahrelang hatte sie mich gequält, indem sie mit Grabesstimme immer wieder gesagt hatte: 'Wir sind ein Wesen, weil wir denselben Namen tragen'" ("For years she had tortured me repeating over and over again in a serious tone that we are one being because we have the same name") (*Untergetaucht*, 386).

80. For example, Jalowicz reports that Koch hoped to influence the political situation by damaging Hitler's "Astralleib" ("astral body") (Jalowicz, *Untergetaucht*, 164). In the last weeks of the war, she invited a Nazi neighbor and forced Jalowicz to hide behind a curtain a few feet from the visitor. Similarly, she insisted that they go to a bomb shelter together and enter through the same door even though their passports bore identical names.

81. When Koch danced with Jalowicz's friend Heller during a social gathering, she seemed "völlig beseelt bei diesem Tanz mit ihrem Traumdoktor, der aussah, wie sich Lieschen Müller einen Filmstar in der Rolle des Frauenarztes vorstellt" ("absolutely transfixed during this dance with a dream doctor who looked like Lieschen Müller images a film star playing the part of a gynecologist") (Jalowicz, *Untergetaucht*, 164). When Jalowicz asked for a nightgown during one of her stays at the Koch home, Koch

mocked her because she herself was used to sleeping in her underwear (Jalowicz, *Untergetaucht*, 115).

82. "So machten das Leute, die später behaupteten, sie hätten von nichts gewußt" (Jalowicz, *Untergetaucht*, 352).

83. See "Die durchschnittliche deutsche Hausfrau interessierte sich dafür, wo sie zu einem erträglichen Schwarzmarktpreis ein Pfund Tomaten herbekam, und kriegte Weinkrämpfe, wenn ihr die Suppe angebrannt war. Sie hatte anti-semitische Klischees im Kopf oder auch nicht, aber die Vorschriften gegen Juden kannte sie nicht" ("The average German housewife was interested in where she could get a pound of tomatoes at an acceptable black market price and had crying fits when her soup was burnt. She had anti-Semitic clichés in her head or not, but she did not know the regulations regarding Jews") (Jalowicz, *Untergetaucht*, 85).

84. See Jalowicz, *Untergetaucht*, 147.

85. "Nur wenn zufällig die Rede auf Politik kam und der Name des Führers fiel, lächelte diese vereinsamte und introvertierte alte Jungfer merkwürdig entzückt und schloss halb die Augen. Bei ihr begegnete mir das Phänomen einer leidenschaftlichen Hitlerbegeisterung am Rande des religiösen Wahns zum ersten Mal" (Jalowicz, *Untergetaucht*, 178; see also 191 and 237).

86. Jalowicz, *Untergetaucht*, 82.

87. "'Ach so, na dann, dann macht es ja nichts.' Einer Jüdin brauchte diese Nazisse ihren Beistand nicht anzubieten" (Jalowicz, *Untergetaucht*, 80).

88. "Auch wir haben Vorurteile gegen alle Nichtjuden" (Jalowicz, *Untergetaucht*, 73; see also 388).

89. "Wer Hitler gewählt hat, soll jetzt die Konsequenzen spüren" (Jalowicz, *Untergetaucht*, 311). See also her response when Koch's father is upset because Russian soldiers stole things from his house: "'Du Scheißnazi,' dachte ich, 'du und deinesgleichen, ihr habt Hitler gewählt, ihr habt diesen Krieg mit angezettelt, und die Durchhalteparolen befolgt'" ("You piece of shit Nazi, I thought, you and people like you, you voted for Hitler, you helped instigate this war and obeyed the calls to persevere") (Jalowicz, *Untergetaucht*, 359).

90. "Endlich wurde mir bewußt, wie viel unverschuldetes Leid der Krieg auch unter den Nichtjuden angerichtet hatte" ("Finally I realized how much undeserved suffering the war had caused also among non-Jews") (Jalowicz, *Untergetaucht*, 379).

91. "'Wenn ich die Möbel nicht kaufe, nimmt sie ein anderer.' Ich gab ihr recht, aber ich war merkwürdig tief ins Herz getroffen" ("'If I don't buy the furniture, somebody else will.' I agreed, but strangely I was wounded deep in my heart") (Jalowicz, *Untergetaucht*, 254).

92. Jalowicz, *Untergetaucht*, 319. See also "Derselbe Piefke, der einen tödlichen Hass gegen den reichen Juden vom Vorderhaus hegte, der ihn vielleicht einmal bei einem Grundstücksverkauf übervorteilt hatte, und der den innigen Wunsch hatte, dass dieser Mann verschwinde, damit er sich dessen Wohnzimmerteppich aneignen konnte – dieser selbe Piefke hatte aber nichts gegen hungernde junge Mädchen, die fleißig arbeiteten, so wie er selbst auch"

("The same stupid boy who harbored lethal hatred for the rich Jew in the house in front who perhaps got the better of him once during a land transaction, and who wishes ardently that this man should disappear so that he can take his living room rug – the same stupid boy had nothing against hungry young girls who worked hard, just like he did") (Jalowicz, *Untergetaucht*, 62).

93. "Allen traditionellen Vorurteilen" (Jalowicz, *Untergetaucht*, 226).

94. See Schaumann, *Memory Matters*, 102.

95. The English translation of *weiter leben*, published in 2001 as *Still Alive: A Holocaust Girlhood Remembered*, differs drastically from the German original. For an analysis of the differences between the two works, see Schaumann "Translation" and McGlothlin, "Autobiographical Revision."

96. Rothberg, *Traumatic Realism*, 129 and 131. Schulte-Sasse also notes the jarring effect of combining the extraordinary with the ordinary, and adds that the "prosaic friction of the mother-daughter story is incompatible with the stakes of the Holocaust story" (Schulte-Sasse, "Living On in the American Press," 473). Schulte-Sasse further points out that Klüger intermingles "a Holocaust story with personal recollections that are too close, and with a narrative attitude that's too far away" (474). See also Finnan, "Gendered Memory?," 278.

97. "Die Kriege gehören den Männern, daher auch die Kriegserinnerungen. Und der Faschismus schon gar, ob man nun für oder gegen ihn gewesen ist: reine Männersache. Außerdem: Frauen haben keine Vergangenheit. Oder haben keine zu haben. Ist unfein, fast unanständig" (Klüger, *weiter*, 12; see also 236).

98. One of the most forceful objections to a feminist approach to the Holocaust was forwarded by Gabriel Schoenfeld, who believes that it would "sever Jewish women, in their minds, from their families as well as from the larger Jewish community" ("Auschwitz and the Professors," 45). In contrast, feminist scholars have argued that gender played a crucial role in the persecution of Jews. In the concentration camps, women were particularly vulnerable as mothers: upon arrival in Auschwitz, children were ordered to stay with their mothers, thereupon pregnant women and mothers who were accompanied by children under the age of fifteen were selected for extermination (see Heinemann, *Gender and Destiny*, 14–15; Hirsch and Spitzer, "Gendered Translations," 5). Ringelheim states that "more Jewish women were deported than Jewish men, and more women than men were selected for death in the extermination camps" (Ringelheim, "The Split between Gender and the Holocaust," 349; see also Quack, "Jüdische Frauen in den dreißiger Jahren," 123) while Rittner and Roth argue that in general "the odds for surviving the Holocaust were worse for Jewish women than for Jewish men" ("Prologue," 2). Ringelheim further notes that in postwar displaced persons' camps "40% of the population was female and 61% was male" ("Women and the Holocaust," 394). In addition to the smaller chance of survival, women were particularly vulnerable to sexual abuse: "prostitution, verbal and physical sexual abuse, and at times rape were experiences special to women in the Holocaust" (*Gender and Destiny*, 17). Furthermore, Baer and Goldenberg

raise the important point that "gender-based experience before the rise of Hitler conspicuously shaped women's responses to the Holocaust" ("Introduction," xiv). For example, since in the beginning Nazi persecution focused on Jewish men, men were perceived to be in greater danger than women and children and thus were often the first to emigrate (Ofer and Weitzman, "Introduction," 6). Women also tended to stay behind to take care of elderly parents and children and were thus less likely to emigrate (Bos, "Women and the Holocaust," 47; see also Kaplan, "Keeping Calm," 48; "Jewish Women," 203; Rittner and Roth, "Prologue," 7). According to Baer and Goldenberg, the ratio of Jews who stayed behind in Germany was "136 Jewish women to every 100 Jewish men" ("Introduction," xix). On gender and the Holocaust, see also Horowitz, "Gender, Genocide, and Jewish Memory," and Goldenberg, who aptly summarized the role of gender in the Holocaust as "different horrors within the same hell" ("Memoirs of Auschwitz Survivors," 327).

99. "Über die Grausamkeit der Aufseherinnen wird viel geredet und wenig geforscht. Nicht daß man sie in Schutz nehmen soll, aber sie werden überschätzt ... Ich glaube, ... daß sie im Durchschnitt weniger brutal waren als die Männer" (Klüger, *weiter*, 146). See also: "weiß doch jeder, daß es keine SS-Frauen gegeben hat" ("Everybody knows that there were no SS women") (146).

100. See Wenk and Eschebach 33. Koonz raises the important point that female guards may have "seemed more cruel because their behavior deviated farther from our conception of 'feminine' models" ("Consequences," 290).

101. "Den Faschismus und den Nazismus als eine männliche Befindlichkeit betrachte ... bei der die Frauen nie mehr als Mitläuferinnen sind und sein können" (Klüger, *unterwegs verloren*, 166).

102. "Binsenweisheit" (Klüger, *unterwegs verloren*, 166; see also 147).

103. See Reese and Sachse, who note that National Socialist race politics was male in its conception, political decision-making process, and implementation, but in concrete settings, such as hospitals and various institutions, female organizations, social workers, and nurses participated in its execution in practical terms ("Frauenforschung und Nationalsozialismus," 94).

104. "Gewiß haben die deutschen Frauen dem Führer zugejubelt, genau so laut wie die Männer. Doch so widerwärtig uns dieser Jubel heute erscheinen mag, so ist er noch kein Verbrechen" (Klüger, *weiter*, 147).

105. "Das Gute ist unvergleichlich und auch unerklärlich, weil es keine rechte Ursache hat als sich selbst und auch nichts will als sich selbst" (Klüger, *weiter*, 133), "das Normale ist Feigheit, und man soll keinen für normales Benehmen verurteilen" (Klüger, *weiter*, 186).

106. "Wenn Feigheit das Normale ist ... dann wäre nur das, was noch unter der Feigheit liegt, das aktive Mitmachen, die Fleißaufgaben für die schlechte Sache, zu mißbilligen" (Klüger, *weiter*, 186). See also her statement on concentration camp inmates who mistreated other inmates: "Wer im KZ die Schläge, die er von oben empfing, nach unten weitergab, hat nur so

gehandelt, wie biologisch und psychologisch zu erwarten" ("A concentration camp inmate who passed on the beatings he received from above to those below him did only what is to be expected biologically and psychologically") (Klüger, *weiter*, 136).

107. Young, *Writing and Rewriting the Holocaust*, 160.
108. On Klüger's decision to write for Germans, see McGlothlin, "Autobiographical Revision," 56. On her German readers, see Bauschinger, "Uns verbindet, was uns trennt." The fact that *weiter leben* became a bestseller in Germany may well be related to Klüger's willingness to engage with Germans and to the fact that she does not offer graphic details of her experience in the camps. As Lorenz points out, Klüger does not "repeat the known descriptions of the concentration camps and makes no attempt to depict the details of the prisoners' daily routine" (Lorenz, "Memory," 211). See also Heidelberger-Leonhard, who believes that readers appreciated a representation of Auschwitz "ohne Gas" ("without gas") ("Ruth Klüger weiter leben," 167). Such omissions can be seen to spare Klüger's readers, but they may also stem from Klüger's desire not to silence or repel her readers through a detailed accounting of atrocities and to avoid concentration camp pornography, or, as Klüger calls it, "Bordellphantasien" ("brothel fantasies") (*weiter*, 236, 238). Furthermore, since Klüger published her memoirs in 1992, there was a certain dispensation from bearing witness (Angerer, "Wir haben ja im Grunde nichts als die Erinnerung," 65), i.e., there was an earlier body of work that had detailed the horrors of the camp.
109. "Anders gesagt, ich schreibe es für Deutsche" (Klüger, *weiter*, 142).
110. The dialogic effect is reinforced by Klüger's deft use of personal pronouns. In particular, her use of "*du*" frequently remains ambiguous, referring both to a figure in the story and the reader. For example, recounting a conversation with her father about Crystal Night, she writes: "Siehst du, ich weiß es noch" ("Look, I still remember") (Klüger, *weiter*, 20). See also "rechts und links von mir standen Menschen, Männer und Frauen, auch Kinder, und sahen beiseite. Oder verschlossen ihre Gesichter, so daß nichts eindringen konnte. Wir haben unsere eigenen Sorgen, behelligt uns bitte nicht" ("To the right and left of me were people, men and women, also children, and looked away. Or shut off their faces so that nothing could enter. We have our own worries, please do not bother us") (Klüger, *weiter*, 185–186), where the "*uns*" refers to both the bystanders and the readers. In addition, Klüger frequently cites the statements of interlocutors: "Meine deutschen Bekannten sagen: . . . " ("My German acquaintances say: . . . ") (Klüger, *weiter*, 23).
111. "Die Leserin (wer rechnet schon mit männlichen Lesern? Die lesen nur von anderen Männern Geschriebenes)" (Klüger, *weiter*, 82). See also 79.
112. See Schneider, who notes that Klüger interrupts every narrative unit with reflective, questioning, appellative interjections before it has a chance to solidify ("Reflexion oder Evokation," 172). See also McGlothlin, who notes Klüger's tendency to move "back and forth between two or more intellectual

positions ... without attempting to resolve their contradictions into one overarching synthetic declaration" ("Autobiographical Revision," 61).

113. "Gestern schrieb ich diese Sätze, heute scheinen sie falsch" (Klüger, *weiter*, 167).

114. Schulte-Sasse argues that "for all Klüger's refusal of teleology and redemption, her twice-written book manifests the hope of a community grounded in the process of exchanging stories" ("Living on in the American Press," 474).

115. "Du solltest lernen zu verzeihen, dir selbst und anderen, dann wär dir besser ... Ich bin kein Vieh, ich kann nicht vergessen. Verzeihen ist zum Kotzen" (Klüger, *weiter*, 278–279).

116. "Immer wieder war von Versöhnung die Rede, die ich den Lesern angeblich angeboten hätte. Das war falsch. Ich bin nicht befugt, den Mord an anderen Menschen zu verzeihen" (Klüger, *unterwegs verloren*, 165). See also her comment in *unterwegs verloren* that *weiter leben* is "too restrained": "in zu gemäßigten Worten ... aufgeschrieben" (Klüger, *unterwegs*, 214). Adelson speaks of Klüger's emphasis on precise irreconcilabilities ("Ränderberichtigung," 95).

117. In his analysis of Holocaust testimonies, Langer argues that "the losses they record raise few expectations of renewal or hopes of reconciliation" (*Holocaust Testimonies*, xi). And yet, one could argue that Klüger does not fit this pattern because her dedication to a dialogue with contemporary Germans holds out hope of reconciliation.

118. "Nur an meinen Unversöhnlichkeiten erkenn ich mich, an denen halt ich mich fest" (Klüger, *weiter*, 279).

119. "Je länger der Weg, desto geringer war die Chance, gehässigen Blicken und Begegnungen zu entgehen. Man trat auf die Straße und war in Feindesland" (Klüger, *weiter*, 16). See also 10.

120. "Es war nicht so leicht, Nazis von Nichtnazis wie Kraut und Rüben zu unterscheiden. Überzeugungen waren ungefestigt, Stimmungen schwankten, Sympathisanten von heute konnten schon morgen Gegner sein und umgekehrt" (Klüger, *weiter*, 17).

121. See Klüger, *weiter*, 44.

122. "Als es im Saal hell wurde, wollte ich die anderen vorgehen lassen, aber meine Feindin stand und wartete, ... Sie redete fest und selbstgerecht, im Vollgefühl ihrer arischen Herkunft, wie es sich für ein BDM-Mädchen schickte und noch dazu in ihrem feinsten Hochdeutsch: 'Weißt du, daß deinesgleichen hier nichts zu suchen hat?" (Klüger, *weiter*, 47).

123. "Sie, im eigenen Haus, den Spiegel ihrer rassischen Reinheit vor Augen, ich, auch an diesem Ort beheimatet, aber ohne Erlaubnis, und in diesem Augenblick ausgestoßen, erniedrigt und preisgegeben. ... Man sieht sich im Spiegel boshafter Augen, und man entgeht dem Bild nicht, denn die Verzerrung fällt zurück auf die eigenen Augen, bis man ihr glaubt und sich selbst für verunstaltet hält. ... Wenn ich mich noch ein einziges Mal unterstehen tät, hierher zu kommen, so würde sie mich anzeigen, ich hätt ja noch ein Glück, daß sie's nicht gleich täte. ... Ich hatte an diesem

Nachmittag für meine Person, in meinem Bereich und ganz unmittelbar erfahren, wie es mit uns und den Nazis stand" (Klüger, *weiter*, 48–49).

124. Klüger, *weiter*, 74.
125. "Theresienstadt sei ja nicht so schlimm gewesen, informierte mich die deutsche Frau eines Kollegen in Princeton, die sich der Gnade der späten Geburt erfreute" (Klüger, *weiter*, 85); "Auschwitz, ja, nach allem was sie gehört habe, sagte Gisela, das müsse arg gewesen sein, aber da sei ich doch nicht so lange gewesen, oder? Mir sei es doch relativ gut gegangen, ich hätte nach Amerika ausreisen können, und das deutsche Nachkriegselend sei mir erspart geblieben. Verglichen mit ihrer Mutter, die den Mann an der russischen Front verlor, hätte meine Mutter, die in Amerika noch zweimal heiratet, doch großes Glück gehabt" (93).
126. Trezise, *Witnessing Witnessing*, 32.
127. "Alle Kriegserlebnisse sollten auf einen einzigen Nenner, nämlich den eines akzeptablen deutschen Gewissens, zu bringen sein, mit dem sich schlafen läßt" (Klüger, *weiter*, 85).
128. "Man sieht schon, diese Aufzeichnungen handeln fast gar nicht von den Nazis, über die ich wenig aussagen kann, sondern von den schwierigen, neurotischen Menschen, auf die sie stießen" ("As you see, these notes barely deal with Nazis about whom I cannot say much, but with the difficult, neurotic people whom they encountered") (Klüger, *weiter*, 56). See also "die Fragen, die Deutsche bei solchen Gesprächen erörtern, um die Täter kreisen, während Juden mehr über die Opfer wissen wollen" ("the questions that Germans discuss in such conversations are concerned with perpetrators whereas Jews want to know more about the victims") (Klüger, *weiter*, 96).
129. "Menschen derselben Generation . . . doch der alte Krieg hat die Brücken zwischen uns gesprengt" (Klüger, *weiter*, 111); "der Frage, was ich mit früheren Nazis gemeinsam habe . . . wir verstehen uns bestens, nicht immer, aber oft . . . Wichtig ist lediglich, daß sie alles erlebt haben" (Klüger, *weiter*, 124).
130. "Das von mir erlebte hatte die draußen nicht einmal berührt. Ich entdeckte das Geheimnis der Gleichzeitigkeit" (Klüger, *weiter*, 145). For other comments on the inalienable differences between Holocaust survivors and Germans of the same generation, see also her comment that families who employed forced labor tend to think fondly of their help and believe that they were treated well whereas she is aware that they are talking about slave labor (158). Klüger further notes that Germans tend to lament the loss of their homeland after the war whereas Holocaust victims celebrated their newfound freedom (173).
131. See Klüger, *weiter*, 189. See also her comment on a German friend who almost lost his mother because she was to be sent to Siberia: "Solche wirren Berührungspunkte sind die Grundlage meiner Freundschaft mit ihm und anderen Deutschen" ("Such confused commonalities are the foundation of my friendship with him and other Germans" (Klüger, *weiter*, 183).

132. "Ich schreib es für die, die nicht mit den Tätern und nicht mit den Opfern fühlen wollen und können" (Klüger, *weiter*, 141).

133. "Antisemiten verkehrten nicht mit Juden, sonst wären sie ja keine Antisemiten gewesen" (Klüger, *weiter leben*, 63).

134. Klein, *Sentenced to Live*, 5.

135. For example, witnessing the bombing of Nuremberg, Cecilie Klein writes, "we saw flames leaping up into the sky above Nuremberg. "Not enough!" Mina and I whispered to each other" (*Sentenced to Live*, 99).

136. "Unwillkürlich mußte ich Vergleiche ziehen, mußte an mein ehemaliges normales Leben denken. War auch ich einmal unberührt vom Leid anderer Menschen gewesen?" "Involuntarily I had to draw comparisons, had to think of my former normal life. Had I too been unconcerned about the suffering of other people?" (Naor, *Krankengymnastin in Auschwitz*, 112).

CHAPTER 7

Conclusion

"The highest one can achieve is to know and to live with the knowledge that it was like this and not any different, and then to see and to wait what will follow from this."[1]

Hannah Arendt

A reading of the life writing of German women during the Third Reich yields a number of insights into what I have called the grammar of complicity. Such a grammar of complicity may manifest in the form of repetitions, formulaic expressions, and rigid structures. But it may also rely on omissions, denial, inconsistencies, non sequiturs, and contradictions as disparate facts resist integration into the dominant storyline. More often than not, the memoirs of non-Jewish German women are marked by narrative ruptures, by conceptual and visual blind spots, and by partial or intermittent silences. Many of these authors are unable to form a coherent narrative of the self that joins their own experiences to larger historical narratives. Many of these narratives testify to processes of splitting or compartmentalization that enabled their authors to cope with what they experienced at the time. They also testify to an erosion of trust and a concomitant inability to form intimate bonds or to talk about traumatic experiences. In turn, this lack of communication could lead to a gradual erosion of any sense of reality to such an extent that ignorance and denial became indistinguishable. Once such a diffusion of reality sets in, it gives rise to a confusion about one's basic motivations and about the consequences of one's actions and thus makes accountability impossible.

In reading women's memoirs about the Second World War, it becomes painfully obvious that they do not easily map onto common periodizations of public discourses on *Vergangenheitsbewältigung*. To be sure, the texts themselves are often difficult to date. Some integrate diaries or notes from the Third Reich into narratives written decades after the war. Some were written immediately after the war but remained unpublished for decades.

Even so, however, it is clear that private memory can indeed be wholly disconnected from public discourses of the past. Some texts were published in the 1970s but offer highly sophisticated analyses of the complicity of average Germans. Conversely, some texts were published in the past ten years, but never engage in a dialogue with the most important insights yielded by decades of highly publicized *Vergangenheitsbewältigung*.

In numerous accounts of the Third Reich, perceptions of gender interfere with conceptualizations of women's agency and accountability. All too often, gender is marshaled to minimize culpability. For example, the literary glorification of the nurse as angel in white makes it all but impossible to inquire about the complicity of actual frontline nurses. Similarly, an exclusive focus on the suffering of rape victims and female refugees tends to preempt any investigation of the complicity of women in the Third Reich. In discussing this project with others, scholars and nonacademics alike, I have often encountered a reluctance to hold the women discussed in these pages responsible. This reluctance is typically motivated by two considerations. Many argue that, compared to the violent actions of their male contemporaries, the contributions women made to Nazi crimes were indirect and often marginal. As Koonz notes, "except for a few thousand prison matrons and camp guards, women did not participate in murder."[2] Frequently, the argument of relative innocence is compounded by references to female victimization. After all, women who supported the Nazi regime and exhibited anti-Semitic prejudice were not spared the suffering that afflicts civilians in times of war. Thus, it follows that they deserve compassion rather than severe judgment. While such evocations of female innocence and suffering exonerate women qua gender, others object that any attempt to hold these women accountable represents a failure to understand the human condition. More often than not, complicity does not rise to the level of criminal behavior. As Ruth Klüger points out, goodness is extraordinary while going along with the policies of a dictatorial regime is normal and one cannot blame people for behaving normally.

To be sure, these are valid and important points. And yet, they are also deeply problematic and ethically unsatisfactory. To begin with, if we focus on the most violent aspects of genocide, we neglect the crucially important network of support, ranging from secretarial work to household chores, that made the efficient implementation of the Holocaust possible. Similarly, if we insist on highlighting women's (all too real) victimization in the Third Reich at the expense of their capacity for agency, we undermine the very feminism we seek to advocate. As Zipfel points out, the price of female innocence is female agency and power.[3] Thus, to insist on women's political impotence during the Third Reich is not only counterfactual but also too high a price to pay. However, the most important, and most controversial, argument concerns not the structural functionality of the Third Reich or the historical reality of gender, but the ethical valence of complicity, particularly if such complicity does not consist of active contributions but rather rests on sins of omission, on silent assent, reluctant compliance, or willful denial. To say that such compliance and assent are to be expected is most certainly true, but it is also a position that offers little hope for the future of democratic governments. It is important to recognize that the Holocaust was not the result of an entire society in the throes of rabid, annihilist anti-Semitism. Rather, it was enough that the violent anti-Semitism of the few was quietly supported by the casual anti-Semitism of the many.[4] As von Kardorff remarked: "I don't know any dyed-in-the-wool Nazis, and yet everything is accepted as though it were unchangeable."[5] Regardless of whether we consider the Holocaust a singular, incomparable event or not, the society that perpetrated the crime of genocide was not unique: it was a society in which substantial subsections of the population "felt betrayed by an alien political establishment, a fraying welfare net, and chronic economic dislocations,"[6] and in which this sense of disenfranchisement entered a perilous alliance with racist and xenophobic sentiments.

Undoubtedly, to ask for active engagement and everyday resistance is asking for a lot. Consider, for example, Hildegard Knef's memoir *The Gift Horse: Report on a Life* (*Der geschenkte Gaul: Bericht aus einem Leben*), in which she pokes fun at what she considers to be the impossibly high expectations of the denazification commission that, she feels, despised her "because of my negligence which has prevented me from emigrating when I was seven years old, from fully comprehending the situation, initiating a revolution, and organizing resistance groups. Instead, I have indulged in growing up while contemptuously neglecting my environment."[7] Knef's statement is certainly self-serving in its desire to exacerbate the impossibility of resistance – note that Knef, who was born in 1925, was not a child but a young adult during the Second World War – but it also reminds us that age is a factor in political decisions. While many of the women whose memoirs are discussed in these pages were no longer children during the Third Reich, they were, almost all of them, very young. And while their gender cannot exonerate them, their youth does constitute a mitigating circumstance. And yet, I would argue that the primary goal of an analysis of life writing from the Third Reich is not to determine whether any particular woman was more or less guilty of sins of commission and omission. Indeed, such a focus misses the most important point. Rather, the challenge consists in embracing the memoir's potential to engage us "in the interval between identification and estrangement."[8] In other words, in parsing the motivations, rationales, and blind spots evident in these narratives, we become apt to interrogate our own society and lives for niches of complicity and for the nooks and crannies of denial. Thus, reading these memoirs can help us become attuned to our own "grammar of complicity," to our ruptured narratives and cropped vision, to our willingness to maintain silence about social taboos and to compartmentalize the strands of a larger narrative that should have remained a unified story.

As Trezise proposes, the "situated views" afforded by the memoir "can never attain to the panorama."[9] And yet, a reading of the corpus of texts selected for this study reveals distinct trends. The maxim that emerges most clearly could be summarized with the German saying "*Wehret den Anfängen*,"[10] that is, exercise resistance when a regime such as National Socialism first begins to organize. As Bridenthal, Grossman, and Kaplan point out, "Nazism did not arrive full blown, with promises of war and gas chambers. It came slowly, step by step."[11] Once the gas chambers were operational, there was indeed little the average citizen could do. But the Nazi genocide of the Jews was preceded by a long line of civil and human rights violations, implemented in the midst of busy cities and in full view of the average German. It is contexts such as these that call for oppositional actions. And if we are tempted to think that the price of resistance is too high, we might remember that some were willing to pay a much higher price. When non-Jewish German physician Ella Lingens Reiner was transported to Auschwitz for helping Jews, she left behind a much-beloved three-year-old son. And yet when her release from Auschwitz was a distinct possibility and she thus stood to save her own life and be reunited with her family, she chose to risk it all to rescue a Jewish inmate from the gas chamber. While this is clearly an example of goodness as a manifestation of extraordinary courage in Klüger's sense, I believe it would be helpful not to confine it to the realm of the miraculous and thus remove it from the reality of everyday life. Instead, it can serve as a reminder that, while heroism is out of reach for most of us, there are numerous, less demanding acts of opposition and resistance that hold the potential to make a difference and thus would go some way toward fulfilling our fundamental obligation toward those demarcated as "others."

Notes

1. "Das Höchste, was man erreichen kann, ist zu wissen und auszuhalten, daß es so und nicht anders gewesen ist, und dann zu sehen und abzuwarten, was sich daraus ergibt" (Arendt, *Elemente und Ursprünge totaler Herrschaft*, 33).
2. Koonz, *Mothers in the Fatherland*, 387.
3. Zipfel, "Wie führen Frauen Krieg?" 460.
4. See Koonz, *Mothers in the Fatherland*, 62.
5. "Ich kenne keinen überzeugten Nazi, und doch wird alles hingenommen, als sei es unabänderlich" (Kardorff, *Berliner Aufzeichnungen 1942–45*, 43).
6. Koonz, *Mothers in the Fatherland*, xviii.
7. "Verachtung ob meiner Nachlässigkeit, die mich daran gehindert, im siebenten Lebensjahr zu emigrieren, die Lage zu überblicken, eine Revolution in die Wege zu leiten, Widerstandsgruppen zu formen und mich statt dessen, die Umwelt schnöde negierend, dem Wachstum hingegeben zu haben" (Knef, *Der geschenkte Gaul*, 128).
8. Trezise, *Witnessing Witnessing*, 80.
9. Trezise, *Witnessing Witnessing*, 80.
10. Literally "defend the beginnings," but often translated as "nip in the bud."
11. Bridenthal, Grossman, and Kaplan, *When Biology Became Destiny*, xii.

Bibliography

Adelsberger, Lucie. *Auschwitz: A Doctor's Story.* Boston, MA: Northeastern University Press, 1995.

Adelson, Leslie A. "Ränderberichtigung: Ruth Klüger und Botho Strauß." *Zwischen Traum und Trauma – die Nation: transatlantische Perspektiven zur Geschichte eines Problems.* Ed. Claudia Mayer-Iswandy. Tübingen: Stauffenburg, 1994. 85–97.

Adler, H. G. *Theresienstadt 1941–1945: Das Antlitz einer Zwangsgemeinschaft.* Göttingen: Wallstein, 2012.

Adler, Hildegard. "Scham und Schuld: Barrieren des Erinnerns in Christa Wolfs und Peter Härtlings *Kindheitsmustern* und im psychoanalytischen Prozess." *Der Deutschunterricht* 35.5 (1983): 5–20.

Agazzi, Elena. "Familienromane, Familiengeschichten und Generationenkonflikte: Überlegungen zu einem eindrucksvollen Phänomen." *Gedächtnis und Identität: Die deutsche Literatur nach der Vereinigung.* Ed. Fabrizio Cambi. Würzburg: Königshausen und Neumann, 2008. 187–203.

Ahonen, Pertti, Gustavo Corni, Jerzy Kochanowski, Rainer Schulze, Tamás Stark, and Barbara Stelzl-Marx. *People on the Move: Forced Population Movements in Europe in the Second World War and Its Aftermath.* New York, NY: Berg, 2008.

Al-Zubi, Hasan. "Coming to an End: The Narrative of Holocaust Autobiographies and Memoirs." *Interactions: Ege University Journal of British and American Studies* 18.1 (2009): 31–42.

Alexijewitsch, Swetlana. *Der Krieg hat kein weibliches Gesicht.* Frankfurt am Main: Suhrkamp, 2015.

Alfers, Sandra. "Voices from a Haunting Past: Ghosts, Memory, and Poetry in Ruth Klüger's *weiter leben: Eine Jugend* (1992)." *Monatshefte* 100.4 (2008): 519–533.

Andreas-Friedrich, Ruth. *Schauplatz Berlin: Tagebuchaufzeichnungen 1945 bis 1948.* Frankfurt am Main: Suhrkamp, 1985.

Angerer, Christian. "Wir haben ja im Grunde nichts als die Erinnerung: Ruth Klügers weiter leben im Kontext der neueren KZ-Literatur." *Sprachkunst* 29.1 (1998): 61–83.

Anonyma. *Eine Frau in Berlin: Tagebuch-Aufzeichnungen vom 20. April bis 22. Juni 1945.* Frankfurt am Main: btb, 2005.

Arendt, Hannah. *Elemente und Ursprünge totaler Herrschaft: Antisemitismus, Imperialismus, totale Herrschaft.* Munich: Piper, 1986.

Ascher, Lisbeth. *Pflege als Begegnung: Eine Krankenschwester erzählt aus ihrem Leben.* Vienna: Facultas, 1999.

Assmann, Aleida. *Generationsidentitäten und Vorurteilsstrukturen in der neuen deutschen Erinnerungsliteratur.* Vienna: Picus, 2006.

Geschichte im Gedächtnis: Von der individuellen Erfahrung zur öffentlichen Inszenierung. Munich: C. H. Beck, 2007.

Das neue Ungehagen an der Erinnerungskultur: Eine Intervention. Munich: C. H. Beck, 2013.

Assmann, Jan. *Das kulturelle Gedächtnis: Schrift, Erinnerung und politische Identität in frühen Hochkulturen.* Munich: Beck, 1992.

Baer, Elizabeth R. and Myrna Goldenberg. "Introduction: Experience and Expression: Women and the Holocaust." *Experience and Expression: Women, the Nazis, and the Holocaust.* Ed. Elizabeth R. Baer and Myrna Goldenberg. Detroit, MI: Wayne State University Press, 2003. xiii–xxxiii.

Baer, Hester. "Sex, Death, and Motherhood in the Eurozone: Contemporary Women's Writing in German." *World Literature Today* 86.3 (2012): 59–65.

Bajohr, Frank. "Vom antijüdischen Konsens zum schlechten Gewissen: Die deutsche Gesellschaft und die Judenverfolgung 1933–1945." *Der Holocaust als offenes Geheimnis: Die Deutschen, die NS-Führung und die Alliierten.* Ed. Frank Bajohr and Dieter Pohl. Munich: C. H. Beck, 2006. 15–79.

Bajohr, Stefan. *Die Hälfte der Fabrik: Geschichte der Frauenarbeit in Deutschland 1914 bis 1945.* Marburg: Verlag Arbeiterbewegung und Gesellschaftswissenschaft, 1979.

Baker, Gary Lee. "Auntie 'Times' and Elvira's Tears: The Montage Effect in Uwe Johnson's *Jahrestage* and Christa Wolf's *Kindheitsmuster.*" *Internationales Uwe Johnson Forum* 3 (1993): 121–138.

Bal, Mieke. "The Rape of Narrative and the Narrative of Rape: Speech Acts and Body Language in *Judges.*" *Literature and the Body: Essays on Populations and Persons.* Ed. Elaine Scarry. Baltimore, MD: Johns Hopkins University Press, 1988. 1–32.

Bamm, Peter. *Die unsichtbare Flagge: Ein Bericht.* Munich: Kösel, 1952.

Bar-On, Dan. *Legacy of Silence: Encounters with Children of the Third Reich.* Cambridge, MA: Harvard University Press, 1989.

Barnett, Pamela R. "Perceptions of Childhood." *Christa Wolf in Perspective.* Ed. Ian Wallace. Amsterdam: Rodopi, 1994. 59–71.

Barnett, Victoria J. *Bystanders: Conscience and Complicity during the Holocaust.* Westport, CT: Praeger, 2000.

Barstow, Anne Llewellyn, ed. *War's Dirty Secrets: Rape, Prostitution, and Other Crimes against Women.* Cleveland, OH: Pilgrim Press, 2000.

Bartov, Omer. *Germany's War and the Holocaust: Disputed Histories.* Ithaca, NY: Cornell University Press, 2003.

Baumgart, Reinhard. "Das Leben – kein Traum? Vom Nutzen und Nachteil einer autobiographischen Literatur." *Literatur aus dem Leben: Autobiographische*

Tendenzen in der deutschsprachigen Gegenwartsdichtung. Ed. Herbert Heckmann. Munich: Carl Hanser, 1984. 8–28.

Bauschinger, Sigrid. "Uns verbindet, was uns trennt: Ruth Klügers *weiter leben und seine Leser.*" *Jüdischer Almanach des Leo Baeck Instituts.* Frankfurt am Main: Jüdischer Verlag, 1996. 126–137.

Bechdolf, Ute. "Den Siegern gehört die Beute: Vergewaltigungen beim Einmarsch der Franzosen im Landkreis Tübingen." *Geschichtswerkstatt* 16 (1988): 31–36.

Beck-Heppner, Birgit. "Frauen im Dienst der Wehrmacht: Individuelle oder kollektive Kriegserfahrung." *Von Feldherren und Gefreiten: Zur biographischen Dimension des 2. Weltkrieges.* Ed. Christian Hartmann. Munich: Oldenbourg, 2008. 103–112.

Beddow, Michael. "Doubts about Despair: Christa Wolf's *Kindheitsmuster.*" *Reflection and Action: Essays on the Bildungsroman.* Ed. James Hardin. Columbia, SC: University of South Carolina Press, 1991. 415–417.

Beevor, Antony. *The Fall of Berlin 1945.* New York, NY: Penguin, 2003.

Behre, Maria. "Die Moralität des Ich-Sagens: Johannes Bobrowskis Prosa als Anregung zum Schreiben bei Christa Wolf." *Germanica* 13 (1993): 115–129.

Benz, Ute, ed. *Frauen im Nationalsozialismus: Dokumente und Zeugnisse.* Munich: Beck'sche Verlagsbuchhandlung, 1993.

Benz, Wolfgang. "Der Generalplan Ost: Zur Germanisierung des NS-Regimes in den besetzten Ostgebieten 1939–1945." *Die Vertreibung der Deutschen aus dem Osten: Ursachen, Ereignisse, Folgen.* Ed. Wolfgang Benz. Frankfurt am Main: Fischer, 1995. 45–57.

Benz, Wolfgang. "Fünfzig Jahre nach der Vertreibung: Einleitende Bemerkungen." *Die Vertreibung der Deutschen aus dem Osten: Ursachen, Ereignisse, Folgen.* Ed. Wolfgang Benz. Frankfurt am Main: Fischer, 1995. 8–13.

Benz, Wolfgang, ed. *Überleben im Dritten Reich: Juden im Untergrund und ihre Helfer.* Munich: dtv, 2006.

Berger, Alan L. and Naomi Berger. *Second Generation Voices: Reflections by Children of Holocaust Survivors and Perpetrators.* Syracuse, NY: Syracuse University Press, 2001.

Berger, Christiane. "Die Reichsfrauenführerin Gertrud Scholtz-Klink." *Sie waren dabei: Mitläuferinnen, Nutznießerinnen, Täterinnen im Nationalsozialismus.* Ed. Marita Krauss. Göttingen: Wallstein, 2009. 103–123.

Berger, Karina. "Expulsion Novels of the 1950s: More than Meets the Eye?" *Germans as Victims in the Literary Fiction of the Berlin Republic.* Ed. Stuart Taberner and Karina Berger. Rochester, NY: Camden House, 2009. 42–55.

Berger, Karina. *Heimat, Loss and Identity: Flight and Expulsion in German Literature from the 1950s to the Present.* Oxford: Peter Lang, 2015.

Berger, Stefan. "On Taboos, Traumas and Other Myths: Why the Debate about German Victims of the Second World War Is Not a Historians' Controversy." *Germans as Victims: Remembering the Past in Contemporary Germany.* Ed. Bill Niven. New York, NY: Palgrave Macmillan, 2006. 210–224.

Bernardoni, Claudia. "Ohne Schuld und Sühne? Der moralische Diskurs über die feministische Auseinandersetzung mit dem Nationalsozialismus." *Töchterfragen: NS Frauen Geschichte.* Ed. Lerke Gravenhorst and Carmen Tatschmurat. Freiburg: Kore, 1990. 127–134.

Bernstein, Sara Tuvel with Louise Loots Thornton and Marlene Bernstein Samuels. *The Seamstress: A Memoir of Survival.* New York, NY: Berkeley Books, 1999.

Biallas, Leonie. *"Komm, Frau, raboti": Ich war Kriegsbeute.* Leverkusen: Drachenmond Verlag, 2004.

Biendarra, Anke. "Gen(d)eration Next: Prose by Julia Franck and Judith Hermann." *Studies in 20th & 21st Century Literature* 28.1 (2004): 212–239.

Bleker, Johanna and Heinz-Peter Schmiedebach. "Vorwort." *Medizin und Krieg: Vom Dilemma der Heilberufe 1865 bis 1985.* Ed. Johanna Bleker and Heinz-Peter Schmiedebach. Frankfurt am Main: Fischer, 1987. 7–9.

Bleker, Johanna. "Medizin im Dienst des Krieges – Krieg im Dienst der Medizin: Zur Frage der Kontinuität des ärztlichen Auftrages und ärztlicher Werthaltungen im Angesicht des Krieges." *Medizin und Krieg: Vom Dilemma der Heilberufe 1865 bis 1985.* Ed. Johanna Bleker and Heinz-Peter Schmiedebach. Frankfurt am Main: Fischer, 1987. 13–25.

Bletzer, Keith V. "A Voice for Every Woman and the Travesties of War." *Violence against Women* 12.7 (2006): 700–705.

Blickle, Peter. *Heimat: A Critical Theory of the German Idea of Homeland.* Rochester, NY: Camden House, 2002.

Blum, Bettina. "'Einen weiblichen Soldaten gibt es nicht': Helferinnen der Wehrmacht zwischen männlichem Einsatz und 'fraulicher Eigenart.'" *Ariadne: Forum für Frauen und Geschlechtergeschichte* 47 (2005): 46–51.

Blumer, Arnold. "Identitätsbildung als Bildschöpfung am Beispiel von Christa Wolfs Roman *Kindheitsmuster.*" *Acta Germanica* 19 (1988): 136–143.

Boa, Elizabeth and Rachel Palfreyman. *Heimat, a German Dream: Regional Loyalties and National Identity in German Culture 1890–1990.* Oxford: Oxford University Press, 2000.

Boa, Elizabeth. "Wolf, *Kindheitsmuster.*" *Landmarks in the German Novel.* Ed. Peter Hutchinson and Michael Minden. Oxford: Peter Lang, 2010. 77–92.

"Labyrinths, Mazes, and Mosaics: Fiction by Christa Wolf, Ingo Schulze, Antje Ravic Strubel, and Jens Sparschuh." *Debating German Cultural Identity since 1989.* Ed. Anne Fuchs, Kathleen James-Chakraborty, and Linda Shortt. Rochester, NY: Camden House, 2011. 131–155.

Bobinac, Marijan. "Am Herzen erblindet: Zur Inszenierung der Geschichte in Julia Francks Roman *Die Mittagsfrau.*" *Zagreber Germanistische Beiträge* 21 (2012): 145–164.

Bock, Gisela. "Ordinary Women in Nazi Germany: Perpetrators, Victims, Followers, and Bystanders." *Women in the Holocaust.* Ed. Dalia Ofer and Lenore J. Weitzman. New Haven, CT: Yale University Press, 1998. 85–100.

Bock, Sigrid. "Christa Wolf: *Kindheitsmuster.*" *Weimarer Beiträge* 23.9 (1977): 102–130.

Bock, Sigrid. "Christa Wolf: *Kindheitsmuster*." *Zum Roman in der DDR*. Ed. Marc Silberman. Stuttgart: Ernst Klett, 1980. 131–151.

Böddeker, Günter. *Die Flüchtlinge: Die Vertreibung der Deutschen im Osten*. Frankfurt am Main: Ullstein, 1996.

Bonner, Withold. "Vielleicht besteht der Krieg nur in der Verwischung der Fronten: Zur Problematik dichotomer Täter- und Opferdiskurse am Beispiel von *Eine Frau in Berlin* (Anonyma) und *Heimsuchung* (Jenny Erpenbeck)." *Jahrbuch Deutsch als Fremdsprache* 37 (2011): 24–41.

Born, Helga. "Das Vergewaltigen war noch in vollem Gange." *Courage: aktuelle Frauenzeitung* 2 (1980): 57–61.

Bos, Pascale R. "Women and the Holocaust: Analyzing Gender Difference." *Experience and Expression: Women, the Nazis, and the Holocaust*. Ed. Elizabeth R. Baer and Myrna Goldenberg. Detroit, MI: Wayne State University Press, 2003. 23–50.

"Feminists Interpreting the Politics of Wartime Rape: Berlin, 1945; Yugoslavia, 1992–93." *Signs* 31.4 (2006): 995–1025.

Bourke, Joanna. *Rape: Sex, Violence, History*. London: Virago, 2007.

Boveri, Margret. *Tage des Überlebens: Berlin 1945*. Munich: dtv, 1970.

Brandt, Jan. "In der Verjüngungsmaschine: Interview mit Jenny Erpenbeck." www .spiegel.de/kultur/literatur/autorin-jenny-erpenbeck-in-der verjuengungsma schine-a-345055.html

Braun, Michael. *Die deutsche Gegenwartsliteratur*. Cologne: Böhlau, 2010.

Bredow, Ilse Gräfin von. *Deine Keile kriegste doch*. Munich: dtv, 1992.

Breiding, Birgit. *Die Braunen Schwestern: Ideologie, Struktur, Funktion einer natio-nalsozialistischen Elite*. Stuttgart: Franz Steiner Verlag, 1998.

Bridenthal, Renate, Atina Grossmann, and Marion Kaplan, eds. *When Biology Became Destiny: Women in Weimar and Nazi Germany*. New York, NY: Monthly Review Press, 1984.

Bridenthal, Renate, Atina Grossmann, and Marion Kaplan. "Introduction: Women in Weimar and Nazi Germany." *When Biology Became Destiny: Women in Weimar and Nazi Germany*. Ed. Renate Bridenthal, Atina Grossmann, and Marion Kaplan. New York: Monthly Review Press, 1984. 1–29.

Brodzki, Bella. "Mothers, Displacement, and Language in the Autobiographies of Nathalie Sarraute and Christa Wolf." *Life/Lines: Theorizing Women's Autobiography*. Ed. Bella Brodzki and Celeste Schenck. Ithaca, NY: Cornell University Press, 1988. 243–259.

Brostrom, Kenneth N. "*Prussian Nights*: A Poetic Parable for Our Time." *Solzhenitsyn in Exile: Critical Essays and Documentary Materials*. Ed. John B. Dunlop, Richard S. Haugh, and Michael Nicholson. Stanford, CA: Hoover Institution Press, 1985. 229–242.

Brown, Adam. "Screening Women's Complicity in the Holocaust: The Problems of Judgement and Representation." *Holocaust Studies: A Journal of Culture and History* 17.2–3 (2011): 75–98.

Brownmiller, Susan. *Against Our Will: Men, Women, and Rape*. New York, NY: Fawcett Books, 1975.

Bruha, Antonia. *Ich war keine Heldin.* Vienna: Europaverlag, 1995.

Brumlik, Micha. *Wer Sturm sät: Die Vertreibung der Deutschen.* Berlin: Aufbau Verlag, 2005.

Burk, Henning, Erika Fehse, Marita Krauss, Susanne Spröer, and Gudrun Wolter. *Fremde Heimat: Das Schicksal der Vertriebenen nach 1945. Das Buch zur Fernsehserie.* Berlin: Rowohlt, 2011.

Burke, James Wakefield. *The Big Rape.* Berlin: World Wide Productions, 1955.

Burke Fessler, Diane. *No Time for Fear: Voices of American Military Nurses in World War II.* East Lansing, MI: Michigan State University Press, 1996.

Burrin, Philippe. *From Prejudice to the Holocaust: Nazi Anti-Semitism.* Transl. Janet Lloyd. New York, NY: The New Press, 2000.

Cabanis, Hertha. *Das Licht in den Händen: Die Geschichte der Bettina.* Stuttgart: Steinkopf, 1951.

Cahill, Ann J. *Rethinking Rape.* Ithaca, NY: Cornell University Press, 2001.

Callamard, Agnes. "Refugee Women: A Gendered and Political Analysis of the Refugee Experience." *Refugees: Perspectives on the Experience of Forced Migration.* Ed. Alastair Ager. London: Continuum, 1999. 196–214.

Camfield, Martha. "Das Zitat als narrative Struktur am Beispiel der Lieder in Christa Wolfs *Kindheitsmuster.*" *Carleton Germanic Papers* 18 (1990): 23–50.

Caruth, Cathy. *Unclaimed Experience: Trauma, Narrative, and History.* Baltimore, MD: Johns Hopkins University Press, 1996.

Casper, Monica J. and Lisa Jean Moore. *Missing Bodies: The Politics of Visibility.* New York, NY: New York University Press, 2009.

Cencig, Elisabeth. "The Jordans: Remembered and Invented Past in Christa Wolf's *Kindheitsmuster* and Alice Munro's *Lives of Girls and Women.*" *International Journal of Canadian Studies* 6 (1992): 63–85.

Chamier, Astrid von and Insa Eschebach. "Ilse Schmidt 'Ich persönlich habe keinen Ton gesagt': Erinnerungsbilder einer ehemaligen Stabshelferin." *WerkstattGeschichte* 10 (1995): 67–72.

Christiansen, Hanna. "Was vom Holocaust erinnert wird hängt davon ab, wie es erinnert wird: Die Erinnerungen der Wehrmachtsangehörigen Ilse Schmidt." www.literaturkritik.de/public/rezension.php?rez_id=4124&ausgabe=200109, September 2001. Last accessed January 2016.

Cohen, Stanley. *States of Denial: Knowing about Atrocities and Suffering.* Cambridge: Polity Press, 2001.

Cohen-Pfister, Laurel. "Rape, War, and Outrage: Changing Perceptions on German Victimhood in the Period of Post-Unification." *Victims and Perpetrators 1933–1945: (Re)Presenting the Past in Post-Unification Culture.* Ed. Laurel Cohen-Pfister and Dagmar Wienroeder-Skinner. Berlin: Walter de Gruyter, 2006. 316–336.

Connerton, Paul. *How Societies Remember.* Cambridge: Cambridge University Press, 1989.

Conze, Susanne and Beate Fieseler. "Soviet Women as Comrades-in-Arms: A Blind Spot in the History of War." *The People's War: Responses to WWII in the Soviet Union*. Ed. Robert W. Thurston and Bernd Bonwetsch. Chicago, IL: University of Illinois Press, 2000. 211–234.

Cooke, Miriam and Angela Woollacott, eds. *Gendering War Talk*. Princeton, NJ: Princeton University Press, 1993.

Cooper, Helen M., Adrienne Auslander Munich, and Susan Merrill Squier. "Introduction." *Arms and the Woman: War, Gender, and Literary Representation*. Ed. Helen M. Cooper, Adrienne Auslander Munich, and Susan Merrill Squier. Chapel Hill, NC: University of North Carolina Press, 1989. xiii–xx.

Cosgrove, Mary. "*Heimat* as Nonplace and *Terrain Vague* in Jenny Erpenbeck's *Heimsuchung* and Julia Schoch's *Mit der Geschwindigkeit des Sommers*." *New German Critique* 39.2 (2012): 63–86.

Costagli, Simone. "Unverhofftes Wiedersehen: Erscheinungsformen des 'deutschen Ostens' in der Gegenwartsliteratur." *Gedächtnis und Identität: Die deutsche Literatur nach der Vereinigung*. Ed. Fabrizio Cambi. Würzburg: Königshausen & Neumann, 2008. 277–291.

Couser, G. Thomas. *Memoir: An Introduction*. New York, NY: Oxford University Press, 2012.

Dahlke, Birgit. "Frau komm! Vergewaltigungen 1945 – zur Geschichte eines Diskurses." *Literatur Gesellschaft DDR: Kanonkämpfe und ihre Geschichte(n)*. Ed. Birgit Dahlke, Martina Langermann, and Thomas Taterka. Stuttgart: Metzler, 2000. 275–311.

Dahlke, Birgit. "Tagebuch des Überlebens: Vergewaltigung 1945 in ost- und westdeutschen Autobiographien." *Autobiography by Women in German*. Ed. Mererid Puw Davies, Beth Linklater, and Gisela Shaw. Oxford: Lang, 2001. 195–212.

Darnstädt, Thomas and Klaus Wiegrefe. "Vater, erschieß mich!" *Die Flucht: Über die Vertreibung der Deutschen aus dem Osten*. Ed. Stefan Aust and Stephan Burgdorf. Munich: Deutsche Verlags-Anstalt, 2002. 21–38.

De Pauw, Linda Grant. *Battle Cries and Lullabies: Women in War from Prehistory to the Present*. Norman, OK: University of Oklahoma Press, 1998.

DeGroot, Gerard J. "Arms and the Woman." *A Soldier and a Woman: Sexual Integration in the Military*. Ed. Gerard J. DeGroot and Corinna Peniston-Bird. London: Pearson Education Limited, 2000. 3–17.

DeGroot, Gerard J. "Lipstick on Her Nipples, Cordite in Her Hair: Sex and Romance among British Servicewomen during the Second World War." *A Soldier and a Woman: Sexual Integration in the Military*. Ed. Gerard J. DeGroot and Corinna Peniston-Bird. London: Pearson Education Limited, 2000. 100–118.

Demetz, Hanna. *Ein Haus in Böhmen*. Frankfurt am Main: Ullstein, 1978.

Deutschkron, Inge. *Ich trug den gelben Stern*. Munich: dtv, 1985.

Didon, Sybille. *Kassandrarufe: Studien zu Vorkrieg und Krieg in Christa Wolfs Erzählungen Kindheitsmuster und Kassandra*. Stockholm: Almqvist & Wiksell International.

Doerr, Karin. "Memories of History: Women and the Holocaust in Autobiographical and Fictional Memoirs." SHOFAR 18.3 (2000): 49–63.

Dollenmayer, David. "Generational Patterns in Christa Wolf's *Kindheitsmuster.*" *German Life and Letters* 39.3 (1986): 229–234.

Dönhoff, Marion Gräfin. *Kindheit in Ostpreussen.* Munich: btb, 1998.

Ritt durch Masuren: Aufgeschrieben 1941 für meinen Bruder Dietrich. Würzburg: Rautenberg, 2008.

Namen, die keiner mehr nennt: Ostpreussen – Menschen und Geschichte. Reinbek bei Hamburg: rororo, 2009.

Douglas, R.M. *Orderly and Humane: The Expulsion of the Germans after the Second World War.* New Haven, CT: Yale University Press, 2012.

Dribben, Judith Strick. *A Girl Called Judith Strick.* Foreword by Golda Meir. Toronto: General Publishing Company, 1970.

Dückers, Tanja. *Himmelskörper.* Berlin: Aufbau, 2004.

Dunant, J. Henry. *A Memory of Solferino.* London: Cassell and Company, 1947.

Duttlinger, Carolin. "The Ethics of Curiosity: Ruth Klüger, *weiter leben.*" *Oxford German Studies* 38.2 (2009): 218–231.

Dwyer, Anne. "Runaway Texts: The Many Life Stories of Iurii Trifonov and Christa Wolf." *Russian Review* 64.4 (2005): 605–627.

Dylewska, Agnieszka. "Grenzen des Schweigens: Grenzsituationen und Kommunikationsphänomen im Roman von Julia Franck *Die Mittagsfrau.*" *Kontinuitäten Brüche Kontroversen: Deutsche Literatur nach dem Mauerfall.* Ed. Edward Bialek and Monika Wolting. Dresden: Neisse, 2012. 325–346.

Eakin, Paul John. "Eye and I: Negotiating Distance in Eyewitness Narrative." *Partial Answers* 7.2 (2009): 1–12.

Ebbinghaus, Angelika, ed. *Opfer und Täterinnen: Frauenbiographien des Nationalsozialismus.* Frankfurt am Main: Fischer, 1997.

Ebert, Jens. "Mein Schmuck ist im Krieg die Tracht und mein Leben der Dienst." *Briefe einer Rotkreuzschwester von der Ostfront.* Ed. Jens Ebert and Sibylle Penkert. Göttingen: Wallstein, 2006. 7–53.

Edvardson, Cordelia. *Gebranntes Kind sucht das Feuer.* Transl. Anna-Liese Kornitzky. Munich: dtv, 1989.

Eichenberger, Elsi. *Als Rotkreuzschwester in Lazaretten der Ostfront: Schweizer Ärztemissionen im 2. Weltkrieg. Teil 3 Smolensk, Kriegswinter 1941/42. Ein Erlebnisbericht.* Ed. Reinhold Busch. Berlin: Frank Wünsche, 2004.

Eichhorn, Svenja and Philipp Kuwert. *Das Geheimnis unserer Großmütter: Eine empirische Studie über sexualisierte Kriegsgewalt um 1945.* Gießen: Psychosozial Verlag, 2011.

Eidukeviciene, Ruta. "(Re)konstruktion der Vergangenheit im neuen deutschen Familienroman (unter besonderer Berücksichtigung des Romans *Die Mittagsfrau* von Julia Franck)." *Literatura* 50.5 (2008): 35–46.

Eigler, Friederike. *Gedächtnis und Geschichte im Generationenroman seit der Wende.* Berlin: Erich Schmidt Verlag, 2005.

"Beyond the Victim Debate: Flight and Expulsion in Recent Novels by Authors from the Second and Third Generation (Christoph Hein, Reinhard Jirgl,

Kathrin Schmidt, and Tanja Dückers)." *Generational Shifts in Contemporary German Culture*. Ed. Lauren Cohen-Pfister and Susanne Vees-Gulani. Rochester, NY: Camden House, 2010. 77–94.

"Critical Approaches to *Heimat* and the Spatial Turn." *New German Critique* 115, 39.1 (2012): 27–48.

Elliger, Katharina. *Und tief in der Seele das Ferne: Die Geschichte einer Vertreibung aus Schlesien*. Reinbek bei Hamburg: Rowohlt, 2010.

Elshtain, Jean Bethke. *Women and War*. New York, NY: Basic Books, 1987.

Engler, Jürgen. "Normalität und Argwohn: Christa Wolf's *Kindheitsmuster*." *Neue deutsche Literatur* 47.2 (1999): 7–14.

Enloe, Cynthia. *Does Khaki Become You: The Militarization of Women's Lives*. Boston, MA: South End Press, 1983.

Ensler, Eve. *Necessary Targets: A Story of Women and War*. New York, NY: Villard, 2001.

Erpenbeck, Jenny. *Heimsuchung. Roman*. Munich: btb, 2010.

Eschebach, Insa, Sigrid Jacobeit, and Silke Wenk, eds. *Gedächtnis und Geschlecht: Deutungsmuster in Darstellungen des nationalsozialistischen Genozids*. Frankfurt am Main: Campus Verlag, 2002.

Eschebach, Insa and Regina Mühlhäuser, eds. *Krieg und Geschlecht: Sexuelle Gewalt im Krieg und Sex-Zwangsarbeit in NS-Konzentrationslagern*. Berlin: Metropol, 2008.

Ettinger, Elzbieta. *Kindergarten*. London: Constable, 1971.

Fell, Christa. "Lenkas Traum: Nachdenken über Christa W." *Hinter dem schwarzen Vorhang: Die Katastrophe und die epische Tradition*. Ed. Friedrich Gaede. Tübingen: Francke, 1994. 243–253.

Ferguson, Frances. "Rape and the Rise of the Novel." *Representations* 20 (1987): 88–112.

Fickert, Kurt J. "Fantastic Precision: The Style of Christa Wolf's *An Illustration of Childhood*." *The International Fiction Review* 17.2 (1990): 124–127.

Finckh, Renate. *Mit uns zieht die neue Zeit*. Baden-Baden: Signal, 1978.

Finckh, Renate and Heike Mundzeck. "Renate Finckh im Gespräch mit Heike Mundzeck." *Der alltägliche Faschismus: Frauen im Dritten Reich*. Ed. Charles Schüddekopf. Bonn: J. H. W. Dietz, 1981. 68–79.

Finnan, Carmel. "Autobiography, Memory and the Shoa: German-Jewish Identity in Autobiographical Writings by Ruth Klüger, Cordelia Edvardson and Laura Waco." *Jews in German Literature since 1945: German-Jewish Literature?* Ed. Pol o' Dochartaigh. Amsterdam: Rodopi, 2000. 447–459.

Finnan, Carmel. "Gendered Memory? Cordelia Edvardson's *Gebranntes Kind sucht das Feuer* and Ruth Klüger's *weiter leben*." *Autobiography by Women in German*. Ed. Mererid Puw Davies, Beth Linklater, and Gisela Shaw. Oxford: Peter Lang, 2001. 273–290.

Fontaine, Karin. *Nationalsozialistische Aktivistinnen (1933–1945): Hausfrauen, Mütter, Berufstätige, Akademikerinnen. So sahen sie sich und ihre Rolle im tausendjährigen Reich*. Würzburg: Köngishausen & Neumann, 2003.

Foucault, Michel. *The Birth of the Clinic: An Archaeology of Medical Perception.* Transl. A. M. Sheridan Smith. New York, NY: Vintage Books, 1994.

Frahm, Ole. "Ein deutsches Trauma: Zur Schamlosigkeit deutscher Opferidentifikation." *German Life and Letters* 57.4 (2004): 372–390.

Franck, Julia. *Die Mittagsfrau. Roman.* Frankfurt am Main: S. Fischer, 2007.

Franck, Julia. "The Wonder (of) Woman." Transl. Alexandra Merley Hill. *Women in German Yearbook: Feminist Studies in German Literature and Culture* 24 (2008): 229–240.

Frankenthal, Käte. *Der dreifache Fluch: Jüdin, Intellektuelle, Sozialistin: Lebenserinnerungen einer Ärztin in Deutschland und im Exil.* Ed. Kathleen M. Pearle and Stephan Leibfried.Frankfurt am Main: Campus, 1981.

Frederick, Sharon and the Aware Committee on Rape. *Rape: Weapon of Terror.* River Edge: Global Publishing, 2001.

Frei, Norbert. *1945 und wir: Das Dritte Reich im Bewußtsein der Deutschen.* Munich: Beck, 2005.

Frieden, Sandra. "In eigener Sache: Christa Wolf's *Kindheitsmuster.*" *The German Quarterly* 54.4 (1981): 473–487.

"Falls es strafbar ist, die Grenzen zu verwischen: Autobiographie, Biographie und Christa Wolf." *Vom Anderen und vom Selbst: Beiträge zu Fragen der Biographie und Autobiographie.* Königstein: Athenäum, 1982. 153–166.

Friedländer, Saul. *When Memory Comes.* Transl. Helen R. Lane. New York, NY: Farrar Straus Giroux, 1979.

"The Wehrmacht, German Society, and the Knowledge of the Mass Extermination of the Jews." *Crimes of War: Guilt and Denial in the Twentieth Century.* Ed. Omer Bartov, Atina Grossmann, and Mary Nolan. New York, NY: New Press, 2002. 17–30.

Friedrichsmeyer, Sara. "Women's Writing and the Construct of an Integrated Self." *The Enlightenment and Its Legacy: Studies in German Literature in Honor of Helga Slessarev.* Ed. Sara Friedrichsmeyer and Barbara Becker-Cantarino. Bonn: Bouvier, 1991. 171–180.

Frietsch, Elke and Christina Herkommen. "Nationalsozialismus und Geschlecht: eine Einführung." *Nationalsozialismus und Geschlecht: Zur Politisierung und Ästhetisierung von Körper, "Rasse" und Sexualität im "Dritten Reich" und nach 1945.* Ed. Elke Frietsch and Christina Herkommer. Bielefeld: transcript, 2009. 9–44.

Fuchs, Anne. *Phantoms of War in Contemporary German Literature, Films and Discourse: The Politics of Memory.* London: Palgrave Macmillan, 2008.

Fuchs, Anne and Mary Cosgrove. "Introduction: Germany's Memory Contests and the Management of the Past." *German Memory Contests: The Quest for Identity in Literature, Film, and Discourse since 1990.* Ed. Anne Fuchs, Mary Cosgrove, and Georg Grote. Rochester, NY: Camden House, 2006. 1–21.

Fürstler, Gerhard and Peter Malina. *Ich tat nur meinen Dienst: Zur Geschichte der Krankenpflege in Österreich in der NS-Zeit.* Vienna: Facultas, 2004.

Gaida, Ulrike. *Zwischen Pflegen und Töten: Krankenschwestern im Nationalsozialismus. Einführung und Quellen für Unterricht und Selbststudium.* Frankfurt am Main: Mabuse, 2011.

Ganguli, Selina. "Patterns of Childhood: Reflections on Christa Wolf's *Kindheitsmuster.*" *Journal of the School of Languages* 7.1–2 (1980): 54–64.

Garraio, Julia. "Vergewaltigung als Schlüsselbegriff einer misslungenen Vergangenheitsbewältigung: Hans-Ulrich Treichels *Der Verlorene* und Reinhard Jirgls *Die Unvollendeten.*" *Mittelweg* 36 (2010): 3–17.

"Hordes of Rapists: The Instrumentalization of Sexual Violence in German Cold War Anti-Communist Discourses." *RCCS Annual Review* 5.5 (2013): 43–63.

Gartmann, Hildegard. *Blitzmädchen: Dokumentarroman.* Wiesbaden: Limes, 1971.

Gättens, Marie-Luise. "Mädchenerziehung im Faschismus: Die Rekonstruktion der eigenen Geschichte in Christa Wolfs *Kindheitsmuster.*" *Der Widerspenstigen Zähmung: Studien zur bezwungenen Weiblichkeit in der Literatur vom Mittelalter bis zur Gegenwart.* Ed. Sylvia Wallinger and Monika Jonas. Innsbruck: Institut für Germanistik der Universität Innsbruck, 1986. 281–293.

"Language, Gender, and Fascism: Reconstructing Histories in *Three Guineas, Der Mann auf der Kanzel,* and *Kindheitsmuster.*" *Gender, Patriarchy, and Fascism in the Third Reich: The Response of Women Writers.* Ed. Elaine Martin. Detroit, MI: Wayne State University Press, 1993. 32–64.

Gebhardt, Miriam. *Als die Soldaten kamen: Die Vergewaltigungen deutscher Frauen am Ende des Zweiten Weltkriegs.* Munich: Deutsche Verlags-Anstalt, 2015.

Gehmacher, Johanna. "Im Umfeld der Macht: populäre Perspektiven auf Frauen der NS-Elite." *Nationalsozialismus und Geschlecht: Zur Politisierung und Ästhetisierung von Körper, 'Rasse' und Sexualität im 'Dritten Reich' und nach 1945.* Ed. Elke Frietsch and Christina Herkommer. Bielefeld: transcript, 2009. 49–69.

Gehmacher, Johanna and Gabriella Hauch. "Einleitung." *Frauen- und Geschlechtergeschichte des Nationalsozialismus: Fragestellungen, Perspektiven, neue Forschungen.* Ed. Johanna Gehmacher and Gabriella Hauch. Innsbruck: StudienVerlag, 2007. 7–19.

Gelfand, Wladimir. *Deutschland Tagebuch 1945–46.* Ed. Elke Scherstjanoi. Berlin: Aufbau, 2008.

Gersdorff, Ursula von. *Frauen im Kriegsdienst 1914–1945.* Stuttgart: Deutsche Verlags-Anstalt, 1969.

Gerstenberger, Katharina. "Fictionalizations: Holocaust Memory and the Generational Construct in the Works of Contemporary Women Writers." *Generational Shifts in Contemporary German Culture.* Ed. Laurel Cohen-Pfister and Susanne Vees-Gulani. Rochester, NY: Camden House, 2010. 95–114.

Geu, Susanne. "Schreiben zum Überleben: Ein Interview mit Julia Franck." www .zeit.de/online/2007/40/interview-julia-franck

Gilliland, Gail. "Self and Other: Christa Wolf's *Patterns of Childhood* and Primo Levi's *Se Questo E Un Uomo* as Dialogic Texts." *Comparative Literature Studies* 29.2 (1992): 182–209.

Gilman, Sander. *The Jew's Body*. New York, NY: Routledge, 1991.

Gilmore, Leigh. *The Limits of Autobiography: Trauma and Testimony*. Ithaca, NY: Cornell University Press, 2001.

Ginsburg, Ruth. "In Pursuit of Self: Theme, Narration, and Focalization in Christa Wolf's *Patterns of Childhood*." *Style* 26.3 (1992): 437–446.

Goedecke, Jonathan. *Flucht und Vertreibung*. Munich: GRIN, 2005.

Goldenberg, Myrna. "Memoirs of Auschwitz Survivors: The Burden of Gender." *Women in the Holocaust*. Ed. Dalia Ofer and Lenore J. Weitzman. New Haven, CT: Yale University Press, 1998. 327–339.

Goodbody, Axel. "*Heimat* and the Place of Humans in the World: Jenny Erpenbeck's *Heimsuchung* in Ecocritical Perspective." *New German Critique* 43.2 (2016): 127–151.

Goschalk, Julie C. "When Children of Holocaust Survivors Meet Children of Nazis." *Second Generation Voices: Reflections by Children of Holocaust Survivors and Perpetrators*. Ed. Alan L. Berger and Naomi Berger. Syracuse, NY: Syracuse University Press, 2001. 336–343.

Grass, Günter. *Danziger Trilogie. Die Blechtrommel. Katz und Maus. Hundejahre*. Munich: Steidl, 1999.

Beim Häuten der Zwiebel. Göttingen: Steidl, 2006.

Gravenhorst, Lerke. "NS-Verbrechen und asymmetrische Geschlechterdifferenz: eine kritische Auseinandersetzung mit historischen Analysen zur NS-Täterschaft." *Nationalsozialismus und Geschlecht: Zur Politisierung und Ästhetisierung von Körper, 'Rasse' und Sexualität im 'Dritten Reich' und nach 1945*. Ed. Elke Frietsch and Christina Herkommer. Bielefeld: transcript, 2009. 86–103.

Gravenhorst, Lerke and Carmen Tatschmurat, eds. *Töchterfragen: NS Frauen Geschichte*. Freiburg: Kore, 1990.

Gravenhorst, Lerke and Carmen Tatschmurat, eds. *Töchterfragen: NS Frauen Geschichte*. Ed. Lerke Gravenhorst and Carmen Tatschmurat. Freiburg: Kore, 1990. 11–13.

Grimm, Reinhold. "Elternspuren, Kindheitsmuster: Lebensdarstellung in der jüngsten deutschsprachigen Prosa." *Vom Anderen und vom Selbst: Beiträge zu Fragen der Biographie und Autobiographie*. Königstein: Athenäum, 1982. 167–182.

Gross, Leonard. *The Last Jews in Berlin*. New York, NY: Bantam Books, 1982.

Grossmann, Atina. "A Question of Silence: The Rape of German Women by Occupation Soldiers." *West Germany under Construction: Politics, Society, and Culture in the Adenauer Era*. Ed. Robert G. Moeller. Ann Arbor MI: University of Michigan Press, 1997. 33–51.

Grossmann, Atina. "Eine Frage des Schweigens: Die Vergewaltigung deutscher Frauen durch Besatzungssoldaten: Zum historischen Hintergrund von Helke Sanders Film *BeFreier und Befreite*." *Frauen und Film* 54/55 (1994): 15–28.

Grossmann, Atina. *Jews, Germans, and Allies: Close Encounters in Occupied Germany*. Princeton, NJ: Princeton University Press, 2007.

Grote, Christiane and Gabriele Rosenthal. "Frausein als Entlastungsargument für die biographische Verstrickung in den Nationalsozialismus? Über Strategien der Normalisierung der nationalsozialistischen Vergangenheit in Deutschland." *Tel Aviver Jahrbuch für deutsche Geschichte* 21 (1992): 289–318.

Grundhewer, Herbert. "Von der freiwilligen Kriegskrankenpflege bis zur Einbindung des Roten Kreuzes in das Heeressanitätswesen." *Medizin und Krieg: Vom Dilemma der Heilberufe 1865 bis 1985.* Ed. Johanna Bleker and Heinz-Peter Schmiedebach. Frankfurt am Main: Fischer, 1987. 29–44.

Gumpert, Gregor. "Noch einmal: Das gemiedene Thema: Zur literarischen Reflexion auf Flucht und Vertreibung 1945." *Internationales Archiv für Sozialgeschichte der deutschen Literatur* 30.2 (2005): 104–116.

Hagemann, Karen. "Home/Front: The Military, Violence and Gender Relations in the Age of the World Wars." *Home/Front: The Military, War and Gender in Twentieth-Century Germany.* Eds. Karen Hagemann and Stefanie Schüler-Springorum. New York, NY: Oxford University Press, 2002. 1–41.

Hagemann, Karen. "Jede Kraft wird gebraucht: Militäreinsatz von Frauen im Ersten und Zweiten Weltkrieg." *Erster Weltkrieg, Zweiter Weltkrieg: Ein Vergleich. Krieg, Kriegserlebnis, Kriegserfahrung in Deutschland.* Ed. Bruno Thoß and Hans-Erich Volkmann. Paderborn: Ferdinand Schöningh, 2002. 79–106.

Hagemann, Karen, "Preface." *Home/Front: The Military, War and Gender in Twentieth-Century Germany.* Eds. Karen Hagemann and Stefanie Schüler-Springorum. New York, NY: Oxford University Press, 2002. ix-xii.

Hagemann, Karen and Stefanie Schüler-Springorum, eds. *Home/Front: The Military, War and Gender in Twentieth-Century Germany.* New York, NY: Oxford University Press, 2002.

Hahn Beer, Edith with Susan Dworkin. *The Nazi Officer's Wife: How One Jewish Woman Survived the Holocaust.* New York, NY: Perennial, 2000.

Halbwachs, Maurice. *On Collective Memory.* Ed., trans., and with an introduction by Lewis A. Coser. Chicago, IL: University of Chicago Press, 1992.

Hammel, Andrea. "The Destabilisation of Personal Histories: Rewriting and Translating Autobiographical Texts by German-Jewish Survivors." *Comparative Critical Studies* 1.3 (2004): 295–308.

Hanley, Lynne. *Writing War: Fiction, Gender & Memory.* Amherst, MA: University of Massachusetts Press, 1991.

Harris, R. "The 'Child of the Barbarian': Rape, Race, and Nationalism in France during the First World War." *Past & Present* 141 (1993): 170–206.

Hartmann, Karl-Heinz. "Erinnerungsarbeit, Hermann Kant: *Der Aufenthalt* (1977), Christa Wolf: *Kindheitsmuster* (1977), Christoph Hein: *Horns Ende* (1985)." *Der deutsche Roman nach 1945.* Ed. Manfred Brauneck. Bamberg: C. C. Buchners, 1993. 188–202.

Harvey, Elizabeth. "Remembering and Repressing: German Women's Recollections of the 'Ethnic Struggle' in Occupied Poland during the Second World War." *Home/Front: The Military, War and Gender in Twentieth-Century Germany.* Ed.

Karen Hagemann and Stefanie Schüler-Springorum. New York, NY: Oxford University Press, 2002. 275–296.

Women and the Nazi East: Agents and Witnesses of Germanization. New Haven, CT: Yale University Press, 2005.

"Homelands on the Move: Gender, Space and Dislocation in the Nazi Resettlement of German Minorities from Eastern and Southeastern Europe." *Women and Men at War: A Gender Perspective on World War II and Its Aftermath in Central and Eastern Europe.* Ed. Maren Röger and Ruth Leiserowitz. Osnabrück: fibre Verlag, 2017. 35–57.

Heer, Hannes. *Vom Verschwinden der Täter: Der Vernichtungskrieg fand statt, aber keiner war dabei.* Berlin: Aufbau, 2004.

Heffernan, Valerie. "Julia Franck, *Die Mittagsfrau: Historia Matria* and Matrilineal Narrative." *Emerging German-Language Novelists of the Twenty-First Century.* Ed. Lyn Marven and Stuart Taberner. Rochester, NY: Camden House, 2011. 148–161.

Heidelberger-Leonard, Irene. "Ruth Klüger *weiter leben* – ein Grundstein zu einem neuen Auschwitz-Kanon." *Deutsche Nachkriegsliteratur und der Holocaust.* Ed. Stephan Braese, Holger Gehle, Doron Kiesel, and Hanno Loewy. Frankfurt am Main: Campus, 1998. 157–169.

Heineman, Elizabeth. "The Hour of the Woman." *American Historical Review* 101.2 (1996): 354–395.

"Gender, Sexuality, and Coming to Terms with the Nazi Past." *Central European History* 38.1 (2005): 41–74.

Heinemann, Marlene E. *Gender and Destiny: Women Writers and the Holocaust.* New York, NY: Greenwood Press, 1986.

Heinsohn, Kirsten, Barbara Vogel, and Ulrike Weckel, eds. *Zwischen Karriere und Verfolgung: Handlungsräume von Frauen im nationalsozialistischen Deutschland.* Frankfurt am Main: Campus, 1997.

Heinz, Annemarie. *Anna, die Soldatin.* Mühlacker: Stieglitz, 1999.

Helbig, Louis Ferdinand. *Der ungeheure Verlust: Flucht und Vertreibung in der deutschsprachigen Belletristik der Nachkriegszeit.* Wiesbaden: Otto Harrassowitz, 1988.

Helbig, Louis Ferdinand, Johannes Hoffmann, and Doris Kraemer. *Verlorene Heimaten – neue Fremden: Literarische Texte zu Krieg, Flucht, Vertreibung, Nachkriegszeit.* Dortmund: Forschungsstelle Ostmitteleuropa, 1995.

Henry, Frances. *Victims and Neighbors: A Small Town in Nazi Germany Remembered.* Foreword by Willy Brandt. South Hadley, MA: Bergin & Garvey Publishers, 1984.

Henry, Nicola, Tony Ward, and Matt Hirshberg. "A Multifactorial Model of Wartime Rape." *Aggression and Violent Behavior* 9.5 (2004): 535–562.

Herbermann, Nanda. *Der gesegnete Abgrund: Schutzhäftling Nr. 6582 im Frauenkonzentrationslager Ravensbrück.* Annweiler: Plöger Medien, 2002.

Herf, Jeffrey. *The Jewish Enemy: Nazi Propaganda during World War II and the Holocaust.* Cambridge, MA: Belknap Press of Harvard University Press, 2006.

Herkommer, Christina. *Frauen im Nationalsozialismus – Opfer oder Täterinnen? Eine Kontroverse der Frauenforschung im Spiegel feministischer Theoriebildung und der allgemeinen historischen Aufarbeitung der NS-Vergangenheit*. Munich: Martin Meidenbauer, 2005.

Herkommer, Christina. "Women under National Socialism: Women's Scope for Action and the Issue of Gender." *Ordinary People as Mass Murderers: Perpetrators in Comparative Perspectives*. Ed. Olaf Jensen and Claus-Christian W. Szejnmann. New York, NY: Palgrave Macmillan, 2008. 99–119.

Herzberger, Magda. *Eyewitness to Holocaust*. Mattoon: Modern Images, 1985.

Herzog, Dagmar, ed. *Brutality and Desire: War and Sexuality in Europe's Twentieth Century*. New York, NY: Palgrave Macmillan, 2011.

Herzog, Dagmar. "Introduction: War and Sexuality in Europe's Twentieth Century." *Brutality and Desire: War and Sexuality in Europe's Twentieth Century*. Ed. Dagmar Herzog. New York, NY: Palgrave Macmillan, 2011. 1–15.

Hesse-Werner, Ingrid. *Als Pommern brannte. Biografische Erzählung*. Norderstedt: Nemesis, 2006.

Higgins, Lynn A. and Brenda R. Silver, eds. *Rape and Representation*. New York, NY: Columbia University Press, 1991.

Higonnet, Margaret Randolph. "Introduction." *Behind the Lines: Gender and the Two World Wars*. Ed. Margaret Randolph Higonnet, Jane Jenson, Sonya Michel, and Margaret Collins Weitz. New Haven, CT: Yale University Press, 1987. 1–17.

Higonnet, Margaret Randolph, Jane Jenson, Sonya Michel, and Margaret Collins Weitz, eds. *Behind the Lines: Gender and the Two World Wars*. New Haven, CT: Yale University Press, 1987.

Hilberg, Raul. *Perpetrators, Victims, Bystanders: The Jewish Catastrophe 1933–1945*. New York, NY: HarperPerennial, 1992.

Hilzinger, Sonja. *Christa Wolf*. Frankfurt am Main: Suhrkamp, 2007.

Himmelstoß, Elisabeth. *Und ich konnte nichts ändern! Odyssee einer Nachrichtenhelferin*. Berlin: E.S. Mittler & Sohn GmbH, 1994.

Hirsch, Helga. *Schweres Gepäck: Flucht und Vertreibung als Lebensthema*. Hamburg: Edition Körber Stiftung, 2004.

Hirsch, Marianne and Leo Spitzer. "Gendered Translations: Claude Lanzmann's *Shoa*." *Gendering War Talk*. Ed. Miriam Cooke and Angela Woollacott. Princeton, NJ: Princeton University Press, 1993. 3–19.

Hoerning, Erika M. "Frauen als Kriegsbeute: Der Zwei-Fronten-Krieg: Beispiele aus Berlin." *Wir kriegen jetzt andere Zeiten: auf der Suche nach der Erfahrung des Volkes in nachfaschistischen Ländern*. Ed. Lutz Niethammer and Alexander von Plato. Berlin: J. H. W. Dietz, 1985. 327–344.

Holub, Robert. "Fact, Fantasy and Female Subjectivity: *Vergangenheitsbewältigung* in Christa Wolf's *Patterns of Childhood*." *Facing Fascism and Confronting the Past: German Women Writers from Weimar to the Present*. Ed. Elke P. Frederiksen and Martha Kaarsberg Wallach. Albany, NY: State University of New York Press, 2000. 217–234.

Höntsch-Harendt, Ursula. *Wir Flüchtlingskinder*. Halle: Mitteldeutscher Verlag, 1985.

Hörnigk, Therese. "Kriegserlebnis und Wandlungsgestaltung in der frühen DDR-Literatur." *Literatur im Wandel: Entwicklungen in europäischen sozialistischen Ländern 1944/45–1980*. Ed. Ludwig Richter, Heinrich Olschowsky, Juri W. Bogdanow, and Swetlana A. Scherlaimowa. Berlin: Aufbau Verlag, 1986. 223–246.

"Gespräch mit Christa Wolf." *Sinn und Form* 41.2 (1989): 241–272.

Horowitz, Sara R. "Gender, Genocide, and Jewish Memory." *Prooftexts* 120.1–2 (2000): 158–190.

Horwitz, Gordon J. *In the Shadow of Death: Living Outside the Gates of Mauthausen*. New York, NY: Free Press, 1990.

Hunt Jentsch, Mary. *Trek: An American Woman, Two Small Children, and Survival in World War II Germany*. Foreword and Epilogue by Steve Mumford. New York, NY: McWitty, 2008.

Huyssen, Andreas. *Twilight Memories: Marking Time in a Culture of Amnesia*. New York, NY: Routledge, 1995.

Jackson, Neil and Barbara Saunders. "Christa Wolf's *Kindheitsmuster*: An East German Experiment in Political Autobiography." *German Life and Letters* 33 (1980): 319–329.

Jackson, Sophie. *Hitler's Heroine: Hanna Reitsch*. Stroud: History Press, 2014.

Jacobs, Ingeborg. *Freiwild: Das Schicksal deutscher Frauen 1945*. Berlin: List, 2008.

Jaiser, Constanze. "Die Zeugnisliteratur von Überlebenden der deutschen Konzentrationslager seit 1945." *Shoah in der deutschsprachigen Literatur*. Ed. Norbert Otto Eke and Hartmut Steinecke. Berlin: Erich Schmidt Verlag, 2006. 107–134.

Jalowicz Simon, Marie. *Underground in Berlin: A Young Woman's Extraordinary Tale of Survival in the Heart of Nazi Germany*. Transl. Anthea Bell. Foreword and Afterword by Hermann Simon. New York, NY: Little, Brown and Company, 2014.

Jalowicz Simon, Marie. *Untergetaucht: Eine junge Frau überlebt in Berlin 1940–1945*. Frankfurt am Main: Fischer, 2014.

Jansen, Odile. "Doppelte Erinnerung: Täter- und Opferidentitäten in Christa Wolfs Rekonstruktion des Traumas der Flucht." *German Life and Letters* 57.4 (2004): 440–455.

Janzen, Frauke. "Erinnerungen der Dritten Generation – Vergangenheitsentwürfe in Julia Franck's *Die Mittagsfrau* (2007)." *Revista de Filología Alemana* 20 (2012): 103–117.

Jaspers, Karl. *The Question of German Guilt*. Transl. E. B. Ashton. New York, NY: Fordham University Press, 2000.

Jirgl, Reinhard. *Die Unvollendeten*. Munich: dtv, 2010.

Johnson, Richard L. "Nazi Feminists: A Contradiction in Terms." *Frontiers: A Journal of Women Studies* 1.3 (1976): 55–62.

Jones, David E. *Women Warriors: A History*. Dulles, VA: Potomac Books, 1997.

Jopling, Lucy Wilson. *Warrior in White*. San Antonio, TX: Watercross Press, 1990.

Jütte, Robert, Wolfgang U. Eckart, Hans-Walter Schmuhl, and Winfried Süß. *Medizin und Nationalsozialismus: Bilanz und Perspektiven der Forschung*. Göttingen: Wallstein, 2011.

Kaplan, Marion A. "Jewish Women in Nazi Germany: Daily Life, Daily Struggles, 1933–1939." *Different Voices: Women and the Holocaust*. Ed. Carol Rittner and John K. Roth. St. Paul, MN: Paragon House, 1993. 187–212.

Between Dignity and Despair: Jewish Life in Nazi Germany. New York, NY: Oxford University Press, 1998.

Kaplan, Marion . "Keeping Calm and Weathering the Storm: Jewish Women's Responses to Daily Life in Nazi Germany." *Women in the Holocaust*. Ed. Dalia Ofer and Lenore J. Weitzman. New Haven, CT: Yale University Press, 1998. 39–54.

Kardorff, Ursula von. *Berliner Aufzeichnungen 1942–45*. Ed. Peter Hartl. Munich: dtv, 1997.

Katscher, Liselotte. *Krankenpflege und Drittes Reich: Der Weg der Schwesternschaft des Evangelischen Diakonievereins 1933–1939*. Stuttgart: Verlagswerk der Diakonie, 1990.

Keegan, John. *A History of Warfare*. New York, NY: Vantage, 1994.

Keil, Ernst-Edmund, ed. *Vertrieben .... Literarische Zeugnisse von Flucht und Vertreibung. Eine Auswahl aus Romanen, Erzählungen, Gedichten, Tagebüchern und Zeichnungen der Jahre 1945–1985*. Bonn: Kulturstiftung der deutschen Vertriebenen, 1985.

Kettenacker, Lothar, ed. *Ein Volk von Opfern? Die neue Debatte um den Bombenkrieg 1940–45*. Berlin: Rowohlt, 2003.

Killius, Rosemarie. *Frauen für die Front: Gespräche mit Wehrmachtshelferinnen*. Leipzig: Militzke, 2003.

Kirsten-Herbst, Ruth. *Mädchen an der Front: Eine Flakhelferin erzählt*. Asslar: Schulte + Gerth, 1985.

Klee, Ernst, Willi Dressen, and Volker Riess, eds. *"The Good Old Days": The Holocaust as Seen by Its Perpetrators and Bystanders*. Transl. Deborah Burnstone. Foreword by Hugh Trevor-Roper. Old Saybrook, CT: Konecky & Konecky, 1988.

Klein, Cecilie. *Sentenced to Live: A Survivor's Memoir*. Preface by Samuel Pisar. New York, NY: Holocaust Library. 1988.

Klüger, Ruth. "Dichten über die Shoa: Zum Problem des literarischen Umgangs mit dem Massenmord." *Spuren der Verfolgung: Seelische Auswirkungen des Holocaust auf die Opfer und ihre Kinder*. Ed. Gertrud Hardtmann. Gerlingen: Bleicher, 1982. 203–221.

weiter leben: Eine Jugend. Munich: dtv, 1994.

Still Alive: A Holocaust Girlhood Remembered. New York, NY: Feminist Press, 2001.

Unterwegs verloren: Erinnerungen. Munich: dtv, 2010.

Knabe, Hubertus. *Tag der Befreiung? Das Kriegsende in Ostdeutschland*. Berlin: Ullstein, 2009.

Knef, Hildegard. *Der geschenkte Gaul: Bericht aus einem Leben*. Munich: Ullstein, 2009.

Knopp, Guido. *Die grosse Flucht. Das Schicksal der Vertriebenen*. Munich: Econ Ullstein, 2001.

Koch, Gertrud. "Blut, Sperma, Tränen: BeFreier und Befreite – ein Dokumentarfilm von Helke Sander." *Frauen und Film* 54/55 (1994): 3–14.

Koepcke, Cordula. *Frauen im Wehrdienst: Erinnerungen von Ingeborg Hecht, Ruth Henry, Christa Meves und ein aktueller Diskussionsbeitrag*. Freiburg: Herder, 1982.

Köhler, Astrid. "Große Form – kleine Form: Gegen den Strich der Familiensaga." *Poetiken der Gegenwart: Deutschsprachige Romane nach 2000*. Ed. Silke Horstkotte and Leonhard Herrmann. Berlin: De Gruyter, 2013. 229–243.

Kohlhaas, Elisabeth. "Weibliche Angestellte der Gestapo 1933–1945." *Sie waren dabei: Mitläuferinnen, Nutznießerinnen, Täterinnen im Nationalsozialismus*. Ed. Marita Krauss. Göttingen: Wallstein, 2009. 148–165.

Komann, Margot. "Wie ich Nationalsozialistin wurde: Eine kritisch feministische Lektüre der Theodore Abel-Akten." *Töchterfragen: NS Frauen Geschichte*. Ed. Lerke Gravenhorst and Carmen Tatschmurat. Freiburg: Kore, 1990. 149–166.

Komar, Kathleen L. "The Difficulty of Saying 'I': Reassembling a Self in Christa Wolf's Autobiographical Fiction." *Redefining Autobiography in Twentieth-Century Women's Fiction: An Essay Collection*. Ed. Janice Morgan. New York, NY: Garland, 1991. 261–279.

Kompisch, Kathrin. *Täterinnen: Frauen im Nationalsozialismus*. Cologne: Böhlau, 2008.

Konsalik, Heinz G. *Der Arzt von Stalingrad*. Munich: Wilhelm Heyne, 2003.

Koonz, Claudia. "The Competition for Women's *Lebensraum*, 1928–1934." *When Biology Became Destiny: Women in Weimar and Nazi Germany*. Ed. Renate Bridenthal, Atina Grossmann, and Marion Kaplan. New York, NY: Monthly Review Press, 1984. 199–236.

Mothers in the Fatherland: Women, the Family and Nazi Politics. New York, NY: St. Martin's Press, 1987.

"Consequences: Women, Nazis, and Moral Choice." *Different Voices: Women and the Holocaust*. Ed. Carol Rittner and John K. Roth. St. Paul, MN: Paragon House, 1993. 287–308.

Kopelev, Lev. *To Be Preserved Forever*. Ed. Anthony Austen. Philadelphia, PA: Lippincott, 1977.

Köpnick, Lutz. "Rettung und Destruktion: Erinnerungsverfahren und Geschichtsbewusstsein in Christa Wolfs *Kindheitsmuster* und Walter Benjamins Spätwerk." *Monatshefte* 84.1 (1992): 74–90.

Köpp, Gabi. *Warum war ich bloß ein Mädchen? Das Trauma einer Flucht 1945*. Munich: Herbig, 2010.

Kornreich Gelissen, Rena with Heather Dune Macadam. *Rena's Promise: A Story of Sisters in Auschwitz.* Boston, MA: Beacon Press, 2015.

Kossert, Andreas. *Kalte Heimat: Die Geschichte der deutschen Vertriebenen nach 1945.* Munich: Pantheon, 2008.

Kraft, Helga W. "Searching for a Motherland: Women Breaking Their Generational Chains in Christa Wolf's *Kindheitsmuster, Sommerstück*, and *Medea. Stimmen.*" *Writing against Boundaries: Nationality, Ethnicity and Gender in the German-Speaking Context.* Ed. Barbara Kosta and Helga Kraft. Amsterdam: Rodopi, 2003. 141–165.

Kramer, Edith. "Hell and Rebirth – My Experiences during the Time of Persecution." *Sisters in Sorrow: Voices of Care in the Holocaust.* Ed. Roger A. Ritvo and Diane M. Plotkin. College Station: Texas A&M University Press, 1998. 129–153.

Krauss, Marita. "Grenzenlose Hingabe: Wie eine Rotkreuzschwester dem Führer an der Ostfront diente." www.faz.net/aktuell/feuilleton/politik/grenzenlose-hingabe-1386361.html. October 17, 2006. Last accessed February 3, 2016.

"Rechte Frauen: Mitläuferinnen, Profiteurinnen, Täterinnen in historischer Perspektive." *Sie waren dabei: Mitläuferinnen, Nutznießerinnen, Täterinnen im Nationalsozialismus.* Ed. Marita Krauss. Göttingen: Wallstein, 2009. 7–19.

Kremer, S. Lillian. *Women's Holocaust Writing: Memory and Imagination.* Lincoln, NE: University of Nebraska Press, 1999.

Krieger, Gerd. "Ein Buch im Streit der Meinungen: Untersuchung literaturkritischer Reaktionen zu Christa Wolfs *Kindheitsmuster.*" *Weimarer Beiträge* 31.1 (1985): 56–75.

Kroll, Frank-Lothar, ed. *Flucht und Vertreibung in der Literatur nach 1945.* Berlin: Gebr. Mann, 1997.

Krystal, John H., Stephen M. Southwick, and Dennis S. Charney. "Post Traumatic Stress Disorder: Psychobiological Mechanism of Traumatic Remembrance." *Memory Distortion: How Minds, Brains, and Societies Reconstruct the Past.* Ed. Daniel L. Schacter. Cambridge, MA: Harvard University Press, 1997. 150–172.

Kuby, Erich. *The Russians and Berlin, 1945.* Trans. Arnold J. Pomerans. New York, NY: Hill and Wang, 1968.

Kuhn, Annette. "Der Traum von einer Erinnerungskultur—meine Gedanken zu dem Bericht der Wehrmachtsangehörigen Ilse Schmidt." Introduction to Ilse Schmidt. *Die Mitläuferin: Erinnerungen einer Wehrmachtsangehörigen.* Berlin: Aufbau Verlag, 1999. 7-12.

Kundrus, Birthe. *Kriegerfrauen: Familienpolitik und Geschlechterverhältnisse im Ersten und Zweiten Weltkrieg.* Hamburg: Hans Christians, 1995.

"Nur die halbe Geschichte: Frauen im Vorfeld der Wehrmacht zwischen 1939 und 1945. Ein Forschungsbericht." *Die Wehrmacht: Mythos und Realität.* Eds. Rolf-Dieter Müller and Hans-Erich Volkmann. Munich: Oldenbourg, 1999. 719–735.

Kuretsidis-Haider, Claudia. "Täterinnen vor Gericht: Zur Kategorie Geschlecht bei der Ahndung von national-sozialistischen Tötungsdelikten in Deutschland und Österreich." *Sie waren dabei: Mitläuferinnen, Nutznießerinnen, Täterinnen im Nationalsozialismus.* Ed. Marita Krauss. Göttingen: Wallstein, 2009. 187–210.

Lamse, Mary Jane. "*Kindheitsmuster* in Context: The Achievement of Christa Wolf." *University of Dayton Review* 15.1 (1981): 49–55.

Langer, Lawrence L. *Holocaust Testimonies: The Ruins of Memory.* New Haven, CT: Yale University Press, 1991.

Langerwey, Mary D. "The Nurses Trial at Hadamar and the Ethical Implications of Health Care Values." *Experience and Expression: Women, the Nazis, and the Holocaust.* Ed. Elizabeth R. Baer and Myrna Goldenberg. Detroit, MI: Wayne State University Press, 2003. 111–126.

Lanwerd, Susanne and Irene Stoehr. "Frauen- und Geschlechterforschung zum Nationalsozialismus seit den 1970er Jahren: Forschungsstand, Veränderungen, Perspektiven." *Frauen- und Geschlechtergeschichte des Nationalsozialismus: Fragestellungen, Perspektiven, neue Forschungen.* Ed. Johanna Gehmacher and Gabriella Hauch. Innsbruck: StudienVerlag, 2007. 22–68.

Lapp, Benjamin. "The Holocaust Survivor as Germanist: Marcel Reich-Ranicki and Ruth Klüger." *Rebirth of a Culture: Jewish Identity and Jewish Writing in Germany and Austria Today.* Ed. Hillary Hope Herzog, Todd Herzog, and Benjamin Lapp. New York, NY: Berghahn, 2008. 113–121.

Lasker-Wallfisch, Anita. *Inherit the Truth: A Memoir of Survival and the Holocaust.* New York, NY: St. Martin's Press, 1996.

Lauckner, Nancy A. "The Treatment of Holocaust Themes in GDR Fiction from the Late 1960s to the Mid-1970s: A Survey." *Studies in GDR Culture and Society.* Ed. Margy Gerber. Washington, DC: University Press of America, 1981. 141–154.

Lauer, Betty. *Hiding in Plain Sight: The Incredible True Story of a German-Jewish Teenager's Struggle to Survive in Nazi-Occupied Poland.* Hanover, NH: Smith and Kraus Global, 2004.

Lawson, Ursula D. "Founders and Inheritors in the Short Story of the GDR." *Selected Proceedings of the Pennsylvania Foreign Language Conference.* Ed. Gregorio Martin. Pittsburgh, PA: Duquesne University Press, 1988. 111–116.

Lechner, Silvester and Alfred Moos. "Ulm – Theresienstadt – Ulm: Einleitung." *Als Krankenschwester im KZ Theresienstadt: Erinnerungen einer Ulmer Jüdin.* Ed. Silvester Lechner and Alfred Moos. Stuttgart: Silberburg, 1988. 7–13.

Leck, Ralph. "Conservative Empowerment and the Gender of Nazism: Paradigms of Power and Complicity in German Women's History." *Journal of Women's History* 12.2 (2000): 147–169.

Lehker, Marianne. *Frauen im Nationalsozialismus. Wie aus Opfern Handlanger der Täter wurden – eine nötige Trauerarbeit.* Frankfurt am Main: Materialis, 1983.

Lehndorff, Hans Graf von. *Ostpreußisches Tagebuch: Aufzeichnungen eines Arztes aus den Jahren 1945–47.* Munich: dtv, 2010.

Lengyel, Olga. *Five Chimneys: A Woman Survivor's True Story of Auschwitz.* Chicago, IL: Academy Chicago Publishers, 1947.

Lepora, Chiara and Robert E. Goodin. *On Complicity and Compromise.* Oxford: Oxford University Press, 2013.

Levine, Michael G. "Writing Anxiety: Christa Wolf's *Kindheitsmuster.*" *Diacritics* 27.2 (1997): 106–123.

Levine, Michael G. *The Belated Witness: Literature, Testimony, and the Question of Holocaust Survival.* Stanford, CA: Stanford University Press, 2006.

Leys, Ruth. *From Guilt to Shame: Auschwitz and After.* Princeton, NJ: Princeton University Press, 2007.

Lezzi, Eva. "Ruth Klüger: Literarische Authentizität durch Reflexion: weiter leben – still alive." *Shoah in der deutschsprachigen Literatur.* Ed. Norbert Otto Eke and Hartmut Steinecke. Berlin: Erich Schmidt Verlag, 2006. 286–292.

Liebrand, Claudia. "'Das Trauma der Auschwitzer Wochen in ein Versmaß stülpen' oder: Gedichte als Exorzismus. Ruth Klügers *weiter leben.*" *Jüdische Intellektuelle im 20. Jahrhundert: Literatur- und kulturgeschichtliche Studien.* Eds. Ariane Huml and Monika Rappenecker. Würzburg: Königshausen & Neumann, 2003. 237–248.

Lifton, Robert Jay. *The Nazi Doctors: Medical Killing and the Psychology of Genocide.* New York, NY: BasicBooks, 1986.

Lilly, J. Robert. *Taken by Force: Rape and American GIs in Europe during World War II.* New York, NY: Palgrave Macmillan, 2007.

Linden, R. Ruth. *Making Stories, Making Selves: Feminist Reflections on the Holocaust.* Columbus, OH: Ohio State University Press, 1993.

Lingens Reiner, Ella. *Prisoners of Fear.* London: Victor Gollancz, 1948.

Linn, Marie-Luise. "Doppelte Kindheit: Zur Interpretation von Christa Wolfs *Kindheitsmuster.*'" *Deutschunterricht* 30.2 (1978): 52–66.

Lipinski, Katja. *Frauen an die Front! Von 1939 bis Kriegsende 1945.* Zweibrücken: VDM Heinz Nickel, 1998.

Livi, Massimiliano. *Gertrud Scholtz-Klink: Die Reichsfrauenführerin: Politische Handlungsräume und Identitätsprobleme der Frauen im Nationalsozialismus am Beispiel der Führerin aller deutschen Frauen.* Münster: Lit Verlag, 2005.

Loeper, Heidrun. *Engpass zur Freiheit: Aufzeichnungen der Frau Hilde Huppert über ihre Erlebnisse im Nazi-Todesland und ihre wundersame Errettung aus Bergen-Belsen.* Manuskriptbearbeitung von Arnold Zweig. Osnabrück: Kontextverlag, 1990.

Longenbach, James. "The Women and Men of 1914." *Arms and the Woman: War, Gender, and Literary Representation.* Ed. Helen M. Cooper, Adrienne Auslander Munich, Susan Merrill Squier. Chapel Hill, NC: University of North Carolina Press, 1989. 97–123.

Lorenz, Dagmar C.G. "Memory and Criticism: Ruth Klüger's *weiter leben.*" *Women in German Yearbook* 9 (1993): 207–224.

Lorenz, Dagmar C. G. "The Interchange between Experience and Literature: German-Jewish Women Writers of the Holocaust." *Facing Fascism and*

Confronting the Past: German Women Writers from Weimar to the Present. Ed. Elke P. Frederiksen and Martha Kaarsberg Wallach. Albany, NY: State University of New York Press, 2000. 171–185.

Lower, Wendy. *Hitler's Furies: German Women in the Nazi Killing Fields.* New York, NY: Houghton Mifflin Harcourt, 2013.

Lubich, Frederick Alfred. "Surviving to Excel: The Last German Jewish Autobiographies of Holocaust Survivors Ruth Klüger, Marcel Reich-Ranicki, and Paul Spiegel." *Modern Judaism* 25.2 (2005): 189–210.

Lühe, Irmela von der. "Das Gefängnis der Erinnerung: Erzählstrategien gegen den Konsum des Schreckens in Ruth Klügers *weiter leben.*" *Bilder des Holocaust: Literatur – Film – Bildende Kunst.* Ed. Manuel Köppen and Klaus R. Scherpe. Cologne: Böhlau, 1997. 29–45.

Luhmann, Susanne. "Gender and the Generations of Difficult Knowledge: Recent Responses to Familial Legacies of Nazi Perpetration." *Women in German Yearbook* 25 (2009): 174–198.

Mahlendorf, Ursula. "Der weisse Rabe fliegt: Zum Künstlerinnenroman im 20. Jahrhundert." *Deutsche Literatur von Frauen.* Vol. 2. Ed. Gisela Brinker-Gabler. Munich: C. H. Beck, 1988. 445–459.

Mahr, Cordula. *Kriegsliteratur von Frauen? Zur Darstellung des Zweiten Weltkriegs in Autobiographien von Frauen nach 1960.* Herbolzheim: Centaurus Verlag, 2006.

Malempré, Sigrid. *Flintenweib: Ostpreußen 1945 – verlorene Kindheit, verlorene Heimat.* Gelnhausen:Wagner, 2010.

Mardorossian, Carine M. "Toward a New Feminist Theory of Rape." *Signs* 27.3 (2002): 743–775.

Marfleet, Philip. *Refugees in a Global Era.* New York, NY: Palgrave Macmillan, 2006.

Marks, Elise. "The Alienation of I: Christa Wolf and Militarism." *Mosaic* 23.3 (1990): 73–85.

Martin, Elaine. "Victims or Perpetrators: Literary Responses to Women's Roles in National Socialism." *Facing Fascism and Confronting the Past: German Women Writers from Weimar to the Present.* Ed. Elke P. Frederiksen and Martha Kaarsberg-Wallach. Albany, NY: State University of New York Press, 2000. 61–82.

Mattson, Michelle. "Mother's Care? Models of Motherhood and Their Ethical Implications in Post-WWII German Literature." *National Women's Studies Association Journal* 21.1 (2009): 101–130.

Maubach, Franka. "Expansion weiblicher Hilfe: Zur Erfahrungsgeschichte von Frauen im Kriegsdienst." *Volksgenossinnen: Frauen in der NS-Volksgemeinschaft.* Ed. Sybille Steinbacher. Göttingen: Wallstein, 2007. 93–111.

Die Stellung halten: Kriegserfahrungen und Lebensgeschichten von Wehrmachthelferinnen. Göttingen: Vandenhoeck & Ruprecht, 2009.

"Love, Comradeship, and Power – German Auxiliaries and Gender Relations in the Occupied Territories." *Women and Men at War: A Gender Perspective on*

World War II and Its Aftermath in Central and Eastern Europe. Eds. Maren Röger and Ruth Leiserowitz. Osnabrück: fibre Verlag, 2017. 157–177.

McClelland, James L. "Constructive Memory and Memory Distortions: A Parallel-Distributed Processing Approach." *Memory Distortion: How Minds, Brains, and Societies Reconstruct the Past.* Ed. Daniel L. Schacter. Cambridge, MA: Harvard University Press, 1997. 69–90.

McCormick, Richard. "Rape and War, Gender and Nation, Victims and Victimizers: Helke Sander's *BeFreier und Befreite.*" *Camera Obscura* 16.1 (2001): 99–141.

McFarland-Icke, Bronwyn Rebekah. *Nurses in Nazi Germany: Moral Choices in History.* Princeton, NJ: Princeton University Press, 1999.

McGlothlin, Erin E. "Autobiographical Revision: Ruth Klüger's *weiter leben* and *Still Alive.*" *Gegenwartsliteratur: Ein germanistisches Jahrbuch* 3 (2004): 46–70.

Meiners, Antonia. *Die Stunde der Frauen zwischen Monarchie, Weltkrieg und Wahlrecht 1913–1919.* Munich: Elisabeth Sandmann, 2013.

Meinhof, Renate. *Das Tagebuch der Maria Meinhof: April 1945 bis März 1946 in Pommern. Eine Spurensuche.* Reinbek bei Hamburg: Rowohlt, 2006.

Melzer, Bernd. "Zu Christa Wolfs Prosaarbeiten der siebziger Jahre." *Wissenschaftliche Zeitschrift der Wilhelm-Pieck Universität Rostock* 31.8 (1982): 9–22.

Merkel, Ulrich. "Selbstreferenz und Selbsterschaffung aus dem Möglichkeitssinn: Beobachtungen zu Struktur und Sprache des Romans der Neuzeit (Moderne, Postmoderne) am Beispiel von Grimmelshausens *Simplicissimus,* Christa Wolfs *Kindheitsmuster,* Wolfgang Hilbigs *Ich.*" *Weimarer Beiträge: Zeitschrift für Literaturwissenschaft, Ästhetik und Kulturwissenschaften* 49.1 (2003): 80–95.

Merley Hill, Alexandra. "Homesick: Longing for Domestic Spaces in the Works of Julia Franck." *German Women Writers and the Spatial Turn: New Perspectives.* Ed. Carola Daffner and Beth A. Muellner. Berlin: De Gruyter, 2015. 133–147.

Merridale, Catherine. *Ivan's War: Life and Death in the Red Army, 1939–1945.* New York, NY: Picador, 2006.

Messerschmidt, James W. "The Forgotten Victims of World War II: Masculinities and Rape in Berlin, 1945." *Violence against Women* 12.7 (2006): 706–712.

Meyer, Beate. "Anpassung, Selbstbehauptung und Verdrängung: Zum Berufsalltag zweier Mitläuferinnen im Nationalsozialismus." *Zwischen Karriere und Verfolgung: Handlungsräume von Frauen im nationalsozialistischen Deutschland.* Ed. Kirsten Heinsohn, Barbara Vogel, and Ulrike Weckel. Frankfurt am Main: Campus, 1997. 166–188.

Meyer, Birgit. "Brief an Lerke Gravenhorst." *Töchterfragen: NS Frauen Geschichte.* Ed. Lerke Gravenhorst and Carmen Tatschmurat. Freiburg: Kore, 1990. 135–140.

Meyer, Franziska. "Sommerhaus, früher: Jenny Erpenbecks *Heimsuchung* als Korrektur von Familienerinnerungen." *Gegenwartsliteratur: Ein germanistisches Jahrbuch* 11 (2012): 324–343.

Miller, Nancy K. "The Entangled Self: Genre Bondage in the Age of the Memoir." *PMLA* 122.2 (2007): 537–547.

Miller, Sarah Lew and Joyce B. Lazarus. *Hiding in Plain Sight: Eluding the Nazis in Occupied France.* Chicago, IL: Academy Chicago Publishers, 2012.

Milton, Sybil. "Women and the Holocaust: The Case of German and German-Jewish Women." *When Biology Became Destiny: Women in Weimar and Nazi Germany.* Ed. Renate Bridenthal, Atina Grossmann, and Marion Kaplan. New York, NY: Monthly Review Press, 1984.

Minden, Michael. "Social Hope and the Nightmare of History: Christa Wolf's *Kindheitsmuster* and *Stadt der Engel.*" *Publications of the English Goethe Society* 80.2–3 (2011): 196–203.

Misztal, Barbara A. *Theories of Social Remembering.* Maidenhead: Open University Press, 2003.

Mitscherlich, Margarete. "Die Frage der Selbstdarstellung: Überlegungen zu den Autobiographien von Helene Deutsch, Margaret Mead und Christa Wolf." *Neue Rundschau* 91.2–3 (1980): 291–316.

Moeller, Robert G. *War Stories: The Search for a Usable Past in the Federal Republic of Germany.* Berkeley, CA: University of California Press, 2001.

"What Did You Do in the War, *Mutti*? Courageous Women, Compassionate Commanders, and Stories of the Second World War." *German History* 22.4 (2004): 563–594.

"The Politics of the Past in the 1950s: Rhetorics of Victimisation in East and West Germany." *Germans as Victims: Remembering the Past in Contemporary Germany.* Ed. Bill Niven. New York, NY: Palgrave Macmillan, 2006. 26–42.

Monahan, Evelyn M. and Rosemary Neidel-Greenlee. *And If I Perish: Frontline U.S. Army Nurses in World War II.* New York, NY: Alfred A. Knopf, 2003.

Moos, Alfred. "Vorwort." *Als Krankenschwester im KZ Theresienstadt: Erinnerungen einer Ulmer Jüdin.* Ed. Silvester Lechner and Alfred Moos. Stuttgart: Silberburg, 1988. 5–6.

Morgenstern, Erika. *Überleben war schwerer als Sterben. Ostpreussen 1944–48.* Munich: Herbig, 2004.

Morris, Madeline. "By Force of Arms: Rape, War and Military Culture." *Duke Law Journal* 45.4 (1996): 651–781.

Morrison, Jack G. *Ravensbrück: Everyday Life in a Women's Concentration Camp 1939–45.* Princeton, NJ: Markus Wiener Publishers, 2000.

Mosse, George L. *Toward the Final Solution: A History of European Racism.* New York, NY: Howard Fertig, 1985.

Mühlhäuser, Regina. *Eroberungen: Sexuelle Gewalttaten und intime Beziehungen deutscher Soldaten in der Sowjetunion 1941–1945.* Hamburg: Hamburger Edition, 2001.

Mühlhäuser, Regina. "Vergewaltigungen in Deutschland 1945: Nationaler Opferdiskurs und individuelles Erinnern." *Nachkrieg in Deutschland.* Ed. Klaus Naumann. Hamburg: Hamburger Edition, 2001. 384–408.

Müller, Heidelinde. *Das literarische Fräuleinwunder: Inspektion eines Phänomens der deutschen Gegenwartsliteratur in Einzelfallstudien*. Frankfurt am Main: Lang, 2004.

Muller Bruml, Hana. "I Was a Nurse in Theresienstadt." *Sisters in Sorrow: Voices of Care in the Holocaust*. Ed. Roger A. Ritvo and Diane M. Plotkin. College Station, TX: Texas A&M University Press, 1998. 23–49.

Münch, Ingo von. *Frau komm! Die Massenvergewaltigungen deutscher Frauen und Mädchen 1944–45*. Graz: Ares, 2009.

Naimark, Norman M. *The Russians in Germany: A History of the Soviet Zone of Occupation 1945–49*. Cambridge, MA: Harvard University Press, 1995.

  Fires of Hatred: Ethnic Cleansing in Twentieth-Century Europe. Cambridge, MA: Harvard University Press, 2001.

Naor, Simha. *Krankengymnastin in Auschwitz: Aufzeichnungen des Häftlings Nr. 80574*. Freiburg im Breisgau: Herder, 1986.

Nawratil, Heinz. *Schwarzbuch der Vertreibung 1945 bis 1948: Das letzte Kapitel unbewältigter Vergangenheit*. Munich: Universitas, 1982.

Neary, Brigitte, ed. *Frauen und Vertreibung: Zeitzeuginnen berichten*. Graz: Ares, 2008.

Neary, Brigitte U. and Holle Schneider-Ricks. *Voices of Loss and Courage: German Women Recount Their Expulsion from East Central Europe, 1944–1950*. Rockport, NY: Picton Press, 2002.

Niethammer, Lutz. *Deutschland danach: Postfaschistische Gesellschaft und nationales Gedächtnis*. Bonn: Dietz, 1999.

Nightingale, Florence. *Notes on Nursing: What It Is, and What It Is Not*. Digireads. com Publishing, 2010.

Niven, Bill, ed. *Germans as Victims: Remembering the Past in Contemporary Germany*. New York, NY: Palgrave Macmillan, 2006.

Niven, Bill. "Introduction: German Victimhood at the Turn of the Millenium." *Germans as Victims: Remembering the Past in Contemporary Germany*. Ed. Bill Niven. New York, NY: Palgrave Macmillan, 2006. 1–25.

Nobile, Nancy. "'Ihr Erbteil': The Legacy of Romanticism in Jenny Erpenbeck's *Heimsuchung*." *Gegenwartsliteratur: Ein germanistisches Jahrbuch* 14 (2015): 61–83.

Ochsenknecht, Ingeborg. *Als ob der Schnee alles zudeckte: Eine Krankenschwester erinnert sich an ihren Kriegseinsatz an der Ostfront*. Recorded by Fabienne Pakleppa. Berlin: Ullstein, 2004.

Ofer, Dalia and Lenore J. Weitzman. "Introduction: The Role of Gender in the Holocaust." *Women in the Holocaust*. Eds. Dalia Ofer and Lenore J. Weitzman. New Haven, CT: Yale University Press, 1998. 1–18.

Ohrgaard, Per. "Ein Foto mit Hut – Bemerkungen zu Christa Wolf: *Kindheitsmuster*." *Orbis Litterarum* 42.3–4 (1987): 375–387.

Oliver, Kelly. *Women as Weapons of War: Iraq, Sex, and the Media*. New York, NY: Columbia University Press, 2007.

Panke-Kochinke, Birgit and Monika Schaidhammer-Placke. *Frontschwestern und Friedensengel: Kriegskrankenpflege im Ersten und Zweiten Weltkrieg. Ein Quellen- und Fotoband.* Frankfurt am Main: Mabuse, 2002.

Panzer, Anneliese. *Ich war fünf und hatte das Leben noch vor mir: Erinnerungen an eine Flucht.* Munich: Brendow, 1999.

Paul, Christa. *Zwangsprostitution: Staatlich errichtete Bordelle im Nationalsozialismus.* Berlin: Hentrich, 1994.

Peitsch, Helmut. *Deutschlands Gedächtnis an seine dunkelste Zeit: zur Funktion der Autobiographik in den Westzonen Deutschlands und den Westsektoren von Berlin 1945 bis 1949.* Berlin: Sigma Bohn, 1990.

Peitsch, Helmut. *Nachkriegsliteratur 1945–1989.* Göttingen: V&R unipress, 2009.

Penkert, Brigitte. *Briefe einer Rotkreuzschwester von der Ostfront.* Ed. Jens Ebert and Sibylle Penkert. Göttingen: Wallstein, 2006.

Pennington, Reina. "'Do Not Speak of the Services You Rendered': Women Veterans of Aviation in the Soviet Union." *A Soldier and a Woman: Sexual Integration in the Military.* Ed. Gerard J. DeGroot and Corinna Peniston-Bird. London: Pearson Education Limited, 2000. 152–171.

Petö, Andrea. "Stimmen des Schweigens: Erinnerungen an Vergewaltigungen in den Hauptstädten des 'ersten Opfers' (Wien) und des 'letzten Verbündeten' Hitlers (Budapest) 1945." *Zeitschrift für Geschichtswissenschaft* 47 (1999): 892–913.

Pflugk-Harttung, Elfriede von, ed. *Frontschwestern: Ein deutsches Ehrenbuch.* Berlin: Bernard & Graefe, 1936.

Pickerodt, Gerhart. "Christa Wolfs Roman *Kindheitsmuster*: Ein Beitrag zur Vergangenheitsbewältigung." *Exile: Wirkung und Wertung. Ausgewählte Beiträge zum fünften Symposium über deutsche und österreichische Exilliteratur.* Ed. Donald G. Daviau and Ludwig M. Fischer. Columbia, SC: Camden House, 1985. 293–307.

Pinkert, Anke. "Pleasures of Fear: Antifascist Myth, Holocaust, and Soft Dissidence in Christa Wolf's *Kindheitsmuster*." *German Quarterly* 76.1 (2003): 25–37.

Piszkiewicz, Dennis. *From Nazi Test Pilot to Hitler's Bunker: The Fantastic Flights of Hanna Reitsch.* Westport, CT: Prager, 1997.

Plavius, Heinz. "Gewissensforschung: Christa Wolf: *Kindheitsmuster*, Aufbau Verlag und Weimar." *Neue Deutsche Literatur* 25.1 (1977): 139–151.

Poutrus, Kirsten. "Ein fixiertes Trauma: Massenvergewaltigungen bei Kriegsende in Berlin." *Feministische Studien* 13.2 (1995): 120–129.

Prager, Brad. "Occupation as the Face of War: Concealing Violence in the Diary *A Woman in Berlin*." *Fighting Words and Images: Representing War across the Disciplines.* Ed. Elena V. Baraban, Stephan Jaeger, and Adam Muller. Toronto:University of Toronto Press, 2012.

Prager, Jeffrey. *Presenting the Past: Psychoanalysis and the Sociology of Misremembering.* Cambridge, MA: Harvard University Press, 1998.

Price, Lisa. "Finding the Man in the Soldier-Rapist: Some Reflections on Comprehension and Accountability." *Women's Studies International Forum* 24.2 (2001): 211–227.

Probert-Wright, Bärbel. *An der Hand meiner Schwester: Zwei Mädchen im kriegszerstörten Deutschland.* Munich: Knaur, 2008.

Probst, Inga. "Auf märkischen Sand gebaut: Jenny Erpenbecks *Heimsuchung* zwischen verorteter und verkörperter Erinnerung." *Geschlechtergedächtnisse: Gender Konstellationen und Erinnerungsmuster in Literatur und Film der Gegenwart.* Ed. Ilse Nagelschmidt, Inga Probst, and Torsten Erdbrügger. Berlin: Frank & Timme, 2010. 67–88.

Proctor, Robert N. *Racial Hygiene: Medicine under the Nazis.* Cambridge, MA: Harvard University Press, 1988.

Pye, Gillian. "Jenny Erpenbeck and the Life of Things." *Transitions: Emerging Women Writers in German-Language Literature.* Ed. Valerie Heffernan and Gillian Pye. New York, NY: Ropopi, 2013.

Quack, Sibylle. "Jüdische Frauen in den dreißiger Jahren." *Zwischen Karriere und Verfolgung: Handlungsräume von Frauen im nationalsozialistischen Deutschland.* Ed. Kirsten Heinsohn, Barbara Vogel, and Ulrike Weckel. New York, NY: Campus Verlag, 1997. 111–128.

Raphael, Jody. "Silencing Reports of Sexual Assault: The Controversy over a Woman in Berlin." *Violence against Women* 12 (2006): 693–699.

Reese, Dagmar. *Growing Up Female in Nazi Germany.* Transl. William Templer. Ann Arbor, MI: University of Michigan Press, 2009.

Reese, Dagmar and Carola Sachse. "Frauenforschung und Nationalsozialismus: Eine Bilanz." *TöchterFragen, NS-Frauen Geschichte.* Ed. Lerke Gravenhorst and Carmen Tatschmurat. Freiburg i.Br.: Kore, 1990. 73–106.

Reeves Sanday, Peggy. "Rape and the Silencing of the Feminine." *Rape: An Historical and Social Enquiry.* Ed. Sylvana Tomaselli and Roy Porter. New York, NY: Basil Blackwell, 1986. 84–101.

Reiter, Andrea. "'Ich wollte, es wäre ein Roman.' Ruth Klüger's Feminist Survival Report." *Forum for Modern Language Studies* 38.3 (2002): 326–340.

Reiter, Margit. *Die Generation danach: Der Nationalsozialismus im Familiengedächtnis.* Innsbruck: Studienverlag, 2006.

Reitsch, Hanna. *Das Unzerstörbare in meinem Leben.* Stegen am Ammersee: Druffel & Vowinckel, 2008.

Reitsch, Hanna. *Fliegen, Mein Leben.* Dresden: Winkelried, 2009.

Reski, Petra. *Ein Land so weit.* Berlin: List, 2008.

Richter, Isabel. "Das Andere hat kein Geschlecht: Politische Gerichtsprozesse in der Weimarer Republik und im Nationalsozialismus." *Bestien und Befehlsempfänger: Frauen und Männer in NS-Prozessen nach 1945.* Ed. Ulrike Weckel and Edgar Wolfrum. Göttingen: Vandenhoeck & Ruprecht, 2003. 175–193.

Rietsch, Jörg. "Versuch über einen Versuch: Gedanken über den Blick auf Geschichte in Christa Wolfs Roman *Kindheitsmuster.*" *Weimarer Beiträge* 38.1 (1992): 68–84.

Ringelheim, Joan. "Women and the Holocaust: A Reconsideration of Research." *Different Voices: Women and the Holocaust.* Ed. Carol Rittner and John K. Roth. St. Paul, MN: Paragon House, 1993. 373–405.

"The Split between Gender and the Holocaust." *Women in the Holocaust.* Ed. Dalia Ofer and Lenore J. Weitzman. New Haven, CT: Yale University Press, 1998. 340–350.

Rippl, Gabriele, Philip Schweighauser, and Therese Steffen. "Introduction: Life Writing in an Age of Trauma." *Haunted Narratives: Life Writing in an Age of Trauma.* Ed. Gabriele Rippl, Philip Schweighauser, and Therese Steffen. Toronto: University of Toronto Press, 2013. 3–18.

Rittner, Carol and John K. Roth. "Prologue: Women and the Holocaust." *Different Voices: Women and the Holocaust.* Ed. Carol Rittner and John K. Roth. St. Paul, MN: Paragon House, 1993. 1–19.

Ritvo, Roger A. and Diane M. Plotkin. *Sisters in Sorrow: Voices of Care in the Holocaust.* Foreword by Harry James Cargas. College Station, TX: Texas A&M University Press, 1998.

Roberts, Louis. "Novel Form in Apuleius and Christa Wolf." *Classical and Modern Literature* 3.3 (1983): 125–138.

Roberts, Mary Louise. *What Soldiers Do: Sex and the American GI in World War II France.* Chicago, IL: University of Chicago Press, 2013.

Röger, Maren. "Sexual Contact between German Occupiers and Polish Occupied in World War II Poland." *Women and Men at War: A Gender Perspective on World War II and Its Aftermath in Central and Eastern Europe.* Ed. Maren Röger and Ruth Leiserowitz. Osnabrück: fibre Verlag, 2017. 135–155.

Rogoff, Irit. "Von Ruinen zu Trümmern: Die Feminisierung des Faschismus in deutschen historischen Museen." *Denkräume zwischen Kunst und Wissenschaft.* Ed. Silvia Baumgart, Gotlind Birkle, Mechthild Fend, Bettina Götz, Andrea Klier, and Bettina Uppenkamp. Berlin: Dietrich Reimer, 1993. 259–285.

Römer, Felix. *Kameraden: Die Wehrmacht von innen.* Munich: Piper, 2012.

Rosenthal, Gabriele, ed. *Der Holocaust im Leben von drei Generationen: Familien von Überlebenden der Shoah und von Nazi-Tätern.* Gießen: Psychosozial-Verlag, 1999.

Rosenthal, Hans. *Zwei Leben in Deutschland.* Bergisch-Gladbach: Bastei-Lübbe, 1980.

Roshnowski, Stanislaw W. "Der Roman als Form des historischen Bewusstseins: *Kindheitsmuster* von Christa Wolf und *Der Aufenthalt* von Hermann Kant." *Literatur im Wandel: Entwicklungen in europäischen sozialistischen Ländern 1944/45–1980.* Ed. Ludwig Richter, Heinrich Olschowsky, Juri W. Bogdanow and Swetlana A. Scherlaimowa. Berlin: Aufbau Verlag, 1986. 430–447.

Roth, John R. "Equality, Neutrality, Particularity: Perspectives on Women and the Holocaust." *Experience and Expression: Women, the Nazis, and the Holocaust.* Ed. Elizabeth R. Baer and Myrna Goldenberg. Detroit, MI: Wayne State University Press, 2003. 5–22.

Rothberg, Michael. *Traumatic Realism: The Demands of Holocaust Representation.* Minneapolis, MN: University of Minnesota Press, 2000.

Rothe, Anne. *Popular Trauma Culture: Selling the Pain of Others in the Mass Media.* New Brunswick, NJ: Rutgers University Press, 2011.

Ruddick, Sara. *Maternal Thinking: Toward a Politics of Peace.* Boston, MA: Beacon Press, 2002.

Rüdiger, Jutta. *Ein Leben für die Jugend: Mädelführerin im Dritten Reich.* Oldendorf: Deutsche Verlagsgesellschaft, 1999.

Rüdiger, Jutta, ed. *Zur Problematik von Soldatinnen: Der Kampfeinsatz von Flakwaffenhelferinnen im 2. Weltkrieg. Berichte und Dokumentationen.* Lindhorst: Askania, 1987.

Ruediger, Wilma. *Frauen im Dienst der Menschlichkeit: Erlebtes im DRK von 1914–Friedland.* Munich: J.F. Lehmanns, 1962.

Rueß, Susanne and Astrid Stölzle, eds. *Das Tagebuch der jüdischen Kriegskrankenschwester Rosa Bendit, 1914 bis 1917.* Stuttgart: Franz Steiner, 2012.

Rupp, Leila J. *Mobilizing Women for War: German and American Propaganda 1939–1945.* Princeton, NJ: Princeton University Press, 1978.

Sakova, Aija. "Fighting Fear with Writing: Christa Wolf's *Kindheitsmuster* and Ene Mihkelson's *Ahasveeruse uni (The Sleep of Ahasuerus)*." *Haunted Narratives: Life Writing in an Age of Trauma.* Ed. Gabriele Rippl, Philip Schweighauser, and Therese Steffen. Toronto: University of Toronto Press, 2013. 211–224.

Salier, Eva. *Survival of a Spirit.* New York, NY: Shengold Publishers, Inc., 1995.

Salus, Grete. *Ein Engel war nicht dort: Ein Leben wider den Schatten von Auschwitz.* Leipzig: Forum Verlag, 2005.

Sander, Helke. "Zuwort zum Vorwort." Introduction to Helke Sander and Barbara Johr, eds. *BeFreier und Befreite: Krieg, Vergewaltigung, Kinder.* Frankfurt am Main: Fischer, 2008. 3–8.

Sander, Helke and Barbara Johr. "Frauen erzählen." *BeFreier und Befreite: Krieg, Vergewaltigung, Kinder.* Ed. Helke Sander and Barbara Johr. Frankfurt am Main: Fischer, 2008. 83–95.

Sander, Helke and Barbara Johr, ed. *BeFreier und Befreite: Krieg, Vergewaltigung, Kinder.* Frankfurt am Main: Fischer, 2008.

Sarti, Wendy Adele-Marie. *Women + Nazis: Perpetrators of Genocide and Other Crimes during Hitler's Regime, 1933–1945.* Palo Alto, CA: Academica Press, 2012.

Sayner. Joanne. *Women without a Past? German Autobiographical Writings and Fascism.* Amsterdam: Rodopi, 2007.

Schaal, Björn. *Jenseits von Oder und Lethe: Flucht, Vertreibung und Heimatverlust in Erzähltexten nach 1945.* Trier: Wissenschaftlicher Verlag, 2006.

Schacter, Daniel L. "Memory Distortion: History and Current Status." *Memory Distortion: How Minds, Brains, and Societies Reconstruct the Past.* Ed. Daniel L. Schacter. Cambridge, MA: Harvard University Press, 1997. 1–43.

Schacter, Daniel L., ed. *Memory Distortion: How Minds, Brains, and Societies Reconstruct the Past.* Cambridge, MA: Harvard University Press, 1995.

Schaumann, Caroline. "From *weiter leben* (1992) to *Still Alive* (2001): Ruth Klüger's Cultural Translation of Her 'German Book' for an American Audience." *The German Quarterly* 77.3 (2004): 324–339.

Schaumann, Caroline. *Memory Matters: Generational Responses to Germany's Nazi Past in Recent Women's Literature.* Berlin: Walter de Gruyter, 2008.

Schenck, E. G. *Vom Massenelend der Frauen Europas in den Wirrnissen des XX. Jahrhunderts.* Bonn-Bad Godesberg: Verlag der Heimkehrer, 1988.

Scherstjanoi, Elke. "Ein Rotarmist in Deutschland." *Wladimir Gelfand. Deutschland Tagebuch 1945–46.* Ed. Elke Scherstjanoi. Berlin: Aufbau, 2008. 315–339.

Schlink, Bernhard. *Guilt about the Past.* Toronto: Anansi Press, 2010.

Schlögel, Karl. "Bugwelle des Krieges." *Die Flucht: Über die Vertreibung der Deutschen aus dem Osten.* Ed. Stefan Aust, and Stephan Burgdorf. Munich: Deutsche Verlags-Anstalt, 2002. 179–196.

Schmatzler, Uta Cornelia. *Verstrickung, Mitverantwortung und Täterschaft im Nationalsozialismus: Eine Untersuchung zum Verhältnis von weiblichem Alltag und Faschismus.* Kiel: L & F Verlag, 1994.

Schmidt, Ilse. *Die Mitläuferin: Erinnerungen einer Wehrmachtsangehörigen.* Berlin: Aufbau, 1999.

Schmidt-Harzbach, Ingrid. "Eine Woche im April, Berlin 1945: Vergewaltigung als Massenschicksal." *Feministische Studien* 3.2 (1984): 51–65.

Schmitz, Helmut. "Family, Heritage, and German Wartime Suffering in Hanns-Josef Ortheil, Stephan Wackwitz, Thomas Medicus, Dagmar Leupold, and Uwe Timm." *Germans as Victims in the Literary Fiction of the Berlin Republic.* Ed. Stuart Taberner and Karina Berger. Rochester: Camden House, 2009. 70–85.

Schmitz, Helmut and Annette Seidel-Arpaci. "Introduction." *Narratives of Trauma: Discourses of German Wartime Suffering in National and International Perspective.* Ed. Helmut Schmitz and Annette Seidel-Arpaci. Amsterdam: Rodopi, 2011. 1–16.

Schneider, Helmut J. "Reflexion oder Evokation: Erinnerungskonstruktion in Ruth Klügers *weiter leben* und Martin Walsers *Der springende Brunnen*." *Zeitschrift für deutsche Philologie* 125 (2006): 160–175.

Schoenfeld, Gabriel. "Auschwitz and the Professors." *Commentary* 105.6 (1998): 42–46.

Scholtz-Klink, Gertrud. *Verpflichtung und Aufgabe der Frau im nationalsozialistischen Staat.* Berlin: Junker und Dünnhaupt, 1937.

Schopmann, Claudia. "Flucht in den Untergrund: zur Situation der jüdischen Bevölkerung in Deutschland 1941–45." *Nationalsozialismus und Geschlecht: Zur Politisierung und Ästhetisierung von Körper, "Rasse" und Sexualität im "Dritten Reich" und nach 1945.* Eds. Elke Frietsch and Christina Herkommer. Bielefeld: transcript, 2009. 285–296.

Schorer, Avis D. *A Half Acre of Hell: A Combat Nurse in WWII.* Lakeville: Galde Press, 2000.

Schubert, Helga. *Judasfrauen.* Munich: dtv, 1995.

Schubert, Katja. "Kein Zivilisationsbruch: Wahrscheinliche Geschichte: *Heimsuchung* (2007) und *Aller Tage Abend* (2012) von Jenny Erpenbeck." *Störfall? Auschwitz und die ostdeutsche Literatur nach 1989*. Ed. Carola Hähnel-Mesnard and Katja Schubert. Berlin: Frank & Timme, 2016. 91–108.

Schubert Lehnhardt, Viola. *Frauen als Täterinnen und Mittäterinnen im Nationalsozialismus: Gestaltungsspielräume und Handlungsmöglichkeiten.* Halle-Wittenberg: Druckerei der Martin-Luther Universität, 2006.

Schuchmann, Kathrin. "Die Zeit scheint ihr zur Verfügung zu stehen wie ein Haus: Heimat und Erinnerung in Jenny Erpenbecks *Heimsuchung.*" *Zagreber Germanistische Beiträge* 22 (2013): 53–69.

Schüddekopf, Charles, ed. *Der alltägliche Faschismus: Frauen im Dritten Reich.* Bonn: J. H. W. Dietz, 1981.

Schulte-Sasse, Linda. "Living On in the American Press: Ruth Klüger's *Still Alive* and Its Challenge to a Cherished Holocaust Paradigm." *German Studies Review* 27.3 (2004): 469–475.

Schwab, Gabriele. *Haunting Legacies: Violent Histories and Transgenerational Trauma.* New York, NY: Columbia University Press, 2010.

Schwarz, Gudrun. *Eine Frau an seiner Seite: Ehefrauen in der SS-Sippengemeinschaft.* Berlin: Aufbau, 2000.

"During Total War, We Girls Want to Be Where We Can Really Accomplish Something: What Do Women Do in Wartime." *Crimes of War: Guilt and Denial in the Twentieth Century*. Ed. Omer Bartov, Atina Grossmann, and Mary Nolan. New York, NY: New Press, 2002. 121–137.

Schwarzer, Alice. *Marion Dönhoff: Ein widerständiges Leben.* Cologne: Kiepenheuer & Witsch, 2008.

Schwendemann, Heinrich. "Tod zwischen den Fronten." *Die Flucht: Über die Vertreibung der Deutschen aus dem Osten.* Ed. Stefan Aust and Stephan Burgdorf. Munich: Deutsche Verlags-Anstalt, 2002. 71–82.

Schwertfeger, Ruth. *Women of Theresienstadt: Voices from a Concentration Camp.* Oxford: Berg, 1989.

Scott, Joan. "Rewriting History." *Behind the Lines: Gender and the Two World Wars.* Ed. Margaret Randolph Higonnet, Jane Jenson, Sonya Michel, and Margaret Collins Weitz. New Haven, CT: Yale University Press, 1987. 21–30.

Seidler, Franz W. *Blitzmädchen – Die Geschichte der Helferinnen der deutschen Wehrmacht im Zweiten Weltkrieg.* Bonn: Wehr & Wissen, 1979.

Seifert, Ruth. "War and Rape: A Preliminary Analysis." *Mass Rape: The War against Women in Bosnia-Herzegovina.* Ed. Alexandra Stiglmayer. Transl. by Marion Faber. Lincoln, NE: University of Nevada Press, 1994. 54–72.

Seithe, Horst and Frauke Hagemann. *Das Deutsche Rote Kreuz im Dritten Reich (1933–1939). Mit einem Abriß seiner Geschichte in der Weimarer Republik.* Frankfurt am Main: Mabuse, 2001.

Sereny, Gitta. "Into that Darkness." *Women and the Holocaust: Different Voices.* Ed. Carol Rittner and John K. Roth. St. Paul, MN: Paragon House, 1993. 270–286.

Shelton, Regina Maria. *To Lose a War. Memories of a German Girl.* Carbondale, IL: Southern Illinois University Press, 1982.

Shephard, Ben. *The Long Road Home: The Aftermath of the Second World War.* New York, NY: Knopf, 2011.

Sibley Fries, Marilyn. "Problems of Narrating the Heimat: Christa Wolf and Johannes Bobrowski." *Cross Currents* 9 (1990): 219–230.

Sichrovsky, Peter. *Born Guilty: Children of Nazi Families.* Trans. Jean Steinberg. New York, NY: Basic Books, 1988.

Sielke, Sabine. *Reading Rape: The Rhetoric of Sexual Violence in American Literature and Culture, 1790–1990.* Princeton, NJ: Princeton University Press, 2002.

Slibar, Neva. "Anschreiben gegen das Schweigen: Robert Schindel, Ruth Klüger, die Postmoderne und Vergangenheitsbewältigung." *Jenseits des Diskurses: Literatur und Sprache in der Postmoderne.* Ed. Albert Berger and Gerda Elisabeth Moser. Vienna: Passagen Verlag, 1994. 337–356.

Smale, Catherine. "'Ungelöste Gespenster'? Ghosts in Ruth Klüger's Autobiographical Project." *Modern Language Review* 104.3 (2009): 777–789.

Smith, Jill Suzanne. "Sounds of Silence: Rape and Representation in Julie Zeh's Bosnian Travelogue." *German Women's Writing in the Twenty-First Century.* Ed. Hester Baer and Alexandra Merley Hill. Rochester, NY: Camden House, 2015. 175–196.

Smith, Sidonie. *A Poetics of Women's Autobiography: Marginality and the Fictions of Self-Representation.* Bloomington, IL: Indiana University Press, 1987.

Smith, Sidonie and Julia Watson. *Reading Autobiography: A Guide for Interpreting Life Narratives.* Minneapolis, MN: University of Minnesota Press, 2010.

Snyder, Maria. "The View from the Parking Lot: Political Landscapes and Natural Environments in the Works of Brigitta Kronauer and Jenny Erpenbeck." *German Women Writers and the Spatial Turn: New Perspectives.* Ed. Carola Daffner and Beth A. Muellner. Berlin: De Gruyter, 2015. 229–245.

Solzhenitsyn, Alexander. *Prussian Nights: A Poem.* Transl. Robert Conquest. New York, NY: Farrar, Straus and Giroux, 1974.

Spieckermans, Anna. "Als Flakwaffenhelferin im Einsatz 1944/45: Ein Bericht." *Feministische Studien* 3.2 (1984): 27–38.

Steinbach, Erika. "Vorwort." *Schwarzbuch der Vertreibung 1945 bis 1948: Das letzte Kapitel unbewältigter Vergangenheit.* Munich: Universitas, 1982. 7–11.

Steinbacher, Sybille. "Einleitung." *Volksgenossinnen: Frauen in der NS-Volksgemeinschaft.* Ed. Sybille Steinbacher. Göttingen: Wallstein, 2007. 9–26.

Stephan, Alexander. "Von Aufenthalten, Hosenknöpfen und Kindheitsmustern: Das Dritte Reich in der jüngsten Prosa der DDR." *Studies in GDR Culture and Society.* Ed. Margy Gerber. Washington, DC: University Press of America, 1981. 127–139.

Stephens, Anthony. "Die Verführung der Worte – von *Kindheitsmuster* zu Kassandra." *Wolf: Darstellung – Deutung – Diskussion.* Ed. Manfred Jurgensen. Berne: Francke, 1984. 127–147.

Stephenson, Jill. *Women in Nazi Germany.* Harlow: Pearson Education Limited, 2001.

Steppe, Hilde. *Krankenpflege im Nationalsozialismus*. Frankfurt am Main: Mabuse, 2013.

Steppe, Hilde and Eva-Maria Ulmer, eds. *Ich war von jeher mit Leib und Seele gerne Pflegerin: Über die Beteiligung von Krankenschwestern an den Euthanasie-Aktionen in Meseritz-Obrawalde*. Frankfurt am Main: Mabuse, 2011.

Stiglmayer, Alexandra, ed. *Mass Rape: The War against Women in Bosnia-Herzegovina*. Transl. by Marion Faber. Lincoln, NE: University of Nevada Press, 1994.

Stone, Brangwen. "Visiting the Hometown, Revisiting the Past: Christa Wolf's *Kindheitsmuster*." *Neophilologus* 96 (2012): 593–609.

Stone, Katherine. "The Pitfalls of Constructing a Female Genealogy: Cultural Memory of National Socialism in Recent Family Narratives." *German Women's Writing in the Twenty-First Century*. Ed. Hester Baer and Alexandra Merley Hill. Rochester, NY: Camden House, 2015. 55–73.

Stone, Katherine. *Women and National Socialism in Postwar German Literature: Gender, Memory, and Subjectivity*. Rochester, NY: Camden House, 2017.

Summ, Erika. *Schäfers Tochter: Die Geschichte der Frontschwester Erika Summ 1921–1945*. Ed. Jürgen Kleindienst. Berlin: Zeitgut, 2006.

Summerfield, Penny. "'She Wants a Gun not a Dishcloth!': Gender, Service and citizenship in Britain in the Second World War." *A Soldier and a Woman: Sexual Integration in the Military*. Ed. Gerard J. DeGroot and Corinna Peniston-Bird. London: Pearson Education Limited, 2000. 119–135.

Szepansky, Gerda. *Blitzmädel, Heldenmutter, Kriegerwitwe: Frauenleben im Zweiten Weltkrieg*. Frankfurt am Main: Fischer, 1986.

Taberner, Stuart. "Representations of German Wartime Suffering in Recent Fiction." *German Wartime Suffering*. Ed. Bill Niven. London: Palgrave, 2006. 164–180.

"Memory-Work in Recent German Novels: What (if Any) Limits Remain on Empathy with the 'German Experience' of the Second World War?" *Germans as Victims in the Literary Fiction of the Berlin Republic*. Eds. Stuart Taberner and Karina Berger. Rochester: Camden House, 2009. 205–218.

Taberner, Stuart and Karina Berger. "Introduction." *Germans as Victims in the Literary Fiction of the Berlin Republic*. Ed. Stuart Taberner and Karina Berger. Rochester, NY: Camden House, 2009. 1–14.

Tanner, Laura. *Intimate Violence: Reading Rape and Torture in Twentieth-Century Fiction*. Bloomington, IN: Indiana University Press, 1994.

Taubitz, Monika. *Treibgut: Eine Kindheit nach dem Kriege*. Würzburg: Bergstadtverlag, 2009.

Taylor, Jennifer. "Ruth Klüger's *weiter leben: eine Jugend*: A Jewish Woman's 'Letter to her Mother.'" *Out from the Shadows: Essays on Contemporary Austrian Women Writers and Filmmakers*. Ed. Margarete Lamb-Faffelberger. Riverside: Ariadne Press, 1997. 77–86.

Thürmer-Rohr, Christina. *Vagabundinnen: Feministische Essays.* Berlin: Orlanda Frauenverlag, 1987.

Tomaselli, Sylvana, and Roy Porter, eds. *Rape: An Historical and Social Enquiry.* New York, NY: Basil Blackwell, 1986.

Toussaint, Jeanette. "Nichts gesehen – nichts gewusst: Die juristische Verfolgung ehemaliger SS-Aufseherinnen durch die Volksgerichte Wien und Linz." *Frauen- und Geschlechtergeschichte des Nationalsozialismus: Fragestellungen, Perspektiven, neue Forschungen.* Ed. Johanna Gehmacher and Gabriella Hauch. Innsbruck: StudienVerlag, 2007. 222–239.

Trevor-Roper, Hugh. *The Last Days of Hitler.* Chicago, IL: Chicago University Press, 1992.

Trezise, Thomas. *Witnessing Witnessing: On the Reception of Holocaust Survivor Testimony.* New York, NY: Fordham University Press, 2013.

Tröger, Annemarie. "Between Rape and Prostitution: Survival Strategies and Chances of Emancipation for Berlin Women after World War II." *Women in Culture and Politics: A Century of Change.* Ed. Judith Friedlander, Blanche Wiesen Cook, Alice Kessler-Harris, and Carroll Smith-Rosenberg. Bloomington, IN: Indiana University Press, 1986. 97–117.

Troller, Norbert. *Theresienstadt: Hitler's Gift to the Jews.* Transl. Susan E. Cernyak-Spatz. Ed. Joel Shatzky. Chapel Hill, NC: University of North Carolina Press, 1991.

Vogt, Lore. "Bericht über den Einsatz als Flakwaffenhelferin." *Zur Problematik von Soldatinnen: Der Kampfeinsatz von Flakwaffenhelferinnen im 2. Weltkrieg. Berichte und Dokumentationen.* Ed. Jutta Rüdiger. Lindhorst: Askania, 1987. 12–86.

Voutta, Antje. "Figurationen des Unwiederholbaren: Literarische Annäherungen an Geburt und frühe Kindheit." *Wiederholen: Literarische Funktionen und Verfahren.* Ed. Roger Lüdeke and Inka Mülder-Bach. Göttingen: Wallstein, 2006. 173–194.

Wachsmuth, Iris. "Tradierungsweisen von Geschlechterbildern: der Umgang mit familiengeschichtlichen Verstrickungen in den Nationalsozialismus." *Nationalsozialismus und Geschlecht: Zur Politisierung und Ästhetisierung von Körper, "Rasse" und Sexualität im "Dritten Reich" und nach 1945.* Ed. Elke Frietsch and Christina Herkommer. Bielefeld: transcript, 2009. 433–441.

Wanning Harries, Elizabeth. "The Mirror Broken: Women's Autobiography and Fairy Tales." *Marvels & Tales* 14.1 (2000): 122–135.

Waxman, Zoe. "Rape and Sexual Abuse in Hiding." *Sexual Violence against Jewish Women during the Holocaust.* Ed. Sonja M. Hedgepeth and Rochelle G. Saidel. Waltham, MA: Brandeis University Press, 2010. 124–135.

Weckel, Ulrike and Edgar Wolfrum. *Bestien und Befehlsempfänger: Frauen und Männer in NS-Prozessen nach 1945.* Göttingen: Vandenhoeck & Ruprecht, 2003.

Weckel, Ulrike and Edgar Wolfrum. "NS-Prozesse und ihre öffentliche Resonanz aus geschlechtergeschichtlicher Perspektive." *Bestien und Befehlsempfänger: Frauen und Männer in NS-Prozessen nach 1945.* Ed.

Ulrike Weckel and Edgar Wolfrum. Göttingen: Vandenhoeck & Ruprecht, 2003. 9–21.

Weedon, Chris. "Childhood Memory and Moral Responsibility: Christa Wolf's *Kindheitsmuster.*" *European Memory and the Second World War.* Ed. Helmut Peitsch, Charles Burdett, and Claire Gorrara. New York, NY: Berghahn, 1999. 238–246.

Weglein, Resi. *Als Krankenschwester im KZ Theresienstadt: Erinnerungen einer Ulmer Jüdin.* Ed. Silvester Lechner and Alfred Moos. Stuttgart: Silberburg, 1988.

Weitzman, Lenore J. "Living on the Aryan Side in Poland: Gender, Passing, and the Nature of Resistance." *Women in the Holocaust.* Ed. Dalia Ofer and Lenore J. Weitzman. New Haven, CT: Yale University Press, 1998. 187–222.

Welzer, Harald, Sabine Moller, and Karoline Tschuggnall. *Opa war kein Nazi: Nationalsozialismus und Holocaust im Familiengedächtnis.* Frankfurt am Main: Fischer, 2003.

Wendt-Hildebrandt, Susan. "*Kindheitsmuster*: Christa Wolf's Probestück." *Seminar* 17.2 (1981): 164–176.

Wenk, Silke and Insa Eschebach. "Soziales Gedächtnis und Geschlechterdifferenz: Eine Einführung." *Gedächtnis und Geschlecht: Deutungsmuster in Darstellungen des nationalsozialistischen Genozids.* Ed. Insa Eschebach, Sigrid Jacobeit, and Silke Wenk. Frankfurt am Main: Campus Verlag, 2002. 13-40.

Whitlock, Flint. *The Beasts of Buchenwald: Karl & Ilse Koch, Human-Skin Lampshades, and the War-Crimes Trial of the Century.* Brule: Cable Publishing, 2011.

Wiesehan, Gretchen. "Christa Wolf Reconsidered: National Stereotypes in *Kindheitsmuster.*" *Germanic Review* 68.2 (1993): 79–87.

Wiesel, Elie. *The Town beyond the Wall. A Novel.* Trans. Stephen Becker. New York, NY: Schocken Books, 1982.

Wiesenthal, Simon. *The Sunflower: On the Possibilities and Limits of Forgiveness.* New York, NY: Schocken Books, 1997.

Wilke, Sabine. "Dieser fatale Hang der Geschichte zu Wiederholungen: Geschichtskonstruktionen in Christa Wolf's *Kindheitsmuster.*" *German Studies Review* 13.3 (1990): 499–512.

"Worüber man nicht sprechen kann, darüber muss man allmählich zu schweigen aufhören: Vergangenheitsbeziehungen in Christa Wolfs *Kindheitsmuster.*" *Germanic Review* 66.4 (1991): 169–176.

Williams, Linda. "The Classic Rape: When do Victims Report?" *Social Problems* 331.4 (1984): 459–467.

Willmot, Louise. "Women in the Third Reich: The Auxiliary Military Service Law of 1944." *German History* 2 (1985): 10–20.

Windaus-Walser, Karin. "Frauen im Nationalsozialismus: Eine Herausforderung für feministische Theoriebildung." *Töchterfragen: NS Frauen Geschichte.* Ed. Lerke Gravenhorst and Carmen Tatschmurat. Freiburg: Kore, 1990. 59–72.

Winkler, Dörte. *Frauenarbeit im Dritten Reich.* Hamburg: Hoffmann und Campe, 1977.

Withuis, Jolande. "Die verlorene Unschuld des Gedächtnisses: Soziale Amnesie in Holland und sexuelle Gewalt im Zweiten Weltkrieg." *Gedächtnis und Geschlecht: Deutungsmuster in Darstellungen des Nationalsozialistischen Genozids.* Ed. Insa Eschebach, Sigrid Jacobeit, and Silke Wenk. Frankfurt am Main: Campus Verlag, 2002. 77–97.

Wolf, Christa. *Kindheitsmuster.* Berlin: Luchterhand, 1983.

Wolters, Wendy E. "A Bridge between My Memories and Yours." *Transformations: The Journal of Inclusive Scholarship & Pedagogy* 16.2 (2005): 118–126.

Wyman, Mark. *DPs: Europe's Displaced Persons, 1945–1951.* Ithaca, NY: Cornell University Press, 1989.

Young, James E. *Writing and Rewriting the Holocaust: Narrative and the Consequences of Interpretation.* Bloomington, IN: Indiana University Press, 1988.

Zahlmann, Christel. "*Kindheitsmuster:* Schreiben an der Grenze des Bewusstseins." *Erinnerte Zukunft: 11 Studien zum Werk Christa Wolfs.* Ed. Wolfram Mauser. Würzburg: Königshausen und Neumann, 1985. 141–160.

Zayas, Alfred Maurice de. *A Terrible Revenge: The Ethnic Cleansing of the East European Germans.* New York, NY: Palgrave Macmillan, 2006.

Zehfuss, Maja. *Wounds of Memory: The Politics of War in Germany.* Cambridge: Cambridge University Press, 2007.

Zipfel, Gaby. "Wie führen Frauen Krieg?" *Vernichtungskrieg: Verbrechen der Wehrmacht 1941–1944.* Ed. Hannes Heer und Klaus Naumann. Hamburg: Hamburger Edition, 1995. 460–474.

"Verdrängte Erinnerungen, verdeckte Überlieferungen: Akteurinnen im Nationalsozialismus." *Mittelweg* 5.2 (1996): 64–73.

"Die Welt ist so schön, und wir zerstören sie." Afterword. Ilse Schmidt. *Die Mitläuferin: Erinnerungen einer Wehrmachtsangehörigen.* Berlin: Aufbau, 1999. 167–191.

Index